Rethinking Political Institutions

Rethinking Political Institutions

The Art of the State

EDITED BY

Ian Shapiro, Stephen Skowronek, and Daniel Galvin

New York University Press

NEW YORK AND LONDON

NEW YORK UNIVERSITY PRESS
New York and London
www.nyupress.org

Library of Congress Cataloging-in-Publication Data
Rethinking political institutions : the art of the state /
edited by Ian Shapiro, Stephen Skowronek, and Daniel Galvin.
p. cm.
Includes bibliographical references and index.
ISBN–13: 978–0–8147–4026–2 (cloth : alk. paper)
ISBN–10: 0–8147–4026–X (cloth : alk. paper)
1. Political science. 2. State, The. 3. Public administration.
4. Constitutional law. 5. Democracy. I. Shapiro, Ian.
II. Skowronek, Stephen. III. Galvin, Daniel.
JF51.R35 2006
320—dc22 2005035677

New York University Press books are printed on acid-free paper,
and their binding materials are chosen for strength and durability.

Manufactured in the United States of America

10 9 8 7 6 5 4 3 2 1

Contents

Introduction

Daniel Galvin, Ian Shapiro, and Stephen Skowronek

Institutions are the art of the state. They give it shape, articulate its relationships, and express its legitimacy. There is no escaping them in the study of politics. No wonder, then, that political science currently plays host to a greater variety of approaches to thinking about the significance of institutions than ever before in its history. Historical, legal-constitutional, economic, philosophical, and sociological perspectives compete for attention. A good bit of that variety, and that competition, is on display in these pages. They capture the state of the art in the study of the art of the state.

In recent years, compilations that showcase the scholarship of one or another of these persuasions have become familiar, as have essays that distinguish practitioners of each and pit their perspectives against one another. Less common are works that lay out problems to which all students of institutions must attend and clear the ground for their mutual engagement. Filling that void seems on its face a fairly straightforward exercise, but, as a practical matter, it is not. It is one thing to bemoan the disciplinary incentives for scholars to place themselves in narrow, relatively closed research circles; quite another to bring their labors into some common orbit. Had we invited this diverse group of scholars to address the potential for mutual engagement directly, we suspect that few would have participated and that much of what we received back would have been airy rhetoric. We asked instead for focused, substantive essays in which scholars consider from their own perspectives the significance of political institutions and the outstanding issues and problems they find emergent in their study. This allowed us to collect an extraordinary group of leading lights, to tap insights from each tradition in a way that was likely to be of interest to proponents of the others, and to present a candid survey of the current thinking.

This is a start, a down payment on the promise of a more direct and fluid exchange. Readers are not given answers; they are rather invited to pull anchor, wander wide, and think for themselves as to where to go next. We trust that there are real gains to be had from the juxtapositions they will encounter along the way and that the effort necessary to consider similar issues from different points of view will be handsomely repaid.

The three headings under which we have grouped the essays do not exhaust the connections to be drawn among them, but this organization does capture a good bit of resonance. Under the first heading, we have collected the essays that take up general conceptual issues regarding the attributes of institutions, the different ways in which they work their effects, and the scope of institutional politics. Notable in the chapters included in Part I is their collective impatience with the current boundaries of institutional study and the analytic frameworks that have defined them. Claus Offe stresses the givenness of institutions in social life and directs the study of institutional operations outward to considerations of social power. Picking up the power theme but directing it to a reconsideration of the rational choice literature, Terry Moe unravels assumptions that have led many to treat political institutions as self-contained and mutually beneficial systems of cooperation and urges us to attend more directly to their imposition on others. John Ferejohn examines a different meaning of the givenness of institutions in politics. He points to analytic conventions that hold institutional structures apart from human behavior and interrogates the ways in which the separability assumption can aid or impair the design and reform of institutions. Boundaries are also at issue in Rogers Smith's and Paul Pierson's essays. Smith argues that political ideas, though not themselves institutions, are indispensable to understanding the political orders that they construct, and Pierson considers the institutional attributes of public policies. The discontent expressed with received conceptions of institutional politics dovetails with the willingness of these authors to hold new definitions in abeyance pending closer attention to the interfaces between institutions and the other elements of the polity of which they are a part. One discerns a common movement from different directions, a movement from thinking about the politics of institutions per se toward thinking institutionally about politics at large.

The essays in Part II approach institutional politics in a more applied fashion, but a similar impulse to lay aside conventional assumptions is apparent. These chapters examine the institutional construction of politics, the empirical reach, operational limits, and observable dynamics of the political formations that they generate. At issue are the ordering capacities of institutions and their impact on change over time. Kathleen Thelen challenges the dominant conception of order and change in time—punctuated equilibrium—in which institutional orderings are temporally bound between brief moments of exogenously induced system transformation. She shows how early institutions set up in Germany to promote vocational training were drawn forward and elaborated across a series of major regime changes, and, in so doing, she calls for closer attention to the dynamics of political contestation and political coalitional change that undergird institutional structures and operations. Margaret Weir looks at issues of order and change in a similar spirit but from the side of the political actor. Questioning the common identification of institutional "feedback" effects with policy reinforcement and system maintenance, she points to the complex and often competing networks of institutions that have emerged over time around issues of labor and the elderly, and in them she finds a multiplication of the opportunities for interest definition, coalition formation, and institutional transformation. In Elisabeth Clemens's essay, the standard bureaucratic model of state-building is delimited by a survey of the many alternative routes taken in the expansion of public authority in America and of the systemic disorganization that they have collectively bred. She explains the emergence, in practice, of a "Rube Goldberg" state featuring a "tangle of indirect incentives, cross-cutting regulations, overlapping jurisdictions, delegated responsibility, and diffuse accountability." Finally, Kent Weaver presents a comparative study of pension support retrenchment in advanced democracies to test arguments about how different institutional structures affect the capacity of states to impose losses on politically salient constituencies. He finds that standard assumptions about the relative capacities of parliamentary and separated systems, though not without foundation, are often overridden by particular rules, temporal contingencies, and innovative informal arrangements.

The institutional construction of politics is not only an empirical question but also a practical and normative one. The chapters in Part III approach the matter more directly from the point of view of constitutional craftsmanship and democratic legitimacy, but the authors make us aware that these traditional issues of political theory are becoming harder to separate from the analytic and empirical issues touched on by others.

Mark Tushnet sets the stage by reconsidering the relationship between constitutional law and politics and by describing an array of constitutional choices that polities make to either strengthen or blur the distinction between the two. The choice of constitutional forms is the theme of Jon Elster's essay as well, but he turns to the subject to raise some empirical and analytic questions about what lies behind these choices. Taking into view different episodes of constitutional choice in French history, he finds acceptance in each instance of provisions of consequence that defy any rational calculation of self-interest by the choosers, and, in so doing, he problematizes the rational basis of institutional construction generally. Working within a very different scholarly tradition and looking at very different material, Keith Whittington has written an essay that cuts the other way. He reexamines the problem of a countermajoritarian difficulty in the American practice of judicial review and finds a number of reasons why legislators might support a practice that ostensibly restricts their governing prerogatives. His reassessment suggests that this age-old bone of contention among America's constitutional and democratic theorists retains its hold because it serves the calculated interests of representatives and electorates alike—because, in other words, it has both democratic and rational warrants. Part III closes with Ulrich Preuss's challenge to traditional ways of thinking about institutional construction. As he sees it, the problems of institutional construction in modern democracies are different from those taken up previously because traditional political theory was principally concerned with how best to establish democracy in the first place. At issue today, he argues, is the cultivation and maintenance of a democratic citizenry capable of sustaining a modicum of rational and informed deliberation, and that, he ventures, is something to be realized less through traditional modes of institution building than through more sustained attention to the institution of citizenship itself.

Though the contributors to this volume do not speak with a single voice, they do convey an overarching message. The reader is witness to an all-fronts assault on the convenient assumptions that have supported separate communities of institutional research. The common impulse in these essays is to expose the limitations of and to challenge the boundaries within which these communities have operated. Our hope is that this volume will promote greater awareness of this outward-reaching spirit and help to sustain it, for we are confident that the important insights and the greatest gains for knowledge now lie on those frontiers.

Several years ago, the Yale Department of Political Science launched a "New Initiative" entitled "Rethinking Political Order: The Nation State in the Emerging World." The aim was to break out of the traditional field categories through which the discipline of political science has organized the study of politics and to promote the development of new research communities that would draw scholars of different background into a discussion of common problems. The initiative set forth five subthemes identifying associated problems that have stood the test of time and are also likely to figure as pressing issues of the near future: Representation and Popular Rule; Order, Conflict, and Violence; Identities, Affiliations, and Allegiances; Crafting and Operating Institutions; and Distributive Politics. The contention is that research communities directed toward these problems will not only cut across the discipline's deepening methodological divides and traditional field specializations but also harness its tremendous diversity of talent and depth of knowledge in tackling them.

To get started, conferences were held on each of the initiative's subthemes. The conference "Crafting and Operating Institutions" was organized by the editors of this volume and held at Yale on the weekend of April 11–13, 2003. Leading scholars were invited to present original papers and were later given the opportunity to revise in light of the conference proceedings. The essays in this volume all began as contributions to that conference. Other participants included Akhil Amar, Charles Cameron, Daniel Carpenter, Craig Cummings, Keith Darden, Anna Grzymala-Busse, Jacob Hacker, Peter Hall, Gregory Huber, Ira Katznelson, Jonathan Koppell, Pauline Jones-Luong, John Lapinski, Rose Razaghian, Theda Skocpol, and Barry Weingast. In one way or another, all contributed to bringing this work to fruition.

Part I

Institutional Study and Its Boundaries

Political Institutions and Social Power
Conceptual Explorations

Claus Offe

The term "institution" is one of the most frequently used and, at the same time, most rarely defined in the social sciences. Social scientists relate to the theoretical concept of institution as ordinary people relate to some established institution: They take the meaning for granted and proceed to make use of it. The question that I want to focus on here concerns the implications of institutions for the generation, distribution, exercise, and control of social power. The question can be elaborated with the help of a quote from Sven Steinmo, one of the initiators[1] of the research program of "historical institutionalism." Steinmo writes: "Institutions define the rules of the political game and as such they define who can play and how they play . . . [institutions] can shape who wins and who loses."[2]

If we replace in this sentence the term "institutions" with the word "power" or "holders of social power," the meaning remains virtually the same. "Institutions" and "power," it seems, are being used almost interchangeably. But that cannot be right, as "holders of power" are clearly actors, while institutions are not. What I want to explore here are the mechanisms through which institutions affect the distribution of social power among actors and are, in a circular way, themselves the result of the exercise of power.

To this end, I start with (1) a set of propositions, distilled out of the theoretical literature on institutions, on which social scientists (including economists) who study institutions seem to be largely agreed. These propositions refer to structural features of all institutions (or of subgroups that form types of institutions). In the next section, I turn to (2) the functions that institutions perform. Section (3) of the chapter deals with the capacity of institutions to endow actors with power and privilege and various trajectories of challenge and change of institutions. It is by mere coincidence that each of these three sections is subdivided into eight propositions.

(1) The Structure of Institutions

(a) Rules vs. Regularities

Institutions are systems of *rules* that apply to the future behavior of actors. They constitute actors and pro-/prescribe their scope and mode of action. These rules can be sanctioned through mechanisms that are specified in the charter, or legal specification, of an institution. These rules are, consciously or habitually, observed and complied with by actors who are aware not only of the rules but also of the fact that these rules are being enforced and deviant courses of action sanctioned. Institutions often impose severe constraints on what actors are permitted to do. In contrast, *regularities* are propositions based upon the observation of patterns in past events that do not have, by themselves, normative qualities; neither can they be sanctioned. A similar distinction can be made between institutions and conventions. Institutions differ from conventions in that the rules that they consist of are potentially contested. Violations of institutional rules can result from an actor's interest and are not just a mistake. While it makes no intelligible sense to challenge the QWERTY convention of organizing characters on a keyboard (as it becomes self-enforcing the moment it is adopted, as deviation is rendered prohibitively costly once the standard is adopted), institutions can meaningfully be challenged and their alteration advocated. "Excessive" challenges may be precluded through an enforcement agency. Formal institutions need guardians and enforcers.

(b) Institution Building vs. Purposive or Instrumental Action

Institutions are often explained and justified in terms of the problems they are designed to resolve or the values they serve. This problem-solving or value-achieving perspective on the origin and change of political institutions, often framed in metaphors taken from medicine or engineering, is deeply misleading. The logic of this perspective is something like this: If you don't like the outcome, get a new set of institutions that yields better results. There are a number of things that are dubious with this perspective. For one thing, there may be outcomes and events for which simply no remedial institution is known. Or the speculation that a specific institutional pattern will result in an equally specific outcome may be erroneous, as "existing empirical knowledge is not adequate for an explicit policy of institutional design."[3] Ethnic conflict in deeply divided societies may be a case in point.[4] Second, institutions (such as corporatist industrial relations systems) may yield desirable results in one evaluative dimension and highly undesirable ones in another, without a neutral metric being available that could measure the net utility of outcomes. It is often also the case that protagonists of institutional innovation make multiple claims, addressed to different constituencies, as to what the proposed innovation is good for. In order to build a winning coalition of supporters, they may need to remain rather unspecific regarding intended outcomes. Third, the utility that institutions generate may be distributed according the pattern of an inverted U. Highly repressive state institutions may first provide for political calm but later reach a tipping point and trigger rebellion. Fourth, the productivity of institution may be context-sensitive, with the context itself being formed by other institutions or conditions. In the absence of such favorable context, one particular institution may not yield the benefits that hence are not due to the institution itself but contingent upon synergetic effects with other institutions. Also, what Goodin has called the "Myth of the Intentional Designer" not only downplays the fact that "typically, there is no . . . designer" but also suggests that if there were one, "social engineers always work with the materials . . . unalterably shaped by the past."[5] Finally, and most important, legislators or other representative actors may be unable or unwilling to adopt institutions even though they are (let us suppose) demonstrably capable of coping with their most serious problems. The patient, as it were, suffers from a disease that renders him incapable of swallowing the pill. A long time ago, Ernst Fraenkel highlighted a case of this "incentive incompatibility" when he observed, shortly before the breakdown of the Weimar constitution, in Germany: "Were the existing legislature capable of passing a constitutional reform, such reform would be superfluous. It is exactly impossibility to have the reform adopted by parliament that makes it necessary."[6] Somewhat less tragically, the patient may be willing to accept the remedy but do so only in exceptional moments of sanity (such as occur after wars, civil wars, or regime breakdowns). Horowitz speaks of "the exceptional character of the occasion for innovation."[7]

What seems to follow from all of these doubts and objections concerning constructivist rationalism in institution building is this: The origin of institutions must be looked for not in terms of purposive rational, consequentialist, and outcome-related but in value rational and deontological terms, or what March and Olsen[8] have termed the "logic of appropriateness."[9] Institutions and institutional changes are more consistently explained in term of the balance of social power that they reflect than in terms of the goals and objectives that they are claimed to serve.

(c) Institutions vs. Traditions

Institutions differ from traditions or mere habits in that those involved in them show at least a rudimentary degree of reflexive awareness of the presence of these institutions and their claim to validity. For instance, institutions and the system of rules of which they consist are codified in law books and other books, they can be taught and theorized, reasons can be given for the validity of these rules and the bindingness with which they shape the action of actors, and so on.

(d) Implicit Theories

Institutions come with an implicit theory about themselves, an "animating idea"[10] that provides reasons for their support and defense. For instance, democratic political institutions are framed in a set of ideas such as popular sovereignty, limitation of state powers, and procedural impartiality, while authoritarian ones invoke collective security, paternalism, or some doctrine promulgated by the political elite concerning the course of history. An institution that is entirely incapable of providing widely accepted reasons for itself is, as it were, intellectually naked (like the proverbial emperor in his new clothes) and, for this reason, in a precarious position and vulnerable to challenge. These implicit theories refer to how people normally behave and what kinds of desires they will pursue.[11]

(e) Priority in Time to Action

Institutions precede the action of actors in time. They are premises of action. They are not created on the spot (as contracts are) but are "given" in the sense that less contingency applies to institutions than to actions. Contracts themselves, as a form that governs major parts of social interaction, have the quality of scripts, that is, of precluding the option of *not* using this form if actors want to put themselves in control of valued goods or services. This quality of being inescapably "given" is what made Durkheim speak of the "noncontractual" features of contracts, of "social facts," and so on (*"chosisme"*).

(f) Anonymity of Origin

In contrast to organizations, institutions do not have founders or authors. To be sure, an individual constitution as an instance of the institutional pattern of constitutional government does have "founding fathers." But this pattern itself, of which individual constitutions are widely varying incarnations, has emerged out of arguments, experiences, demands, movements, discourses, and theories that evolved and came to prevail in seventeenth- and eighteenth-century Europe. Rather than as a result of individual decisions or founding acts, they evolved and came into being as a result of some collective manifestation of "communicative power."[12] As widely observed practices, they "emerge" anonymously under certain conditions and contexts, which later historians then usually explain as having created a specific institutional pattern. There may have been heroes, protagonists, or prophets, as well as theorists who elaborated and explained the reasons for the validity of an institution. But any ascription of an institution to a personal and hence mortal creator would expose it to the risk of being later denounced as an arbitrary or self-interested, at any rate as a by-now obsolete invention of that particular person, or to the risk of sectarianism, the recognition of which is limited to the followers of a particular person. Anonymity is also a defining element of institutions in that they refer to actors in terms of offices, rules, resources, and so forth, never in terms of persons and names of persons.[13] Institutions such as the school, the family, the joint stock company, the political party, and the state and its bureaucracy owe their robustness and proclaimed timelessness to the fact that we cannot tell who "invented" them. In that sense, "fatherlessness" is an asset, as is the myth of parthenogenesis in the case of the founder of Christianity. Similarly, human reason itself, rather than some personal founder, is held to be, according to contractarian political theory, the source of the state as an institution.

(g) Contested Values

Institutions regulate the distribution of values the access to which and the distribution of which are intensely contested.[14] The access to wealth and income, the control of physical violence, the recognition of individuals as member of a group, authority over and solidarity within the group, sexual relations, generational relations, the access to social and physical security, health, education, knowledge, esthetic values, and spiritual salvation are all items on a list of potential conflicts in which the stakes and hence the potential for disruptive violence can be very high.[15] Institutions can best be thought of as regimes that regulate the productions and distribution of these and other values—which is why they are the potential object of distributive conflict initiated by actors who desire a different pattern of the distribution of and access to these values.

(h) Theorists' Proposed Typologies of Institutions

Typologies of institutions can be based on institutional fields and their respective core values (religion/salvation, schools/education). They can also proceed along the formal/informal or legal/moral/ethical divide.[16] Or they can proceed according to a hierarchy of "basic" institutions (such as constitutions), intermediary institutions (statutory laws), and operative institutions (administrative decrees).[17] Such hierarchies usually also imply a hierarchy of robustness, or resistance to change, as in the hierarchy of political community, regime form, and legislation[18] or the hierarchy of basic versus incremental policy changes.[19]

(2) Functions of Institutions

(a) Formative Impact upon Actors

Institutions shape actors' motivational dispositions; goals and procedures are "internalized" by actors, who adopt goals, procedures, and interpretations of the situation that are congruent with the institutional patterns. Institutions shape actors so that they (many or even most of them) take these institutions for granted and comply with their rules. Institutions have a formative, motivation-building, and preference-shaping impact upon actors. They subsume and subordinate the individual, shape his tastes and desires, and promulgate habitual codes of conduct. In order for an institution to make the transition from an idea, a blueprint, or a vision to an actually existing arrangement widely enacted in social practices, the set of rules, forms, and constraints must "sink in," "take root," "make sense," become "taken for granted," and meet with the recognition and support of those who come to live with and under the institution in question. Institutions have less to do with strategy, choice, and instrumental rationality (as organizations do) and more with emergence, growth, and intrinsic valuation.[20] Institutions are part of the stock of "common knowledge," even of those who are unfamiliar with particular organizations that form instances of institutions. Even if I never attend church or a stock exchange, I still have an idea of what these institutions are thought to be good for and how people act when they are involved in the institution.[21]

(b) Congruent Preference Formation

By virtue of this formative effect, as well as the shaping of actors' expectations, institutions can provide for predictability, regularity, stability, integration, discipline, and cooperation. In the absence of institutions, actors would not be able to make strategic choices, because they would lack the information about what kind of action to expect from others, which they need to know in order to pursue their own benefit.[22] More broadly and regardless of the special case of strategic action, institutions fulfill a requirement, as philosophical anthropologists[23] have argued, that results from a basic and constitutive deficiency of human nature: Human beings are not only naked in the literal sense (and therefore in need of clothing and shelter); they are also "naked" in the metaphorical sense that they are lacking instinct-based behavioral programs that would provide them with guidance in responding to the challenges of the physical and the social world. Because human behavior is not naturally and fully governed by instinctual mechanisms (as is the case with all animals), humans, in order to cope with the destructive potential of their "fearsome naturalness,"[24] need rules (or "culture") to compensate for this deficiency. Freudian social psychology (*Civilization and Its Discontents*) follows a similar idea of "requisite repression," an idea that has later come to be challenged by the Freudian Left[25] and complemented by the notion of institutions that perform not just the function of "necessary" but, beyond that, of unnecessary or "surplus" repression.

From Aristotle to John S. Mill to contemporary theories of deliberative democracy, we find the notion of institutions' (and, in particular, constitutions') capacity for congruent preference-building. Good constitutions generate good citizens and enhance the capacities that are accorded to them in constitutional texts. The viability and robustness of institutions are in turn thought to be contingent upon the loyalty and supportive disposition of citizens toward those institutions, because no institution is capable of ensuring its durability through formal sanctions alone. Institutions are dependent upon requisite sectoral virtues and informal codes of conduct, such as honesty and competitiveness in business, impersonal neutrality in bureaucracy, noncorruptibility in politics, trust and affection in family life, collectivity orientation in the professions, learning efforts in schools, dutiful preparedness for self-sacrifice in military combat organizations, and so on. They also shape expectations of what others are likely to do, as well as a sense of collective identity among those who belong to and live in or under an institution. No institution can function unless such corresponding informal codes of conduct and sector-specific ethos are observed by participants. One important function of institutions is to inculcate such loyalty.

At the same time, institutions are necessary in order to avoid states of ambiguity, anomie, and disorientation. It is only through political institutions that we can avoid the political nightmares of cycling majorities and arbitrary rule, and only through economic institutions that we can limit defection and opportunism, the absence of trust, and the uncertainty about the constraints that govern gain-seeking modes of behavior. As Goodin has put it succinctly, "there can be a market in anything only if there is not a market in everything."[26]

Some institutions are more stringent than others. "Only in the limiting case will [institutions] restrict the [feasible] set to one alternative. . . . The institution may establish the general parameters for the interaction (by excluding some strategies) but allow for considerable flexibility in the choice of strategies within that framework."[27] However, the actual range of choice of individuals need not be greater in the second than in the first case, as the institutionally mediated perception of the "normal" mode of action, the conformist discipline with which a code of conduct is observed, may be so narrow and rigid that actors spontaneously adopt a strict self-discipline (or "auto-governementality"), thus acting as if the feasible set actually consisted of just one alternative. But many institutions leave considerable leeway for variations that follow from the values and interests of those who make use of institutions and build organizations premised on them. This variability of actually observable practices implies that explanations of action and outcomes based on the independent variable of underlying institutional patterns must rely on a soft and probabilistic notion of causation.

(c) Economizing on Transaction Costs

In particular, institutions increase the efficiency of transactions as they help to economize on search, negotiation, and enforcement costs of market and nonmarket interaction.[28] To the extent that institutions are capable of cultivating their corresponding codes of conduct and the respective ethical dispositions, a by-product of their functioning is the avoidance of the costs of conflict and conflict resolution. Needless to say, the shape of institutions and their change cannot be explained, in a functionalist manner, by the objectives to which their operation turns out to contribute. However, with this proviso in mind, we can predict the kinds of transaction cost problems that will result from the weakness or failure of institutions in certain environments. For instance, in a society where exchange and interaction are limited to the members of tribes and primordial groups, tolerable levels of transaction costs will be obtained even in the absence of formal institutions. Personal knowledge of transaction partners will facilitate cooperation by virtue of tradition and informal rules alone. In contrast, "modern" societies provide opportunities and incentives to interact with "strangers" whom we do not know nor expect to ever come to know as persons. In such a posttraditionalist context, the only safeguard actors can have against the opportunism and defection of other actors is based upon institutions, the failure of which thus seems to be a much more serious problem in modern societies than in traditional ones.

(d) Frictionless Self-Coordination

Institutions shape action by providing opportunities and incentives to actors so that a spontaneous order (*kosmos,* or spontaneous regularities, vs. *taxis,* or intentionally designed rules) results.[29] For instance, market institutions inculcate such virtues as prudence, diligence, punctuality, self-control, and self-attribution of both success and failure, thereby triggering spontaneous patterns of self-coordination. Rather than prescribe a particular course of action, institutions focus the attention of actors on what is relevant and irrelevant, what preferences are to be pursued and incentive or opportunities responded to, what resources employed, and so on. Institutions "act on the manner in which [individuals] regulate their own behavior," which is why the institutionalization of liberty through "liberalism [represents] a specific rationality of government," which cultivates "suitable habits of self-regulation."[30]

(e) Continuity

By virtue of their formative impact upon individuals, as well as their contribution to social order, institutions can be self-perpetuating: The longer they are in place, the more robust they grow, and the more immune they become to challenges. Institutions can breed conservatism. Innovation becomes more costly, both because those living in institutions have come to take them for granted and because those who are endowed by them with power and privilege resist change. For both of these reasons, they set premises, constraints, and determinants for future developments and thus become "path dependent" and limit change to the mode of (at best) incremental adjustment.

(f) Failure and Breakdown of Institutions

One way in which institutional failure may happen is through a more or less accidental change of conditions in the external world that undermines the viability of institutional patterns or limits their ability to function. If that happens, rules and institutionalized goals and power relations are rendered untenable, whether because of some emerging discrepancy between an institutional complex and its economic, demographic, or technological environment or because of an evolving lack of fit between institutional complexes, such as the incompatibility between institutions of higher education and labor market institutions. There is simply no "meta-institution" that is capable of coordinating sectoral institutional arrangements. In either of these cases, actors who have so far complied with institutional practices will start a process of (potentially self-accelerating) defection. An example from the German political economy is the assumption, built into the institutional pattern of wage bargaining, that semicentralized multiemployer bargaining ("*Flächentarifvertrag*") in the long term converges with the interests of both workers and employers and also enhances the productivity and competitiveness of the economy as a whole, thus creating the conditions of its own sustainability. However, labor market crises, regional disparities, international competition, and not least the consequences of German unification have shattered this presumed equilibrium of interests. Another example is the institutions of family life in African societies, the rules of which prescribe that the care for young children must be taken over by specified members of the wider family in (the presumably relatively rare) case these children become orphans. However, as a direct consequence of the HIV epidemic, this situation has ceased to be rare, and the family-based institutions of vicarious care have turned out to be overburdened and are beginning to break down. These are just two examples of how institutions may lose their "fit" with the external context conditions on which they depend, and hence their viability.

(g) Another Case of "Path-Departure" and Institutional Breakdown

Other cases of institional breakdown grow out of the failure, or loss of moral plausibility, of the implicit theory of a just social order that comes with any institution. Institutions can implode because of a shortage of the moral resources and loyalties that are needed for their support. For instance, the notion of a just gender division of labor, congealed in the "male breadwinner" family pattern, has come under pressure from individualistic and egalitarian normative ideas. The same syndrome of normative ideas has made the "collectivist consensus," on which the Bismarckian institutions of contributory pay-as-you-go old-age pensions are based, falter. Here, we observe the breakdown of institutions as a result of their internal loss of a sense of "appropriateness"[31] and justice. In the conceptual jargon of sociologists, the two cases (f) and (g) can be labeled "crisis" versus "conflict," or failure of systems integration *versus* failure of social integration, respectively.

(h) Institutional Transformation and a Gestalt Switch.

What used to be seen and taken for granted as a valid and well-functioning arrangement is now being looked upon and challenged as a pattern that represents a frozen power structure inherited from a remote and now obsolete past. For instance, the privileged position of the five permanent members of the UN Security Council is a result of the fact that these five states are the victorious powers of the Second World War and also share among them a monopoly on the (legitimate) possession of nuclear

weapons. However, both the post–World War II configuration of the international system and the Cold War have become a matter of the past, and
this nuclear monopoly has become entirely nominal and increasingly ficti-
tious. Moreover, one of the permanent members can now afford, because
of its unparalleled military power, to ignore and bypass Security Council
decisions. The entire arrangement can therefore be discredited as the
unwarranted projection of past power relations onto the present, thus
cementing relations of power that cannot be justified under present conditions any longer.

(3) Social Power, as Provided by Institutions and
as Challenging Institutions

Social power manifests itself in a mode of action that has the effect of setting parameters for the action of other social actors, be it in favorable or
unfavorable ways, as seen by those others. In either case, the exercise of
power is conflictual, controversial, and contested. In this conflict, some
legitimating norm of (political, social, economic) justice is invoked and
appealed to. The exercise of power affects others in ways that are perceived
by them to be justice-relevant, either fulfilling or violating standards of
justice. Given the controversial and essentially contested nature of these
standards, I take it as axiomatic that any institution can be criticized for
failing to live up to some version of justice. Note that this definition of
power excludes two (arguably entirely fictive) phenomena that played a
role in nineteenth-century political thought: the "administration of
things" (as opposed to "rule over men," as elaborated by Saint-Simon and
adopted into Marxism by Engels), which supposedly affects objects other
than social actors, or social actors in an essentially uncontroversial way,
and the exclusively private and self-referential action that is of no consequence whatsoever to other actors.[32] We can thus say that social power
evaporates when externalities of action are either universally and unequiv-
ocally beneficial or entirely absent.

Apart from these two (highly idealized) limiting cases, any formal institution does involve three kinds of power. First, it relies on the power of
policing and enforcement agents, or guardians, including the socialization
agents, media, and so on, that perform tasks of the educational propaga-
tion of institutional patterns and related ideas and implicit theories. Second, institutions preserve power relations as they contain patterns of

privilege, power, and control that are biased in favor of some actors in some institutional field and work to the disadvantage of others. Third, there is the virtual power of those who might have reasons (for instance, reasons following from 2(f) or 2(g)), to defect from, obstruct, or challenge institutional patterns and replace them with new ones. This triad of power phenomena that is embedded in institutional patterns can be illustrated using the famous line by Bertolt Brecht (*Threepenny Opera*, scene 9), who lets one of his protagonists ask the rhetorical question "What is breaking into a bank compared to founding a bank?" The robbing of a bank is an act that the "guardians" are obviously called upon to deal with. The (by Brecht's implication, far greater) "crime" of founding and operating a bank is the power structure embedded in the institution of banking, namely the power with which the institution of banking endows some economic actors at the expense of other actors. But Brecht's speech act that puts matters in this way makes sense only in a "revolutionary" per-spective—a perspective, that is, that envisions the exercise of a kind of power that would be capable of overpowering the institutional pattern that is represented by the "bank" and replacing it with some different kind of credit mechanism.

Institutions endow specific actors with power. They place players in a position that allows them to take arguably unfair advantage of others or to exclude others from the participating in the decision-making process even when the decision to be made affects them in significant ways (or what-ever other justice-related complaint may be raised against them). The gen-eralization that I want to suggest is a model according to which institutions operate in a tripolar field of power conflicts that unfold among the guardians (enforcers and educators), beneficiaries, and poten-tial challengers.

The dynamics of this power conflict surrounding institutions can range from vehement to latent. The latter applies if an institution consists of a set of rules that nobody needs to enforce because nobody violates it; that nobody can claim to involve unfair privilege or exclusion; and that nobody finds worth criticizing or challenging. It is not easy, I submit, to think of an example of an institution to which all of this applies and that is, in fact, an "institution," rather than a widely shared habit or a perfectly self-enforcing convention. Perhaps equally rare are instances of the other extreme of open and vehement contest. Which leads me to the question of how the three parties that are hypothetically involved in the dynamics of social power concerning institutional rules manage to conceal, accommodate, or disperse this conflict. What follows is a typology of situations and modes in which institutions cope with power-related contests and challenges.

(a) Institutions in which the bias of privilege is not obvious to participants but that endows some actors with benefits at the expense of some excluded, discriminated, or misrepresented interest will escape any serious challenge, particularly if the guardians can point to allegedly universal and nondiscriminatory incidence of benefits flowing from the institution. "Rule" is being camouflaged as "technically competent administration." In this configuration, the power implications of the institutional pattern can just be perceived by the outside observer, rightly or not.

(b) Even if some bias in favor of beneficiaries of holding power is widely perceived and objections concerning the justice of the arrangement raised, the institutional rules and procedures may be such that an open and promising challenge of the institutional pattern is not expected to have any chance of success. This may be so because a set of ideas and an institutional blueprint on the basis of which some critical alliance of challengers might crystallize is missing. This is the situation analyzed by theories of power that focus upon its "second" face (nondecisions and exclusionary agenda-setting),[33] as well as its "third" face (manipulative interference with awareness of interests).[34] Challenging the (dis)empowering effects of the institution may appear either unpromising, given the weakness of opponents, or not "worth the effort," given the negative sanctions that are to be expected from the guardians. As potential sources of critique are silenced and disorganized, the power of the privileged is rendered invisible.

(c) Some institutions are highly flexible and open to self-revision. Some eighteenth- and nineteenth-century political thinkers believed it desirable to provide for a process of a radical ongoing "synchronization" of institutions so that the legacy of unfair distributional patterns that is inherent in inherited institutions could be effectively neutralized. For instance, according to Rousseau, each time the Assembly comes together, it should affirm the validity of the constitution and alter it if it is no longer unanimously supported. After all, why should we, those presently alive, allow defunct generations to exercise power over us? But this solution is deceptive, because the neutralization of inherited unfairness would be tantamount to granting comfortable opportunities to present holders of social power. An institution that is in constant need of affirmation is not really an institution, because it fails to shape preferences and expectations in durable ways. While the inherited playing field on which we find ourselves may be far from level, treating it constantly as a tabula rasa may well leave us in an even more tilted terrain. Holding fast to inherited institutions and their effect of "long-distance" self-binding can protect us from the dangers of an overly direct impact of present power relations upon renovated institutions. This conservative approach certainly does not neutralize whatever power effects are built into institutions, but it at least helps to preserve the potential of institutions for creating predictability and stability and for economizing on transaction costs. The same logic applies to the requirement of supermajorities for institutional change. The advantage of synchronization must be balanced against the dual disadvantage of just empowering present holders of veto power and the unpredictability of the behavior of everyone else. Even highly unfair institutions may be able to command the loyalty and compliance of actors because these have reason to believe that any transition to better ones will be prohibitively costly and because existing institutions are at least familiar and reasonably calculable; they are "the best we have" and can hope for for the time being.[35]

An example of how an excessive flexibility of institutions can have quite dubious effects is the opportunistic manipulation of electoral laws,[36] that is, laws that normally do not partake of the rigidity accorded to constitutional rules proper. If every ruling party could use its majority to push through parliament the combination of electoral rules that best serves its interest in being re-elected, this strategy of opportunistically rewriting institutional rules would hardly be seen as enhancing fairness. The same applies to governing elites' self-serving manipulation of rules governing federalism (examples from Nigeria and India come to mind) and the devolution of government functions. Institutions that can be opportunistically switched off and on, or altered in the pursuit of strategic considerations, are an oxymoron. Institutions perform their function only if they are protected by some degree of "requisite rigidity" and are designed in accordance with principles (what I have called their "implicit theory") that allow us to value them for their intrinsic rather than their instrumental value (if perhaps only because their long-term causal effects are hidden behind a veil of ignorance).

(d) A way out of this dilemma might be the reliance on mechanisms that allow for the institutionalization of institutional change, subjecting it to procedural constraints. All constitutions contain ("meta-") rules that specify the procedures according to which they can be amended and changed. In addition, they often constitute agents, such as constitutional courts, and prescribe rules with which any binding (re-)interpretation of formal institutions must comply. To be sure, there is no guarantee that the space for self-revision thus provided, as well as the political determination to use it, will ever be sufficient to heal even the most blatant power privileges that are built into institutional arrangements.[37]

(e) Another option to appease challengers and to neutralize any alleged power content of institutional forms is to provide for a choice of parallel institutional forms that apply to the same field of action (i. e., the coexistence of public and commercial mass media and schools, business corporations and cooperatives, state and federal legislative competences), as well as the liberal option of opting out (e. g., of the representational monopoly of trade unions or employers' associations). The power-neutralizing effect of these pluralization/liberalization options is, however, bound to be limited at best, because the choices that are made available are likely to be used in ways that reflect the status and privilege of those who make them, as in the opposition of public health systems and private health insurance.

(f) In rare cases, institutions show the capacity for accommodating challenges without thereby exposing their core rules and actors to challenge. The Roman Catholic Church is perhaps the most impressive example of an institution that has been capable of preserving both the continuity of the institutional core of the *una sancta* and ongoing adjustment and self-revision. Another instance of the Lampedusa principle ("changing things so that everything stays the same") is that of European monarchies: They have shown an amazing capacity for being constitutionalized and democratized, so that, arguably, today at least half of European consolidated democracies are in fact monarchies, not republics. Similarly, the legal institutions that make up *les droits de l'homme,* while originally destined to refer to the rights of French males, have gradually come to apply to all human beings through the creeping diffusion of an original "animating idea." It is at least not evident that today's liberal democracies belong to this small group of exceptionally "ultrastable" institutions, given the fact that the moral context condition of liberal democracy, the sovereign nation-state, together with the patriotic loyalty to shared principles and a common destiny that it evokes in citizens, is in the process of evaporating. On the other hand, many liberal democracies have at times shown great capacities for co-opting and incorporating both ideas and elites whose sources were those political forces that were most likely to challenge some given distribution of power and privilege.

(g) Other institutions are even less capable of adjusting to challenges, although the need to respond to these challenges and the evidence of unfairness is widely understood. Often institutions, or those responsible for their management and enforcement, are trapped in their obsession with continuity and their refusal to concede change. This behavior is well known in authoritarian regimes, which sometimes (have good reasons to) fear that concessions will lead to breakdown, while not appreciating the fact that the failure to grant such concession is even more likely to lead to breakdown. The logic of this dilemma is not entirely absent from liberal democracies. To illustrate, let me return to the case of a Bismarckian system of contributory old-age pensions based upon contributions shared equally by employers and employees. It is a well-understood mathematical certainty that this system cannot yield, as it is legally committed to do, income-graduated pensions above the poverty line under conditions of a rapidly aging population with high levels of unemployment. It is also well understood that any attempted continuation of this system involves massive distributional injustices in favor of the retired and at the expense of the presently active generation. Yet, the electoral situation of any incumbent government makes it unfeasible (and politically virtually suicidal) to do either of the two things that evidently need to be done: to cut the benefits of the retired generation and/or to impose substantial additional burdens (which will not be shared by the employers) upon the employed of the active generation, the revenues from which can then serve to finance the transition to a funded system. In Germany, this configuration of constraints has been known for thirty years; had a revision of the pension system been initiated in the mid-1970s, the needed cuts in benefits and rises in contributions might have been spread over time and painlessly absorbed. Yet, liberal democracies are not made (at least not all of them) for policies with a thirty-year time horizon; instead, they are tied to medium-term electoral cycles that provide strong incentives to dump the externalities of presently unresolved problems onto future generations. These, in turn, become the victims of procrastination as they lack the time slack that is needed to cope with them.

To be sure, this is an extreme case of democratic institutional rigidity and the incapacity to adopt adequate and timely responses to challenges. But there are other examples of institutional arrangements being trapped in the sense that some paths are more difficult to depart from than others. The economic institutions of capitalist market societies can serve as an example of structurally precluded path-departure.[38] As far as political institutions are concerned, let us consider the example of five basic design alternatives of constitutional democracies. These are:

1. Federalism versus a unitary form of state
2. Direct democracy through referenda versus representative legislative bodies
3. Majority voting versus proportional representation
4. Parliamentary versus presidentialism
5. Intergovernmentalism versus supranational federalism (in the context of European integration)

The hypothetical argument I want to suggest (but cannot support here with any empirical evidence) is that the "transition probabilities" (or direction of entropy) between the first and the second of these design alternatives are quite asymmetrical. Some alterations of an institutional setup are uphill, others downhill. That is to say, it is easily conceivable that the government of a centralized state finds it in its interest and manages to mobilize support to pursue strategies of devolution and power sharing, but it is only under very exceptional conditions that the reverse takes place and a federal system generates a defederalizing reform. In order for uphill institutional innovations to materialize, some actors (federal states, the electorate, members of a duopoly of political parties, parliaments, nation-states) must be willing to deliberately disempower themselves, whereas they stand to gain power when reforms are adopted in the opposite direction.

(h) One limiting case of institutional change is "deinstitutionalization." Whereas all the previous cases in this section have dealt with either the continuity of institutions or processes by which one institutional pattern is replaced by another one, the case of deinstitutionalization is special in that rules are being abandoned *without* being replaced by some alternative institutional pattern. Social action that used to be governed by binding rules now becomes—and is, by some, recommended to be made—a matter of unrestrained, inventive, and unilateral ad hoc decision making. In the early twenty-first century, the map of the world is littered with deinstitutionalized states, or state ruins. This condition does not apply only to the most obvious cases, Afghanistan and Iraq. It also applies to Serbia, where none of the three prerequisites of statehood, namely fixed territorial borders, an effective regime covering this territory, and a population with a sense of loyalty toward this regime, is firmly in place.

It is interesting and arguably symptomatic to follow the use of the term "deinstitutionalization" in both positive and normative social science. The earliest use I was able to detect occurred in the late 1970s, when the term was introduced by specialists on the reform of psychiatric institutions (in the wake of the Italian Basaglia debate). In that usage, deinstitutionalization was equivalent to dehospitalization, which was both observed as a trend and (arguably somewhat frivolously) recommended as a left-libertarian reform strategy. From this highly specialized usage, the term spread to other social services (such as the rehabilitation of drug users and criminals) and to social policy studies in general.[39] From there, it was adopted as a key analytical concept by specialists in the fields of sociology of the family,[40] leisure activities, and religion. In the 1990s, the career of the concept continued in such diverse field as education and vocational training, development studies, organization and management, the economics of transformation societies, political culture (including the development of voting behavior and political parties), the formation of political elites, political decision making (e. g., through ad hoc committees rather than constituted parliamentary committees), international relations, and new types of military conflict, which are increasingly carried out by noninstitutional actors other than by (alliances of) states and their armies. The widely shared neoliberal belief that institutional constraints of markets, and in particular labor markets, are the prime obstacle to growth and prosperity points in the same direction. Other phenomena emerging in the institutionally uncharted terrain include "nongovernmental" and "nonprofit" organization, both of which are symptomatically designated in negative terms, that is, in terms of what they are *not* within the context of familiar institutional patterns.

In fact, we can observe in many of these fields symptoms of institutional decomposition, the common denominator of which might be described as the erosion of encompassing rules and their enforcement mechanisms, stable hierarchies, consolidated patterns of specialization and cooperation, "animating ideas" and hegemonic notions of normal patterns of the life course, and widely recognized frameworks of constraints and codes of conduct. Needless to say, such erosion is not just widely observed but also welcomed and promoted by the proponents of two ascendant public philosophies: libertarian varieties of social, economic, and political postmodernism, with their standard suspicion that institutions are mostly pretexts for rent-seeking or rigidities that interfere with efficiency, and communitarian social philosophies and political doctrines, with their emphasis on moral communities, identities, and the neo-Tocquevillean belief that what is needed for the coordination of social action is not so much institutions (with their implicit dangers of centralization and majority tyranny)[41] as the revitalization of community virtues and resources such as "social capital." So it is unsurprising that the kind of social scientists who are interested in the study, as well as the fair and appropriate design, of institutions often show sympathies with left-of-center liberal republicanism, in Europe better known as social democracy.[42]

It is also worth noting that, while the concern with institutions, their stability and credibility, has been a typical concern of conservative political thinkers, this concern seems now to have shifted its political base to the political left, while economic and political libertarians have adopted and made use of (some of) the political left's principled skepticism and suspicions concerning the illegitimate social power that is built into, as well as at the same time hidden by, institutions. The anti-institutional quest for unrestrained self-actualization, once having been proclaimed by leftist countercultural revolutionaries, is easily taken over by free-market libertarians. The reverse side of the anti-institutional libertarian advocacy of the market is the claim that institutionally unrestrained power should be used arbitrarily and to its full extent. For instance, populism is a political practice that is more concerned with understanding what "the people" feel and want than with observing the constraints of the institutions of representative political institutions. To the extent that these various projects succeed, it is no longer institutions that "structure politics" and "shape who wins and who loses"; it is power, sheer and naked, for the understanding of which institutionalist approaches may be no longer needed nor helpful.

One concluding remark: In the 1990s, the concept of "totalitarianism" has been revived and employed in the retrospective historical and comparative analysis of both the Nazi and the Stalinist regimes. As to the former, it has been argued by contemporaries of the National Socialist regime[43] that this regime represented an extreme form of "deinstitutionalization." Not only did it lacked a constitution; it even lacked a rule of succession for its top leadership, as well as even a rudimentary set of rules specifying the working relations between the four rival power centers of state, army, party, and industry. Everything that happened was based on decisions, virtually nothing on rules with any meaningful binding power, to say nothing about legal rights. Something similar might be argued concerning Stalin's Soviet Union. Both of these cases serve to demonstrate, if in different ways, how the "fearsome naturalness" of human action can unfold as a result of the radical erosion of institutions.

NOTES

Thanks for helpful criticism and hints are due to the organizers and participants of the conference, as well as to Ellen Immergut, Peter A. Kraus, Johanna A. Offe, and Rainer Schmalz-Bruns.

1. Sven Steinmo, Kathleen Thelen, and Frank Longstreth, eds., *Structuring Politics: Historical Institutionalism in Comparative Analysis* (New York: Cambridge University Press, 1992).

2. Sven Steinmo, "Institutionalism," in Neil J. Smelser and Paul B. Baltes, eds., *International Encyclopedia of the Social and Behavioral Sciences* 11 (Oxford: Elsevier, 2001), 7555.

3. Johan P. Olsen, "Institutional Design in Democratic Contexts," *The Journal of Political Philosophy* 5, 3 (1997): 221.

4. Donald L. Horowitz, "Constitutional Design: An Oxymoron?" in Ian Shapiro and Stephen Macedo, eds., *Designing Democratic Institutions, Nomos XLII* (New York: New York University Press, 2000), 254; cf. Claus Offe, "Political Liberalism, Group Rights and the Politics of Fear and Trust," in Claus Offe, *Herausforderungen der Demokratie* (Frankfurt am Main/New York: Campus, 2003), 321–334.

5. Robert E. Goodin, "Institutions and Their Design," in Introduction to Goodin (ed.), *The Theory of Institutional Design* (Cambridge: Cambridge University Press, 1996), 28–30.

6. Ernst Fraenkel, "Verfassungsreform und Sozialdemokratie," reprinted in Fraenkel, *Zur Soziologie der Klassenjustiz und Aufsätze zur Verfassungskrise 1931–32* (Darmstadt: Wissenschaftliche Buchgesellschaft, 1968 [1932]), 102.

7. Donald L. Horowitz, "Constitutional Design: An Oxymoron?" in Ian Shapiro and Stephen Macedo, eds., *Designing Democratic Institutions, Nomos XLII* (New York: New York University Press, 2000), 275.

8. James March and Johan P. Olsen, *Rediscovering Institutions: The Organizational Basis of Politics* (London: Collier Macmillan, 1989).

9. Cf. also Olsen, "Institutional Design in Democratic Contexts."

10. Goodin, "Institutions and Their Design," 26.

11. In the present demographic crisis, the first Chancellor of the West German state, Konrad Adenauer, is often quoted as saying that "people are always going to have children." This implicit theory undergirding the viability of welfare state institutions is evidently no longer true, any more than the assumption that people will always seek to participate in politics by solidly identifying with one political party.

12. Jürgen Habermas, *Faktizität und Geltung* (Frankfurt: Suhrkamp, 1992), ch. 8.

13. It is symptomatic that totalitarian regimes not only demolish all inherited institutions/constitutions as soon as they come to power but also attach political power to persons rather than to roles and offices. Thus the quasi-constitutional Nazi law, which was in fact the utter perversion of constitutionalism, of August 1, 1934, stipulates that the joint powers of the President and the Chancellor shall now be in the hands of "Adolf Hitler" and that the law becomes effective at the time of death of the (then nominally still president) Hindenburg.

14. Claus Offe, "Designing Institutions for East European Transitions" in Robert E. Goodin, ed., *The Theory of Institutional Design* (Cambridge: Cambridge University Press, 1996), 199–226.

15. Cf. Shmuel N. Eisenstadt, "Social Institutions: The Cconcept," in David Sills, ed., *International Encyclopedia of the Social Sciences* 14 (1968), 409–421.

16. Douglass C. North, *Institutions, Institutional Change, and Economic Performance* (Cambridge: Cambridge University Press, 1990).

17. Elinor Ostrom, *Governing the Commons: The Evolution of Institutions for Collective Action* (Cambridge: Cambridge University Press, 1990), 50–55.

18. David Easton, *A Systems Analysis of Political Life* (New York: Wiley, 1965).

19. Peter A. Hall, *Governing the Economy: The Politics of State Intervention in Britain and France* (New York: Oxford University Press, 1986).

20. Cf. Jack Knight, *Institutions and Social Conflict* (Cambridge: Cambridge University Press, 1992).

21. "One of the main features of institutional rules is that they are socially shared. The knowledge of their existence and applicability is shared by the members of the relevant group or community" (ibid., 68).

22. Ibid., ch. 3.

23. Arnold Gehlen, *Urmensch und Spätkultur: Philosophische Ergebnisse und Aussagen* (Bonn: Athenäum, 1956).

24. Ibid.

25. Herbert Marcuse, *One-Dimensional Man: Studies in the Ideology of Advanced Industrial Society* (Boston: Beacon Press, 1964).

26. Goodin, "Institutions and Their Design," 23.

27. Knight, *Institutions and Social Conflict*, 58–59.

28. North, *Institutions, Institutional Change, and Economic Performance.*

29. Friedrich A. Hayek, *Law, Legislation and Liberty,* 1 (London: Routledge, 1973).

30. Barry Hindess, "Politics as Government" (ANU: unpublished manuscript, 2001), 2, 4, 11.

31. March and Olsen, *Rediscovering Institutions.*

32. John Stuart Mill, *On Liberty* (London: Longmans, Green, Reader and Dyer, 1875).

33. Peter Bachrach and Morton S. Baratz, *Power and Poverty: Theory and Practice* (New York: Oxford University Press, 1970).

34. Stephen Lukes, *Power: A Radical View* (London: Macmillan, 1974); John Gaventa, *Power and Powerlessness: Quiescence and Rebellion in an Appalachian Valley* (Oxford: Clarendon Press, 1980).

35. It is this web of beliefs on which the viability of state socialist authoritarian regimes depended and they they have been able to effectively inculcate in their citizens. As a consequence, many of them have preferred to play with the proverbial "devil we know."

36. Cf. Carles Boix, "Setting the Rules of the Game," *American Political Science Review* 93, 3 (1999): 609–624.

37. For example, according to German constitutional jurisprudence (revised in early 2005), the *Grundgesetz* does not permit the adoption of a mode of financing tertiary education that would rely to a significant extent on the payment of tuition fees. As a consequence, a condition is likely to remain immune to political challenge in which not only is the university system massively underfunded, but also the universe of taxpayers subsidizes, with highly regressive distributional effects, the human capital formation of the middle class whose offspring will continue to attend universities for free.

38. Lindblom analyses the market as a mechanism "for repressing change through an automatic punishing recoil." "The market might be characterized as a prison. For a broad category of political/economic affairs, it imprisons policy making and imprisons our attempts to improve our institutions." See Charles E. Lindblom, "The Market as Prison," *Journal of Politics* 44, 2 (1982): 325, 329.

39. The earliest book-length treatment in which the concept plays a central role is Paul Lerman, *Deinstitutionalization and the Welfare State* (New Brunswick, NJ: Rutgers University Press, 1981).

40. Hartmann Tyrell, "Ehe und Familie— Institutionalisierung und Deinstitutionalisierung," in Kurt Lüscher et al., eds., *Die "postmoderne" Familie* (Konstanz, 1988), 145–156.

41. Cf. Peter L. Berger and Richard Neuhaus, *To Empower People: The Role of Mediating Structures in Public Policy* (Washington, DC: American Enterprise Institute for Public Policy Research, 1977).

42. Bo Rothstein, *Just Institutions Matter: The Moral and Political Logic of the Universal Welfare State* (Cambridge: Cambridge University Press, 1998), is an example.

43. Franz Neumann, *Behemoth: The Structure and Practice of National Socialism* (Toronto/New York: Oxford University Press, 1944).

2

Power and Political Institutions

Terry M. Moe

More than a decade ago, I attended a conference at Yale on the rational choice theory of political institutions, where I presented a paper that took issue with the way the theory was then developing.[1] The problem, as I saw it, was that the theory tended to view political institutions as structures of voluntary cooperation that resolve collective action problems and benefit all concerned, when in fact the political process often gives rise to institutions that are good for some people and bad for others depending on who has the power to impose their will. Institutions may be structures of cooperation, I argued, but they may also be structures of power. And the theory should recognize as much.

I didn't get a standing ovation at the conference. But in the broader community of scholars I was hardly alone in thinking that power is essential to an understanding of political institutions. Jack Knight soon published a book-length analysis arguing that institutions are mainly explained by distributional conflicts—and power—rather than collective benefits.[2] Even by then, major studies relying on rational choice reasoning had already made power central to their analyses of political institutions,[3] and in the years since this kind of work has continued to grow and reach a broad audience.[4] Indeed, power is so commonly featured in this literature that it is now easy to believe—as I suspect most scholars in the field do—that power is an integral part of the theory, on a par with cooperation in explaining political institutions.

But it really isn't. However much power might be discussed, the fundamentals of the theory have not changed. They take their orientation from the same framework that guides all economic theory: voluntary exchange among rational individuals. They identify the key challenge as one of understanding whether rational individuals will cooperate in the face of collective action problems. And their explanations are built around mutual gains, credible commitments, self-enforcing equilibria, and other concepts that flow from the logic of voluntary choice. This is the analytic core of the theory, the root source of its logic, language, and formalization.

There are two problems here. The first is that power is a peripheral component of the theory. The rational choice theory of political institutions is really a theory of cooperation that, with elaboration, can be used to say something about power. As Mancur Olson rightly notes, "We need to understand the logic of power"—and the current theory of voluntary exchange is not designed to do that.[5]

The second problem reinforces the first. It is that, because power is so obviously important to politics and so commonly a part of institutional analysis, the literature gives the sense that power *is* being given equal (or at least appropriate) weight in the overall theory. There is a good deal of confusion about the relative analytic roles of power and cooperation, and this confusion undermines efforts to right the imbalance.

Of course, maybe there is just one problem here: that I am confused. And I expect that more than one rational choice theorist will tell me so. But I have participated in this field for a long time now, and I think it's fair to say that, if I am confused, I'm not alone. There is much to be gained, therefore, in clarifying how power and cooperation are dealt with in this literature, and in encouraging an appropriate balance between the two.

Institutions as Structures of Cooperation

Prior to the 1980s, social choice theory had shown that collective decisions are prone to instabilities, and that voting can easily lead to chaos in which virtually any alternative can beat any other given the right manipulation of the agenda.[6] A puzzle remained, however, because voting processes in the real world of government are usually quite stable. Why so much stability? The answer, as Kenneth Shepsle and Barry Weingast so elegantly showed, is that voting typically occurs within a structure of rules that limit the agenda and bring about stability.[7]

Thus began the positive theory of political institutions. The early focus on agenda control was only natural given the dilemmas of social choice. Yet agenda control was regarded as important not simply because it brings stability to chaos, but also because of its clear connection to political power: whoever controls the agenda can engineer voting outcomes to his or her own advantage, and thus gain power over policy. Indeed, the classic works on agenda control by William Niskanen and by Thomas Romer and Howard Rosenthal were not centrally about chaos and stability.[8] They were studies of institutionally based power that showed how particular actors—bureaus in the former case, school boards in the latter—used agenda control to get their way in politics.

By the early 1980s the rudiments of a power-based theory seemed to be in place. The public choice literature was already well developed; and in addition to its work on agenda control, its work on rent-seeking also put the spotlight on power. Rent-seeking focused on the power of interest groups over public policy, and on the social inefficiencies that arise from lobbying and special-interest policies.[9] While the subject of this work was policy rather than institutions, the overlap was substantial and unavoidable. Policies that create tariffs and quotas in international trade, for example, are essentially just creating institutions—rules, agreements, organizations. Thus, while the rent-seeking literature is often portrayed as an interest-group theory of public policy, it also offers a (nascent) theory of political institutions—arguing that they are beneficial to some, harmful to others, and socially inefficient.

Prior to the new institutionalism, then, rational choice theory was already providing power-based explanations for governmental structure. Its analytic center of gravity, however, was about to change. The stimulus was the rise of a new body of theory within economics that sought to explain the existence and properties of economic organization.[10] Once economists trained their sights on issues of organization, their new analytic tools—among them transaction cost economics, agency theory, and theories of repeated games—transformed the intellectual terrain of their discipline. Political scientists soon began applying these tools to political institutions, and the new institutionalism was off and running.[11]

As in economics generally, the basic framework in this literature is one of voluntary exchange among autonomous actors. But its distinctive focus is on cooperation. How can individuals who are self-interested and opportunistic overcome their collective action problems to cooperate for mutual gain? The answers take the form of institutions—usually involving rules and other formal structures, but sometimes consisting solely of informal arrangements (rooted in norms, for instance)—which allow participants to mitigate obstacles to collective action, commit to cooperative agreements, and realize gains from trade. As such, institutions emerge as good things, and it is their goodness that ultimately explains them. They exist and take the forms they do because they make people better off.[12]

Consider the familiar principal-agent relationship between an employer and a potential employee. The principal has limited time and knowledge, and he can gain by hiring someone with expertise to do the work. The agent can gain by getting paid. But despite the prospect of mutual gain, it is not easy for them to cooperate. The agent has interests of his own—for example, in leisure or professionalism—that give him incentives not to do what is best for the principal. He also has an informational advantage that makes such shirking possible: for he has expertise the principal does not have, takes actions the principal cannot observe, and has personal qualities—his levels of honesty, diligence, and the like—that are largely hidden. A bad worker has incentives to use the information asymmetry to pass himself off as a good worker, while a good worker may have a hard time convincing the principal of his true type. As a result, the principal has reason to distrust his agent, to pay him less than a good agent is worth, and perhaps not to hire anyone at all.

These actors face a collective action problem. The principal and a good worker could both benefit from cooperation, but the information asymmetry prevents them from fully realizing gains from trade. The way around the problem is for the principal to devise an efficient set of rules, incentive structures, and monitoring mechanisms that—by mitigating the information asymmetry and bringing the agent's interests into alignment with the principal's—represents a mutually beneficial arrangement to which both parties can credibly commit, and is either self-enforcing or enforceable by a third party such as the courts. This arrangement is an institutional solution (a simplified version of the business firm) that makes cooperation possible. The actors choose it and stick with it because they both benefit, and this is what explains the institution's emergence, its specific form, and its ultimate stability.[13]

I have used the principal-agent framework for illustration, but the logic is characteristic of the new economics of organization more generally. Transaction cost economics, for example, leads to the same basic conclusions. Efforts by both actors to strike a beneficial deal are confounded by the same information asymmetry, creating high transaction costs. And efforts to minimize these costs lead to the same sorts of institutional solutions that help them cooperate for mutual gain. All roads lead to Rome.

Given this perspective on institutions, how does power fit in? The literature offers no clear answer. In our principal-agent example, it might seem obvious that the employer exercises power over the employee. But the institutional solution to their cooperation problem has to be mutually beneficial, and could just as well be designed by the agent. This is true even of whatever formal authority the employer gains under the new institution; for authority is endogenous to their agreement and beneficial to the agent as well as the principal. The principal, by this logic, has no special power just because he is on top.

An alternative view is that the agent actually wields power in this relationship, using his informational advantage to circumvent the principal's control and pursue his own ends. Such information-based power is well recognized in the study of bureaucracy, going back to Max Weber.[14] But if we turn to the basics of the theory, the real import of asymmetric information is not that it somehow empowers the agent, but that it creates problems for the principal *and* the agent and is *bad for both of them*. Yes, the agent's expertise gives him leverage and allows him to shirk. But this is why the principal distrusts him and may not want to deal with him at all. The source of his power is the source of his undoing. His challenge is to find a way—an institutional solution—to overcome the handicap of his power and get the principal to cooperate with him for mutual gain. This is what the analysis is really about. Not agent power, but cooperation for mutual gain.

In political science, the new economics of organization has been applied to a broad range of political institutions, from legislatures to bureaucracies to international organizations to the basic framework of democracy.[15] Power is often part of these analyses. But with a few exceptions, which I discuss below, it is included because it is obviously relevant to institutional politics and can't be ignored, not because the theories are designed to explore its exercise and consequences. The most basic arguments are about how self-interested actors can make voluntary choices to overcome collective action problems and cooperate for mutual gain. Often the focus is specifically on credible commitments and self-enforcing agreements, two major ingredients that can make cooperation possible.

A good example is Barry Weingast and William Marshall's analysis of the internal organization of Congress.[16] In effect, their logic begins with a stylized state of nature in which legislators make decisions by majority rule. These actors face a collective action problem. All want policies beneficial to their own districts, but they can't get them without the support of colleagues whose interests are often very different. Efforts to construct the coalitions needed for countless bills over time are threatened by endless haggling, frequent reneging, complexity, uncertainty, and other sources of heavy transaction costs. Most coalitions never form, and the gains from trade are foregone—to the disadvantage of all.

The solution, Weingast and Marshall argue, is to reduce transaction costs dramatically through a set of internal structures—committees with strict jurisdictions and gate-keeping powers, for example—that facilitate credible commitments and promote regular cooperation. This institutional solution, they claim, is the structure that has emerged to govern the modern Congress, and it is stable because it is self-enforcing—that is to say, because legislators find it beneficial and have no incentive to defect.

The rational choice literature is more diverse than this one illustration can suggest. But the theme is a general one, and it has put its distinctive stamp on the way institutions are studied and understood. This is succinctly revealed in the observations of scholars who have sought to provide perspective on the literature as a whole. Consider, for example, Shepsle's summary remarks in an influential early article on the nature of political institutions:

> The argument developed only briefly here is that cooperation that is chancy and costly to transact at the level of individual agents is facilitated at the level of institutions. Practices, arrangements, and structures at the institutional level economize on transaction costs, reduce opportunism and other forms of agency "slippage," and thereby enhance the prospects of gains through cooperation, in a manner generally less available at the individual level. Institutions, then, look like ex ante agreements about the structure of cooperation.[17]

Thematically, things have not changed over the years. In a recent compendium on the discipline of political science, Weingast offers the following overview of the literature on why institutions exist and take the forms they do:

> In brief, the answer is [that individuals] often need institutions to help capture gains from cooperation. In the absence of institutions, individuals often face a social dilemma, that is, a situation where their behavior makes all worse off. . . .
>
> Appropriately configured institutions restructure incentives so that individuals have an incentive to cooperate. . . . The essence of institutions is to enforce mutually beneficial exchange and cooperation.[18]

Power and Domestic Institutions

It might seem easiest to argue the importance of power when political institutions are the creations of predatory rulers or international hegemons. So let's begin at the other end of the spectrum, with political institutions that are created through democratic politics under constitutional rules of the game. On the surface, these contexts would appear to give cooperationist theories the greatest possible advantage and a power critique its greatest challenge.

What kinds of institutions do democracies normally create? Political scientists tend to rivet their attention on the key authoritative institutions—legislative, executive, and judicial—set up by the constitution, or on the framework of democratic rules themselves. The great bulk of government, however, is composed of bureaucratic agencies—unexciting as this may sound—and they are designed and adopted by public officials who make decisions under prevailing rules of the game. To simplify the discussion, these are the institutions I'll be focusing on here.[19]

It is easy to see that these most common of democratic institutions are often *not* cooperative or mutually beneficial for many of the people affected by them. They involve the exercise of power. This is so even if the democratic rules of the game are assiduously followed in their creation and design. A prime reason is that the public authority employed to create and design them can be exercised by whatever coalitions gain the necessary support in the legislature (often a majority). Whoever wins has the right to make decisions on behalf of everyone, and whoever loses is required by law—backed by the police powers of the state—to accept the winners' decisions. This means that any groups that prevail under the formal rules can legitimately use public authority to impose bureaucratic institutions that are structurally stacked in their own favor, and that may make the losers worse off, perhaps by a lot.[20]

In the voluntaristic framework of the new economics, which often makes good sense in competitive contexts of economic choice, people who expect to lose from any proposed institutional arrangement *can simply walk away.* This is what guarantees (in theory) that such structures will be mutually beneficial. The losers don't have to participate. But in democratic politics, *they can't leave,* at least not unless they are prepared to leave the country, which is typically not a practical option. So when they lose under the democratic rules of the game, they have to suffer the consequences—

and the winners are well aware of this. The latter can impose the institutions they want. There is nothing to stop them. They don't need to cooperate.[21]

Alternative Views

There are other ways of looking at institutional politics that put a more positive, cooperationist spin on these issues, and they are worth considering—in part because they represent familiar lines of reasoning, and in part because they are sources of confusion that need to be clarified. Two stand out.

The first is rooted in Coasian models of economic exchange, in which freely bargaining actors can arrive at a point on the Pareto frontier that is efficient and beneficial to all concerned. In a political context, the idea is that, when public policies (and institutions) help some interests and hurt others but expand the size of the pie, the winners can compensate the losers through some form of bargain and both can be better off. When policies are inefficient and don't expand the size of the pie, bargaining will lead to their rejection. The vision is one of cooperation and mutual gain.

This argument doesn't wash, however. Consider the best-case scenario in which a policy (such as free trade) stands to make both sides better off once compensation payments are made, and the support of both sides is needed for passage. The problem is that such bargains tend to involve enormous transaction costs and are difficult if not impossible to arrange. The transaction costs arise not only from difficulties in identifying the relevant actors, amounts, and conditions, but also from difficulties in arriving at agreements that are mutually credible and enforceable despite the uncertainties of democratic politics. As Thrainn Eggertsson notes, "[I]n the real world, high costs of negotiating and enforcing such agreements prohibit them: seldom do winners voluntarily compensate the losers."[22] If the losers' support is not necessary for passage of the policy, things are of course brighter for the winners, who do not need to bargain at all. Society is allegedly better off with the new policy and the bigger pie. But the winners now have no incentive to compensate the losers—who are worse off, and stay worse off.[23]

Now consider the flipside of the above scenario. Let's assume that a powerful group is in a position to impose a special-interest policy that is inefficient for society, making the size of the pie smaller but the winning group itself better off. According to the Coasian argument, the losers would prevent this inefficient policy from being adopted by paying off the winners. But here too, for the same reasons as in the first case, the transaction costs will typically be prohibitively high, and most bargains will not actually happen. The inefficient policy will be enacted, the winners will win, and society as a whole will be worse off. (Even if the bargain does happen, the losers still wind up worse off than under the original status quo, and the winners get a bundle for simply threatening to use the power of public authority.)

Note the logic at work here. The argument that bargaining will somehow save institutions from social inefficiency, an argument that essentially defends the cooperationist theme of the new economics, runs smack into the logic of the new economics itself. A political bargain to produce an efficient policy—or prevent an inefficient one—is only likely to succeed in a Coasian world in which transaction costs are small and unimportant. But the defining claim of the new economics is that transaction costs tend to be large and important.[24] Indeed, this is the foundation of its analysis of institutions. If transaction costs in politics are large and important, however, then many political bargains are likely to be untenable, compensations are likely to go unpaid, political outcomes are likely to be inefficient, and there are likely to be losers as well as winners.

Now consider a second line of reasoning that also puts a positive spin on democratically created institutions. This one arises from the familiar notion that government is based on a social contract. The idea here is that, while certain groups may be losers when new institutions are created within democratic politics, they are not really losers (or do not expect to be) in the grander scheme of things. They accept the overarching framework of democratic rules; and although they know they may lose on particular decisions, they expect to be better off than they would be outside the framework—under some other constitution, say, or no constitution at all. Thus, particular domestic institutions may not be to their liking, but this is part of the larger deal, and the system as a whole is good and beneficial.

This argument might carry some weight if a political system were analogous to what Oliver Williamson calls a "governance structure" in the economic realm.[25] Governance structures are relational contracts in which actors agree to procedures that allow them to adjudicate disputes, adjust to new developments, and otherwise ensure that their original agreement is maintained over time in a changing environment. The actors know that particular decisions may not go their way, but they participate because they see the entire arrangement and its stream of decisions as beneficial.

What makes such stylized governance structures different from political systems, however, is that they are voluntary. People agree to participate, and they can walk away if they believe they are not better off. Political systems are different. Centuries of political philosophy notwithstanding, there is no social contract in any meaningful sense that can account for the foundations of government.[26] In all modern societies, people are typically born into the formal structure of their political systems, do not agree to it from the outset, and cannot leave if they find it disadvantageous (unless they leave the country). This being so, the fact that some groups lose in domestic politics—and have new institutions thrust upon them that they do not want—cannot be glossed over by saying that they have agreed to the larger system. They haven't.

Another problem with the social contract argument is that it substitutes oranges for apples. A theory of institutions should be able to explain how bureaucratic agencies emerge from the political process and why they take the forms they do. If the theory implies that institutions are cooperative and mutually beneficial, then surely this conclusion should apply to bureaucratic organizations (where it fails). But the social contract argument shifts attention to the democratic framework itself. While it recognizes that bureaucratic organizations may not be cooperative and mutually beneficial, it implicitly contends that the *framework* is the institution we ought to be focusing on, and that this institution *is* cooperative and mutually beneficial. Even if this claim were true (and it isn't), it does nothing to address the original challenge to the theory—that bureaucracies often violate the theory's expectations—and nothing to move us toward a theory that accounts for the kinds of institutions that arise out of democratic politics. Instead, it confuses the issue by creating ambiguity around what we mean by "institution" and what we are trying to explain.

Theories of Bureaucracy

These sorts of ambiguities are not unique to the social-contract argument. They pervade virtually all aspects of what the new economics has to say about political institutions. Consider the rational-choice theory of public bureaucracy, which attempts to explain precisely the kinds of domestic institutions that we have been discussing thus far.

Here the seminal work is by Matthew McCubbins, Roger Noll, and Barry Weingast, who use a principal-agent approach to explain the structure of American bureaucracy.[27] How, they ask, can an "enacting coalition" of legislators and interest groups ensure that its favored policies are faithfully carried out by its bureaucratic agents? The solution takes the form of structure: a rational coalition will impose rules, decision procedures, and reporting requirements that are strategically designed to constrain the bureaucracy to do what it wants. Their explanation of bureaucratic structure, then, arises from the efforts of legislators and their allies to control the bureaucracy.

In another major work, Murray Horn wants to explain the same things that McCubbins, Noll, and Weingast do.[28] But he focuses less on the principal-agent problem facing the enacting coalition than on the exchange relationship between legislators and interest groups, and thus on the agreement that gives rise to the enacting coalition itself. Actors on both sides of the exchange have something to trade. Interest groups have campaign contributions and other resources to offer legislators; legislators have the authority to create policies and agencies beneficial to the groups. Attempts to cooperate for mutual gain, however, are undermined by transaction costs. Most important, the legislators have a hard time guaranteeing that any benefits provided today will endure over time because they can't commit future legislatures (possibly controlled by opponents) to uphold the deal. And the less credibly legislators can promise future benefits, the less the groups will want to pay in the current period. To overcome this commitment problem, legislators create agencies that—by structural design—are not only constrained to pursue the groups' interests, but also insulated from unwanted future influences.

These two theories are self-conscious applications of the new economics, but neither does much to clarify how bureaucratic institutions are cooperative and mutually beneficial. There is much to be gained from exploring this, so let me offer a reconstruction of their arguments that I think is consistent with the logic of their work. In both analyses there are inevitably losers in the politics by which bureaucratic agencies are created. The authors make nothing of this. Nevertheless, the enacting coalition is only one faction of legislators and interest groups. Other factions are losers and may be worse off because of the coalition's choices. The same is true for portions of the larger population, who must live with the institutions being thrust upon them. In this fundamental sense, the bureaucracy cannot be viewed as a structure of cooperation.

This is only half the story, however. Even if the bureaucracy is coercive, in the sense that it is imposed by winners on losers, these analyses correctly point to two cooperative elements that explain how structural choices emerge out of politics. The first is that legislators and groups in the enacting coalition must arrive at an agreement that overcomes their collective action problems. This agreement, which is largely about the structural contours of the agency, is cooperative and mutually beneficial. The second element is the principle-agent relationship between legislators and the bureaucratic agency. If the legislators are to get the performance they want from the agency, they must solve the "principal's problem" by designing an efficient structure that is acceptable to the bureaucrats. Because of the acceptability criterion, which is fundamental to any principal-agent relationship, this agreement too can be viewed as cooperative and mutually beneficial.[29] The bureaucracy thus arises out of two founding agreements, a coalitional agreement among legislators and interest groups and a principal-agent agreement among legislators and bureaucrats. These agreements are interrelated—each presupposes the other—and can jointly be viewed as a nexus of contracts that create the new institution.

Both power and cooperation are essential, therefore, to any effort to understand public agencies. Bureaucracies are institutions that are imposed by winners on losers. But they are also cooperative and mutually beneficial for the subset of actors who agree to their creation. Each property, in fact, is fundamental to the other. It is precisely because they cooperate that the winners are able to use public authority to impose their will on the rest of society. And it is the prospect of exercising this power that motivates the winners to cooperate.[30]

With this as background, let's step back and consider two basic ambiguities that plague the new economics, at least as it applies to political institutions. First, what are the institutions being explained? Second, who are the actors for whom these institutions are cooperative and mutually beneficial?

When attention is confined to private firms, the situation being analyzed is self-contained: all the action is "internal." The firm is a nexus of contracts among owners, managers, and workers, who enter into voluntary agreements about the organization and its structure that apply *to them* and govern *their own* behavior. In effect, the institution is their agreement, and they are creating the institution *for themselves*. It only makes sense, then, that they—the "insiders"—are the relevant population by which we determine whether the institution is cooperative and mutually beneficial.

Suppose we apply this same line of reasoning to public agencies. On the surface, what we are trying to explain is exactly the same: the organization and its structure. But the underlying agreement that creates an agency does not consist of the people we would at first blush think are its insiders, namely, the bureaucrats who make up the agency. The agreement includes the bureaucrats plus all the legislators and interest groups in the enacting coalition. It is this much larger and very different "institution" that is the political analogue to the business firm. And all these political players—bureaucrats, winning legislators, winning interest groups—are its insiders. They are the ones who have cooperated in creating an agency that is beneficial *for them.* If we view them as the relevant population, then, the institution can be said to be cooperative and mutually beneficial.

This perspective identifies an important sense in which bureaucracies *are* structures of cooperation. Yet it fails to recognize what is truly fundamental about them: that they are created through a process of collective choice in which the victorious insiders get to impose their institutional creations on society as a whole. The cooperative agreement that they reach among themselves is not just an agreement that applies to them and governs their own behavior. It is an agreement that applies to *everyone* and governs *everyone's* behavior. This being so, defining the institution in terms of the agreement among insiders ignores the fact that, once the agreement becomes law, everyone must follow its rules. They can't walk away.

There are other confusions as well. Consider what happens when we try to explain a public agency's stability. The new economics would have us focus on the overarching agreement among the firm's insiders and on whether they have incentives not to defect from the deal. But in politics this doesn't make much sense. Once an agency is created, it becomes a legal entity in its own right, and its survival and structure are protected by democratic rules of the game. In the American system, for instance, the policymaking process is filled with veto points, making new legislation difficult to achieve and blocking relatively easy. The upshot is that, while a strong coalition may have been necessary to create the agency, protecting it from formal change is much easier—and can be carried out by a weaker coalition, a different coalition, or by ad hoc voting partners who come to the agency's aid in time of need. Thus the stability of the agency itself is *not* contingent upon maintaining the original agreement or preventing members from defecting from the enacting coalition. The only part of the agreement that needs to live on is the agency, which can live forever as long as no new legislation is passed.

In the end, whether a political institution is considered cooperative and mutually beneficial, as well as how we want to think about its stability, depends on what we mean by "institution" and which actors we count as the relevant population. These are not matters of objective truth, but matters of analytical choice. The argument I presented earlier, that domestically created political institutions are inherently coercive, is also not a straightforward matter of truth. It was founded on a conceptual choice, which I left ambiguous: I was looking at institutions and their relevant populations in the broader sense just outlined, not in the narrower sense that a business-based application of the new economics seems to imply. The claims I made were correct, given my implicit definitions. But a new economics claim that political institutions are cooperative and mutually beneficial is also correct, based on alternative interpretations of those same terms. While there can be no right way to define our concepts, we do need to be clear about them, and thus clear about what we are saying. When we are, it turns out that both power and cooperation play essential roles in explaining how public agencies emerge from democratic politics, how they get designed, and what their consequences are.

I want to close by returning to the ambiguity at the heart of all principal-agent relationships: the question of whether, in a relationship of cooperation and mutual benefit, principals and agents might still be thought of as exercising power over one another. In the discussion above, I ignored this ambiguity to avoid complicating a basic point that needed to be clarified: that cooperation occurs among insiders, who use their cooperation to exercise power over others. This point is relatively easy to drive home, because the kind of power involved makes someone worse off. When we talk about power within a principal-agent relationship, however, we no longer have this advantage, because both the principal and the agent come out ahead. If power is being exercised, it is more difficult to recognize and more difficult to distinguish from cooperation.

The usual interpretation of the bureaucratic theories we just considered is that they are theories of political control—theories, that is, of how the legislature controls the bureaucracy. Indeed, the McCubbins, Noll, and Weingast argument is a major component of what is often called the congressional dominance theory.[31] It would be easy to infer, based on the language employed, that these must be theories of power. Yet this is true only in a superficial sense. For if we take their analytic frameworks seriously, the power presumed to be exercised by the legislature over the bureaucracy is embedded in relationships that are cooperative and mutually beneficial, and the explanation of bureaucratic structure is rooted in cooperationist theory. These are theories of cooperation that talk the language of power, but without recognizing or dealing with the key ambiguity involved.[32]

I will revisit this principal-agent ambiguity in a later section. For now, I simply want to observe that if we can find a way to think clearly about power within principal-agent relationships, and if we decide that power is being exercised, then cooperation *among the insiders* actually has a power dimension to it. This being so, a theory of institutions would need to recognize a key role for power not simply in the efforts of insiders to impose their institutional creations on everyone else, but also in their efforts to arrive at agreements among themselves.

Power and Institutions in the State of Nature

If power is essential to an understanding of institutions in orderly, rule-governed contexts, what about contexts that lack an overarching set of constitutional rules—because the rules do not exist, say, or because they are vague or in transition or the subject of struggle?

In these sorts of anarchic settings, public authority and government do not exist, and they cannot be used by some groups to impose their will on others. On the surface, this might seem to brighten the prospects for cooperation, and it is tempting to make parallels to the state of nature that economists often assume: a marketplace in which autonomous actors are free to make choices and enter into agreements as they see fit. Given such a scenario, it might seem that any agreements would be cooperative and mutually beneficial.

But the economists' state of nature implicitly assumes an overarching system of law that guarantees property rights and enforces contracts. The existence of such a system obviously reduces the likelihood of theft and violence, promotes social order, and enhances cooperation and exchange. It also violates what we mean by a state of nature, for its actors are playing by rules imposed and enforced from above.

What happens when there aren't any rules? The answer is that social actors are plunged into a Hobbesian world in which people are nominally free to make their own decisions and enter into cooperative arrangements—but everyone is also vulnerable to predation by everyone else, and the weak are particularly vulnerable to predation by the powerful. They are free to be robbed, free to be murdered, free to be enslaved.

The absence of government cuts both ways, then. It removes public authority from the political equation and thus eliminates the immediate means by which the winners impose new institutions on the losers in domestic politics. Yet it also removes the framework of rules that can guarantee order in society, protect property rights and contracts, and promote trade and cooperation. And in eliminating such rules, it creates opportunities for the exercise of other types of power that do not depend on public authority for their force.

The Rise and Development of National Institutions

In their attempts to explain the origin of political institutions, rational choice theorists often begin with a state of nature—which is sometimes Hobbesian and sometimes not—and ask about the prospects for cooperation. How can self-interested individuals overcome their collective action problems and all the dangers of the state of nature to arrive at basic rules for the conduct of their affairs?[33] Until the new economics burst on the scene, the accepted answers were essentially negative. Hobbes, of course, had argued that the solution was an all-powerful Leviathan. And Olson had argued that rational individuals would usually not cooperate in pursuit of common interests, and that selective incentives or coercion would typically be required to get them to organize.[34] (Even then, they would not really be cooperating.)

With the new economics, the pendulum swung hard the other way. Theories of repeated games, whose technology was just becoming available, showed that the prospects for cooperation are much brighter when people interact with one another again and again over time, and pointed toward a variety of factors—the strategies of the players, the "shadow of the future," reputations, the ability to commit, and so on—that determined whether cooperation would occur.[35] The rise of transaction cost economics and agency theory, which linked cooperation to formal institutions, was an integral part of all this. Both took advantage of the same technology, and their cooperationist logic reinforced the same themes. Before long, cooperation was the basis for a new theory of political institutions.

As the theory has grown over the years and been applied to a range of institutional topics, some of the most influential work has dealt with how the fundamentals of democracy emerge out of state-of-nature-like contexts in which rules of governance are absent, problematic, or in flux. A notable example is a widely cited article by Douglass North and Barry Weingast on the rise of democracy in seventeenth-century England.[36]

Their account takes the following form. The English kings needed money for their military campaigns (and other things) but had difficulty raising funds. The problem was that, however solemn their promises to repay loans from financial elites, their own sovereignty allowed them to renege on any deals—so their promises were not credible, and fund-raising deals that could have been mutually beneficial often did not materialize. In effect, the kings were too powerful for their own good, and they were suffering the consequences. As were financial elites. There was, however, an institutional solution to their dilemma. The solution was to "tie the king's hands" by devising a new system of governance that transferred significant legal powers to parliament and an independent judiciary. This dilution of monarchical power was good for kings because they could now raise money by making credible promises to repay loans. And it was good for the moneyed interests (represented in parliament) because they could now make loans, be repaid, and have their property rights protected. The institutional solution—the basic framework of democracy—was thus cooperative and mutually beneficial, and it was stable because neither side had an incentive to defect.[37]

The notion that democratic institutions arise as cooperative solutions to collective action problems can be found in other influential works as well. In his study of transitions to democracy in Eastern Europe and Latin America, for example, Adam Przeworski argues that democracies emerge when opposing groups see elections as giving them a fair chance of competing for office, and when they believe that—even if they stand to lose on occasion—they can still advance their own interests over time.[38] When these conditions are met, the groups can agree to abide by a set of democratic rules. Democracies are thus self-enforcing structures of cooperation and mutual benefit.

But this begs an important question: who are the insiders for whom the agreement is cooperative and mutually beneficial? In Przeworski's case, the insiders are the two opposing groups, and his analysis shows that, under certain circumstances, they can arrive at a solution that involves elections. Yet in any real-world context, these two groups would not represent the preferences of all citizens, and there is no guarantee that the unrepresented would be better off as a result of the deal. They never agreed to it. What we do know is that two groups powerful enough to be threats to one another, and probably to national peace and stability, have forged an agreement that is imposed on everyone else. It is cooperative and mutually beneficial *for them,* but not necessarily for others.

In North and Weingast's argument, the situation is more involved. As I have told their story—consistent with the theoretical lesson usually associated with it—the insiders would appear to be a select group of elites, namely, the king and the moneyed class. If so, it would be *their* agreement. The new democratic institutions would be cooperative and mutually beneficial for them, but not necessarily for ordinary people, who were not part of the deal. But the story that North and Weingast actually tell is more complicated. For although tying the king's hands proves to be a good thing for monarchs over the long haul, the monarchs themselves did not see it that way ex ante. They fervently *resisted* having their hands tied, and only violence and revolution settled the issue. Democratic institutions had to be *forced* on the monarchy. The rise of British democracy had at least as much to do with power as with cooperation—but this is nowhere reflected in the theoretical lesson we are supposed to take away from the analysis.

This same literature on the rise of the state also advances an important companion theme. The idea is that democratic institutions promote economic growth, that economic growth is good for everyone, and that this makes democracy attractive to those who choose institutions.

The connection between institutions and economic growth has been explored most influentially by North.[39] In a series of publications that won him a Nobel Prize, North's institutional theory departs significantly from neoclassical economics in explaining why some economies succeed and other do not. The argument is multifaceted, but its main lesson is simply this: that political institutions have profound effects on economic growth, and if rulers are able to adopt the *right* institutions—if they are able to get property rights right—then the economy will grow and everyone in society can benefit, including the ruler.

North recognizes that rulers usually do not choose this productive path—in part because it can threaten their hold on political power—and that they often create institutions that are predatory and socially inefficient instead. The coercive power of the state, he says, is necessary in order to impose a good framework of rules that encourage productive cooperation, but the conundrum is that "if the state has coercive force, then those who run the state will use that force in their own interest at the expense of the rest of the society."[40] This problem might be mitigated when the circumstances are right—for example, when leaders have long time horizons and expect to gain from economic growth. Yet history shows that circumstances are often otherwise.

But while North is unflinching about the downside of political institutions, this is not what his analysis is really about. His aim is to understand the connection between institutions and economic growth, and "the central focus is on the problem of human cooperation—specifically the cooperation that permits economies to capture the gains from trade that were the key to Adam Smith's *Wealth of Nations*."[41] The theory he seeks to displace is neoclassical economics, and "what has been missing is an understanding of the nature of human coordination and cooperation."[42]

Power and predation are not irrelevant to North's way of thinking, then, but they are not in the same league with cooperation. They may not even be of secondary importance. For when arguing how neoclassical economics can best be modified once cooperation is taken into account, he points not to issues of power and predation but to issues of incomplete information and subjective perceptions. "There is nothing the matter with the rational actor paradigm," he maintains, "that could not be cured by a healthy awareness of the complexity of human motivation and the problems that arise from information processing. Social scientists would then understand not only why institutions exist, but also how they influence outcomes."[43] Indeed, in later articles distilling his theoretical views on the development of institutions, the arguments he lays out—and the research agenda he goes on to develop—have nothing to do (directly) with power and predation, but a lot to do with perceptions, attitudes, culture, and knowledge, and with bringing cognitive science to bear on the study of institutions.[44]

Most of the rational choice literature shows a similar ambivalence toward power, recognizing its relevance yet pushing it to the analytic periphery. In particular, there seems to be widespread agreement among rational choice theorists that

- the coercive power of the state is often necessary for enforcing cooperative agreements and creating institutions (contract law, property rights) that promote them;

- a state powerful enough to use coercion toward such positive ends can also use it predatorily; and
- this dilemma of state power must somehow be resolved—for example, by tying the king's hands—if cooperative, mutually beneficial outcomes for society are to be realized.

The role of these insights, however, is typically to provide a better understanding of cooperation and mutual gain (and democracy and economic growth), not to shed light on the pervasive and often troubling ways that power can shape political institutions, and not to promote a broader theory that brings cooperation and power into balance.[45]

A relatively small number of rational choice scholars have given power much more serious attention. They have done so in different ways, however, and their separate attempts—while often laudable in themselves—have not produced much coherence in the aggregate. Some have emphasized power in the context of empirical work, where attention centers mainly on the details of particular cases.[46] Others have offered theoretical arguments about particular aspects of power, but without launching a more generalized attack on mainstream theory.[47]

A few, however, have attempted to develop broader arguments about the need for integrating power into the theory of institutions. I put myself in this category,[48] but here I want to focus on a small group of scholars—Robert Bates, Margaret Levi, Jack Knight, and Mancur Olson—who write about how the state and its institutions develop from more primitive beginnings.[49]

Bates has the most in common with North. He devotes considerable attention to power and its often destructive effects, but his ultimate concern is with how power is used to promote cooperation, mutual gain, and the institutions that make them possible. This is the thrust of his seminal work on Africa, in which he shows how Kenya's leaders used their power to get property rights right, with beneficial results.[50] It is also the theme of his more recent *Prosperity and Violence,* which shows how "violence becomes domesticated . . . and is used not to predate or to destroy but rather to strengthen the productive forces of society."[51] Even so, his larger theme is that power and cooperation are inextricably intertwined, and that institutions can not be understood unless this is recognized.

Levi's departure from North is more striking. Her focus is not on the positive, but rather on the broader consequences that power can have for political institutions and citizens. From the beginning of the new institutionalism, she has been the strongest proponent of a power-based theory, arguing that political institutions are shaped by power asymmetries and that they protect and promote the interests of the powerful.[52] Cooperation is essential too, she makes clear, but it is bound up with the exercise of power. In *Of Rule and Revenue*, for example, a central theme is that rulers are typically predatory but can extract resources from their citizens most efficiently when the latter engage in "quasi-voluntary compliance," which may require rulers to adopt institutions with a degree of public legitimacy.[53] Another theme is that cooperation is a key means by which rulers ally themselves with other elites so that all can extract resources most efficiently from the larger population. The insiders, in other words, cooperate to plunder those who are not part of the deal.

Levi and Bates push the envelope by bringing power to center stage. But neither takes on the more fundamental task of challenging the analytics of rational choice. Knight was the first to do this in a systematic way.[54] Beginning with the basics of individual choice and strategic interaction, he argues that institutions are "not best explained as a Pareto-superior response to collective goals or benefits, but, rather, as a by-product of conflicts over distributional gains,"[55] and he aims to show how a theory of institutions can be rooted in bargaining relationships and the power asymmetries that shape their outcomes.

Knight's analysis is admirably ambitious, and it succeeds in calling attention to fundamentals. But it does not readily serve as a springboard for change. One reason is that it focuses on informal social institutions and doesn't devote much attention to the formal political institutions that make up the state. More important, its bargaining analysis almost always turns out to be an analysis of how rational individuals struggle to distribute *gains*—with no one losing—rather than an analysis of redistribution (or coercion or violence) in which some individuals gain and others lose. Particularly for this latter reason, it remains ambiguous what kinds of analytic changes Knight is really proposing, and whether a bargaining framework—which rational choice theorists use to understand the voluntary division of gains, not the imposition of losses on involuntary victims—is appropriate for the job.

Knight, Levi, and Bates are all political scientists, and this should come as little surprise. Power has long been central to the way political scientists think about politics, and it is only natural that, when rational choice rose to prominence, some of them would try to fit power into a rational choice framework. It is not at all natural for economists to do such a thing. Their theory and research are tightly constrained by the analytics of voluntary exchange, and even when they turn their attention toward politics they tend to either avoid the subject of power entirely or to explore it in a limited way that fits their framework of voluntarism.[56]

This being so, it is significant that perhaps the most provocative argument for a power-based theory of the state—Olson's *Power and Prosperity*—comes from one of the world's most prominent economists and is clearly intended to influence the thinking of other economists.[57] Published two years after Olson's untimely death, this is a work he had been developing for years and had yet to perfect. Partly for this reason, I suspect, it is not as tightly argued as it might have been.[58] Even so, Olson was a creative and iconoclastic thinker, and this work is a bold attempt to make power a central concern of economic theory.

For our purposes, Olson makes two noteworthy contributions here. The first is his power-based theory of the state, which elaborates ideas developed in his earlier work.[59] A major theme is that even autocratic leaders sometimes have incentives to use their power for social good. But Olson puts the spotlight on coercion, corruption, inefficiency, and predation—viewing them as the norm and rightly at the center of theory. He stands out, moreover, because he builds his theory on simple and insightful conceptual distinctions—between encompassing and special interests, between roving and stationary bandits—that allow for a logical analysis that is focused, simple, and potentially far-reaching. Unfortunately, he also stands out by making little constructive use of the new economics, aside from his own work on collective action; and as a result, the concerns that play key roles in the rest of the literature—about credible commitments, the tying of hands, and the like—are not well integrated into his analysis, which is almost purely his own. He compounds the problem by ignoring Bates, Levi, Knight, and others, and indeed dismissing all work on power but his own as "only a jumble of ad hoc arguments and some fancy jargon."[60]

His second contribution, at any rate, is potentially more important than the theory he develops: he launches an attack on voluntarism itself, arguing that an adequate theory of the state must get beyond the usual bargaining framework and develop a logic of coercion and force. He devotes an entire chapter—destined, he thinks, to be the "most interesting part of the book" to economists[61]—to a critique of voluntarist theories of government. The content of his critique leaves much to be desired, for it focuses on the Coasian claims of the Chicago School,[62] and it speaks with confusion about—but mainly ignores—the new economics and its cooperationist theories of institutions, which are his real competition here. So this part of his analysis is an opportunity missed. Even so, what he tries to do is exactly what the field needs.

The International System

The international system is the paradigmatic state of nature, an anarchy in which there is no overarching authority, property rights are ultimately unprotected, and every nation is out for itself. While various schools of thought organize debate within the field, there is widespread agreement on the importance of power; and it is the realist school, which portrays the international system in stark terms of power and self-interest, that is the benchmark theory against which all others try to establish their validity and earn attention and support.

The rise of the new economics has presented realism with a major challenge. The pioneering work comes from Robert Keohane, who argues that international institutions are cooperative means by which nation-states can overcome their collective action problems to realize gains from trade.[63] He agrees that powerful nations like the United States create institutions to promote their own interests. But he also argues that other nations only join these institutions because they benefit from them, and he emphasizes that the structural means by which institutions bring about cooperation—chiefly by providing information, rules, and principles that reduce transaction costs, enhance decentralized enforcement, and increase interaction—make it easier for members to pursue shared interests and reap mutual gains.

Keohane's work has stimulated a flood of scholarship on the prospects for international cooperation, and in the process the new economics has profoundly shaped the intellectual perspective of the field. Whether the subject is international trade or war and peace, and however much power enters the equation, the language of institutional analysis is one of credible commitments, self-enforcing agreements, and cooperation for mutual benefit. A mainstream example is Milner's *Interests, Institutions, and Information,* which explores the impacts of domestic politics on international cooperation.[64] A less obvious (but more telling) example is Martin's influential study of economic sanctions, *Coercive Cooperation.* Martin clearly acknowledges the coercive role of sanctions and threats, but the purpose of her book is to "examine the conditions under which states cooperate to impose economic sanctions,"[65] and its "major finding . . . is that considerations of credibility provide the most explanatory leverage."[66] International institutions enter the picture as "useful commitment mechanisms" and are "positively associated with the level of cooperation achieved."[67]

Even realists, who tend to discount institutions as epiphenomena of power, often find themselves speaking the same language—and singing the same tune. In a widely cited article, for instance, Stephen Krasner argues that the institutional system is driven by power; and he points the way toward a broader theory rooted in the new economics that can explain how power is used to promote national interests.[68] His accompanying analysis, however, shows how nations faced with coordination problems (in the area of telecommunications policy) can move from inefficient outcomes to the Pareto frontier, and how the more powerful nations have disproportionate influence over which point on the frontier is chosen. The role of power, then, simply determines how the gains from cooperation are divided up. All of the cooperating nations are made better off in the process. There are no losers.

Krasner is not alone in arguing the importance of power, but then relying on a theory of cooperation that directs attention away from all the bad things that power can do (at least to the nations being victimized by it). For example, a recent consortium of researchers involved in what they call the Rational Design Project is concerned with mapping out and explaining the institutional structure of the international system, and they explicitly acknowledge the need for an expanded theoretical framework that takes power into account. But even for them, power mainly has to with distribution problems, coordination problems, and choices among multiple equilibria, not with nations being forced to do things that are against their interests. Indeed, it is one of their premises that "over the long haul states gain by participating in specific institutions—or else they will abandon them."[69]

The logic of voluntarism is also central to the literature on international bargaining. Even though this work is often about war and about how aspects of power can affect bargaining outcomes, the basic framework is one of cooperation and mutual gain. In a prominent summary of the bargaining literature, Robert Powell puts it this way:

> Bargaining is about deciding how to divide the gains from joint action. That is, coordinated action frequently increases the size of the "pie"—for exam-

ple, the exchange of goods often creates gains from trade; revising the territorial status quo peacefully rather than through the costly use of force means that the resources that would have been destroyed by fighting can now be divided. The existence of potential gains from acting jointly creates an incentive to cooperate.[70]

A recent book by Lloyd Gruber stands apart from the rest. Gruber takes the mainstream to task for building a cooperationist theory of international institutions that largely ignores power, and he launches a challenge that is truly fundamental: arguing that nations sometimes join international institutions even when they expect to be worse off for doing so. What looks like cooperation often hides the underlying exercise of power.[71]

Gruber's argument is based on an insightful idea that is both simple and correct. Some nations, he notes, are so important in a given sphere of activity—as nations with large economies are in international trade—that when one or more of them decide to "go it alone" in creating a multinational institution, other nations may eventually choose to join even if they never wanted such an institution in the first place and expect to be worse off. This may seem inconsistent with rational behavior, but it actually isn't. For the key issue is: worse off compared to what?

This is where the novel insight comes in. When the prime movers band together to form an institution—say, to promote free trade and the coordination of their economic policies—nations that oppose such a development are faced with a fait accompli. The original status quo has been taken away from them, and the new reality is that this new institution does exist. They can either join or be left out in the cold—but they can't go back to the way things were. If they now decide that joining makes them better off than not joining, they will voluntarily become members. But they expect to be worse off than if the institution had never existed in the first place.

Gruber marshals evidence for his argument by studying NAFTA and the European Monetary System. He shows that in both cases there were prime movers (the United States and Canada for NAFTA, Germany and France for the EMS) that engineered a new status quo, as well as nations that preferred not to have any institution at all (Mexico for NAFTA, Italy and Britain for the EMS) but joined nonetheless once the original status quo was taken away from them. Other scholars may or may not agree with Gruber's empirical conclusions, as it is difficult to calculate each nation's expected benefits under alternative scenarios. Even so, his argument is provocatively subversive. For it not only suggests how power can worm its way into the very foundations of "voluntary" choice, but also asserts that institutions may not be cooperative and mutually beneficial even for the insiders that willingly join them.

Power

If power is fundamental to institutions, we need to think about it as rigorously as we now think about cooperation, and we need to integrate both into a common rational choice framework. While it may sound naïve to say so, my own view is that this is not exceedingly difficult to do, at least from an analytical standpoint. The difficulty lies in overcoming mind-sets that have prevailed among economists and political scientists for decades.

Economists aren't very interested in studying power. It is true that their theories of voluntary exchange point them in other directions; but economists created these theories, and they have always been free to modify, reinterpret, or expand them to allow for a more far-reaching analysis of power. They haven't done so because they haven't wanted to, not because there is something inherent to economics that prevents them.[72] Political scientists *are* interested in studying power, as it is central to much of what they want to explain. But the community power debates of the 1960s, combined with the large and contentious philosophical literature on power, seem to have convinced much of the discipline that power can not be defined or studied rigorously.[73] And when rational choice took the field by storm, its theories of voluntary choice and cooperation reinforced these jaded notions.

So how can power be made more fundamental to rational choice? I don't presume to have a perfect solution up my sleeve. Nor do I mean to trivialize the complex issues that the concept of power ultimately raises. But in the few pages remaining, I do want to set out some simple ideas about how we might proceed in putting power to more productive use.

A good first step is to recognize that the definitional problems surrounding the concept do not have to be entirely resolved for theoretical progress to be made. After all, there is still no agreement on what an institution is. Some scholars see institutions as rules of the game, others see them as formal organizations, others as patterned behavior, still others as "myths" and ideational structures.[74] But these differences haven't prevented the theory of political institutions from making tremendous progress over the last twenty years. I suspect the same will prove true for different notions of power. We simply need to move ahead.

We can do this most effectively by focusing first on power's most egregious expressions, coercion and force—precisely as Olson has argued.[75] It might seem that these aspects of power are flatly inconsistent with voluntary choice and thus outside the framework entirely. How, then, can rational choice deal with them? The answer, perhaps surprisingly, is that it already does—but in a confusing way. If this confusion can be cleared up, there is no reason that these aspects of power can not become an integral part of rational choice theory. No technical innovations are really required.[76]

To see why, consider a stylized situation in which a criminal presents his victim with a classic choice: "your money or your life." An economist might say that this is just another case of voluntary exchange. If the victim chooses to hand over his wallet, he is simply acting on his preferences and making a rational choice. He would rather lose his money than his life. There is no need to introduce power into the analysis, because voluntary exchange already explains the outcome. The common sense response, however, is that the exchange between criminal and victim is obviously not voluntary. The criminal is using threats of violence, and he is coercing the victim to give up his money against his will. The economist can rejoin, though, that it actually *is* the victim's will to give up the money, and common sense is thus thrown into doubt by a semantic dispute over what the victim's "will" really is.

There is no right or wrong here. Whether the exchange is voluntary or coercive depends on how you look at it. There is, however, an analytical means of cutting through the confusion. This is to recognize that the victim's will is being expressed relative to a specific agenda of alternatives. And the criminal is now controlling the agenda. Before the criminal walks up, the victim lives peacefully with his wallet in his own pocket and his life not subject to threat. This is the original status quo. When the criminal arrives on the scene, however, the victim is presented with two alternatives—give up his money or give up his life—and they compose his entire choice set. He cannot choose the original status quo, which requires that he be left alone, because the criminal has taken this alternative away from him. The victim "voluntarily" gives up his wallet when faced with the power-constrained choice set, because he is better off giving up his money than getting killed. But he is worse off than he would be under the original status quo—which he can no longer have, thanks to the criminal's exercise of agenda power.

This is the kind of power Gruber is talking about.[77] It is a form of agenda control in which one actor denies the status quo to others in order to steer them into accepting alternatives more to his liking. Most instances of institutional power that we discussed earlier are of this type as well. For when legislators and interest groups impose institutions on the broader population, or when rulers adopt predatory institutions to extract resources from citizens, these insiders are revoking the original status quo and giving outsiders two choices: play by the new rules or be punished by the police powers of the state. The outsiders cannot go back to the way things were. They must now choose from the power-constrained choice set and from that alone. They may (and probably will) choose to "cooperate." But they may also be worse off than before the institutions were imposed.

A related type of agenda control operates to protect the status quo rather than change it. This can occur, for example, when actor A uses his agenda power not to deny actor B the original status quo, but rather to deny him other alternatives that he would actually find preferable—alternatives that A wants to prevent being adopted. This is the kind of power that Peter Bachrach and Morton S. Baratz highlight in their classic critique of pluralism, in which they argue that political elites often maintain their positions not by winning conflicts against opponents, but by using agenda control to keep conflictual alternatives off the table entirely.[78] This kind of power has a lot to do with the stability of political institutions. Recall, for example, that public bureaucracies can usually survive (regardless of what happens to their enacting coalitions) as long as no legislation is passed to kill them. Supporters who play pivotal roles in the policy-making process, then, can use agenda control—even if they are a distinct minority—to keep reform proposals off the table and thus to prevent change from even coming up for a vote.

Both types of agenda control help to clear up confusion and make power more analytically tractable.[79] In the first case, A exercises power by denying B the original status quo and constraining him to choose an alternative he otherwise would *not* prefer. In the second, A exercises power by denying B attractive alternatives to the status quo and preventing him from adopting changes he otherwise *would* prefer. Note that in both cases B is making voluntary choices within the power-constrained choice set— but at the same time he may be a victim of coercion or force, because A is setting limits on his options and engineering his choices. B is better off by reference to the constrained choice set—but at the same time he may be worse off by reference to the alternatives denied him. He is cooperating and reaping gains from trade—but at the same time he may be a victim of manipulation and even predation. There is nothing contradictory about these apparently contradictory claims. They are all equally valid descriptions of the same choice situation, and they can all be recognized and explored using the logic of rational choice. We simply need to be clear about our frames of reference.

Even if we are, semantic squabbles are inevitable. The analytics may lead us to agree, for example, that B is worse off relative to the original status quo denied him by A; yet some might call this coercion and some might not, depending on the extent of B's loss, whether A intended for it to happen, and other considerations. Given the plasticity of ordinary language, there is no avoiding these ambiguities. But the important point is, they don't matter much. What matters is that we have an objective basis for saying that B is worse off—and indeed for measuring the magnitude of his loss—even in cases when the mainstream explanation would point to cooperation and mutual gain.

Ironically, coercion and force are the easiest aspects of power to deal with. This is because they are essentially negative (B is made worse off) and readily distinguished from cooperation and mutual gain. Other aspects of power are more challenging because the boundaries are less clear. Suppose we agree that much of what we mean by power has to do with one actor intentionally shaping the choice-set of another.[80] Then what do we make of an apparently simple case of positive inducements: a situation, for example, in which rich nation A gets poor nation B to accept troops on its territory by paying a large sum of money? The standard explanation would see this as a voluntary exchange that makes both nations better off. But is it also an exercise of power? After all, A influences B's choices by adding an attractive alternative to B's choice set, and this allows A to get what it wants. Other nations, moreover, may find their future decisions heavily constrained by A's success in stationing troops on B's soil: a spillover effect that is surely what A wants as well.

Principal-agent relationships give rise to the same sorts of questions—and it is in this context that the ambiguity at the heart of these relationships needs to be understood. As I discussed earlier, if we explain bureaucratic structure as deriving from the efforts of a legislative principal to control the behavior of its bureaucratic agent, then the structure may be characterized as cooperative and mutually beneficial. Yet the legislature is clearly using structure to constrain the agency from doing what it would otherwise want to do, such as pursuing policies more to its own liking. And the agency is clearly using its informational advantage to shape the beliefs and available choices of the legislature. So while both benefit from the final outcome *relative to some baseline*, both are also actively engaged in controlling the other's agenda—and they can be construed as making each other worse off relative to *other* baselines.

Generalizing the analysis of power to situations of mutual gain raises subtle issues, and to address them fully would require more extensive treatment than I can undertake here. Fortunately, some of this ground has already been covered, notably by Randall Bartlett, whose *Economics and Power* is a comprehensive attempt to show how these and other aspects of power can be integrated into economic theory.[81] Bartlett's perspective—and mine—is that, given the right frames of reference, there is no contradiction between mutual gain and the exercise of power, and that both are often going on at once. Indeed, it is in seeing them as integral components of the same relationship that we gain a better, more fully rounded understanding of it. And a better theory.

I should add, finally, that whether we think of power in general terms or focus more narrowly on coercion and force, the exercise of power doesn't just occur in political institutions. It also occurs in business firms and throughout the private sector, and is relevant to how these institutions get structured, how they perform, and how people are affected. Current theory largely ignores this, emphasizing voluntary agreement and implying that all actors can easily walk away when dissatisfied—which provides a stark contrast with the public sector. This is a contrast I have used several times, for heuristic purposes, to drive home basic theoretical points. But the fact is, severe constraints on choice and high costs of exit are often facts of life in the private sector too—especially when competition is weak and monopoly strong—and the theory needs to recognize as much. Were it to do so, its rosy view of business firms would no longer be so rosy.[82]

Conclusion

The rational choice theory of political institutions has been extraordinarily productive over the last few decades, and much of what it reveals about political institutions is valid and important—namely, that their creation, design, and consequences have a lot do with the efforts of social actors to find cooperative solutions to collective action problems. Yet political institutions are more than just structures of cooperation. They are also structures of power, and the theory does not tell us much about this. As a result, we get a one-sided—and overly benign—view of what political institutions are and what they do.

This problem is not well understood, and indeed is typically not seen as a problem at all. For there is a widespread sense in the literature that, because power is so frequently discussed, it *is* being taken into account and is just as fundamental to the theory as cooperation. Confusion about these matters is a problem in itself, and is actually the more serious one—because it not only prevents well conceived movements for change, but also undermines the motivation for any change at all. If a theory that truly integrates power and cooperation is to be developed, the key prerequisite is simple clarity.

It might seem that the cooperationist theory would be at its clearest and most compelling in explaining institutions created under democratic rules of the game. But this is not the case. As the new economics has been transported from business firms to democratic institutions, the logic of the analysis has gotten muddled. Key concepts and components—like what the relevant institutions are and which actors count as the relevant population—do not make the transition very well. They get used in different ways across the two sectors, and indeed in various ways within the public sector itself, and this alters the meaning of what is actually being argued. Even the most basic of claims—about cooperation, mutual benefit, stability—become unclear.

When these issues are untangled, and when familiar but distracting arguments (about Coasian bargaining, about the social contract) are dealt with and dismissed, it turns out that the usual cooperationist explanations are valid—but only for some of the players and part of the overall story—and that power is essential to the story too. In effect, the new economics focuses on the political insiders: the legislators, interest groups, and bureaucrats who are the winners of the democratic struggle, and who use public authority to create and design the bureaucratic institutions that fill out democratic government. Their relationships are indeed cooperative and mutually beneficial—*for them.* But they use their cooperation to impose institutions on the political losers, and indeed on everyone else in society, and these outsiders are not part of the deal. In democratic politics, cooperation and power are two sides of the same coin: cooperation makes the exercise of power possible, and the exercise of power often motivates the cooperation.

To focus on cooperation alone, then, is to miss the essence of what is going on as democratic institutions are being created and designed. Much the same can be said about their stability over time. Once they are set up, they become legal entities in their own right, protected by the rules of the game, and they can survive with only periodic backstopping from much smaller and perhaps very different bands of supporters. The new economics' focus on the stability of the original cooperative agreement—and on whether it is self-enforcing—misconstrues what often accounts for the survival of political institutions. Usually, they are stable because of the agenda power of current supporters, not because the original agreement lives on.

When we turn our attention to the rise of state institutions from more primitive beginnings, or to the rise of institutions in the international system, it might seem that the cooperationist theory would be less dominant and more accommodating to notions of power. And in some sense it is. The literature is very much concerned with predation, confiscation, war, and other aspects of power. Yet all this attention to power has not paid off. Power is typically just an add-on to the underlying cooperationist theory, playing a peripheral role that leaves the fundamentals of voluntarism and mutual benefit unchanged. Predation and other downsides of power are acknowledged, but the focus tends to be on cooperative solutions that lead to democracy, the rule of law, protection of property rights, and economic growth.

A few scholars have sought to put power and cooperation on a more equal footing, and they deserve credit for their pioneering work. But it would be stretching things to call their collective efforts a research program, because they do not build upon one another and do not share an analytic roadmap of where they are going or why. They have done much to highlight the importance of power, but less to show how it can be incorporated into the fundamentals of the theory.

The task of integrating power into the theory might seem daunting, but it doesn't need to be—except perhaps at the margins, where positive inducements create unavoidable ambiguities. If we resist the temptation to be overly ambitious at the outset, we should be able to deal in a manageable way with important aspects of power. The most effective way to proceed, in my view, is to focus first on power's most egregious expressions: coercion and force. While they may appear to be quite outside the existing theory, indeed the antithesis of voluntary choice, a little clarification suggests that they can be understood by reference to the familiar analytics of agenda control and constraints on choice and that exploring coercion and force is mainly a matter of adopting the right frames of reference.

There is no need for new analytic tools, and no reason that a theory of voluntary choice cannot accommodate these extreme versions of power. For "voluntary" does not have an absolute meaning within the theory, and it can readily take on features of coercion and force under the right conditions. That the new economics has paid so little attention to these (or any other) aspects of power is not because the tools and concepts are unavailable, but simply because rational choice theorists have channeled their attention elsewhere. Progress requires little more than a new mind-set and an interest in following its lead.

The spillover effects are likely to be substantial and very beneficial. Rational choice theorists will be better equipped to speak to the power issues that political scientists who are more historically and empirically oriented have been studying with great success over the past few decades.[83] They will also be better equipped to learn from these scholars, and to see the value in expanding rational choice theory to incorporate the power dynamics—associated with path dependence, for example, and with critical junctures—that the empirical literature has shown to be important to political institutions.[84] With power a newly shared concern, rational choice theorists and historical institutionalists will have more in common than ever before, and the theoretical and the empirical are likely to come together in far more productive ways.

For now, it is probably wise not to push for a dramatic expansion of what the existing theory is expected to include. The new economics and game theory are not yet very good at handling dynamics, and it may be that, at least for the foreseeable future, they will be limited in what they can do to model certain aspects of power. But that is okay. The short term goal is simply to get power on the agenda of rational choice and to move toward a theory that is no longer so focused on cooperation and the positive side of what political institutions are and do. This is a manageable objective—and if achieved, a major step forward.

NOTES

This chapter is reprinted with the permission of Cambridge University Press. See Terry M. Moe, "Power and Political Institutions," *Perspectives on Politics* 3, 2 (June 2005): 215–233.

1. Terry Moe, "Political Institutions: The Neglected Side of the Story," *Journal of Law, Economics, and Organization* 6 (1990): 213–253.

2. Jack Knight, *Institutions and Social Conflict* (New York: Cambridge University Press, 1992).

3. Douglass C. North, *Structure and Change in Economic History* (New York: Norton, 1981); Douglass C. North, *Institutions, Institutional Change, and Economic Performance* (New York: Cambridge University Press, 1990); Robert H. Bates, *Beyond the Miracle of the Market* (New York: Cambridge University Press, 1989); Margaret Levi, *Of Rule and Revenue* (Berkeley: University of California Press, 1988); Margaret Levi, "A Logic of Institutional Change," in Karen Schweers Cook and Margaret Levi, eds., *The Limits of Rationality* (Chicago: University of Chicago Press, 1990).

4. Bates, *Beyond the Miracle of the Market;* Mancur Olson, Jr., "Dictatorship, Democracy, and Development," *American Political Science Review* 87 (September 1993): 567–576; Mancur Olson, Jr., *Power and Prosperity* (New York: Basic Books, 2000).

5. Olson, *Power and Prosperity*, 2.

6. Kenneth J. Arrow, *Social Choice and Individual Values* (New York: Wiley, 1963 [1951]); Richard D. McKelvey, "Intransitivities in Multidimensional Voting Models and Some Implications for Agenda Control," *Journal of Economic Theory* 12 (1976): 472–482.

7. Kenneth A. Shepsle, "Institutional Arrangements and Equilibrium in Multidimensional Voting Models," *American Journal of Political Science* 23 (1979): 27–59; Kenneth A. Shepsle and Barry R. Weingast, "Structure-induced Equilibrium and Legislative Choice," *Public Choice* 37 (1981): 503–519.

8. William A. Niskanen, *Bureaucracy and Representative Government* (New York: Aldine-Atherton, 1971); Thomas Romer and Howard Rosenthal, "Political Resource Allocation: Controlled Agendas and the Status Quo," *Public Choice* 33, 4 (1978): 27–43.

9. James M. Buchanan, Robert D. Tollison, and Gordon Tullock, eds., *Toward a Theory of the Rent-Seeking Society* (College Station: Texas A&M Press, 1980).

10. Oliver Williamson, *The Economic Institutions of Capitalism* (New York: Free Press, 1985).

11. Terry M. Moe, "The New Economics of Organization," *American Journal of Political Science* 28 (1984): 739–777.

12. Barry R. Weingast, "Political Institutions: Rational Choice Perspectives," in Robert E. Goodin and Hans-Dieter Klingemann, eds., *A New Handbook of Political*

Science (New York: Oxford University Press, 1996); Barry R. Weingast, "Rational-choice Institutionalism," in Ira Katznelson and Helen V. Milner, eds., *Political Science: The State of the Discipline* (New York: Norton, 2002).

13. John W. Pratt and Richard J. Zeckhauser, *Principles and Agents* (Boston: Harvard Business School Press, 1985).

14. Max Weber, *The Theory of Economic and Social Organization,* translated by A. M. Henderson and Talcott Parsons (New York: Oxford University Press, 1947).

15. Robert Axelrod and Robert O. Keohane, "Achieving Cooperation under Anarchy: Strategies and Institutions," *World Politics* 38 (1985): 226–254; Yoram Barzel, *A Theory of the State* (New York: Cambridge University Press, 2002); Bates, *Beyond the Miracle of the Market;* Robert H. Bates, *Prosperity and Violence: The Political Economy of Violence* (New York: Norton, 2001); Randall Calvert, "Rational Actors, Equilibrium, and Social Institutions," in Jack Knight and Itai Sened, eds., *Explaining Social Institutions* (Ann Arbor: University of Michigan Press, 1997); Gary W. Cox and Mathew D. McCubbins, *Legislative Leviathan* (Berkeley: University of California Press, 1993); Avner Greif, "Self-enforcing Political Systems and Economic Growth: Late Medieval Genoa," in Robert H. Bates, Avner Greif, Margaret Levi, Jean-Laurent Rosenthal, and Barry R. Weingast, eds., *Analytic Narratives* (Princeton: Princeton University Press, 1998); Avner Greif, Paul Milgrom, and Barry R. Weingast, "Commitment, Coordination, and Enforcement: The Case of the Merchant Guilds," *Journal of Political Economy* 102 (1994): 745–776; Murray J. Horn, *The Political Economy of Public Administration* (New York: Cambridge University Press, 1995); Robert O. Keohane, *After Hegemony: Cooperation and Discord in the World Political Economy* (Princeton: Princeton University Press, 1984); Levi, *Of Rule and Revenue;* Mathew D. McCubbins, Roger G. Noll, and Barry R. Weingast, "Administrative Procedures as Instruments of Political Control," *Journal of Law, Economics, and Organization* 3, 2 (1987): 243–277; Paul R. Milgrom, Douglass C. North, and Barry R. Weingast, "The Role of Institutions in the Revival of Trade: The Medieval Law Merchant, Private Judges, and the Champagne Fairs," *Economics and Politics* 2, 1 (1990): 1–23; North, *Structure and Change in Economic History;* North, *Institutions, Institutional Change, and Economic Performance;* Douglass C. North, "Five Propositions about Institutional Change," in Jack Knight and Itai Sened, eds., *Explaining Social Institutions* (Ann Arbor: University of Michigan Press, 1995); Douglass C. North and Barry R. Weingast, "Constitutions and Commitment: The Evolution of Institutions Governing Public Choice in Seventeenth Century England," *Journal of Economic History* 49 (1989): 803–832; Elinor Ostrom, *Governing the Commons* (New York: Cambridge University Press, 1990); Adam Przeworski, *Democracy and the Market* (New York: Cambridge University Press, 1991); Barry R. Weingast, "The Economic Role of Political Institutions: Market-preserving Federalism and Economic Development," *Journal of Law, Economics, and Organization* 11 (1995): 1–31; Barry R. Weingast, "The Political Foundations of Democracy and the Rule of Law," *American Political Science Review* 91 (June 1997):

245–263; Barry R. Weingast and William Marshall, "The Industrial Organization of Congress: Or, Why Legislatures, Like Firms, Are Not Organized as Markets," *Journal of Political Economy* 96 (1988): 765–800.

16. Weingast and Marshall, "The Industrial Organization of Congress."

17. Kenneth A. Shepsle, "Institutional Equilibrium and Equilibrium Institutions," in Herbert F. Weisberg, ed., *Political Science: The Science of Politics* (New York: Agathon, 1986),74.18. Weingast, "Rational-choice institutionalism," 670.

19. My argument is about the politics of structure, and its logic would apply just as well to the structure of taxation policy, of transfer payments, of public programs, and the like.

20. Moe, "Political Institutions."

21. The same conclusions about winners, losers, and coercive power can also apply to the private sector—when there is monopoly, for example, or when workers lack exit options. As I note later on, power is relevant to an understanding of institutions in both sectors.

22. Thrain Eggertsson, *Economic Behavior and Institutions* (New York: Cambridge University Press, 1990).

23. See also Avinash K. Dixit and John Londregan, "Redistributive Politics and Economic Efficiency," *American Political Science Review* 89, 4 (1995): 856–866; Avinash K. Dixit and John Londregan, "The Determinants of Success of Special Interests in Redistributive Politics," *Journal of Politics* 58, 4 (1996): 1132–1155; Gary D. Libecap, *Contracting for Property Rights* (New York: Cambridge University Press, 1986).

24. Oliver Williamson, *The Economic Institutions of Capitalism* (New York: Free Press, 1985).

25. Ibid.

26. Russell Hardin, "Contractarianism: Wistful Thinking," *Constitutional Political Economy* 1 (1990): 35–52.

27. McCubbins, Noll, and Weingast, "Administrative Procedures as Instruments of Political Control."

28. Murray J. Horn, *The Political Economy of Public Administration* (New York: Cambridge University Press, 1995).

29. While the acceptability criterion may seem odd in a governmental setting, as the legislators have the legal right to impose any structure they want, the relationship is still voluntary: Existing bureaucrats can quit or transfer, potential bureaucrats can refuse to apply for the jobs, and so on. This being so, the structural solution can be thought of as cooperative and mutually beneficial.

30. I emphasize this aspect of power and its connection to cooperation because it is simple and speaks to the core logic of the new economics. But, as I discuss later on, it is not the only way that power can shape the emergence and design of institutions.

31. Terry M. Moe, "The Positive Theory of Public Bureaucracy," in Dennis C.

Mueller, ed., *Perspectives on Public Choice: A Handbook* (New York: Cambridge University Press, 1997).

32. Other work on political control does the same. See, e. g., David Epstein and Sharyn O'Halloran, *Delegating Powers* (New York: Cambridge University Press, 1999); John D. Huber and Charles R. Shipan, *Deliberate Discretion? The Institutional Foundations of Bureaucratic Autonomy* (New York: Cambridge University Press, 2002).

33. Russell Hardin, *Collective Action* (Baltimore: Johns Hopkins University Press, 1982).

34. Mancur Olson, Jr., *The Logic of Collective Action* (Cambridge, MA: Harvard University Press, 1965).

35. Robert Axelrod, *The Evolution of Cooperation* (New York: Basic Books, 1984); Michael Taylor, *The Possibility of Cooperation* (New York: Cambridge University Press, 1987); Hardin, *Collective Action;* David Kreps, *Game Theory and Economic Modeling* (New York: Oxford University Press, 1990).

36. North and Weingast, "Constitutions and Commitment."

37. See also Hilton L. Root, "Tying the King's Hands: Credible Commitments and Royal Fiscal Policy during the Old Regime," *Rationality and Society* 1 (1989): 240–258.

38. Przeworski, *Democracy and the Market.*

39. North, *Structure and Change in Economic History;* North, *Institutions, Institutional Change, and Economic Performance.*

40. North, *Institutions, Institutional Change, and Economic Performance,* 59.

41. Ibid., 9.

42. Ibid., 11.

43. Ibid., 111.

44. Douglass C. North, "The Historical Evolution of Polities," *International Review of Law and Economics* 14, 4 (1994): 381–391; North, "Five Propositions about Institutional Change"; Chris Mantzavinos, Douglass C. North, and Syed Shariq, "Learning, Institutions, and Economic Performance," *Perspectives on Politics* 2, 1 (2004): 75–84.

45. See, for example, Barry R. Weingast, "The Economic Role of Political Institutions"; Weingast and Marshall, "The Industrial Organization of Congress"; Greif, "Self-enforcing Political Systems and Economic Growth."

46. Jean-Laurent Rosenthal, *The Fruits of Revolution* (New York: Cambridge University Press, 1992); Walter Korpi, "Contentious Institutions: An Augmented Rational-action Analysis of the Origins and Path Dependency of Welfare State Institutions in Western Countries," *Rationality and Society* 13, 2 (2001): 235–283.

47. John Umbeck, "Might Makes Right: A Theory of the Function and Initial Distribution of Property Rights," *Economic Inquiry* 19 (1982): 38–59; Taylor, *The Possibility of Cooperation;* Russell Hardin, *One for All: The Logic of Group Conflict*

(Princeton: Princeton University Press, 1995); Leonard Wantchekon, "The Paradox of 'Warlord' Democracy: A Theoretical Investigation," *American Political Science Review* 98 (2004): 1, 17–34.

48. Moe, "Political Institutions: The Neglected Side of the Story."

49. Bates, *Beyond the Miracle of the Market;* Bates, *Prosperity and Violence;* Levi, *Of Rule and Revenue;* Margaret Levi, "The Predatory Theory of Rule," *Politics and Society* 10, 4 (1981): 431–466; Levi, "A Logic of Institutional Change"; Knight, *Institutions and Social Conflict;* Olson, "Dictatorship, Democracy, and Development"; Olson, *Power and Prosperity.* See also Barzel, *A Theory of the State,* who might be included in this group, but whose overall argument I find less persuasive.

50. Bates, *Beyond the Miracle of the Market.*

51. Bates, *Prosperity and Violence,* 26.

52. Levi, "The Predatory Theory of Rule"; Levi, "A Logic of Institutional Change."

53. Levi, *Of Rule and Revenue;* see also Margaret Levi, *Consent, Dissent, and Patriotism* (New York: Cambridge University Press, 1997).

54. Knight, *Institutions and Social Conflict.* Randall Bartlett, *Economics and Power* (New York: Cambridge University Press, 1989), preceded Knight in offering a book-length treatment of how power might be integrated into the fundamentals of economic theory, but his analysis is not specifically about political institutions. See also Keith M. Dowding, *Rational Choice and Political Power* (Aldershot, UK: Edward Elgar, 1991); Brian Barry, "Power: An Economic Analysis," in Brian Barry, ed., *Power and Political Theory* (New York: Wiley, 1976); David A. Baldwin, *Paradoxes of Power* (Oxford: Basil Blackwell, 1989).

55. Knight, *Institutions and Social Conflict,* 19.

56. Bartlett, *Economics and Power.*

57. Olson, *Power and Prosperity.*

58. See, for example, David M. Woodruff, Review of Mancur Olson, *Power and Prosperity: Outgrowing Communist and Capitalist Dictatorships* (New York: Basic Books, 2000), *East European Constitutional Review* 10, 1 (2001): 97–103.

59. Olson, *The Logic of Collective Action;* Mancur Olson, Jr., *The Rise and Decline of Nations* (New Haven: Yale University Press, 1982); Olson, "Dictatorship, Democracy, and Development"; Martin C. McGuire and Mancur Olson, "The Economics of Autocracy and Majority Rule: The Invisible Hand and the Use of Force," *Journal of Economic Literature* 34, 1 (1996): 72–96.

60. Olson, *Power and Prosperity,* 46.

61. Ibid., 47.

62. Gary Becker, "A Theory of Competition among Pressure Groups for Political Influence," *Quarterly Journal of Economics* 98 (1983): 371–400.

63. Keohane, *After Hegemony.*

64. Helen V. Milner, *Interests, Institutions, and Information: Domestic Politics and International Relations* (Princeton: Princeton University Press, 1997).

65. Lisa L. Martin, *Coercive Cooperation: Explaining Multilateral Economic Sanctions* (Princeton: Princeton University Press, 1992), 10.

66. Ibid., 11–12.

67. Ibid., 12.

68. Stephen D. Krasner, "Global Communications and National Power: Life on the Pareto Frontier," *World Politics* 43 (April 1991): 336–366.

69. Barbara Koremenos, Charles Lipson, and Duncan Snidal, "The Rational Design of International Institutions," *International Organization* 55 (Autumn 2001): 768.

70. Robert Powell, "Bargaining Theory and International Conflict," *Annual Review of Political Science* 5 (2002): 2.

71. Lloyd Gruber, *Ruling the World* (Princeton: Princeton University Press, 2000).

72. Jack Hirschleifer, "The Dark Side of the Force," *Economic Inquiry* XXXII (1994): 1–10; Bartlett, *Economics and Power.*

73. For discussions of the conceptual and methodological issues involved, see, for example, Nelson W. Polsby, *Community Power and Political Theory,* 2nd ed. (Berkeley: Institute of Governmental Studies Press, 1980); Roderick Bell, David V. Edwards, and R. Harrison Wagner, eds., *Political Power* (New York: Free Press, 1969); Steven Lukes, *Power: A Radical View* (London: Macmillan, 1974); Peter Morriss, *Power: A Philosophical Analysis* (New York: Manchester University Press, 2002).

74. Peter A. Hall and Rosemary C. R. Taylor, "Political Science and the Three New Institutionalisms," *Political Studies* 44 (December 1996): 952–973.

75. Olson, *Power and Prosperity.*

76. See also Bartlett, *Economics and Power,* and Barry, "Power: An Economic Analysis," who fit coercion and force within an economic framework, and John Roemer, ed., *Analytical Marxism: Studies in Marxism and Social Theory* (New York: Cambridge University Press, 1986), who provides a economic analysis of Marxist notions of exploitation.

77. Indeed, he says, "What I have been calling go-it-alone power is really just another form of agenda control" (Gruber, *Ruling the World,* 275), and he recognizes that agenda control can be put to more general use in the analysis of power.

78. Peter Bachrach and Morton S. Baratz, "Two Faces of Power," *American Political Science Review* 56 (December 1962): 947–952.

79. We might also think of power in terms of A's ability to affect the reversion levels available to B, an idea suggested to me by Gary Miller. If we adopt a broad notion of agenda control, though, influence over reversion levels might well be regarded as a type of agenda control.

80. Note that this notion of power is similar to Dahl's famous definition: that A has power over B to the extent that he can get B to do something that he otherwise would not do. I am not arguing here for a specific definition but simply focusing

the discussion on a general feature of power that is clearly important. One might argue that other features, such as A's ability to shape B's values, should be part of the definition of power, too. Robert A. Dahl, "The Concept of Power," *Behavioral Science* 2 (1957): 201–215. See, for example, Lukes, *Power: A Radical View*, and Bartlett, *Economics and Power*.

81. Bartlett, *Economics and Power*. Other writers have also offered insightful ideas on integrating power into economic theory. See Dowding, *Rational Choice and Political Power*; Keith M. Dowding, *Power* (Minneapolis: University of Minnesota Press, 1996); Barry, "Power: An Economic Analysis"; and Baldwin, *Paradoxes of Power*.

82. When the new economics of organization first emerged, sociologists immediately attacked it for overlooking the role of power in private organizations, including firms. See, for example, Charles Perrow, "Markets, Hierarchies, and Hegemony: A Critique of Chandler and Williamson," in Andrew Van de Ven and William Joyce, eds., *Perspectives on Organization Design and Behavior* (New York: Wiley, 1986), and Arthur Francis, Jeremy Turk, and Paul Willman, eds., *Power, Efficiency, and Institutions* (London: Heineman, 1983).

83. See Paul Pierson and Theda Skocpol, "Historical Institutionalism in Contemporary Political Science," in Ira Katznelson and Helen V. Milner, eds., *Political Science: The State of the Discipline* (New York: Norton, 2002); Hall and Taylor, "Political Science and the Three New Institutionalisms"; and Korpi, "Contentious Institutions."

84. See Paul Pierson, "Increasing Returns, Path Dependence, and the Study of Politics," *American Political Science Review* 94, 2 (2000): 251–267.

3

Practical Institutionalism

John Ferejohn

1. Introduction

There are practical reasons to try to understand how institutions work in order to use them to help shape our collective lives together.[1] Hobbes and many others have thought that problems of cooperation and coordination make it difficult for members of large and complex societies to pursue even widely shared purposes. A natural response to these "organizational" problems is to try to construct institutions that will permit a society to coordinate the activities of its dispersed and distrustful people. A great deal is known about traditional collective action problems and how they might be solved or at least mitigated. But, institutions can do more than permit people to coordinate their activities in order to achieve their goals. They can also help to create and transform the goals themselves and, beyond that, help transform the identities and self conceptions of the agents. To the neo-Hobbesian, these further possibilities are nuisances that make unnecessarily difficult the solution of collective action problems. If aspirations of the agents cannot be held fixed, it will be very hard to understand the sense in which a problem is "solved" at all. But, from a wider perspective, the wider potentiality of institutions offers the inviting prospect that new kinds of collective issues can be recognized and addressed.[2] Part of the aim of this essay is to try to envision some of these wider opportunities.

Practical institutionalism promises intellectual leverage for politically directed change, but that leverage comes at a price. That price is denominated in empirically approximate or incorrect assumptions about institutional structures and human motivation and the connections between them. It is a price that practitioners as well as social scientists and political theorists have sometimes thought worth paying, and so, at times, one can even explain some institutional changes as the deliberate effort of political leaders to impose or reform institutions to achieve specific purposes. The fact that some of the basic assumptions of practical institutionalism are likely to be wrong may limit its promise in ways that need to be understood. Certainly, conservatives since Edmund Burke have thought that such simplifications are disabling: They doubt that humans are really capable of successfully manipulating institutions precisely because we lack the intelligence to understand how they work and have to rely on dangerous abstractions. Such doubts may or may not be warranted; they can be answered only empirically. In any case, I will try to examine one kind of assumption that has seemed necessary to practical institutionalism, the idea that institutions can be represented as separable, in some sense, from the environments in which they work.

Engineers often make incorrect (because approximate) assumptions about the properties of the materials they use to construct buildings, but except in unusual circumstances those approximations are good enough for the practical purpose at hand. Specifically, they assume that the performance of these materials is independent of the designs which those materials implement: for example, that steel rods perform in a bridge the way they do in laboratory test equipment. This assumption permits knowledge of materials gained in a laboratory or computed from theoretical models to be used to assess how a building, a rocket, or a bridge will perform in various circumstances. Materials may fail in structures, of course, and sometimes these failures can be traced to unanticipated interactions among them within the structures in which they are embedded. But, the occurrence of occasional failures of this type is not thought to justify abandoning the independence hypothesis in general.

Practical institutionalism is concerned with engineering human institutions and faces more or less similar problems. Practical institutionalists since Hobbes have assumed that behavior is more or less separable from institutions—that one can describe facts about behavior that are, in some sense, invariant across institutional contexts. This is not to deny that people are influenced by institutional structures. Institutional influences are, however, assumed to be channeled through the maintained assumptions about human behavior. So, if individuals are deeply resistant to being put at risk of death, as Hobbes thought, they remain so under any institutional configuration, and their response to institutional circumstances is guided in part by this resistance. Similarly, economists typically assume that people are utility maximizers in any institutional context in which they are embedded and, usually, that their preferences can be specified independently of their institutional location.[3]

To say that institutions are separable from behavior is, at minimum, to say that it is possible to vary institutional context while holding behavioral dispositions fixed. It is to deny that there is a relation of necessity between institutions and behavior. This is a conceptual or definitional matter. For example, "democracy" could be understood, or defined, in two ways: narrowly, as a description of certain institutional configurations (e. g., voting rules, systems of representation) or broadly, as a pattern of expectation and dispositions (e. g., people see each other as equals, expect to be able to play a role in public life if they choose, are more or less inclined to vote in elections, are inclined to join associations to pursue common projects; officials listen to their constituents and willingly leave office if they lose an election), together with certain institutional configurations. A nation is not a democracy in this second sense unless its people are democratic in a kind of cultural sense. Democracy understood in the first or institutional sense is separable from behavior, but if it is understood in the second sense, it is not.[4]

Conceptual separability does not require that there be no causal connections between institutions and behavior; it could be the case that adopting democratic institutions makes it more likely that people will come to behave democratically. Or, things could go the other way around. But, the existence of causal relations still permits the conceptual distinction between democratic institutions and democratic behavior even if, under strict causal determination, they would never occur separately in fact. I shall use the term "separability" to denote the denial of causal linkages between institutions and behavior. Separability is the idea that one can vary institutions while holding behavior dispositions and beliefs, or indeed any number of other things, fixed empirically. So, causal separability entails the absence of causal relations between institutions and preferences or beliefs. It is a strong empirical claim about the way the world is, and, as such, it is likely to be wrong.

Of course, any specific characterization of human behavior can be wrong. There is no help for that but to try to learn more. But, we can specifically be wrong in assuming the causal separability of behavior from institutional contexts. And, if we are wrong in this way, the dispositions of agents may interact directly with designed institutions, making assumptions about them wrong and perhaps self-fulfilling or self-defeating. This is a matter not only of our approximate knowledge of how people act but of the possibility that human behavior, however described, may somehow be causally connected to the institutions in which it is embedded. Falsely assuming separability can lead to the construction of institutions that perform in completely unforeseen manners. Indeed, it seems possible to understand some of the disastrous institutional experiments of the past two centuries as a result of the failure to take this prospect into account

2. Designing Institutions

It may, of course, be objected that institutions are not normally designed at all but develop or evolve according to causal or other processes. This is the common view of the evolution of the British constitution or of the constitution of the Roman Republic, each of which is said to have emerged from a succession of struggles among social orders or classes. The practical perspective takes what I shall call the "design stance" toward institutions.[5] It may be distinguished from the causal stance, exemplified by the British and Roman examples, and the interpretive stance. If we seek to explain the structure of the U.S. Constitution, it seems nature to assume the design stance—a posture that Publius assumes in the *Federalist*—and see constitutional structures as the deliberate creations of framers in Philadelphia. The designer, in this case, is a group with complex internal dynamics, and, of course, the design had to be made sufficiently attractive to the people to achieve ratification. Because of such constraints, the design perspective can be quite rich and its implications difficult to work out.[6]

Even so, no one really thinks that the initial structure of the U.S. Constitution can be explained as purely as the result of design without any reference to either contextual or causal factors. An older generation of historians emphasized the economic causes of the Constitution, seeing it as a set of protections that more or less had to emerge from existing structures of property or capital. Contemporary historians more often point to the contingency of decisions at Philadelphia (or during the ratification process): Things might have gone differently,[7] depending on who was in attendance, or as the result of political moves during the ratification debates, each of which has more of a causal than a design aspect.[8] And, we could certainly imagine a political account that focused on the constrain-

ing properties of the voting institutions or committees or agenda formation processes employed either in Philadelphia or in the ratifying conventions. In these ways, institutional changes may be explained causally:
Forces operating within institutions and contexts produce institutional
changes without any intentional steering or design. Moreover, there may
be processes operating in the environment of institutions that select for
those that competitively successful.

Finally, we may also speak of the interpretive perspective that sees institutional change as governed by the development of norms or values that
arise or evolve within the ordinary functioning of an institution.[9] Again,
using an American example, the framers of the U.S. Constitution resisted
the idea of adding a bill of rights to their proposed constitution because
many of them thought that such a listing would be dangerously exclusive,
with respect to unlisted rights, and was, anyway, superfluous. Indeed,
Hamilton asked rhetorically in the *Federalist*: What is the constitution
itself but a bill of rights? But, starting with the Pennsylvania ratification
debates, the defenders of the proposed constitution encountered enormous public skepticism and hostility when making this argument. And,
over the course of the ratification arguments, the framers were forced to
retreat from this position and promised to propose just such a bill of
rights in the form of amendments once the new constitution was ratified.

One could, of course, see this as a mere tactical maneuver aimed at getting the constitution accepted. But, I think it as likely that Madison came
sincerely to believe, by 1789, when the first Congress convened, that the
constitution needed such an explicit statement of protected liberties in
order to realize what he then, in 1789, understood as the republican exper-
iment and not merely as a compromise to get the thing accepted. On this
account, Madison came to see (interpret) the purpose of the Constitution
differently from his view in 1787 and saw that the inclusion of explicit
rights in the Constitution was the best interpretation of the constitutional
project launched in Philadelphia. And, whether or not Madison himself
actually held this new belief in 1789, the subsequent history of American
constitutionalism (and the development of the Supreme Court as a rights-
protecting institution) cannot be explained without recognizing the emergence of such immanent (and eventually widely shared) values.[10] In effect,
then, the interpretive stance is the design stance, but with respect to emergent or immanent goals rather than goals that are fixed prior to the design
of the institution.

Thus, while the causal and interpretive stances point to different accounts of institutional structure and change, both are compatible with the design perspective. Adam Smith's invisible hand argument can be taken as exemplary: Smith argued that markets produce efficient allocations because of the aggregate effects of certain low-level causal mechanisms (that independent decision makers would reliably seek to maximize wealth given fixed prices). The operation of these underlying mechanisms (somehow) causes prices to adjust in ways that allow markets to be understood from a design perspective: as institutions "designed" to produce efficient allocations in some circumstances. When those circumstances do not hold, and allocations are inefficient, the design perspective can tell economists how to reshape markets to attain efficiency in these distorted circumstances.

The same point holds for interpretive perspectives. Political theorists since Hegel have argued that interpretive activities that generate values and beliefs leading to institutional reform and replacement can be seen as designed—as directed toward (immanent) objectives, often an objective invisible to the agents themselves (except perhaps near the end of the historical sequence itself). One need not endorse so strong a view, however: It would be enough to believe that, at any particular point in time, people come up with ideas about how to reform their institutions on the basis of their current interpretation of the values served by those institutions. In this sense, different design perspectives could be contemplated depending on the whether designers are situated in history or stand outside it.

The practical orientation to institutions—seeing institutions as designed to achieve certain purposes—implicates us immediately in two questions: We wish to know the effects of various conceivable institutional structures in producing things that are of value to us, and we want to know how to produce and reform institutions, or how to keep them in place if we have them. These questions can be addressed theoretically, of course, but in the end I believe that we will not be satisfied with purely theoretical answers but will demand empirical evidence of one sort or another.

Institutions may be valued either intrinsically or instrumentally, and this matters for what we want to know about them. Democracy, human rights, and the rule of law may be thought to be somehow intrinsically important to a good life independent of any other effects they may produce. Perhaps they permit or enhance human autonomy, either at the level of the individual or the community, or they are required by some deeper value of moral equality. Or perhaps there is no other value they serve; they are just a part of what it means to have an acceptable collective life. If we value an institution for its own sake, then it does not matter so much what further effects it produces. We would want to find out how to produce and sustain it regardless of its further consequences.

This is not to say that side effects of intrinsically desirable institutions are without interest. We might wish to minimize the bad consequences of an otherwise desirable institution. Or we might wish to appeal to an institution's side consequences in order to persuade others, who do not value it as we do, to accept it nevertheless. We would still be interested in the question of how to bring it into existence or how to make it stable and robust to external events. As part of the answer to these questions, we would also be interested in how to secure people's allegiance to the institution, and perhaps how to motivate them to fight to defend it. And, to secure patriotic attachment, we might need to appeal to the further effects of an institution, even if it is one that we value intrinsically.

Of course, for instrumentally valued institutions, we would be most interested in whether the alleged benefits are real, or in the conditions under which those benefits are produced. Such institutions will be worth having only if their effects are reliably produced, valuable and substantial. So, from an instrumental perspective, it would be important to a defense of democracy, or a parliamentary form of democracy, that such institutions actually tend to produce economic growth or to reduce economic or social inequalities, or lead to some other desirable consequences; or at least that democratic institutions tend to produce these effects more reliably or at less cost than competing alternatives. Then, if these effects turned out to be real, we would have further interests in the same kinds of studies that are important for intrinsically valued institutions—how best to institute the system, secure allegiance to it, make it robust against interfering events.

3. The Standard Model

By taking the practical viewpoint, we accept the notion that institutions can be appraised abstractly by or on behalf of the human beings that inhabit them. Among these features are those that permit people to evaluate how things are going. If we wish to establish markets in order to try allocate resources efficiently, for example, we normally judge efficiency according to preferences that are independent the institution itself. This can be understood as requiring what I have called causal separability: It amounts to denying that institutions themselves have causal effects on values or preferences.

Within political science, much of the formal study of institutions has occurred within the narrow terrains of the study of legislative and electoral behavior. In those settings, it has made sense to think of politicians seeking objectives under constraints in manner that is abstractly similar to economic agents. But, there are some important differences, too. First, while economists take the content of preferences to be egoistic and more or less materialistic, that is a more controversial assumption in political settings. True, some writers, following Marx and Beard and the Chicago school of economics, have seen materially self-interested behavior as more or less normal within the political domain. The notion of office-seeking politicians is only a step away from this view. But, many others take seriously the claims of politicians to seek other kinds of goals and see materialism as descriptively inadequate. At the very least it seems necessary to take account of policy motivated politicians who can be described as seeking to further their views of the public interest. Of course, such goals can be redescribed so as to fit an hedonic interpretation, but this attribution seems arbitrary. Moreover, in view of collective actions within parties, it is a little difficult to see self-interest as the basis for ideological behavior.[11]

Still, these caveats having been made, institutions have the same functional role in these models that they do in economics: They serve to constrain the choices available to the actors embedded in them. Different electoral systems confront voters with different ballot choices, for example. And, rules for forming or deciding on agendas limit the moves available to various legislative actors. The actors, whatever preferences they have (whether hedonic or ideological), seek to fulfill them subject to institutional and physical constraints. So, as in economics, political scientists who take formal approach to institutions have tended to assume that institutions can be characterized separately from the preferences held by their occupants. And, as is the case with economic institutions, the fact that actors make choices subject to institutional constraints implies that (equilibrium) outcomes can be described as (partly) a function of those institutional arrangements.

Subject to some technical caveats, this implies that the agents will be able to form induced preferences over alternative institutional structures.

These induced preferences are usually taken to be instrumental in nature: The reason an actor prefers institution A to institution B is that the equilibrium outcome under A is preferable to the outcome that would result from B, from that actor's viewpoint.[12] So, as Riker noted, the question of choosing among institutions arises naturally in this setup.[13] And all the familiar modeling issues arise: What are the rules governing institutional choice? Are institutional choices made by the same agents who populate the institution, by others outside the institution, or by a designer standing above the fray?

However these issues are resolved, the standard approach neatly separates two questions, asking, first, what are the effects of an institution (which treats the institution itself as exogenous to the choices made by agents operating within it) and, second, what explains the design of the institution itself (which rests on the notion that institutions themselves are endogenous)? Shepsle called these the question of institutional equilibrium and that of equilibrium institutions, and he illustrated an important and quite natural sense in which these two questions are closely linked and that the standard model can be extended to answer the second question.[14] The idea is that agents can form preferences over institutions that are conditioned on how those institutions work to produce outcomes.[15] Here is a simple example where we take voting agendas as exemplary institutions.

Assume that there is a population, N, and an exogenous commitment to using majority rule to decide controversial questions. Suppose, for example, that the population has cyclic producing preferences among outcomes—which we write as xMyMzMx (where xMy means that x beats y in a majority vote)—and that voting is conducted according to a fixed agenda (or order of voting) on the alternatives (where A is the set of agendas). For example, let agenda $((x,y),z) \in A$ require that x is voted against y and the winner against z. For this agenda, given the cycle described earlier, z is the outcome because xMy in the first vote and then zMx.[16] It is easy to see in this case that for every outcome, there is an agenda that will support it as the outcome. So, y will be the outcome of $((x,z),y)$, and x the outcome of $((y,z),x)$. Thus, if voters evaluate agendas in terms of the outcomes they produce, their (induced) preferences over the set of agendas will exhibit a majority cycle; in effect, the cycle over outcomes induces or reproduces a cycle over agendas. Riker called this the heritability problem, and it is not special to the use of majority rule itself; it is true for nearly every voting rule[17] and extends to other kinds of institutions, as well. This line of thinking suggests that there is a kind of infinite regress problem that is inherent in the endogenous choice of institutions.

But, heritability is a problem that depends on a "closed system" postulate that assumes not only that the agents can predict accurately how institutions will work but also that preferences over institutions are induced from preferences over outcomes (produced by those institutions). Lacking any other information about preferences at the prior stage of institutional choice, it seems natural enough to derive them from agents' preferences over outcomes. Natural or not, this amounts to assuming that preferences will remain stable across different circumstances of choice. Or, to put it another way, preferences are assumed to be separable from situations of choice so that actors may anticipate accurately how they will behave once institutions are put into place, for any set of institutions that may be designed. This assumption, separability, seems very strong, and we explore it in the next section.

4. Separability Hypotheses

A basic assumption of the standard model employed in economics and game theory, as well as in positive political theory, is the notion that institutions are separable from behavior. Institutions are supposed to constitute barriers or constraints within which agents choose actions. Market institutions confront agents with budget sets, and they must choose best actions within those sets. Legislative institutions confront actors with rules specifying how to form motions, when to vote, what must be done in secret, when actions can legally be taken. Agents then can formulate their plans within these constraints. Games are supposed to be made up of rules that constrain the plays that actors can make.

There is a deep objection to this hypothesis that I will not discuss in detail: the notion that human institutions are themselves composed of behaviors or anticipated behaviors and so the very notion of separability is somehow incoherent. The structure and valuations of the prisoner's dilemma, for example, is produced by the threats and promises of the police, and these, if they are not actual behaviors, are predictions of future contingent actions. There is a sense that human institutions may always be characterized in this way. The budget set faced by a consumer in general equilibrium models is produced by the aggregated behavior of everyone else, which has the effect of fixing prices and wealth levels for each individual. Even technological constraints are (mostly) determined by past and perhaps current actions of economic agents. There may be some brute physical aspects that enter in, but human action takes place mostly within contexts composed of past, current, and anticipated future actions.

For the present, whatever it is that institutions "are," we assume that they constrain behavior and so in that sense can be described separately from behavior. In partial equilibrium consumer theory, the consumer chooses her consumption plan on the assumption that the prices she faces are fixed or parametric, even though those prices are really summaries of the behavior of other economic agents. Something like the same analytical tactic is employed in game theory, where there is an explicit recognition that each person's best action depends on the actions of others. When an actor is calculating her best reply, she takes (her information about) the preferences of the others as fixed, independent of institutional structure and her own actions. Similarly, in a Nash equilibrium, each player takes the actions of others as fixed or parametric. A weak form of separability— conceptual separability—is all that is assumed in these analytical concepts, if not in the game itself. The structure of the game is assumed to be describable in terms separate from the attributes of the agents. Sometimes this is expressed by assuming that we can write down a "game form" that describes all the moves available to the agents but not the payoffs they will receive. Conceptual separability amounts to saying that game can be reduced to a game form together with payoff (preference) information.

While this seems a fairly innocuous assumption, causal separability is much stronger. There are three general ways in which causal separability might fail or at least be controversial. First, it might be that institutions have a direct causal effect on preferences. Second, institutions themselves may change as a direct result of the actions of the players. Third, institutions and behavior might be connected normatively; that is, an institution might produce a set of norms that will guide choice behavior of agents within the institution, independent of preferences. In a sense, these failures of causal separability are not problems of game theoretic representations. We can, in certain sense, model each of them within a game theoretic setup by enlarging the game in the appropriate manner. But they pose problems of interpretation, which I comment on here.

First, installing a particular institution might somehow establish certain preferences or dispositions in the players. How this happens might be complex and depend on facts outside the game itself. The game of chess is somehow predicated on the notion that the players want to win. This is not a conceptual requirement. One can easily imagine a teacher playing against a novice and making moves, in part, to produce pedagogically useful situations. They are still playing chess in the sense that they conform to the rules governing play. But, the teacher is not playing it to win. There is a sense in which the activity they are engaged in is not really "playing" chess but some other kind of activity; maybe they are playing another game that shares the game form of chess but has different payoffs. The explanation for the teacher's mode of activity is that he is trying to teach the student how to play the game successfully, and so his role as teacher causes him to adopt certain "preferences" as to how the game should be played.

Jon Elster's example of sour grapes is an example of a class of cases in which preferences are caused by a psychological adjustment mechanism of some kind.[18] The fox, seeing that the grapes, which she had desired, are inaccessible to her, comes not to prefer them. Or, we could consider the case of someone whose preference for drinking wine increases with each additional drink. Suppose a person prefers to have one glass of wine with dinner so that she may do some useful work afterward. She knows that, having had one drink, she will then prefer to have another rather than working afterward and will tend to act on that new preference. Here, the mechanism of preference change seems to be chemically based rather than based in a strange or defective deliberative process as in the case of the fox. The sour grapes example is perhaps not so troubling since it is difficult even to say whether the fox wants grapes at all—sometimes she does (if she can get them) and sometimes she doesn't (if she cannot). The change in the fox's preferences seems to be an immediate direct causal consequence of the change in the availability of the grapes. The sense of causation is psychological and, therefore, deliberatively inaccessible to the fox. And, if this is so, it is hard to see what it is that fox wants. We lack any kind of normative leverage on the choice.

The case of a moderate wine drinker is perhaps more troubling: She hopes to drink one glass of wine, knowing that, after having that drink, she will want another. In the case of the wine drinker, there is an intervening chemical process that predictably transforms her preferences in a certain way. Her preferences depend on her chemical state, and so she no longer has deliberative access to her initial (moderate) preferences after having had a drink. It has seemed natural to many that in this case somehow the preferences of the person before drinking anything are somehow her "real" preferences or at least are the ones that ought to be respected. But, that analysis depends on some background assumptions about the effects of alcohol, and perhaps some normative judgements, too, and if the same story were told about Prozac or some other therapeutic chemical this interpretation would no longer so natural.

In both cases, it is hard to see how the agent should act. It seems that a person who wants a single glass of wine has a strategic problem: Unless she can figure out a way to stop her future self from acting on *her* preferences,[19] it is not possible to get her most preferred alternative: dinner with a single glass of wine. But, with the fox it is hard to say that there is even a strategic problem to be addressed. After all, whatever the situation, she will end up with an outcome she prefers or is at least satisfied with (either with grapes if available or without them if not). But what should the fox do if she was to be in position costlessly to make the grapes available? That seems to depend on additional information that is not provided in the myth: in particular on whether the fox prefers the situation of having grapes available—and therefore consuming grapes—to not having access to grapes at all. As with the drinking example, it is customary to think of the fox's preferences when the grapes are not reachable as being somehow distorted or malformed. That is a natural if not inevitable interpretation, and one that a Stoic might resist.

Second, it seems that sometimes choices themselves can influence or change institutions. The standard view already envisions two levels of choice: Within the institutional structure, people take actions guided by the belief that the institutional rules are fixed, but at a higher, "constitutional" level, they choose the institutional rules. Something like this two-level story is sometimes told, for example, about the practices of American law, or of constitutional law generally. Ordinary legislation is supposed to take place within a fixed constitutional framework, whereas constitutional lawmaking occurs on a different and higher track, perhaps according to different rules.[20]

But this may not be an accurate account of the structure of law. Is it really the case that ordinary legislative actions cannot affect constitutional constraints, or that citizens and officials don't expect that constitutional change can occur from the bottom up? Suppose, for example, that ordinary lawmakers, acting in response to a crisis, simply start enacting legislation that had previously been thought unconstitutional. They do this on the belief that the new circumstance of crisis makes it clear that prior constitutional understandings are overly restrictive and either temporarily or permanently inappropriate. Such efforts might well be challenged, of course, in constitutional courts if those have the authority to overturn legislation. But if this occurs, the constitutional court may well reach the same understanding as the legislators. And, whether or not the legislation is challenged, it seems clear that the constitutional rules have been changed and that they have been changed from the bottom.

It is possible, of course, to represent this situation as an expanded game in which, following some event (a crisis), beliefs change in such a way that a different equilibrium can be supported in the subgame that follows the crisis than was accepted in the subgame that would have occurred without a crisis. In this representation, there is no causal relation between actions and institutions. But I guess that there is still a quite natural sense in which that dependence is real: a sense that in some circumstances, the legislators or the people, by the choices they make, can force or cause alterations in its higher law or constitution.

Finally, let's consider normative connections between institutions and behavior. Rousseau and others have suggested that people ought to behave differently in public than in private-choice situations. In *The Social Contract*, Rousseau argued that people could make collective choices on the basis of their own private preferences—the aggregation of these would form what he called the "will of all"—or they could make those choice on the basis of public-regarding judgments, whose aggregation revealed what he called the "general will."[21] From Rousseau's perspective, much of the problem of institutional design was to ensure that people would vote on the basis of the public interest and not on the basis of their private or factional interests. So, for example, he imposed restrictions on the lawmaking process with this aim in mind: He required that questions posed to the assembly be general in the sense that they make no mention of individuals, places, or occupations. He also required the use of a secret ballot, aiming to prevent bribes and corruption. And, he forbade debate and communication among voters, fearing that such interaction would permit seductive rhetoric to deflect the people from the pursuit of public purposes.

Rousseau did not, as far as I can see, say that the choice of these institutional features literally changed preferences. He thought that each citizen's preferences already contained both self-regarding and public-regarding components. Rousseau thought that all people had a weak and imperfect view of the pubic good, as well as a powerful and clear view of their own private interests. Indeed, he thought that all people's visions of their own interests are so strong and palpable that they tend to obscure completely people's vision of the public interest. And this phenomenon would only get worse in a tumultuous public debate. That is why he thought it dangerous to ask the assembly to make judgments that might directly affect the wellbeing of some particular part of the population. Making such judgments would tempt people to use inappropriate standards for choice, to engage in heated and manipulative rhetoric, to bribe, threaten, and cajole their fellows. Much better to pose abstract and principled questions in which people cannot see their private stakes so clearly and must instead focus on issues that affect them all as citizens. The point of designing good public institutions is to make it more likely that citizens will act on the basis of the public interest, what Rawls later called public reason, than vote on the basis of private or partial considerations.

But, though Rousseau himself may not have regarded his institutional recommendations as having a causal effect on preferences, there seems no strong reason to resist this interpretation. A neo-Rousseaian view, for example, might say that certain preferences are either brought into being ex nihilo by the design of new institutions or else are a part of what constitutes the institution itself. When a new game is designed, it is not well described as a mere set of rules governing play; the very design of the game sets in train processes that cause the players to have or develop certain dispositions, such as intentions to adhere to the rules or to try to prevail over opponents within the frame of the game. And, to act in this way, the play of the game usually requires the acquisition of skills and requires that actors submit to the discipline of obtaining those skills. The game itself has the effect of embedding its players in a new normative field, and the norms at work in that field are usually not part of the austere institutional definition of the game. Those norms tell how the game is to be played well, not how it is to be played at all.

I am not saying that these further norms can be clearly foreseen from the beginning or that they are unique. I doubt that Dr. Naismith foresaw the slam dunk or even the jump shot, and so one can wonder whether he should even be considered the father of modern basketball. Modern paternity might better go to Julius Erving or Hank Luchetti. But, my guess is that once the peachbasket was put on the pole and people started playing the game, he and his fellows rapidly fell into (normative) disputations as to how best to play the game, that they came to judgments as to what kinds of skills were most valuable and whom they wanted to be on their team. In a sense, the institution of basketball itself induces its participants to make evaluative or normative judgments as to how the game should be played.

Deciding to make certain choices in a legislature rather than within a market is, by the same token, not adequately described by simply listing the rules of procedure and jurisdiction of that legislature. Rather, there is a presumption that those elected to serve in the legislature will generally try to pursue public purposes by the use of legitimate public means. The effective pursuit of such purposes, when those elected must confront others with different judgment and conflicting interests, requires the development of skills and abilities relevant to that pursuit. These skills are, on most accounts of legislatures, quite different from the skills that are valued in the marketplace. The arts of discussion and deliberation are different in the two settings, and different arguments are effective.

Indeed, as Aristotle and others recognized, one reason to put a certain institution in place, or to use public institutions to make certain kinds of decisions, is that the skills and abilities that institution requires are valued for their own sake. The perspectives and skills associated with public deliberation and decision making are, on this conception, an important part of living a good life. John Stuart Mill's justification of democracy takes this line: Democracy improves the skills, habits, and characters of its citizens, as well as (possibly) producing better decisions.[22] But, whether one regards citizenship norms as valuable or simply as a foreseeable consequence of institutionalization, it seems clear that institutions can have the effect of generating norms that may themselves guide future behavior.

None of these remarks is intended to undercut the notion of causal separability as a tactical modeling device. Theorists have made a great deal of analytic progress in analyzing institutional effects by invoking it as a simplifying assumption. Moreover, at least the last two objections to separability have answers of a kind within the standard model. One can redefine preferences over a larger class of states or events and restore the separability idea from a formal viewpoint. But, the newly constructed set of alternative states becomes pretty unwieldy, and the agents' preferences over these states are hard to interpret. Moreover, it is hard to believe that people actually form and act on such preferences. So I think it is better to recognize and accept the substantive issues raised by these objections as forming research questions of substantive interest in their own right.

A full appraisal of institutions is hampered by maintaining causal separability as a kind of fundamental constraint. I think that Mill was right that a part of the reason for wanting to have democracy, for example, is to change the way we are as citizens: to get us to adopt habits of arguing, listening, and forming opinions as morally autonmous agents. But, changing our actions in a stable and robust way, as Pascal argued, tends to change what we want and value. Eventually, it seems to me, good studies of the differences that institutions make must take such influences into account.

5. Conclusion

Separability assumptions are too useful to be abandoned, but, as strong causal statements, they are very likely to be wrong. It cannot really be true that humans can be understood in the radically "unsituated" way that sep- arability implies. Aristotle was right that man is a social or political animal. But, Hobbes was also right to think that humans can imagine changing institutions while holding onto some of their personal characteristics—at least for a short time. Surely, our institutions as part of our environment have causal relevance to what we want and believe and, indeed, who we are. But, we know very little about these causal processes, and surely the study of institutions requires that we be prepared to examine not merely their intended effects but also other consequences that may predictably follow. These further effects may, of course, temper our enthusiasm for design, or they may offer new opportunities. It is hard to say in advance.

In any case, such study offers a new prospect on institutions whether or not they are designed or "found." We can aspire to master and control our institutions more effectively, but to do that we need to take a perspective that is somewhat independent of the institutions themselves. It hard to see how we could think about doing this without holding some things fixed, that is, maintaining some kind of separability assumption_without, that is, an Archimedean point. But there is no reason for us to take that fixed point as anything more than a provisional assumption that permits us to getting started in evaluating, criticizing, and reforming institutions.

NOTES

1. There are many social scientists who would protest that their commitments are purely scientific or descriptive. This may be well be the case, and, in any case, informative scientific and descriptive studies are essential to the normative or practical perspective pursued here. I doubt, moreover, that a purely descriptive preoccupation would explain very well which institutions are studied. But I leave this speculative worry aside.

2. The remarkable spurt of constitutional development in postwar Europe,

especially among the defeated nations, is testimony to a belief that new institutions could correct recent horrors. Especially notable is the creation of constitutional courts with powers to review and strike down legislation in Germany and Italy. The ensuing development of German and Italian constitutional law has, if anything, exceeded the aspirations of the designers of those institutions. Surely many of these institutional developments must be seen as transformative of goals and identities and not merely as solution to neo-Hobbesian problems. For some descriptive information see John Ferejohn and Pasquale Pasquino, "Constitutional Courts as Deliberative Institutions: Toward an Institutional Theory of Constitutional Justice," in Wojciech Sadurski, ed., *Constitutional Justice East and West* (The Hague: Kluwer Law International, 2002), 21–36.

3. The independence notion is most clearly seen in social-choice theory, which describes institutions as functions that operate over the space of preferences. But it is visible as well in literatures on implementation theory and game theory.

4. We could, of course, speak of democratic institutions in the second sense, but we would have to recognize that democratic institutions are no more than a necessary condition for democracy—if, indeed, they are even that.

5. This language is borrowed from Daniel C. Dennett, *The Intentional Stance* (Cambridge, MA: MIT Press, 1987). The idea is that we can and do assume different stances or perspectives when trying to understand complex processes such as the operations of the brain or the mind. I think the same is true when trying to direct or control social processes.

6. See for example Jack Rakove, *Original Meanings* (New York: Knopf, 1996).

7. It was surely important that most of the delegates to the Convention were already committed to quite radical changes in the Articles of Confederation. Riker argues that there was a process of self-selection involved in choosing the delegates. Perhaps, too, the absence of the New York delegation when some crucial decisions were taken mattered. Indeed, Madison's own design perspective led him to propose much more drastic constitutional changes than he managed to get his colleagues in Philadelphia to accept; he needed to confront more or less causal constraints in acting as a designer.

8. Some historians argue that the refusal of supporters of the new constitution to accept conditional ratification was crucial to its acceptance and that that maneuver might well have failed. Rakove, *Original Meanings*.

9. It is important to emphasize that this is a noncausal notion. We think of a value as emerging within a practice if participants come to see the point of the practice in a new way. They then tend to seek different purposes within the institution and to appraise the institution or practice from a new perspective. This is an internal idea of the kind I discuss at some length in John Ferejohn, "External and Internal Explanation," in Ian Shapiro, Rogers Smith, and Tarek Masoud, eds., *Problems and Methods in the Study of Politics* (Cambridge: Cambridge University Press, 2004).

10. The same story can be told about democratic as well as liberal norms. See Gordon S. Wood, *The Radicalism of the American Revolution* (New York: Knopf, 1992).

11. This is not to make the strong claim that ideology is independent of self-interest. Indeed, it is to say no more than revisionist Marxists have: that the connection between material self-interest and political preferences and beliefs is psychologically complex.

12. This assumption is not at all necessary. Agents could value institutions directly, for their own intrinsic benefits. In that case, induced preferences over institutions would reflect both instrumental and intrinsic valuation, and one would expect to see tradeoffs among these sources. Or, there may be externally imposed restraints (perhaps of constitutional origin) that limit the institutions that may be put in place.

13. William H. Riker, "Implications from the Disequilibrium of Majority Rule for the Study of Institutions," *American Political Science Review* 74 (June 1980): 432–446.

14. Kenneth A. Shepsle, "Institutional Equilibrium and Equilibrium Institutions," in Herbert F. Weisberg, *Political Science: The Science of Politics* (New York: Agathon, 1986).

15. Specifically, agents are assumed to form rational expectations about how those institutions will work.

16. In the example, I assume for ease of illustration that individuals vote sincerely. The same phenomenon can be described if they vote strategically.

17. Though not for unanimity rule or, more generally, for rules in which some players have absolute vetoes (as everyone does in unanimity rule).

18. Jon Elster, *Sour Grapes* (Cambridge: Cambridge University Press, 1990).

19. Perhaps by making sure that there is only a single glass of wine in her house.

20. When considering a proposed constitutional rule, one needs rationally to anticipate how the ordinary legislative process would work under the new rule. And, in the standard story, this anticipation would be governed by assuming that people under the new rule will not see themselves as influencing the constitutional rules directly. The difficulty of maintaining this posture is evident: How is it possible for us to be engaged in constitutional politics at a moment in time without recognizing that others in the future will have that opportunity as well? Surely, as part of engaging in constitutional politics at a moment in time, we need to recognize the possibility of engaging in it once again.

21. Jean-Jacques Rousseau, *The Social Contract* (London: Orion Books, 1993).

22. John Stuart Mill, *Considerations on Representative Government (Great Books in Philosophy)* (Prometheus Books, 1991).

4

Which Comes First, the Ideas or the Institutions?

Rogers M. Smith

The Challenge

This essay addresses one of the central challenges of institutional analyses, particularly of contemporary "historical institutional" analyses, more particularly of my own efforts to conduct such analyses. I write on this topic especially due to awareness of unresolved tensions in those efforts. I have also been influenced by two important recent discussions of the same issues authored by leading historical institutional scholars. These are Robert Lieberman's essay "Ideas, Institutions, and Political Order: Explaining Political Change" and Karen Orren and Stephen Skowronek's *The Search for American Political Development*, a landmark elaboration of ideas advanced in various published essays which already provided much of the foundation for Lieberman's thinking and my own.[1]

Here I agree with these authors that persuasive political analyses must encompass the interrelationships of institutions and ideas, rather than treat either in relative isolation, and that important political changes often result from the interaction of "multiple orders," each with partly autonomous, sometimes clashing developmental dynamics (interactions that Orren and Skowronek term "intercurrence"). I argue, however, that we need to define more fully what constitutes an "order" that might be part of "multiple orders," and we need to clarify further the relationships of ideas and institutions within such orders. I agree with Orren and Skowronek, and against Lieberman and some of my own earlier work, that it is not useful to treat ideological "traditions" or "ideational orders" as themselves "institutional orders." But I continue to insist, more strongly than Orren and Skowronek, that we need analyses of traditions of ideas if we are to understand the purposes that, on their account and mine, give institutional orders much of their character, coherence, and significance.

I illustrate this argument by building on the account of race in America that Desmond King and I have recently advanced.[2] We contend that, among the multiple orders in the United States, there have been at least two evolving "racial orders," one a "white supremacist" racial order or set of linked orders, the other a "transformative egalitarian" racial order or set of orders (the varying descriptions depend upon whether one stresses the continuities or the differences in the stages of these developing systems). Each order or set of orders has been made up of interrelated ideational and institutional components. These orders are important for American political development because of both their conflicts with each other and their interactions with others of America's "multiple orders."[3] Analysis of the ideas that partly constitute these rival institutional orders and their conflict in the late nineteenth century can, for example, explain why, *pace* Orren and Skowronek, the rise of the "separate but equal" Jim Crow system should be seen as a significant instance of political "development." That system represented an enduring change in the preexisting white supremacist institutional order, made necessary by the success of the more egalitarian order in getting its principles formally enshrined in the Constitution via the postwar Amendments. To say this is not to deny at all that Jim Crow remained a kind of white supremacist system. It is to say that it was a significantly different kind of white supremacist system from the one that had prevailed when most African Americans were slaves and few free blacks had even nominal citizenship.

But, though I am positioning the analysis of ideas and institutions in this essay midway between what I see as the positions recently taken by Lieberman and Orren and Skowronek, I suspect these differences (unlike our different interpretations of racial history) are more matters of formulation and emphasis than substance. Hence I regard the arguments here as extensions of, not as challenges to, the basic theoretical positions laid out in these recent historical institutional works, though others must judge how far that is the case. I do so while acknowledging that these authors have raised important concerns about some of my own writings—because the problems they have raised are ones that also trouble me. Let me begin with those concerns, then turn to my thoughts for addressing them and how those thoughts build on and, perhaps, carry further the important accounts of institutional analysis provided by these authors.

Having been trained initially in the history of political ideas, I have long been aligned with those political scientists who stress that "ideas matter" in politics, and I have been pleased in recent years to see resurgent arguments to that effect, especially among comparative politics scholars.[4] Historical institutionalists like Orren and Skowronek and Lieberman have courteously but forcefully argued, however, that those of us who focus on ideas have not done an adequate job of developing theoretical frameworks that find an appropriate place for political institutions, which are entities that embody ideas but are clearly more than just ideas.[5] Without necessarily opposing my claims that American political culture displays not just Louis Hartz's "liberal" tradition but also in fact "multiple traditions," these scholars have contended that it is unwise to place traditions of ideas at the center of political analysis, with institutions given a rather unclear, more marginal position. I have not wholly conceded that my focus on "multiple traditions" mandates neglect of political institutions.[6] I have stressed, like others, that the purposes, rules, roles, and patterns of behavior found in institutions all represent incarnations of the ideas of those who participate in them and that the creation and maintenance of institutions cannot be understood apart from the ideas of the members of the political coalitions that do the creating and maintaining.[7] But it remains true that the center of gravity in my earlier work has been more traditions of ideas than the sorts of institution-centered analyses that these scholars, especially Orren and Skowronek, recommend.

I now think that the ideal point for that center of gravity may lie somewhere between what I have done and what more pure "institutionalists" like Orren and Skowronek generally do. That sense has arisen from reflections on how I have discussed racial identities over the years. In a number of works, I have tried to show that racial ideologies, especially doctrines of white supremacy, constitute analytically distinguishable and historically continuous traditions in American political discourse, along with and intertwined with (among other things) the liberal, republican, and democratic conceptions other scholars have long featured.[8] That work was very much part of the argument that "ideas matter."

But, as my explorations of American racial history have proceeded, I have increasingly stressed that racial identities have been not something that emerged rather organically from social experiences or ideological traditions. Like many others, I have begun to argue that, to a considerable degree, American racial identities have actually been created by relatively autonomous governmental institutions that labeled some as "white," some as "black," some as different races.[9] Those institutional arrangements—antebellum state civil and criminal laws, late-nineteenth- and early-twentieth-century state Jim Crow laws, federal census rules, immigration and naturalization statutes, judicial rulings on all of the above, police enforcement of all of the above, political parties structured to express and preserve all of the above, and more—never simply embodied any single ideological tradition or, indeed, the outlook of any single American group, at least not in straightforward "transmission belt" fashion.[10] They have instead often been compromises negotiated among groups with partly compatible but partly contrasting racial conceptions.

Those compromises have varied from state to state, and from one arena of regulation, such as naturalization, to another, such as school segregation. The compromises have also been partly amended over time in different locations in distinct, often inconsistent ways. But because those compromise results have had official status in defining racial identities, these institutional arrangements can plausibly be seen as more central to the construction of racial identities in America than any particular ideological tradition. In other words, these *institutions* have been more the direct source of racial constructions than socially widespread racial *ideas*. They have given concrete content to racial identities in ways that have often varied from the background racial ideologies that admittedly helped generate those laws—at least, so I have argued, seeking to drive home how much race has been not a biological or a purely cultural but instead a specifically political phenomenon in America.

And yet, even though there is truth in every point just made, I have also been aware that this account may overstate how relatively autonomous American political and legal racial institutions have been from dominant ideological traditions in American society, at least at various crucial junctures. Consider, for example, the 1790 naturalization act, the law that first officially proclaimed that one had to be "white" to be eligible for U.S. citizenship, if one did not already possess it via a legal birthright. Consideration of this example is hard, because we have only scanty records of the first Congress in general, and we have no records of any debate over this provision. We therefore cannot be certain what the members of the first Congress thought about it. But the scholarly consensus, which I have no grounds to attack, is that they probably did not think about it much at all. The sense that citizenship ought to be limited to "whites" was so widely shared among the members of the convention that it did not need discussion.[11]

Where did that consensus come from? The most likely explanations focus on the interactions of expansionist Europeans with indigenous peoples in Africa and North America and on the efforts of British American colonists, in particular, to enslave the labor of the former and seize the lands of the latter, even as they tried to ally with at least some other European immigrants in establishing new, comparatively inclusive republics. In the process of carrying out these economic and political endeavors, European-descended Americans found it useful to have everyday shorthand ways to distinguish those they were with from those they were against. And one convenient device for doing so was to invoke predominant variations in skin color by terming themselves "whites" and the others "blacks" or "red men." This was such a widespread social practice by the time of the first Congress that, rather than invoke anything more complicated (such as "European-descended," because many sorts of people were born in Europe), it probably seemed easier just to write "white" into the law. Various states had already done so, and Congress followed suit.[12]

If so, then that law must be seen as a relatively unconscious and undiluted manifestation of dominant ideological traditions in early American political society. This racial naturalization restriction then went on to become a thorn in the sides of late-nineteenth- and early-twentieth-century courts, especially, as judges labored hard to decide who was "white." That fact alone has rightly been interpreted as indicating that this law represented a legal construction of race that courts then defined further, and in varying ways. But American judges ultimately arrived at an approach that made common-sense social views definitive of what "white" meant. That stance suggests, again, that the legal system's authoritative notions of racial identity should perhaps be best understood as direct expressions, or at least as efforts at direct expressions, of broader intellectual and social traditions, not as something that played much of an independent role in defining what "whiteness" and "race" were.[13]

And if that is right, then I seem to have come full circle. In my past work, I've stressed race as an ideological tradition, a product of ideas more than governmental institutions, and then as a relatively autonomous legal construction, a product of governmental institutions more than ideas, but I have been unable to rest secure in either account. So I feel compelled to ask, which should we really say comes first, the ideas or the institutions— both in point of time and, more important, in explanatory power for understanding phenomena like racial statuses and their role in American politics, including American political changes over time?

Given the limits of my own efforts, let me turn now to the salutary advice my fellow historical institutionalists have offered recently about how to understand the relationship of ideas and governmental institutions—especially since they have also used examples from American racial history.

Learning from Others

In his 2002 *American Political Science Review* article, Robert Lieberman engages in what is in some respects a rapprochement between the sort of work he has done previously and what I have done.[14] That rapprochement is grounded on insights from Orren and Skowronek, though it is distinct from their position. Previously, in *Shifting the Color Line,* Lieberman placed institutions alone at the center of his analysis: He argued that "the problem of race in American society—the very fact that we divide ourselves into racial groups and that assignment to one or another race plays such a large role in shaping the lives of citizens—is a consequence of political institutions." Though he certainly recognized the existence of racial beliefs and attitudes, he stressed how institutions not only "create the conditions in which people can act on their beliefs and interests" but also "help to define those beliefs and interests." Out of the wealth of ideological positions present in society, political institutions privilege some beliefs and interests and provide incentives that can actually generate others. If we attend to "the role of institutions in the construction of racial inequality," Lieberman maintained, we might find that the role of ideas is both limited and much more an institutional product than a cause. As he put it, "the status of racial groups in society results not necessarily from the mobilization of racist ideology but from the normal workings of social and political arrangements."[15] Accordingly, his analysis is focused extensively on the institutional "racial structure" of American politics and other features of governmental institutions, without much attention to racial beliefs or ideologies at all.

In his 2002 essay, after maintaining that my work gives analogously short shrift to governmental institutions, Lieberman self-consciously strives to bring ideas and institutions together within a single framework of analysis. He argues: "neither ideas nor institutions can rightly claim priority in an account that purports to explain significant political change."[16] Rather, it is frequently their friction-ridden interaction that produces changes. Sometimes those changes are not at all predictable from the apparent trajectory of the ideas or institutions alone.

His example here involves the 1964 Civil Rights Act, which he reads as embodying a victory for champions of "color-blind" ideologies over advocates of both racist and egalitarian race-conscious ideological traditions, and the Equal Employment Opportunity Commission, a compromise institution created to placate racial egalitarians but denied the enforcement powers apparently needed to make it effective. Lieberman contends that the ironic results of the multiple "ideational and institutional orders" that shaped civil rights policy was that the high expectations of progress toward racial equality raised by the 1964 Civil Rights Act, combined with the inability of the EEOC to enforce antidiscrimination laws directly, eventually generated executive branch promotion and judicial enforcement of a range of race-targeted measures. These measures could provide some concrete progress toward expanded opportunities for racial minorities, and they were also structured politically in ways that could limit direct legislative and administrative confrontations with powerful conservative constituencies. Lieberman's analysis is concise but complex, calling attention to three strains of racial ideology (white supremacist, colorblind, and race-conscious egalitarianism); the power of the South in Congress; the diverse problems of coalition-building and maintenance that Democrats and Republicans faced; the challenges of bringing change within a fragmented national state and federal system; and more. The pressures, constraints, and opportunities arising from these overlapping but often clashing "ideational and institutional" orders are all presented as necessary elements in producing the surprising result that he seeks to explain—the rise of affirmative action out of apparently contrary commitments both to color-blindness and to weak enforcement.

Perhaps these elements are all necessary, but, as Lieberman acknowledges, the approach lacks the simplicity and elegance to which social scientists aspire.[17] More important for current purposes, it still leaves "ideational" and "institutional" orders as distinct things, whose relationships are instantiated but not fully theoretically explained. Though Lieberman follows Orren and Skowronek in stressing that "the likelihood of significant, extraordinary political change" is increased by greater "friction among multiple political orders," he provides an elaboration of the "dimensions" of order (and disorder) divided into three "clusters": first, "governing institutions," including conventional state institutions; second, the "organizational environment," including "political parties and party systems, the organization of interests, nongovernmental organizations, and the like"; and third, "the ideological and cultural repertoires that organize and legitimate political discourse"—in short, the ideas.[18]

This characterization of "multiple orders" still leaves ideologies as things that somehow exist *apart* from the parties, statutes, governmental agencies, and other institutions that, in his concrete analysis, are also said partly to embody them. Is this "apartness" merely analytical, or genuinely ontological, or . . . what? Lieberman's valuable essay leaves this issue unclear, so it does not fully escape the danger he rightly sees in works that focus on ideologies—that ideas are sometimes treated as "free-floating bits of knowledge and conjecture, detached from considerations of structure and power."[19]

Though Orren and Skowronek pioneered the argument about the significance of friction among "multiple orders" on which Lieberman builds, they would surely view his effort to give "ideational orders" equal status to "institutional" ones as unwise. In their recent book, they reiterate and extend their earlier insistence that if we wish to understand what can truly be called political development, we must embrace the central role of institutions, rather than approach issues of development through "culture" alone. As they persuasively contend, "cultural causes of change (or no-change) will always work, at least in part, through institutions."[20] And institutions, they insist, "are not ideas," even though they are "often carriers of ideas." Ideas can change while institutions persist.[21]

Orren and Skowronek therefore define "development" as "a durable shifting in governing authority," with "governing authority" referring not only to power but also to institutional possession of enforceable, legally recognized "mandates" for control of human behavior, including authority to compel outsiders as well as insiders to follow the prescriptions of governing institutions.[22] On this definition, analysis of authoritative governing institutions *must* be central to accounts of political change, for it is significant, durable, and (usefully) empirically discernible shifts in such institutional arrangements that constitute political development. Ideas usually figure prominently in accounts of the constitution and transformation of those institutions, and for Orren and Skowronek, too, institutions often do help to constitute the ideas and interests of political actors. But to treat traditions of ideas as "orders" comparable to institutional orders would render less clear just what historical institutionalists are supposed to focus on—governing institutions—and why—to grasp empirically verifiable shifts in those institutions.

Among a number of helpful applications of their approach, Orren and Skowronek discuss Reconstruction and its significance for American political development. They argue persuasively that Reconstruction did indeed constitute "political development of the first magnitude" in a momentous regard: It terminated the legal, political, and economic institutions of chattel slavery that had prevailed since colonial times.[23] But advocates of Reconstruction sought to do more, to overcome all the disabilities imposed by slavery. The quest to do so set the governing Republicans in Congress against the Democrats, the Southern states and often the Northern states, and often also the presidency and the courts. Given all this opposition, Orren and Skowronek argue, though Republicans extended the franchise to blacks as a tactic to retain their own power, especially in the North, that formal change was never accompanied by a sufficiently broad transformation in Southern local governments, judicial postures, electoral coalitions, and party compositions to become self-sustaining, as it did in the North. Thus, they maintain that I was wrong to suggest in *Civic Ideals* that egalitarian human rights positions prevailed in the passage of the postwar Amendments but then were subsequently defeated by resurgent advocates of racial hierarchy. Instead, Southern black voting never really represented a genuine, durable political development. Its demise amid what others term the rise of Jim Crow segregation really represented the collapse of a failed effort at change, not real change in itself. Northern black voting did constitute real development, but it was never reversed.[24]

Though, as discussed later, I have some important differences with this argument, in most respects it seems to me more right than wrong. My interest in it here, however, is in what it tells us when considered as an application of an "intercurrence among multiple orders" explanation of political development, and what it tells about the place of ideas, particularly racial ideas, in such explanations. Analyzed as such an application, Orren and Skowronek's discussion of Reconstruction points to a lacuna in their theoretical work to date.

Although they have carefully and persuasively defined "political institutions," "governing institutions," and "political development," they have not so clearly defined what constitutes an "order" for purposes of "multiple order" analyses. They have stated that "political order" in general may be defined as "a constellation of rules, institutions, practices and ideas that hang together over time" as other things change.[25] It seems reasonable to infer that these traits can be expected to be features of all particular political institutional "orders." Their examples also show that "orders" include formal governmental institutions, like Congress, the presidency, and the judiciary, and so they include the ideas embedded in the roles, goals, and rules that characterize those institutions. "Political orders" also encompass political institutions that lack legal governing powers, such as political parties; Orren and Skowronek note that, though all institutions might be deemed "political" in that they seek to order the behavior of their members, a wide range of institutions may become "political" in a further sense. They attempt to control the behavior of individuals and institutions outside their bounds.[26] All these at least occasionally political institutions also embody ideas about their purposes and about the appropriate identities and practices of their participants.

But just when do we say such institutions actually are parts of a "political order"? Are all political institutions, as well as all governing institutions, themselves automatically political "orders"? Are institutions that sometimes seek to order the conduct of outsiders, sometimes not, therefore sometimes in and sometimes out of political orders? Can institutions be part of "multiple orders" simultaneously—so that Congress, for example, can be part of what Orren and Skowronek call the "free-exercise order," even as it may also be chiefly in alliance with a partisan "political order" and even while it constitutes in itself the national legislative "political order"?[27] Is there room for what Lieberman terms "ideational orders" on top of the "governing" and "political" institutional clusters present in both Orren and Skowronek's and his analysis?

Orren and Skowronek's writings make it plausible to answer all of these questions except the last affirmatively. That very fact, however, raises doubts about the concreteness and clarifying power of the concept of political "orders." And, since development is supposed to be explained by intercurrence among these orders, indeterminacy in this key concept can endanger Orren and Skowronek's commendable efforts to give greater theoretical specificity and empirical verifiability to scholarship on American political development.

We can get further insights into their thinking about what counts as a "political order" by returning to their analysis of Reconstruction. They argue that in the Reconstruction era, the "key developmental issues" centered along a "single divide" between the former masters and their political and institutional allies on the one hand and the former slaves and those who, for one reason or another, supported them on the other. The resulting developmental struggles occurred chiefly between the courts, traditional defenders of property rights, and Congress, custodian of novel enforcement powers under the Thirteenth Amendment. This former mas-ter-versus-former-slave, law-versus-politics, court-versus-Congress divi-sion became the axis of alignment for other institutions depending on how they responded to expanded congressional authority—so that states, Democrats, and, to some degree, presidents all aligned against Congress, while the Republican Party sided with it and the freedmen, and the mili-tary tended to go with the flow.[28]

This is a persuasive account, but just what elements in it count as polit-ical "orders" operating intercurrently, with considerable friction? Obvious candidates include traditional legal doctrines of property rights, new con-stitutional legal rules, Congress, the courts, the presidency, the military, both political parties, state and local governments, and the more diffuse political organizations or at least political networks of former masters and former slaves. Yet, though all these, except perhaps the last, probably should be considered political "orders" as Orren and Skowronek speak of them, at least for some purposes, to analyze Reconstruction simply through listing such orders clearly presents a "forest and trees" problem. Not all orders are of equal importance for all topics. In regard to Recon-struction, Orren and Skowronek contend that the big story is how these various orders were aligned into coalitions that took different positions on, ultimately, what to do about the claims of the freedmen and their for-mer masters. They also focus especially on the "starkly institutional" clashes between Congress and the Court rather than "the partisan engage-ment with President Johnson."[29] But do the pro-former-slaves and pro-former-masters claims and coalitions aligned with Congress and the Court, respectively, constitute all or parts of "political orders," or are they simply particular, shifting mobilizations of existing actors, institutions, and "orders" around a dominating single issue? And, though ideas are undeniably featured here, are "ideational orders" any part of this account?

I am not sure how Orren and Skowronek would answer or how they should answer all these questions, though, again, I read them as skeptical about the utility of "ideational orders." But it is one of the many contribu-tions of their work that it can prompt us to seek such answers. So I now provide mine, again building on the arguments that Desmond King and I have recently made.

Political Orders and American Racial Orders

Because political conflicts during Reconstruction did indeed center on issues of former slaves and former masters, it initially seems reasonable to suggest that, above all, the orderings of political powers and statuses that generated the identities of "former slaves" and "former masters" should constitute the key political orders in a "multiple orders" analysis of that era. But what exactly are the enduring, empirically discernible institutional "orders" that defined some as "former masters" and others as "former slaves"? To say that surviving and new institutions constituted persons as bearers of abolished identities seems odd.

When discussing the antebellum period, in contrast, it is straightforward to say, as Orren and Skowronek do, that there had long been an entrenched "master/slave" political order in American life.[30] We can point to an array of common-law rules enforced by courts; an array of statutes passed by state and national legislatures that were themselves constituted by representative structures that embodied distinctions between masters and slaves; an array of political parties with positions on slavery; and an array of other institutions, such as churches and eleemosynary organizations, that sometimes took such positions—all of which collectively made up an enduring structure of governing authority that, on balance, sustained slavery, and hence master/slave identities, up to the Civil War. Antebellum actors in the political order of slavery also regularly invoked religious and scientific ideas that defined and justified these roles, legal rules, and organizational goals, claiming both legal and moral mandates to uphold the slave system. There were also many who opposed slavery, and in the first half of the nineteenth century they had some mixed but real successes in creating laws that kept the institution out of some states and limited it in other ways.

One might reasonably analyze the resulting arrangements as one great "political order" of slavery, an order that generated within itself sources of resistance and opposition in the form of antislavery mobilizations. Such internal generation of friction and conflict is something Orren and Skowronek rightly stress when they discuss the theoretical difficulties of focusing too exclusively on concepts of "path dependency," "feedback," and "fit."[31] Alternatively, one might want to see the antebellum period as displaying instead two dialectically related but analytically distinct "proslavery" and "antislavery" political orders, the latter including the federal and state laws that banned slavery in much of the North, as well as the international slave trade, along with the courts, political parties, electoral interests, and ideologies aligned in enforcement of those laws. We might perhaps finesse that contrast without making the concept of a "political order" too elastic by saying that antebellum America constituted a "political order" of masters and slaves that contained within it component proslavery and antislavery political orders, along with other political orders. I leave for another time the question of whether it really matters if we see the proslavery and antislavery orders as separate things or as subordinate elements in one larger system.

But once the Thirteenth Amendment abolished slavery, wiping out all its explicit national, state, and local judicial and statutory supports in one fell swoop, it becomes less clear how we can talk about what Orren and Skowronek present as the key divide in Reconstruction politics. Perhaps we should describe the United States as having after 1865 a grand "antislavery political order," enshrined in constitutional rules, championed by Congress and sometimes by parts of the executive branch and the judiciary, but one that faced powerful internal resistance from many other parts of America's multiple "political orders" that for one reason or another chose to ally themselves with the former slave owners. The upshot of the resulting conflicts then would seem to be the partial consolidation of this great "antislavery order," including its extension to Northern black enfranchisement, but with other major extensions successfully checked. Though Orren and Skowronek use the language of "political orders" sparingly once they move into close analysis of Reconstruction, their argument seems consistent with this depiction.

But this way of framing the period seems unduly narrow to capture what the institutional and individual political actors at the time thought they were fighting over and what in fact resulted. It seems strained and artificial to talk about the battles that followed the abolition of slavery as essentially clashes between the interests of former slaves and former masters. The Fourteenth and Fifteenth Amendments, especially, redefined the terrain of conflict as struggles over how far the United States would go toward establishing not just an antislavery political order but also a political order of racial equality. This was an obviously related but nonetheless meaningfully distinct issue, and it is one that cannot be analyzed without more explicit consideration of racial ideas and interests than Orren and Skowronek's framing lead them to undertake.

They do note that, despite common institutional interests, Presidents Lincoln, Johnson, and Grant varied on how strongly they opposed congressional assertions of expanded authority. Those variances must be explained in part, I have argued, by the fact that although all three presidents championed the creation of an antislavery political order, Johnson was far more adamant than the other two in his opposition to the creation of a racially egalitarian one.[32] To understand Reconstruction simply or even essentially as a conflict between proponents of an antislavery order and the adherents of an older, embattled but resistant proslavery, or at least pro-former masters, alliance creates difficulties in grasping the role of key actors like Johnson and also key institutions like the presidency.

Reconstruction may need to be framed additionally, perhaps alternatively, as a clash between two opposing racial "political orders" that played out in struggles involving other American political institutions. King and I have suggested that these two racial orders may be termed, first, the "transformative egalitarian racial order" elaborated by the postwar Amendments, which leave open the question of just how egalitarian the new racial order is to be but which clearly move in an egalitarian direction.[33] This order included the numerous champions of greater racial equality in Congress and the Republican Party; some federal and state courts and elected officials; and also African American political organizations and many Northern churches and other reform groups.

The dynamics of this "transformative egalitarian racial order" cannot be grasped without attending to the multiple and complex but on the whole more egalitarian racial ideologies advanced by these groups, ideologies that helped define the order's purposes in terms of ideas that were built into the legal rules and civic roles it generated. Some of those ideas represented true embrace of full racial equality. Some paternalistically viewed African Americans as less developed people who would one day be equal after an extended period of tutelage. Others favored more romantic conceptions of races as having inherently distinct characters or "souls" that all nonetheless had value for the advancement of humanity.[34] A significant part of the difficulty in realizing the egalitarian aspirations expressed in the postwar Amendments lies in the partly conflicting views advanced by the different members of the coalition seeking egalitarian change, then and ever since.

But the greatest difficulties came from outside. The "transformative egalitarian racial order" was opposed from its inception by an older but still evolving "white supremacist racial order." That order probably grew up originally chiefly to justify and institutionally reinforce slavery and tribal displacement in the colonial era, but it had long since gained institutional embodiments in many geographic and social arenas in American life where slavery was absent, as Orren and Skowronek note.[35] Many of these institutional embodiments, such as Northern state laws that barred free blacks from entering their jurisdictions, were abolished by Reconstruction statutes and constitutional amendments, but many other forms of institutionalized racial discrimination, such as segregated schools and transportation facilities, were not clearly invalidated. And the great inequalities in the economic and political resources possessed by American whites and blacks generated under slavery remained, of course, largely unaltered. Champions of these arrangements dominated the Democratic Party and also included many judges who enforced what they took to be still-good law; many state and local officials often concerned about their own governing prerogatives as well as white supremacy; most Southern churches and white vigilante groups; and sometimes presidents anxious about excessive congressional power or, again in Johnson's case, aghast at the prospect of genuine racial equality.

This "white supremacist" order, too, cannot be understood without attention to the ideologies that provided its defining sense of proper political purposes, legal rules, and civic roles. I still think it important that its adherents felt increasingly bolstered by the Darwin-inspired reinvigoration of intellectual defenses for racial discrimination in the late nineteenth century.[36] It was in part because even many of those allied with the Union cause came to think that the full equality apparently promised by the Fourteenth Amendment, in particular, ran contrary to racial "instincts" engrained by history and evolution that they could accept the rebuilding of white supremacy, so long as it was modified to be formally consistent with the new constitutional requirements of civil and political equality. And, for at least some supporters of segregation, the aim truly was to prepare blacks eventually for full and equal citizenship, if that proved possible—something that was never the goal of the form of white supremacy that prevailed before the end of slavery.[37]

Let me also note that recasting Reconstruction (and much subsequent American political development) as involving clashes between an internally divided "transformative egalitarian" racial order and an evolving "white supremacist" order seems to fit well with Orren and Skowronek's insights concerning "intercurrence" as an engine of political change. Again, after the Thirteenth Amendment, though we can speak of a political coalition in support of the interests of former masters, it is hard to show that a "proslavery" institutional "order" still existed in the United States. There were no longer any governing institutions that could plausibly claim legal mandates to pursue and enforce "proslavery" purposes, rules, and roles. Instead, we are forced to analyze Reconstruction struggles as essentially internal resistance on behalf of the interests of former masters *within* what had become officially an "antislavery" political order. Not only does this approach have trouble explaining antislavery white supremacists like Johnson; it also does not clearly involve "intercurrence" between distinct "orders."

In contrast, it is perfectly reasonable, even in light of the postwar Amendments, to speak of a surviving and adapting "white supremacist" political order in late-nineteenth-century America. The participants in this order generally granted that slavery was void and that blacks had to have some more rights than in the past; the constitutional successes of the egalitarian transformative order made those positions inescapable. But they were not prepared to succumb wholly to this rival racial order. Reinforced by the new intellectual defenses of racial hierarchy, they insisted that it was still constitutionally legitimate to maintain modified forms of legal support for white superiority, so long as blacks could be said to have some minimum of "equal protection" against certain kinds of invidious discrimination. We can then quite coherently see in Reconstruction "intercurrent" conflicts between the "transformative" and "white supremacist" racial orders in American life, conflicts that generated two distinct initiatives toward political "development" in Orren and Skowronek's sense, each with mixed success. The postwar Amendments represented a genuine shift in durable governing authority to antislavery legal systems and also the abandonment of direct, explicit racial exclusions. This latter shift gained enough local support in much of the North so that the small numbers of blacks there could vote on an enduring basis. Parts of the "transformative egalitarian racial order" were, then, successfully established in ways that constituted real "development."

But the shift toward abolition of direct racial exclusions was not strong enough to prevent adherents of the still-surviving white supremacist racial order from resurging and extending their domains in the late nineteenth century, in ways that also represented genuine but very different "development." These adherents significantly, successfully, and durably recast overt white supremacy as the facially egalitarian "separate but equal" Jim Crow regime that soon became quite firmly entrenched. It reinstated black disfranchisement and jury exclusion, but now through mechanisms that were no longer explicitly racially discriminatory—even though their legislative defenders often championed them in unmistakable white supremacist terms. In that sense, Southern black enfranchisement can indeed be seen as a failed dimension of a developmental shift that in other regards was much more enduringly successful, as Orren and Skowronek contend. But, if we attend to both the contending racial orders in the period, we can recognize that Jim Crow disfranchisement was an element of a significantly new form of white domination, instead of simply a replay of old-style direct racial exclusions. And, when we recognize this type of disfranchisement as one dimension of similar, pervasive changes in the "white supremacist" racial order, then I think we must accept that this racial order had undergone meaningful development, development necessitated, again, by the intercurrent pressures generated by the constitutional achievements of the "transformative egalitarian" racial order. Though I was wrong in *Civic Ideals* to describe such disfranchisement *simply* as a "resurgence" of older racial hierarchies, it is also not right, I think, to see in it no more than an essentially unbroken continuation of the old proslavery order.

And the ongoing struggles between these two racial orders, each evolving as a result of internal tensions and dynamics as well as the fractious relationships with the other order and with other orders that constituted American political life, have been a large part of the story of American political development ever since. In the 1960s, especially, aided by favorable circumstances and alliances, the "transformative egalitarian racial order" gained important new victories, so that the Jim Crow version of the "white supremacist" racial order came to be almost as definitively repudiated in law as slavery had been.[38] But powerful legacies of that racial order have nonetheless survived in some areas of American law, and even more in a variety of other institutions, such as Congress, state and local powers under federalism, economic and educational institutions,and aspects of the criminal justice system. So, regrettably, the framework of clashing racial orders remains highly significant for understanding American politics today.

Summing Up

If much of what I have written here is roughly right, what does it imply for the main issues raised here: What constitutes a "political order," how should we analyze "ideas" in relation to "institutions," and should we think of racial identities, in particular, as chiefly the products of ideological traditions or of political and legal institutions?

First, it implies that we should define "political orders" by building on Orren and Skowronek's definitions of "political institutions" and "governing institutions" and "development." We should insist that, although there may be lots of "political orders," and although particular institutions will be part of more than one political order at any given time, still there are some high threshold requirements for being counted a significant political order. Anything worthy of that name must have among its components at least some "governing institutions" that can assert legal authority to enforce their goals, rules, and policies against at least some outsiders. These governing institutions must also, however, be parts of relatively enduring coalitions that include "political institutions" such as parties and other politically active organizations if they are to be potent enough to count as important "political orders." And, though such institutions and organizations might become part of a political order for many overlapping reasons, any political order worthy of the name *must* have some defining overarching purposes that are expressed in the rules, policies, and roles it promulgates. Therefore, I still place more stress than Orren and Skowronek on understanding the (again, often overlapping rather than identical) ideologies of the participants in every political order—for those ideologies partly explain both why the different components of the political order adhere to it and why its central objectives are what they are. The traditions of ideas that come to be embodied, often in compromised and altered forms, in institutions must be understood if those institutions are to be understood.

Not just racial orders, then, but everything worthy of being counted as a nontrivial "political order" needs to be analyzed with attention to the ideas that help define its purposes and principles, such as "Whiggish" or "democratic tribunal" doctrines of executive power, or "common-law" or "higher-law" notions of judicial authority, or "republican" or "liberal" or "Anglo-Saxon manifest destiny" ideologies of the status and aims of American citizenship. But, even so, I am now not inclined to go so far as to treat "ideational orders" as "political orders" on the same plane with the presidency or the separation of church and state, as Lieberman has been tempted to do. Orren and Skowronek (and sometimes Lieberman) are right to argue that it is useful to employ concepts with relatively concrete empirical referents and that, to analyze political development well, it is vital ultimately to reach and explain governing institutions. If governing institutions are not undergoing any real changes, it is hard to say that important political changes have been, as yet, fully realized, even if things are happening that may eventually bring them about. Conversely, if governing institutions are undergoing such durable changes, then surely we must say that meaningful development is occurring.

It is because I agree with Orren and Skowronek that governing institutions are so vital in our analyses that I favor defining "political orders" as *always* including at least some such institutions. And, though traditions of ideas or ideologies are in my view also constitutive elements of such orders, their study cannot properly lead us too far away from institutions. Traditions of ideas and ideologies are always carried by particular organizations or sets of organizations within the coalition that constitutes a political order. For purposes of explaining political change, they must be analyzed in those sort of historical political contexts. Ideas can produce political change only when particular, identifiable political institutions, groups, and actors advance them.

This does not mean that we might not fruitfully analyze the internal logical and rhetorical properties, including the inherent tensions, in the ideologies that are borne by particular participants in "political orders." Such analyses can be useful for normative inquiry—and they can also be valuable as means to identify problems that may be manifested in political conflicts. But if such idea-centered analyses are to contribute to historical institutional analyses of political development, they must eventually be explicitly connected with the purposes, rules, and roles defined by political and governing institutions, and with problems manifested in the relations among the multiple orders those institutions comprise. In short, analysis of ideas as constitutive components of governing institution-centered "political orders" seems the most promising way to bring "ideas" and "institutions" together in useful explanatory frameworks.

Finally, what about the relatively autonomous role of political and legal institutions in constructing racial identities? The implication of the arguments here is that, in tracing the origins of racial ideas, we probably do have to spend some time outside governing institutions and even look beyond most political institutions to the broader social practices, economic arrangements, and arenas of scientific inquiry and cultural expression where racial conceptions are often first articulated. To be sure, those locations always exist in some relationship to governing and political institutions, and those relationships will, I believe, often help to illuminate what is going on in social, economic, scientific, and cultural institutions. Still, many of the racial ideas we see in politics did not emerge directly therein, so their birth sites must be found elsewhere.

Yet, I continue to think that, out of the multiplicity of racial ideas that people have generated in these less political places during the course of American political development, some have mattered much more than others both for shaping American politics and for shaping personal and group senses of identity, status, and opportunities. The ideas that have mattered most have been the ideas that have been embraced by various political movements and governing institutions and used to define the goals and laws established by different "political orders" at different times. And, in the process of becoming definitive of the goals of a particular political order, such as state-level structure of white supremacy in the antebellum period or the complex and shifting Jim Crow system of the twentieth century, racial ideas drawn from different arenas have often been compromised, reshaped, and revised. This means that the laws that express those revised ideas have worked to redefine and reconstitute American racial identities and statuses, at least to some degree. Whether those redefinitions are great enough to lead us to reject a political "transmission belt" view of racial identities—whether it matters that in one state a person of one-quarter African ancestry ended up being labeled "white," while in another a person of fifteen-sixteenths European ancestry was considered "black," or whether what really matters is simply that the laws in one way or another labeled us as "black" or "white"—those are questions of judgment, and the answers may depend on what questions concern us at particular moments.

One advantage of the approach to political analysis that I have endorsed here, however, is that it gives us a useful framework for asking all such questions—for considering what it might mean to say that "ideas" or "institutions" come first in explaining political outcomes and political development; for identifying evidence that racial and other ideas have originated more "outside" than "inside" the operations of "political orders"; for using the conflicts among those political orders to determine when and why really meaningful political change, true developmental shifts in governing authority over race and other matters, have occurred. It does so, I think, by going further in the direction Robert Lieberman has recommended, seeking to place the analysis of "ideas" and "institutions" within a single analytical frame. And, in so doing, in my view, it closes at least some of the apparent gap between the sort of "multiple traditions" analyses I have previously undertaken and the "multiple orders" approach that Orren and Skowronek recommend.

If so, we may actually have some encouraging evidence of cumulative progress in historical institutional work. But most readers seem to find me more persuasive as a critic of theories of progress than as a proponent, so, having stepped into that hopeful realm, let me stop here. To go any further is likely to mean an even more hasty retreat.

NOTES

I am grateful to Jacob Hacker and Desmond King for their comments on an earlier version of this essay.

1. Robert C. Lieberman, "Ideas, Institutions, and Political Order: Explaining Political Change," *American Political Science Review* 96 (2002): 697–712; Karen Orren and Stephen Skowronek, *The Search for American Political Development* (New York: Cambridge University Press, 2004).

2. Desmond S. King and Rogers M. Smith, "Racial Orders in American Political Development," *American Political Science Review* 99 (2005): 75–92.

3. King and I contend that these racial orders have been among the most important for American political development, so that no "APD" analysis can be adequate if it does not take them into account, at least to the extent of showing that race is *not* an important factor in the political phenomena being analyzed.

4. E. g., Peter A. Hall, "The Role of Interests, Institutions, and Ideas in the Comparative Political Economy of the Industrialized Nations," in Mark I. Lichbach and Alan S. Zuckerman, eds., *Comparative Politics: Rationality, Culture, and Structure* (Cambridge: Cambridge University Press, 1997); Sheri Berman, *The Social Democratic Movement: Ideas and Politics in the Making of Interwar Europe* (Cambridge, MA: Harvard University Press, 1998); Mark Blyth, *Great Transformations: Economic Ideas and Institutional Change in the Twentieth Century* (Cambridge: Cambridge University Press, 2002).

5. Lieberman, "Ideas, Institutions, and Political Order," 700; Orren and Skowronek, *The Search for American Political Development*, 25, 76–77, 83, 182, 214n5.

6. Rogers M. Smith, *Civic Ideals: Conflicting Visions of Citizenship in U.S. History* (New Haven: Yale University Press, 1997), 507n5.

7. Cf. Howard Gillman, "The Court as an Idea, Not a Building (or a Game): Interpretive Institutionalism and the Analysis of Supreme Court Decision-Making," in Cornell W. Clayton and Howard Gillman, eds., *Supreme Court Perspectives: New Institutionalist Approaches* (Chicago: University of Chicago Press, 1999), 65–87; Alex Wendt, *Social Theory of International Politics* (Cambridge: Cambridge University Press 1999).

8. E. g., Smith, *Civic Ideals.*

9. E. g., Rogers M. Smith, "Black and White after Brown: Constructions of Race in Modern Supreme Court Decisions," *University of Pennsylvania Journal of Constitutional Law* 5 (2003): 709–733.

10. See, e. g., Joel Williamson, *New People: Miscegenation and Mulattoes in the United States* (New York: Free Press, 1980); Melissa Nobles, *Shades of Citizenship: Race and the Census in Modern Politics* (Stanford: Stanford University Press 2000), 25–84.

11. James Kettner, *The Development of American Citizenship, 1608–1870* (Chapel Hill: University of North Carolina Press, 1978), 236–237; David P. Currie, *The Constitution in Congress: The Federalist Period, 1789–1801* (Chicago: University of Chicago Press 1997), 88–89; Charles R. Kesler, "The Promise of American Citizenship," in Noah M. J. Pickus, ed., *Immigration & Citizenship in the 21ˢᵗ Century* (Lanham, MD: Rowman and Littlefield, 1998), 19.

12. See, e. g., Ian F. Haney López, *White by Law: The Legal Construction of Race* (New York: New York University Press 1996), 42–43; Thomas G. West, *Vindicating the Founders: Race, Sex, Class and Justice in the Origins of America* (Lanham, MD: Rowman and Littlefield, 1997), 168–171.

13. See, e. g., Haney López, *White by Law,* 49–109.

14. Lieberman, "Ideas, Institutions, and Political Order."

15. Robert C. Lieberman, *Shifting the Color Line: Race and the American Welfare State* (Cambridge, MA: Harvard University Press, 1998), 11.

16. Lieberman, "Ideas, Institutions, and Political Order," 709.

17. Ibid., 698.

18. Ibid., 703.

19. Ibid., 700.

20. Karen Orren and Stephen Skowronek, "In Search of Political Development," in David F. Ericson and Louise B. Green, eds., *The Liberal Tradition in American Politics: Reassessing the Legacy of American Liberalism* (New York: Routledge, 1999), 29–31, 38–39; Orren and Skowronek, *The Search for American Political Development,* 76.

21. Orren and Skowronek, *The Search for American Political Development,* 83.

22. This definition, found in Orren and Skowronek, *The Search for American Political Development,* 83–84, 123–125, refines a previous version offered in Orren and Skowronek, "In Search of Political Development," 37–38.

23. Orren and Skowronek, *The Search for American Political Development,* 136.

24. Ibid., 136–143.

25. Ibid., 14.

26. Ibid., 83–84.

27. Ibid., 144.

28. Ibid., 137–139. In fact, U.S. representatives also invoked other constitutional bases for their endeavors, especially the long-dormant "republican government" clause. See William M. Wiecek, *The Guarantee Clause of the U.S. Constitution* (Ithaca: Cornell University Press 1972), 172–208, 220–230; Smith, *Civic Ideals,* 296–297).

29. Orren and Skowronek, *The Search for American Political Development,* 139.

30. Ibid., 133–136.

31. Ibid., 102–108.

32. Smith, *Civic Ideals,* 302–304.

33. King and Smith, "Racial Orders in American Political Development."

34. George M. Fredrickson, *The Black Image in the White Mind: The Debate on Afro-American Character and Destiny, 1817–1914* (New York: Harper and Row, 1971), 39–41, 101–110.

35. Orren and Skowronek, *The Search for American Political Development,* 135.

36. Smith, *Civic Ideals,* 291–295.

37. Ibid., 291–295, 347–365, 375–379, 417–418, 433–435.

38. I suspect that analyzing modern civil rights policy in terms of the clash between a "transformative egalitarian racial order" and a surviving "white supremacist racial order" would shed additional light on how affirmative-action measures could emerge from apparent agreement on weak enforcement of statutes that require color-blindness. Proponents of the pivotal "color-blindness" position have always included some who seek to preserve the nation's racial inequalities but others who genuinely wish to see them transformed by appropriate means, and the latter can oppose or favor affirmative action under difference circumstances. I cannot, however, work out this account here.

5

Public Policies as Institutions

Paul Pierson

To paraphrase Richard Nixon, we are all institutionalists now. Institutions stand at the heart of much theorizing and explanation in the social sciences. Analysts working from a variety of perspectives have produced compelling work, emphasizing and explicating the tremendous significance of institutional arrangements for political and social outcomes.[1] Indeed, the various "new institutionalisms" that have sprung up in the social sciences are now decades old. Yet, despite all this attention there remain large holes in our understanding of institutions. This chapter explores one: the effects of large-scale public policies.

Public policies are not always treated as institutions, but I will argue that there are good reasons for doing so. Given the current focus of political scientists on institutions, such a formulation can foster interest in policy effects. At the same time, it provides a basis for extending many of the arguments about institutional effects to the examination of policy effects. Such a move is important, because it allows social scientists to grapple more systematically with one of the most striking features of modern social life: the tremendously expanded significance of government activism. Consider, for instance, the United States. Typically described as a "laggard," this "weak" state nonetheless generates tax revenues of almost one-third of GDP—a figure that represents only the tip of the iceberg of government activity. These revenues are generated through a staggeringly complex tax code that itself constitutes a formidable apparatus of policy activism.[2] The American regulatory state, moreover, presents a vast array of rules that permeates economic and social activity. The state sets down prohibitions and requirements for everything from hiring practices to the design of entryways for private buildings to the kinds of wording prohibited or required on consumer packaging. Most of the politically generated "rules of the game" that directly help to shape the lives of citizens and organizations in modern societies are, in fact, public policies.

Somehow, these realities of contemporary political life have made very little impact on the institutionalist turn in the social sciences. Whether because scholars have been distracted by contemporary rhetoric about the "retreat of the state" or because of political scientists' preoccupation with formal institutions, the reality and political implications of the state's ubiquitous role in modern societies have largely evaded our systematic attention. Political scientists working on a range of substantive issues have, however, begun to focus on policy effects. As I document later, there is now considerable evidence that specific policy interventions often have very substantial and enduring political consequences. The task ahead is to think more clearly about why and when particular kinds of policy structures have certain kinds of effects. Recognizing that policies are important instances of political institutions allows scholars to tap the rich insights of institutional analysis to enhance our understanding of activist government. This facilitates the development of sharper hypotheses about policy effects. It also generates greater recognition that those who study quite distinct substantive issues are also engaged in what should be a shared research program.

The task of this essay is to outline why it makes sense to think about a shared research program on policy effects and to indicate some of the lines along which such a program might progress. The argument is presented in four stages. I consider first the question of whether it makes sense to treat public policies as institutions. Section II takes up, and rejects, two justifications for *not* focusing scholarly attention on the effects of policy structures. Section III outlines, in admittedly very cursory fashion, what political scientists currently know about policy effects. Section IV offers some ideas about how a more self-conscious research program on policy effects, drawing on various strands of institutionalist theory, might proceed.

Are Public Policies Institutions?

In a widely utilized definition, Douglass North describes institutions as "the rules of the game in a society or, more generally . . . the humanly devised constraints that shape human interaction."[3] For the individuals and social organizations that make up civil society, public policies are clearly very central rules that govern their interactions. These rules specify rewards and punishments associated with particular behaviors, ranging from eligibility for specific forms of government largesse on the one hand to large fines, incarceration, or even death on the other. Leaving aside the informal institutions typically explored by sociologists, the institutions that impinge on the modern citizen most directly and intensively as she goes about her daily life are in fact public policies, *not* the formal political institutions that have preoccupied political scientists.

Many political scientists would respond that it is formal political institutions that warrant attention because these are the rules of the game for *politics*. The test for arguments about policy effects is to show that they do indeed matter for politics. Unlike formal institutions, the influence of policies on politics is necessarily indirect. If policies as institutions matter for political scientists, it is because the influence of policies on social actors—on who they are, on what they want, on how and with whom they organize—is such that it changes the way these actors engage in politics.

Why Haven't Policy Effects Received More Attention?

If there is a good case to be made for regarding major public policies as potentially consequential institutions, why have social scientists made only limited steps in this direction? There are two plausible defenses for the paucity of efforts. First, one could argue that since policies, unlike formal institutions, are relatively easy to change (or "plastic"), they are essentially epiphenomenal. Second, it could be argued that the sheer range and heterogeneity of policy interventions makes the development of a successful research program on policy effects impossible. Only the second of these objections, in my view, raises a serious challenge.

The first argument represents a particular version of the challenge that is often applied to institutional arguments more generally: What if the institutions, and their effects, simply reflect some more fundamental causal forces (e. g., the power of political elites)?[4] In this case, one should expect that the institutions themselves are likely to change as these other variables change; they exert no independent effects. Institutions, to be causally significant, need some staying power. Hannan and Freeman made this key observation in their path-breaking work on organizational ecology, although their focus was on organizations rather than institutions:

Structures that adapt swiftly and effortlessly are unlikely to shape processes of historical change. Another way of putting this is that if organizations are the building blocks of modern societies . . . inertia is what gives them this quality. If organizations are plastic, then only the intentions of elites matter.[5]

Implicitly, the view that public policies are highly plastic underpins much research in political science. Standard accounts treat policies solely as dependent variables. Soss and Mettler nicely describe this dominant view as a "systems theory" approach, in which the political process transforms social "inputs" into policy "outputs."[6] Policies are seen as reflecting, rather than modifying, core political processes. Thus, most of the contemporary literature on American politics treats policy as highly responsive to shifts in public opinion.[7] Moreover, even when these arguments about responsiveness are challenged, it is typically a matter of *who* policies respond to (e. g., elite or mass opinion), rather than the prospect that the policies themselves may have important effects.[8]

It is sometimes suggested that the challenge that institutions are epiphenomenal applies with particular force to public policies. Formal political institutions possess greater staying power, because obstacles to revision are higher. As Robert Goodin has put it, modern polities possess "a system of 'nested rules,' with rules at each successive level in the hierarchy being increasingly costly to change."[9] On this account, formal institutions call out for special attention because they are the most durable—and thus most consequential—institutional structures.

It is true that revisions of public policies often confront fewer, or more modest, veto points than do revisions of formal political institutions. The extent of this difference should not be exaggerated, however. Formal barriers to change in constitutional systems are not always so high. And, in systems of fragmented political authority, such as those found in the United States, Canada, and the European Union, formal obstacles to policy revision may be quite substantial. In some cases, public policies may expressly outline difficult revision procedures; for instance, Canada's earnings-related pension scheme can be revised only with the agreement of the federal government and at least seven provinces representing two-thirds of the population, making it "more difficult to amend than most sections of the constitution of the country."[10]

More important, it would be a grave mistake to argue that the staying power of institutions, including public policies, rests largely on the

strength of veto points. Even in situations where the balance among political actors or other relevant features of the social context has undergone
significant change, a number of other features of institutions may make
revision difficult. It is worth exploring these factors in a bit of detail, since
they not only indicate the flaws in views that treat institutions as highly
plastic but point to some important dimensions of policy effects.[11]

One source of potential resilience, heavily emphasized in recent choice-
theoretic work on formal political institutions, is the significance of coordination problems.[12] Actors are better off if they have reliable expectations
about the behavior of others. Institutional choice, in these models, is seen
as primarily a matter of actors converging on a focal point that solves their
coordination problems. These actors may disagree about the "best" outcome, but they are eager to reach a shared understanding. Even coordination around some less-desired outcome is often better than no
coordination at all. Expectations about what others will do are thus crucial
in driving behavior toward a coordinated outcome—and keeping it there.
In these accounts, once institutions have been selected, they have considerable staying power because of the difficulty of coordinating around an
alternative.[13]

Coordination models can, of course, be applied to policies as well as to
formal political institutions. Particular policy structures can reduce uncertainty about the behavior of various actors, generating more stable expectations that facilitate social action. Recent studies in comparative political
economy, discussed in more detail later, highlight the ways in which policy
regimes create frameworks in which a large range of key economic actors
can develop relatively stable expectations about their interactions.[14]

Probably of greater importance than coordination effects, however, are
the ways in which policy structures, once in place, can actually shift both
the distribution of political actors and their policy preferences. Coordination models emphasize that actors may come to see particular changes as
difficult. Broader arguments about feedback effects point to the ways in
which influential actors may come to view particular changes as *undesirable*. By altering incentives and resources among social actors, public policies can profoundly alter the political terrain over time.[15] What changes
are not just actors' expectations about what is possible but also the kinds
of actors that are around, their capacities, and their policy preferences. As
I discuss in more detail in the next section, major public policies may create social environments that select for certain kinds of actors over time,
altering the structure of political debates in the future. At the same time,

policies create incentives that induce substantial investments, both tangible and intangible.[16] To the extent that these investments are specific to a particular policy arrangement, they may greatly alter the future preferences of social actors with respect to a range of political issues.

These kinds of policy effects are of great theoretical significance, because they mount the most fundamental challenge to the "policies are epiphenomenal" argument. If policies have the capacity to shift the composition of actors in a society, their resources, and their preferences, then the case for a research program focused on policy effects is strong. Thus, Section II turns to a more detailed look at this issue, beginning with existing empirical research.

What about the second concern, however? Even if it is granted that policy effects may be considerable, perhaps methodological or theoretical difficulties make a research agenda focused on those effects unpromising. There are valid grounds for this concern, because the universe of public policies is both heavily populated and extremely heterogeneous. Governments make many, many rules of widely varied types. The range of such efforts is indicated by the widespread employment of typologies in public policy literatures, which typically distinguish regulations, public expenditure, and tax subsidies, with endless further distinctions drawn within and across each of these types of policies.

This heterogeneity stands in striking contrast to the key topics considered in the study of formal political institutions. Political scientists who study democratic regimes have achieved a large degree of consensus about the composition of a relatively short list of core institutional arrangements—regime type (parliamentary vs. presidential), federalism, electoral laws, and so on—as well as the key dimensions of each of these arrangements. To be sure, there are fierce debates about the effects of these arrangements. Yet, there is widespread agreement concerning what needs to be debated. This consensus encourages the concentration of intellectual energies. This in turn has facilitated the development of a sophisticated literature on institutional effects.[17]

It is far more difficult to achieve such a level of consensus and focus when studying policy effects. The number of distinct policies is much larger, and many of these involve multiple components that can vary in often subtle ways. Moreover, as the comparative literatures exploring policy regimes and complementarities make clear (see later discussion), policy effects often stem from configurations of government action, making it far more of a challenge to pin down the impact of discrete policies. All of these features make it difficult to develop categories and pursue meaningful comparisons.

These are, in fact, big problems. Combined with the higher priority that literatures on policy in political science have placed on explaining policy *outcomes*, they largely account for the still fairly limited progress of research on policy *effects*. Yet, the nature of this objection also needs to be noted. Unlike the first objection, this one does not deny the significance of policy effects. It simply says that studying them is difficult. The objection, and the practice it leads to, is a variant of the thinking lampooned in the standard joke: A drunk man rationalizes searching for his keys under the lamppost, even though he lost the keys somewhere else, by insisting that it makes sense to search where the light is good. If there are good reasons to think that public policies may have substantial capacities to remake politics, then we need to look more in the dark corners, while figuring out how to improve the lighting. I return to this issue in Section IV, but first I want to push further with the case for the significance of policy effects.

What Do We Know about Policy Effects?

Political scientists working on a range of empirical issues have shown growing interest in the ways public policies can reconfigure politics.[18] Students of both comparative and American politics have identified considerable evidence of policy effects. Among comparativists, much of the focus has been on "policy regimes" that engender distinct patterns of interest group formation and distinctive distributions of public opinion, thus reinforcing divergent and enduring political coalitions. In the comparative study of welfare states, Gosta Esping-Andersen's pathbreaking work emphasized the distinct policy configurations generated in the "liberal," "social democratic," and "conservative" worlds of welfare capitalism.[19] Although Esping-Andersen traced these different regimes to distinct constellations of political power, he argued that the establishment of these policy regimes had enduring political effects.

Arguments about regime effects have become standard in this literature.[20] Huber and Stephens, in their remarkably comprehensive treatment of welfare-state development, strongly emphasize the impact of early policy initiatives in shaping long-term political processes:

As each policy is put into place it transforms the distribution of preferences; as the regime increasingly entrenches itself, it transforms the universe of actors. The economic and political costs of moving to another regime become greater, and conversely the returns of staying on the same track become greater.[21]

Here is their account of the impact of early policy initiatives on public opinion, which they term "the policy ratchet" effect:

Until the era of retrenchment, it was rare for secular conservative parties to roll back welfare state reforms instituted by social democratic or Christian democratic parties. Indeed they generally accepted each new reform after it has been instituted, and the new center of gravity of the policy agenda became defined by the innovations proposed by the progressive forces in society. The reason for the change in posture of the conservative parties was that the reforms were popular with the mass public, especially the broad-based policies in the areas of pensions, education, and health care. . . . The support for policies quickly broadened once citizens enjoyed the benefits of the new policies, and thus the mass opposition to cutbacks in the policies was much broader than the mass support for their introduction. *Thus, the new policy regime fundamentally transforms the preferences of the population.*[22]

Recent comparative work among political economists has also emphasized the impact of policy regimes. These are typically depicted as parts of distinctive "varieties of capitalism" involving policies, formal and informal institutional arrangements, corporate organizations, and patterns of interest intermediation.[23] A key emphasis in this work is the idea of "institutional complementarities." Institutions are complementary when the value of each institution (including public policies) is enhanced by the presence of the others. This emphasis on the ways in which policies and other institutional arrangements mutually reinforce each other explains the macro or "regime" focus of much of this research. It is not single policies operating in isolation that generate major effects but clusters of policies with strong elective affinities.

Comparative research has begun, at least haltingly, to explore micro-level links between policies and important political variables as well. This is an important development, since much of the previous research had simply sketched out what these micro-level mechanisms connecting macro variables might look like, without investigating these connections directly. Iversen and Soskice argue that strong social-insurance states promote the development of specific skills in the workforce. They demonstrate, in turn, that this effect has consequences for political behavior. Countries with large groups of workers with these skills, who need social insurance to protect against risks associated with their investments in nontransferable skills, will exhibit higher levels of public support for expansive social programs.[24]

Research in American politics has also begun to generate substantial evidence of large-scale policy effects. Not surprisingly, given its focus on processes that unfold over substantial stretches of time, this has been especially true in the field of American political development. Building on Theda Skocpol's work on early initiatives in social policy, which showed their significance for political life, Jacob Hacker's recent study breaks important new ground in demonstrating the scope of policy effects.[25] By focusing on the regulatory and tax policies that support the "private" or "hidden" welfare state, he extends an appreciation for policy effects beyond the range of previous studies. By systematically tracking the implications of early policy initiatives over roughly five decades, he provides a particularly compelling examination of the ways in which initial policy arrangements profoundly influenced interest group structures, the preferences of key political groups, and the range of possibilities open to future policymakers.

Hacker's analysis of the interests of employers is particularly revealing. Political economists often present the policy preferences of business actors as almost hardwired—something innate in their status as employers. Yet, Hacker shows that in the United States the same employers developed dramatically different viewpoints on the desirability of social insurance in health care (vehemently opposed) and retirement (largely supportive). Early divergences in policy structures were key factors, Hacker demonstrates, in altering the developing stances of employers in these two areas. This occurred not only because established policy structures changed what employers thought they could get but because these structures gradually changed what employers perceived as desirable.

Just as in the study of comparative politics, micro-level arguments have recently surfaced in work on American politics. Campbell's study of Social Security policy and the elderly and Mettler's analysis of the G.I. Bill of Rights both offer strong evidence linking policy structures to political behavior.[26] Campbell demonstrates that the expansion of Social Security heightened levels of political activity among the elderly (and, most strikingly, among the less affluent elderly). Mettler's survey of World War II veterans reveals significant effects of the G.I. Bill on levels of participation and political attitudes.

Thus, we have considerable empirical research, focused on both the micro and the macro levels, suggesting that policy effects can be substantial. There is now strong support for E. E. Schattschneider's insistence that "new policies create a new politics."[27] There has been less progress, however, in transforming this into a coherent and cumulative research program. We have repeated demonstrations of the significance of policy feedback. Yet, in sharp contrast to the literature on formal political institutions, we have relatively few clear propositions about when we should expect what kinds of effects. Of course, there have been even fewer sustained efforts to subject these propositions to systematic empirical tests. In the next section, I suggest how progress on these fronts might be made.

Advancing a Research Program on Policy Feedback

Social scientists probably do not take as much time as they should to consider what kinds of strategies are likely to generate successful research programs, with "success" defined here broadly as the production of a cumulative contribution to knowledge.[28] Two factors that greatly enhance the prospect for successful research programs are density and clarity. By density I mean that the topic must attract the attention of a community of scholars. By clarity I mean that scholars must identify a (fairly) clear proposition or set of propositions as a focal point for research on that topic. With density comes the opportunity to subject a particular set of observations to alternative methodologies and repeated scrutiny. Equally important, it allows researchers to greatly increase the number of empirical observations they can consider. As Mahoney has argued, this collective enterprise can surmount many of the methodological limitations that a single qualitative study may confront.[29] Clarity enhances efforts to repeatedly evaluate, and refine, particular claims. It also facilitates the application of claims across a wider empirical terrain, involving subjects that might have important points of similarity that would otherwise be missed.

Clarity and density are synergistic. Density encourages the development of clarity, as the concentration of research (and the competition it produces) pushes analysts to make sharper propositions. Clarity encourages the development of density by catching and focusing the attention of other analysts, helping members of a potential research program recognize that they can be part of a broader scholarly conversation, and demonstrating how findings in one empirical study can be of the greatest relevance to those examining related areas.

As noted earlier, research on policy feedback has made significant progress over the past decade. The subject has certainly generated growing attention, and, thanks to some superb scholarship, there is an increasingly strong case to be made for the significance of policy effects. Yet, insufficient density and clarity have placed significant limits on the prospects for a sustained research program organized around policy effects. Two interconnected factors have undercut the development of density. First, as I discussed at the outset, policy structures are highly diverse, and research is scattered across different policy areas. This scattering could be a source of strength, since it would facilitate the development of systematic and wide-ranging comparisons about policy effects.[30] The scattering of research across different policy domains becomes a weakness, however, when it is coupled with a lack of dialogue across these investigations. Those who study specific policy areas are generally interested primarily in that substantive area. There is as of yet only a limited recognition that scholars working in different policy areas are part of a collective inquiry into the significance of policy effects.

The heavy emphasis on qualitative research in studies of policy effects reinforces this tendency. Typically, these efforts are what might be called demonstration projects. They are designed to show that a particular policy or small set of policies was politically significant in the area or areas studied. They are not projects designed to produce or evaluate propositions about variation in policy effects—although they may spur such developments. Scattered research focused on addressing debates within a particular policy area fosters a situation in which discrete studies often remain discrete, rather than contributing as much as they might to a cumulative research program.

The same factors that have limited the development of density in the study of policy feedback have undercut the development of clarity. Because scholars have typically sought to make the case that "policy makes politics" in the particular policy area they are examining, they have explored *all* of the policy effects they consider to be significant. These can be highly diverse.[31] Policies can channel resources to (or from) particular actors, shift incentives that affect a range of relevant behaviors, facilitate or impede specific forms of collective action, and influence public opinion through a number of different mechanisms.

Most existing research has focused simultaneously on a number of these factors in order to show the large effects of policy. It has not attempted to fashion or evaluate propositions about what factors influence the size of particular kinds of policy effects. Yet claims of the sort "policies that do *x* will tend to produce political effect *y*" are more likely to yield the clarity and density that will facilitate more cumulative research. In short, progress requires a shift away from demonstration projects. We need to focus on those types of effects that we have reason to think will be large and identifiable over a range of issues and for which we have theoretical grounds for developing clear hypotheses about the nature, scale, and variation of these effects.

Very briefly, I want to suggest four possible areas for developing promising hypotheses about policy effects. The four areas are the composition and resources of interest groups, the population of social actors, the preferences of organized social actors, and patterns of public opinion. Each of these areas involves variables of considerable interest to political scientists, and in each case there is sufficient existing research to suggest that policy effects may be quite significant.

The Composition and Resources of Interest Groups

The standard "systems theory" approach sees interest groups as contributing political inputs (e. g., lobbying) that results in policy outputs. Yet, there is now substantial evidence that we often need to turn that causal arrow around. Policies often come first, providing the foundation for particular patterns of collective mobilization.[32] Policies can create major incentives to organize, and to organize in particular ways. They can also confer substantial resources on particular types of groups. These resources include direct and indirect financial subsidies, as well as organizational infrastructure and crucial information that private actors can "piggyback" on in their efforts to generate collective action. External help of this kind can be especially important in addressing the high start-up costs and coordination problems that are often crucial to overcoming the formidable initial obstacles to successful collective action.[33]

The social science literature on collective action and the structure of interest groups pays relatively little attention to policy structures. At the same time, we have numerous studies that have demonstrated that these structures can be highly consequential. A research agenda focused on specifying the mechanisms through which policy arrangements influence patterns of interest group formation and maintenance seems a highly promising focus for comparative research.

Policy Environments and the Population of Social Actors

Major public policies can be powerful instruments for changing the population of actors in a social system. Just as formal political institutions, such as electoral arrangements, constitute "environments" that can shift the population of political parties over time, policy arrangements may shape the survival prospects for particular kinds of actors. These changes may take place slowly over a considerable period, but they may have marked long-term political effects. For example, certain kinds of employers (e. g., small businesses) that employ certain kinds of strategies are more likely to flourish in particular policy environments.[34] As noted earlier, criminal justice policy in the United States is selectively (and, in many cases, permanently) removing a considerable and politically distinctive segment of the electorate from the voting population every year. As we accumulate more knowledge about policy effects, we are in a position to start systematically examining how certain kinds of policies, operating over the long term, may alter populations of social actors in politically consequential ways.

The Preferences of Social Actors

As was discussed earlier, Hacker's analysis of employers demonstrates how public policies can alter actor preferences regarding political agendas. There are multiple sources of these effects. A crucial dimension, however, is the generation of investments in human and physical capital and specific organizational forms. Once these investments have been made, they increase the benefits of particular policy arrangements over potential competitors. This dimension of policy effects has the added advantage of being both theoretically and empirically tractable. Theoretically, recent work has shown the connections of a broad literature on asset specificity to the structure of policy arrangements.[35] Empirically, many of the investments that public policies can induce can be measured systematically, both over time and cross-nationally.

It is worth emphasizing that all three of these topics for research share a focus on how structures of public policy influence the development and organizational expression of "interests" in civil society. Indeed, an important benefit of this research agenda is that it could focus attention on, and potentially reinvigorate, the analysis of interests and interest groups—a dimension of political life that has been largely neglected in recent scholarship, both in American and in comparative politics. A quarter-century ago, Terry Moe made a strong plea for something close to this research agenda in the conclusion to his classic work on interest groups: "whereas past research would automatically view governmental officials as targets of influence, future research must turn the tables and explore the influence of governmental officials on the internal policymaking processes of groups, or their various roles in determining whether groups will emerge, the extent to which they will prosper, and how they will be structured."[36] While there is an important difference between focusing on policymakers (as Moe suggests) and focusing on policies as crucial institutional arrangements, he rightly points to the need to see the vast undertakings of government as a source, not just a consequence, of politically active interests.

Patterns of Public Opinion and Political Behavior

Finally, one of the most promising recent developments in the study of policy effects has been the emergence of research that systematically links policy structures to important aspects of public opinion and political behavior.[37] Like other work on policy effects, however, these efforts have typically focused on a single setting. The goal has been to demonstrate that a particular policy alters political behavior. In fact, these works have often identified multiple mechanisms through which behavioral effects may be generated. Policies can, for example, provide resources that facilitate or impede participation. They may create "stakes" that give individuals incentives to participate. They may create framing effects that influence what actors see and what they do not, which issues attract their attention and how they feel about those issues, whom they see as their allies and opponents, as well as whether they feel that their grievances are legitimate and will be treated as legitimate.

The range of these possibilities, along with the persuasive evidence already assembled, points to the promise of this topic. It also, however, suggests the need for a research agenda that, again, specifies the mechanisms that link policy to behavior and develops propositions about the features of policy and political context that produce variations in these effects. We are poised for a second generation of work on policy effects oriented around these questions. What is needed is the clarity of focus and the density of activity that can yield a sustained and cumulative program of research. Given what we now know about the profound impact of government activism on the character of political life, these issues warrant a central place in the contemporary study of institutions.

NOTES

1. For a good overview see Peter Hall and Rosemary C. R. Taylor, "Political Science and the Three New Institutionalisms," *Political Studies* 44 (1996): 936–957.

2. Jacob Hacker, *The Divided Welfare State: The Battle over Public and Private Social Benefits in the United States* (Cambridge: Cambridge University Press, 2002); Christopher Howard, *The Hidden Welfare State* (Princeton: Princeton University Press, 1997).

3. Douglass C. North, *Institutions, Institutional Change, and Economic Performance* (Cambridge: Cambridge University Press, 1990), 3.

4. Jonas Pontusson, "From Comparative Public Policy to Political Economy: Putting Political Institutions in Their Place and Taking Interests Seriously," *Comparative Political Studies* 28 (1995): 117–147; Gerard Alexander, "Institutions, Path Dependence, and Democratic Consolidation," *Journal of Theoretical Politics* 13 (2001): 249–270.

5. Michael T. Hannan and John Freeman, *Organizational Ecology* (Cambridge, MA: Harvard University Press, 1989), 33.

6. Joe Soss and Suzanne Mettler, "Beyond Representation: Policy Feedback and the Political Roots of Citizenship," paper prepared for delivery at the Midwest Political Science Association Meetings, Chicago, April 2003.

7. John Mark Hansen, "Individuals, Institutions, and Public Preferences over Public Finance," *American Political Science Review* 92 (2000): 513–531; James Stimson et al., *The Macropolity* (Cambridge: Cambridge University Press, 2000); Benjamin Page and Robert Shapiro, *The Rational Public: Fifty Years of Trends in Americans' Policy Preferences* (Chicago: University of Chicago Press, 1992).

8. Lawrence Jacobs and Robert Shapiro, *Politicians Don't Pander: Political Manipulation and the Loss of Democratic Responsiveness* (Chicago: University of Chicago Press, 2000).

9. Robert E. Goodin, "Institutions and Their Design," in Robert E. Goodin, ed., *The Theory of Institutional Design* (Cambridge: Cambridge University Press, 1996), 202.

10. Keith G. Banting, "The Welfare State as Statecraft: Territorial Politics and Canadian Social Policy," in Stephan Leibfried and Paul Pierson, eds., *European Social Policy: Between Fragmentation and Integration* (Washington, DC: Brookings Institution Press, 1995), 278.

11. For an extended discussion see Paul Pierson, *Politics in Time: History, Institutions, and Social Analysis* (Princeton: Princeton University Press, 2004), ch. 5.

12. John M. Carey, "Parchment, Equilibria, and Institutions," *Comparative Political Studies* 33 (2000): 735–761; Gary Cox, *Making Votes Count: Strategic Coordination in the World's Electoral Systems* (Cambridge: Cambridge University Press, 1997); Russell Hardin, *Liberalism, Constitutionalism, and Democracy* (Oxford: Oxford University Press, 1999); and Barry Weingast, "Rational Choice Institutionalism," in Ira Katznelson and Helen Milner, eds., *The State of the Discipline* (New York: Norton, 2003), 660–692.

13. Hardin, *Liberalism, Constitutionalism, and Democracy.* For a nice critique of this line of argument see Gerard Alexander, "Institutions, Path Dependence, and Democratic Consolidation," *Journal of Theoretical Politics* 13 (2001): 249–270.

14. Peter Hall and David Soskice, eds., *Varieties of Capitalism* (Oxford: Oxford University Press, 2001).

15. Jacob Hacker and Paul Pierson, "Business Power and Social Policy: Employers and the Formation of the American Welfare State," *Politics and Society* 30 (2002): 277–325.

16. Pierson, *Politics in Time,* ch. 5.

17. Josep Colomer, *Political Institutions: Democracy and Social Choice* (Oxford: Oxford University Press, 2001); Arend Lijphart, *Patterns of Democracy: Government Forms and Performance in 36 Countries* (New Haven: Yale University Press, 1999).

18. Arguments about what is now often termed "policy feedback" are usually traced back to sources such as Lowi and Wilson. Theodore Lowi, "American Business, Public Policy, Case Studies, and Political Theory," *World Politics* 16 (1964): 677–715; James Q. Wilson, "The Politics of Regulation," in James Q. Wilson, ed., *The Politics of Regulation* (New York: Basic Books, 1980), 357–394. These arguments, however, are really about the structure of *issues* and the associated (diffuse or concentrated) winners and losers. They are not arguments about how specific structures of public policy can influence politics. Recent strands of work on this topic stem largely, in my view, from lines of argument set down by Theda Skocpol and her collaborators in the 1980s, e. g., Margaret Weir and Theda Skocpol, "State Structures and the Possibilities for 'Keynesian' Responses to the Great Depression in Sweden, Britain, and the United States," in Peter B. Evans, Dietrich Rueschemeyer, and Theda Skocpol, eds., *Bringing the State Back In* (Cambridge: Cambridge University Press, 1985), 107–162. For an overview see Paul Pierson, "When Effect Becomes Cause: Policy Feedback and Political Change," *World Politics* (1993): 595–628.

19. Gosta Esping-Andersen, *The Three Worlds of Welfare Capitalism* (Princeton: Princeton University Press, 1990).

20. Duane Swank, *Global Capital, Political Institutions, and Policy Change in Developed Welfare States* (Cambridge: Cambridge University Press, 2002); Evelyn Huber and John Stephens, *Development and Crisis of the Welfare State: Parties and Policies in Global Markets* (Chicago: University of Chicago Press, 2001); and Paul Pierson, ed., *The New Politics of the Welfare State* (Oxford: Oxford University Press, 2001).

21. Huber and Stephens, *Development and Crisis of the Welfare State,* 32.

22. Ibid., 28–29, emphasis added.

23. Hall and Soskice, *Varieties of Capitalism;* Herbert Kitschelt, Peter Lange, Gary Marks, and John D. Stephens, eds., *Continuity and Change in Contemporary Capitalism* (Cambridge: Cambridge University Press, 1999).

24. Torben Iversen and David Soskice, "An Asset Theory of Social Policy Preferences," *American Political Science Review* 95 (2001): 875–894.

25. Theda Skocpol, *Protecting Soldiers and Mothers* (Cambridge, MA: Harvard University Press, 1992); Jacob Hacker, *The Divided Welfare State: The Battle over Public and Private Social Benefits in the United States* (Cambridge: Cambridge University Press, 2002).

26. Andrea Louise Campbell, *How Policies Make Citizens: Senior Political Activism and the American Welfare State* (Princeton: Princeton University Press, 2003); Suzanne Mettler, "Bringing the State Back In to Civic Engagement: Policy Feedback Effects of the G.I. Bill for World War II Veterans," *American Political Science Review* 96 (2002): 367–380.

27. E. E. Schattschneider, *Politics, Pressures, and the Tariff* (New York: Prentice-Hall, 1935).

28. See James Mahoney and Dietrich Rueschemeyer, eds., *Comparative Historical Analysis in the Social Sciences* (Cambridge: Cambridge University Press, 2003).

29. James Mahoney, "Knowledge Accumulation in Comparative Historical Research: The Case of Democracy and Authoritarianism," in James Mahoney and Dietrich Reuschemeyer, eds., *Comparative Historical Analysis in the Social Sciences* (Cambridge: Cambridge University Press, 2003), 131–174.

30. Although it is notable that many important areas of policy feedback have so far received almost no attention. There has been some clustering around topics in social policy and political economy (not surprisingly, the places where the most theoretical and empirical progress has occurred). The political effects of many other areas of policy development deserve systematic scrutiny. Hacker, Mettler, Pinderhughes, and Skocpol offer one clear example: "incarceration rates in the United States have quadrupled since 1975, over the course of an era featuring a vigorous anti-crime policy agenda and strict sentencing laws. As a result, 4.7 million individuals are currently prohibited from voting due to their status as felons, and in some states, as ex-felons. Christopher Uggen and Jeff Manza found that such

disenfranchisement likely altered the outcomes of several gubernatorial and U.S. Senate elections and at least one presidential election." Jacob Hacker, Suzanne Mettler, Dianne Pinderhughes, and Theda Skocpol, "Public Policy as a Cause and Effect of Inequality: The United States in Comparative and Historical Perspective," Background Memorandum by the 'Policy Feedbacks' Working Group, APSA Task Force on Inequality and American Democracy, March 2003.

31. Pierson, "When Effect Becomes Cause"; Soss and Mettler, "Beyond Representation."

32. Theda Skocpol's ongoing research on associational life in the United States provides strong evidence linking preexisting policy structures to successful formation and maintenance of interest groups.

33. Terry M. Moe, *The Organization of Interests: Incentives and the Internal Dynamics of Political Interest Groups* (Chicago: University of Chicago Press, 1980); Gerald Marwell and Pamela Oliver, *The Critical Mass in Collective Action: A Micro-Social Theory* (New York: Cambridge University Press, 1993).

34. Hacker and Pierson, "Business Power and Social Policy"; Huber and Stephens, *Development and Crisis of the Welfare State.*

35. Iversen and Soskice, "An Asset Theory of Policy Preferences."

36. Moe, *The Organization of Interests,* 230.

37. Campbell, *How Policies Make Citizens;* Iversen and Soskice, "An Asset Theory of Preferences"; Mettler, "Bringing the State Back In to Civic Engagement."

Part II

Institutional Structure and Political Change

6

Institutions and Social Change
The Evolution of Vocational Training in Germany

Kathleen Thelen

This chapter examines key developments in the evolution of vocational-training institutions in Germany from the late nineteenth century to the present and uses this as a window on questions of social and institutional change.[1] Whereas earlier generations of institutional analysis focused primarily on the effects of different institutional configurations on public policy and other outcomes, a growing number of studies have turned their attention to the question of how institutions themselves develop and evolve over time.[2]

For both of the two most prominent perspectives on institutions in political science—rational-choice institutionalism and historical institutionalism—the favored conceptualization of change is based on a punctuated-equilibrium model. Borrowed from evolutionary biology via Stephen Krasner, this model emphasizes moments of "openness" and rapid innovation followed by long periods of institutional stasis or "inertia."[3] This model emphasizes discontinuous change and, in consequence, tends to draw a sharp analytic distinction between the analysis of institutional innovation (usually in the context of some exogenous "shock") and that of institutional reproduction. The model is sometimes invoked in connection with claims about strong contingency and the importance of agency at institutional "choice points" and, conversely, the primacy of structure over agency in periods of institutional stability or stasis.[4]

This chapter casts doubt on the analytic utility of strong punctuated-equilibrium models of this sort. Sometimes institutional change *is* abrupt and discontinuous, but very often it is not. Against the idea of alternating periods of stasis and rapid, radical change, there often seems to be too much continuity through putative "breakpoints" in history *and* too much gradual change beneath the surface of apparently stable formal institutional arrangements. An examination of the evolution of German vocational-training institutions provides an opportunity to explore both aspects and serves as the basis for elaborating an alternative, political-coalitional, perspective on institutional stability and change. I argue that institutional development is best understood as a process of mobilizing support among social and political actors to construct, revise, or sustain specific institutional arrangements.[5] Institutions are not (or certainly not only) subject to periodic renegotiation (in the context of historical "breakpoints"), but are the object of ongoing political contestation. Institutions evolve as shifts in the political coalitions on which they rest inspire or compel changes—sometimes abrupt and discontinuous but more often incremental and cumulative—in the form these institutions take and the functions they perform in society.

The Case of German Vocational Training

In the literature on political economy, the German training regime is typically held up as an exemplary case of a "collectivist" system for skill formation that solves a number of knotty coordination problems that typically plague private-sector training regimes.[6] The German model features a strong system for plant-based apprentice training that encourages firms to invest in skill formation (among other things, by furnishing solutions to various collective action problems) and also provides important guarantees that apprentices will receive high-quality training (above all, through strong mechanisms for monitoring and enforcement). More generally, Germany's vocational-training system has been characterized as a crucial component in a larger institutional package that not only is compatible with strong and encompassing unions but actively supports a particular (and traditionally very successful) type of "diversified quality production" that reconciles strong unions with strong performance in world manufacturing markets.[7]

The German training system has been invoked as a classic illustration of a number of different theoretical perspectives. From a functional perspective, German vocational-training institutions are seen as facilitating employer coordination around a "high-skill equilibrium."[8] From a power-distributional perspective, the system has been assumed to be a reflection of working-class strength.[9] And from a cultural perspective, it has been seen as one of many institutions that embody a distinctly German mode of self-governance that operates through the country's "social partners" (unions and employers) and without much direction from the state.[10]

Looking at these institutions from today's vantage point, we can see that each of these characterizations contains an important element of truth. However, historically speaking, they are all wide of the mark. The core institutional innovation around which the German system came to be built was a piece of piece of legislation passed in 1897 by an authoritarian government that was designed to shore up a reactionary artisanal class (of small-employer master-craftsmen) that could serve as a political bulwark against the surging and radical working-class movement. Against prominent functionalist arguments, these institutions were not designed with the economic interests of the industrial sector in mind—and they were certainly not meant to reconcile strong unions with anything. Against the power-distributional perspective, organized labor played no role in the genesis of these institutions, and in fact the Social Democratic Party opposed the original legislation. And, against the cultural perspective, the kind of social partnership of which these institutions are now seen to be a part was really nowhere on the horizon.

How did we get from there to here? Well, certainly *not* through a wholesale breakdown of the old institutions and their replacement with new ones. Indeed, one of the striking features of the system is the resilience of core elements even in the face of a series of rather significant "ruptures" over the twentieth century—which in this particular case include defeat in two world wars, foreign occupation, and several regime changes, including into and out of fascism. These are precisely the kinds of historic "breakpoints" that many punctuated-equilibrium models might hypothesize to be moments of sharp change. In fact, against the backdrop of many such theories, the question that one would have to ask is how these institutions—created, after all, for an independent artisanal class that in most countries just vanished with industrialization—actually made it to the present at all, given the magnitude of some of these intervening events and developments.

For understanding the continuities, the kinds of positive-feedback arguments advanced by Pierson (this volume) and others provide a useful starting point, because, as we will see, they can tell us a great deal about how key actors were constituted and the kinds of strategies they pursued with respect to training. In the case at hand, the existence in Germany of a system for skill formation that was monopolized by the artisanal sector hastened the demise of skill-based unions by denying them any hope of controlling the market in skills, thus providing unintended support for the triumph and consolidation of industrial unionism. More consequentially still, as the ranks of Germany's unions swelled with workers who had been certified under the artisanal system, organized labor developed a strong interest in democratizing rather than dismantling a system it had originally opposed. Thus, the German case is a powerful illustration of the way in which feedback effects set in motion by the operation of one set of institutions affect neighboring realms in ways that stabilize those institutions.[11]

However, if one told this purely as a tale of positive feedback, one would miss much of what is in fact interesting and important about the way in which these institutions were also transformed through political contestation, and specifically through the incorporation of groups whose role in the system was unanticipated at the time of their creation. The original legislation provided a framework for training in the artisanal (handicraft, or *Handwerk*) sector only—excluding industry. Key skill-dependent sectors such as metalworking and machine building were forced to work around these institutions as they developed their own training practices. In a case of what Schickler has called institutional "layering," an industrial system was created alongside and parallel to the handicraft system, and the interaction of the two altered the overall trajectory of institutional development, pulling the system in the Weimar years away from the decentralized and rather unsystematic training characteristic of the older *Handwerk* model and toward a much higher degree of centralization, standardization, and uniformity—elements that are now considered defining features of the German system.[12]

Equally important, the function and role of the vocational-training system in the German political economy were transformed in important ways through the eventual incorporation of labor. Although the Social Democratic Party had opposed the 1897 legislation, the later (post–World War II) incorporation of unions into a variety of parapublic corporatist institutions recast the purposes of these institutions even as they contributed to institutional reproduction by bringing the system in line with new economic and political conditions. Institutional survival, that is to say, depended not just on positive feedback or inertia but also on a process of institutional adaptation to accommodate powerful new actors and to address new imperatives, both economic and political. The following sections do not attempt a comprehensive history of the evolution of the German training system[13] but rather follow the German system through several putative breakpoints to document how ongoing renegotiations of the form and scope of these institutions could, over time, cumulate into their political and functional transformation.

Genesis and Evolution of the German Vocational-Training System

To provide a comprehensive analysis of the genesis and evolution of the German system, from its origins in 1897 to the present, would go well beyond the bounds of this chapter. Instead, I lift out aspects of a broader analysis that provide insights into observed continuities in the system in the face of abrupt changes in the political and social landscape and that also illustrate modes of change that are gradual but cumulatively transformative. I draw some insights from the literature on policy feedback,[14] which is crucial to understanding how actors initially on the periphery over time came to be invested in institutions not of their own making. However, in contrast to some of the more mechanical treatments (e. g., emphasizing "lock-in"), I elaborate an explicitly political account that shows how shifts in the political coalitions on which institutions rest can drive significant change in the functions and roles performed by these institutions.

The account focuses special attention on two actors—unions and skill-intensive industrial firms (specifically, the organized machine industry)—that played a key role in both the survival and the transformation of Germany's vocational-training system. Neither of these actors was a part of the original coalition behind the founding legislation (for handicraft training) of 1897. However, both became enormously important "carriers" of the system that evolved out of that legislation—at the same time, however, their participation drove the development of these institutions forward in ways that were completely unanticipated by their founders.

Institutional Design: Political Origins of the Apprenticeship System

The crucial starting point in Germany was the original legislation of 1897 that created a system of apprentice training under the control of the organized artisanal or handicraft (*Handwerk*) sector, that is, self-employed master craftsmen who were also in some cases employers of wage earners and in any event trainers of apprentices whom they also used as a source of cheap labor.[15] The political background for this legislation was the enormous growth in the late nineteenth century of the Social Democratic labor movement, which had elevated the "social question" to the top of the German government's agenda. Along with the better-known carrot-and-stick policies (labor repression and the precocious introduction of comprehensive social insurance), the Imperial government's policy toward the artisanal sector was a third key response to the social democratic threat.[16] Members of the German artisanate had skillfully appealed to conservatives by portraying themselves as the only political force capable of holding the line against rampant liberalism on the one hand and working class radicalism on the other. The authoritarian government of the day was receptive to such appeals and had a strong interest in shoring up a healthy, conservative small-business sector as a bulwark against political polarization and working-class radicalism.

Legislation during the 1870s and 1880s had played to the interests of the artisanate by granting its guilds more authority in regulating apprenticeship and by adjudicating conflicts among masters, journeymen, and trainees.[17] However, by the 1890s, policymakers had become intensely aware of the weaknesses of innovations built around the voluntary guilds, which were subject to classic collective-action and free-riding problems.[18] The result was a much more comprehensive intervention, the Handicraft Protection Law of 1897, which organized the artisanal sector into a network of handicraft chambers (*Handwerkskammern*) with compulsory membership and endowed these chambers with extensive parapublic powers to regulate the content and quality of apprenticeship training. Among other things, the chambers were authorized to set limits on the number of apprentices handicraft firms could take, to establish the required length of training, and to revoke the privileges of firms whose training was not up to their standards.[19]

This legislation was crucial to stabilizing plant-based training in the handicraft sector. The existence of a recognized, parapublic, and, above all, compulsory system for certifying skills and for monitoring apprenticeship meant that a fair amount of training would actually take place in artisanal firms.[20] This stands in sharp contrast to other countries, such as Britain where, in the absence of reliable monitoring capacities (and indeed, in the context of ongoing conflicts over skill with unions), apprenticeship deteriorated at the turn of the century into cheap "boy labour."[21] All signs are that German apprenticeship was headed in this same direction after the liberalization of 1869, but the 1897 law brought "real progress" in mitigating the problem of exploitation associated with so-called overbreeding of apprentices (*Lehrlingszüchterei*).[22]

Impact on Labor and Industry: Implications for Training Policy in the Weimar Years

The importance of this system of skill formation reverberated well beyond the handicraft sector and had a significant effect on the structure and strategies of both organized labor and industry. For labor, the most important consequence was effectively to rule out organizational strategies premised on attempting to control the supply of skills in the economy. The German labor movement was not "born" centralized, and, in fact, near the turn of the century, unions hung in the balance between two more or less equally plausible alternatives—craft- (or at least skill-) based organizations versus industrial organization. The Metalworkers Union, which famously embraced industrial unionism at its 1891 congress, remained very heavily skewed toward skilled workers throughout its early history, and certainly up through World War I. Most of the delegates at the 1891 congress were representing associations of skilled workers, both "single-craft" and "mixed."[23] In 1913, still only about 20 percent of the members of the Metalworkers Union were unskilled or semiskilled workers.[24] The rest were skilled workers, and separate craft groupings maintained their own identities under the overarching rubric of the industrial union. Wage agreements as late as 1919 (featuring different rates for separate crafts) reflected this fact.[25]

In comparative perspective, the question that emerges, therefore, is why the identities and continuing craft attachments of the various occupational groupings in Germany did not prevent skilled workers from throwing their lots in with social democratic unions that were explicitly committed to industrial organization. Clearly, one of the factors that discouraged workers from organizing around skills (and associated strategies based on controlling skilled labor markets) was the fact that union expansion occurred in a context in which the "space" for regulating skills was already rather decisively occupied—by the handicraft chambers. This was crucial for the future of vocational training, because it meant that in Germany (as in Britain), labor strength was premised substantially on the

skills their members commanded, but (unlike in Britain) without skill formation itself being contested across the class divide, that is, with unions
trying to limit apprenticeship in order to control the supply of skills.

In addition, Germany's social democratic unions recruited heavily from
among the ranks of journeymen who had received their training in the
handicraft sector but who had left that sector for (usually higher-paying)
jobs in industry.[26] In the early industrial period, the vast majority of
skilled factory workers were drawn directly from the artisanal sector,[27] and
Handwerk continued to train large numbers of industrial workers
throughout the late nineteenth century and into the twentieth. Schönhoven notes that in 1913, 80 percent of the membership of the Metalworkers Union (DMV) consisted of skilled workers who had served an
apprenticeship (*gerlernte Berufsarbeiter*).[28] At the level of leadership as
well, the early DMV was composed of a "group of men who all came from
apprenticed trades" (*aus gelernteen Berufen*).[29] In short, as the ranks of
Germany's social democratic unions filled up with skilled workers who
had received their credentials in the handicraft system, the unions developed a strong interest not in dismantling that system but rather in controlling or comanaging the system of firm-based training that it
represented.

This "acquired" investment on the part of unions in a training system
not of their own making (a "feedback effect" generated directly by the
operation of handicraft training itself) helps explain how that system survived a first historic rupture, namely Germany's defeat in World War I and
the accompanying, rather abrupt, transition to democracy including the
full incorporation of the working class. The Weimar Republic's first
(Social Democratic) government was intensely interested in reforming the
full range of economic institutions, including those for vocational training. Already in 1919 the unions advocated stripping the handicraft chambers of their monopoly and introducing a more democratic structure,
including full union participation in overseeing and administering plant-
based skill formation.[30] As Heinrich Abel notes, what is most interesting
here is that German unions had no trouble with the idea of firm-based
training; in fact, they called for more firms to undertake it.[31] This stands
in contrast to the position of socialist unions in other countries, notably
Sweden, which preferred school-based vocational education and which
were skeptical of firm-based training as inherently biased toward
employer interests. Clearly this was an option for German unions, too, as
the public vocational-school system was already far more developed in

Germany than anywhere else.[32] However, by this time, Germany's unions were themselves invested in a system through which a large number of their members had earned their own credentials.

Thus, already in the Weimar years, German unions had emerged as ready allies of those segments of capital (and there were some; see later discussion) that had their own reasons for wanting to break into the system of skill formation that had been created for and was being monopolized by master craftsmen. This was not an alliance that could be stabilized or consummated in the Weimar period, but it is important that, from early on, German unions were themselves invested in a system of plant-based training—and therefore were pursuing strategies that were quite different from those of social democratic unions elsewhere that were deeply skeptical of all forms of firm-based training and advocated instead publicly managed school-based vocational training for blue-collar workers.

For industry, the consolidation of a system for skill formation in the *Handwerk* sector in the late nineteenth century had had equally important implications. It was, in the first place, a benefit, because, in contrast to other countries where skills were an enormous bottleneck in the early industrial period, emerging manufacturing industries in Germany could rely on a relatively steady stream of certified skilled workers from the artisanal sector. German industry's dependence on *Handwerk*-based skills was in fact virtually absolute until at least the 1880s and diminished only very slowly in subsequent decades.[33] However, beginning in the 1890s, large firms in the most modern and skill-intensive industries (machine building firms such as Maschinenfabrik Augsburg Nürnberg (M.A.N.), Ludwig Loewe and Company, Borsig, and Koenig and Bauer) began to complain that they were pushing up against the limits, both qualitative and quantitative, of the skills provided by the artisanal sector.[34]

Responding to the perceived inadequacies of craft training, these firms embarked on strategies aimed at internalizing skill formation at the firm level and incorporating training into complementary plant social policies and internal labor markets. In contrast to the traditional *Meisterlehre* model (on-the-job training by working alongside a master craftsman), apprentices would be trained in somewhat larger groups and, initially at least, separate from the production process.[35] Since the idea was to train and then retain skilled workers, these firms linked plant-based training programs to other company-based social policies designed to tie workers to the firm.[36] Such policies bore a strong resemblance to strategies being pursued at exactly the same time in Japan and which in that case subsequently developed into a stable, alternative company-based system of skill formation.[37]

However, in Germany, the premier training firms in the late nineteenth and early twentieth centuries were hobbled by their inability to certify the skills their training conferred. After 1897, the only way to become certified as a "skilled worker" in Germany was through the artisanal (*Handwerk*) chambers.[38] There existed no similar authority or officially recognized framework to certify industrial training, and this became a huge source of irritation for those firms that were engaged in such training. Large machine firms like M.A.N. and Loewe could offer prospective apprentices all manner of privileges and benefits. However, what they could not do was confer the status and rights that accompanied skill certification through the *Handwerk* chambers—something that youth and, especially, their parents valued for the opportunities it opened in the labor market as a whole.[39] Already in 1902, the Association of Berlin Metal Industrialists sought (unsuccessfully) to secure official recognition and certification for industrial apprenticeship in Berlin and accreditation for the training workshops of that city's premier industrial training firms—AEG, Borsig, Loewe, and others.[40] When this failed, individual industrial firms sometimes made arrangements with their local craft chambers to examine and certify their apprentices.[41] However, such ad hoc arrangements were not stable, and indeed, higher failure rates among industrial apprentices simply fueled conflict with *Handwerk,* for example, over the composition of the examination boards and the types of skills to be tested.[42]

In light of these problems, large industrial firms that depended heavily on skills organized among themselves to demand the creation of a parallel system for promoting and certifying industrial training under the collective control of the Industry and Trade Chambers (which were to be endowed with powers equal to those of the Handicraft Chambers). A first important step in the development of industrial training was undertaken, in 1908, with the founding of the German Committee for Technical Education (*Deutscher Ausschuß für Technisches Schulwesen,* or DATSCH) under the joint sponsorship of the Association of German Engineers (*Verein Deutscher Ingenieure,* VDI) and the Association of German Machine-Building Firms (*Verband Deutscher Maschinenbauanstalten,* VDMA).

In the subsequent period (and transition to democracy after World War I), the machine industry was labor's nature ally on the employer side when it came to reforming apprenticeship. Like organized labor, large firms that were heavily dependent on skills had their own reasons for wanting to break the artisanal chambers' monopoly on skill certification. In 1918, DATSCH (at the time under the leadership of M.A.N. director Gottlieb Lippart) had set out an eight-point reform program "to overcome *Handwerk*'s hegemony" in this area through targeted cooperation with the unions. During World War I, unions had floated ideas for the reform of vocational training that at least in certain industrial circles were seen as "quite reasonable." Members of DATSCH endorsed proposals that called for joint (union-employer) oversight of a system of training (for industry as well as for *Handwerk*), calling them a "worthwhile framework" for reform.

Comprehensive (national-level) reforms along these lines languished during the Weimar years and ultimately foundered on the unified opposition of handicraft producers and heavy industry. Handicraft producers sought to maintain their monopoly in training certification and also understood clearly that union participation would undermine their ability to use apprentices as a source of cheap labor. Heavy industry relied less heavily on skill to begin with and (related to this) was more virulently anti-union than were skill-intensive sectors that had reluctantly come to terms with organized labor. Thus, heavy industry, too, opposed reforms that would tie it to more costly training arrangements than it needed and especially rejected any system that gave organized labor a place at the table.

Despite the political stalemate, however, in fact tremendous progress was achieved on a more or less voluntary basis in the 1920s through a combination of the collective-bargaining strategies of unions and the policies of the machine industry though its influential trade association, the *Verband Deutscher Maschinenbauanstalten,* or VDMA. In contrast to Britain (where resurgent craft unionism reinstated significant wage differentials between skilled and unskilled workers in the tight skilled-labor markets just after the war), in Germany the institutionalization of collective bargaining along industrial lines produced a sharp reduction in wage differentials, especially between 1919 and 1921.[43] The resulting labor market imperfections provided strong incentives for firms to invest in training.[44] With unskilled labor relatively expensive and skilled wages held back, firms faced strong incentives to move up-market and to invest in worker training. Meanwhile, the poaching problems that typically plague firm-based training were mitigated by somewhat looser labor markets for most of the Weimar years, while industrywide bargaining further reduced incentives for workers to engage in job-hopping.

Turning to the content of such collective bargains reveals that union bargaining went beyond the issue of pay to seek to regulate also the conditions and terms of training.[45] Contracts that covered apprentices included provisions that limited the number of allowable apprentices, provided for oversight of training and for vocational school attendance, laid out the rights and responsibilities of apprentices and firms, and established the length of apprenticeship.[46] Since these are all things that in the *Handwerk* sector would have been overseen by the chambers, union collective-bargaining policies provided a kind of functional substitute, offering "an answer to the questions that had been left unanswered by the industrial code."[47] In addition, unions had a strong interest in ensuring that the skills taught by training firms were general rather than firm-specific, not just because portable skills would enhance the market position of their members but also as part of their ongoing battle against "yellow" (company) unionism in this period.

Parallel to this and equally important, the Association of German Machine Building Firms (VDMA), which had helped to create DATSCH and which had actively sponsored its efforts in the area of training, underwent an important shift in the early 1920s. The large machine producers that had dominated the VDMA (and also set the terms of debate on training) were displaced by ever-larger numbers of smaller producers from the so-called industrial *Mittelstand.*[48] The changing composition of the VDMA and DATSCH advanced the cause of collectivism and skill standardization tremendously, for it drove an extremely consequential shift in the goals and activities these organizations were pursuing in the area of training. The large companies that had dominated the VDMA before the war had been organizing their strategies around stabilizing internal labor markets and thus had focused their energies primarily on the issue of certification for their own in-plant training facilities. By contrast, the smaller firms that poured into the VDMA in the Weimar years did not—could not—maintain stable internal labor markets. They sought instead to promote the creation of a pool of skills on which they could all draw, thus bringing the issue of skill standardization to the fore.

The 1920s in fact mark the high point of DATSCH's most intensive efforts at developing a framework for standardized, uniform training in industry.[49] The organization's pioneering efforts to systematize and rationalize industry-based training earned it considerable prestige and established it as a widely recognized authority in this area. Together with the VDMA and the Association of German Metal Industrialists (VDM), DATSCH worked out a "model" apprentice contract for the entire machine industry.[50] In the 1920s, DATSCH produced an inventory of skilled trades for the metalworking industries (including a number of new, specifically industrial trades), with profiles of the content of skills required for each. The organization also generated and disseminated standardized training materials, including very detailed training courses (*Lehrgänge*) for the various trades, beginning with the most common— machine builders, fitters, toolmakers, patternmakers, molders, smiths, and precision mechanics. The evidence from this period suggests that these materials were disseminated and used on a relatively wide basis.[51]

In short, and as in the case of labor, the existence of the handicraft system had an important formative impact on the interests and strategies developed by the organized machine industry. The handicraft system served both as a foil against which large machine builders railed (above all, for the way it prevented them from controlling the content of training) but also as a model (in its structure) for skill-dependent industrial firms to emulate.[52] The strategies pursued by the machine industry stabilized core aspects of the system (because machine firms defined their interests and strategies within the logic of that system), while also creating new pressures for changes in that system. The new coalition of interests during the Weimar years helped move the system toward greater skill standardization, which at the time was consistent with the different interests of the small producers that had begun to dominate the VDMA—and which is now considered a hallmark and defining feature of the German system as a whole.

National Socialism and Beyond

The next big rupture in German history—the advent of National Socialism—was associated with important developments in vocational training, but again what is striking is how innovations under the Nazis built on rather than replaced preexisting structures. The years of National Socialism saw not a fundamental reconfiguration but rather the massive consolidation of the system that had been developing on a voluntarist basis in the Weimar years but whose expansion had been limited by divisions both between industry and labor and, especially, among different segments of capital. Some of the political obstacles that had frustrated attempts in the

Weimar period to institute a unitary and comprehensive national system for skill formation were swept away through brute repression; in particular, the elimination of the unions removed the need to reach an accommodation with organized labor on this subject. Cleavages between *Handwerk* and industry were dealt with through policies that alternately played to and overran the interests of the Handicraft Chambers. And, finally, the differences of opinion on training among various segments of industry that had characterized the Weimar years gave way to a new unity, forged in the context of their joint attempts to defend managerial prerogatives against unwanted encroachments by Nazi party functionaries.

The national-socialist state presided over two important developments: a massive expansion of training and the introduction of standardization to render such training uniform across the entire economy. The expansion of training in the first two years of the regime was connected to measures to combat unemployment, but starting in 1935 the goals shifted to rearmament and mobilization for war. The government provided direct subsidies for training, but, in addition, and in a move that the "free" (social democratic) unions had once advocated but that no Weimar government had ever seriously considered, state policy also required firms in the iron, metal, and construction industries that employed ten or more workers to train apprentices.[53] In addition—and against opposition and foot-dragging by *Handwerk*—the Industry and Trade Chambers were granted powers equivalent to those of the handicraft chambers to test and certify industrial skills, and the exam for industrial workers (*Facharbeiter*) was accorded the same recognition and status that the journeymen's exam in the craft sector had long enjoyed, including the right of certified industrial workers to be admitted to the Master exam.[54] These measures produced a dramatic rise in the overall number of youth in training; the number of apprentices taking industrial *Facharbeiter* exams rose from a little under 24,000 in 1937 to more than 110,000 only two years later.[55]

The other aspect of vocational-training policy, skill standardization, was similarly designed to facilitate the regime's war machinery. Broadbased, standardized training would generate a supply of skilled workers who could be deployed flexibly to deal with increased production demands and with continuous changes in production as more and more men were called up (and, later, as production sites were dispersed to shield them from attack). For this task the Economics Ministry turned to DATSCH, which served as the government's main advisory organ for training matters. Building on its previous experience and efforts, DATSCH was charged with developing skill profiles and regulatory instruments (*Ausbildungsordnungen*) that would be disseminated on a national level.[56] Since apprentices could be trained only in recognized occupations and on the basis of standardized training materials that DATSCH developed, these measures imposed a much higher degree of uniformity across sectors than ever before, ensuring that everyone certified as a "skilled mechanic" (for example) possessed the same technical skills and theoretical knowledge irrespective of the firms or sector in which he had received his training.[57]

As mentioned earlier, many employers previously had resisted the imposition of a broad-based training system based on skill standardization, and one of the most important developments of the Nazi period was the unity of interests that was forged among business on the training issue. Whereas the main threat to managerial prerogatives in the area of training throughout the Weimar years had been organized labor, under the Nazis business confronted an equally meddlesome intruder in the form of the German Workers Front (DAF), which sought to claim jurisdiction over employment relations in general and in-plant training in particular.[58] The national-socialist state's bold moves in the area of training had the effect of recasting the debate entirely: The apparatus for a more uniform and standardized system of training at the national level was now a fact; the question was who was going to run it. The story of training in the Nazi period thus became one in which organized business rushed to occupy the regulatory space created by Nazi training policies and then to defend it against the DAF.[59]

Key firms from heavy industry such as Krupp and Gutehoffnungshütte had opposed all training reform in the Weimar years, and under National Socialism they remained decidedly unenthusiastic about submitting to regulations set out by the DATSCH and the Industry and Trade Chambers (IHK). However, as DAF's party functionaries attempted to insert themselves into training matters at the expense of business self-regulation through the chambers, these firms came around. As Frese puts it, "the activities of the [National-Socialist Party and Labor Front in this area] strongly encouraged firms to change their attitude."[60] In other words, the firms that had resisted collectivist solutions in the Weimar years faced a completely different situation and set of choices under the Nazis. The elimination of unions facilitated greater employer unity on this question by eliminating one of the sources of disagreement among them in the

Weimar years, while DAF's incursions into treasured areas of managerial prerogatives pushed them toward greater unity to defend business self-government.

Defend it they did, and mostly successfully, as a result of support from the Economics Ministry, which had also opposed Party influence in these areas.[61] Training deteriorated in the 1940s under the pressure of war production, but the legacy that remained and that had a profound impact on postwar developments was that of a unified national system for apprenticeship training built on the handicraft model but superseding that model by incorporating and applying the technical/organizational innovations that had been developed on a voluntary basis by industry in the 1920s. Equally important, developments in the Nazi years laid the basis for the resurrection of the old system after the war—for it was under the banner of employer self-regulation (against the state) that business convinced the occupying powers to allow vocational-training policy to be reconstructed along much the same lines in the postwar period.

Vocational Training in Postwar Germany

Defeat in World War II and subsequent foreign occupation did not bring significant institutional innovation; on the contrary, the vocational-training system was if anything revived and reinforced without much public deliberation at all. In the context of high youth unemployment and worries about German youngsters coming under the influence of radicals—either on the right or the left—German companies won praise for reestablishing apprentice training programs quickly and unbureaucratically.[62] Already in October 1950, the Ministry of Labor reported 1,011,805 registered apprentices (in industry and *Handwerk*).[63]

The fact of apprenticeship brought with it, of course, the issue of regulation and oversight, and here too industry and handicraft associations reemerged and assumed their traditional roles somewhat organically and, as Abel puts it, "in the absence of the state."[64] All three of the western occupying powers had their doubts about the separation of technical and vocational education from general education, and also about having the former under the control and dominance of employers. At the same time, however, the Allies were also united in their desire to break up concentrated powers of the state and to establish decentralized nodes of authority, and in this context the reestablishment of business self-government looked like a good thing. German employers emphasized wherever possible the ways in which their interests resonated with the values of the occupying powers (particularly the Americans), underscoring the role that private capital and employer self-government could play in limiting state power and guarding against a return of authoritarianism.[65] The head of the department for vocational training of the national organization of Industry and Trade Chambers, Adolf Kieslinger (a man who had occupied basically the same position in the late Weimar and then also the Nazi periods) never tired of insisting that "vocational training is not the task of the state" (*die Berufsausbildung ist nicht Staatsaufgabe*).[66]

The main debates of the 1950s and 1960s regarding plant-based training all turned on the same basic line of cleavage. Employers and their political allies defended the principle of employer self-governance (and the subsidiarity principle)[67] as the only viable way to prevent bureaucratization and to preserve the "elasticity" of the system in the face of changing market and technical conditions.[68] Unions and their political allies, by contrast, returned to the position they had first embraced in the Weimar period. Defining vocational training as a "public task," they sought to subject it to more democratic control and increased participation rights for employee representatives.[69]

What is as striking as the disagreements, however, are the many aspects of the existing system that were *not* controversial—including (as before) labor's endorsement of firm-based training and, indeed, its acceptance of the clear primacy of firm-based over complementary classroom vocational instruction. The union official in charge of vocational training in the 1950s, Josef Leimig, was completely convinced of the value of firm-based training.[70] Like other union functionaries with responsibilities in this area, Leimig had earned his own credentials in the system and had a "traditional understanding" of the concept of a skilled vocation (*Beruf*).[71]

Labor's position on the value of firm-based training should not be taken for granted. A 1952 report submitted to the American High Commissioner on Germany had specifically criticized the German training system as overly grounded in an economic rather than an educational logic and noted that German business appeared to rely rather heavily on the cheap productive labor of apprentices.[72] However, far from picking up on such critiques, German unions if anything joined with industry representatives in a spirited defense of plant-based training and warned against vocational education becoming overly "bookish" (*Verschulung*).[73] Thus, rather than call for a complete overhaul of the country's training system, unions instead returned to demands they had first articulated in 1919, fixing their hopes on legislation to guarantee organized labor full parity codetermination rights within the system[74]—and while they waited and lobbied for overarching legislation on codetermination, the system of in-plant training under chamber auspices was simply rebuilt.

Organized labor did not become a full participant in the system until much later, in 1969, when the Social Democratic Party first joined the governing coalition. However, the new Vocational Training Law of that year (*Berufsbildungsgesetz*, BBiG) did not fundamentally shake up traditional training practices. The law brought training in industry and *Handwerk* under a single national framework and gave unions a stronger voice in the overarching regulatory functions surrounding the definition and elaboration of training regulations and occupational certifications. But, despite this and enhanced participation rights within the relevant employer chambers, much of the infrastructure at the level of the firm remained exactly the same. Since 1969, there has been ongoing skirmishing between unions and employers over the extent of labor participation and about financing arrangements. However, by the contemporary period, organized labor had become a full and fully engaged partner in administering the German vocational-training system and in some ways had developed into the staunchest defender of the system in the face of current difficulties. Labor's full cooperation today in administering and promoting plant-based training signals the completion of a long process of institutional conversion that transformed institutions originally designed (in the 1890s) to defeat organized labor into institutional pillars of a particular, and in some ways a particularly strong, variety of social partnership a hundred years later. This is perhaps a good point at which to return to some of the theoretical issues sketched out at the beginning of this chapter and to which the case of German vocational training seems well suited to speak.

Conclusions

A single case study of this sort cannot, of course, provide a rigorous test of competing theories of institutional reproduction and change. However, a study of the German vocational-training regime offers insights relevant to three broad debates in the literature on institutions concerning (1) institutional design, (2) institutional reproduction, and (3) institutional change. The conclusion deals with each of these points in turn.

Institutional Design and Institutional Effects

First, this case study speaks to theories of institutional design and underscores Robert Bates's cautionary note not to "confound the analysis of the role of institutions with a theory of their causes."[75] Looking at German vocational-training institutions from today's vantage point, analysts quite reasonably (and correctly) portray this system as part of a high-wage, high-quality production regime that reconciles strong unions with strong performance in export markets. However, as the history shows, this was not the obvious endpoint of a trajectory that could have been foreseen in the late nineteenth century. As Pierson notes, the point is not that institutions are not designed by purposive actors with particular interests; clearly they are.[76] The point, rather, is that "changes in the broader social environment and/or in the character of the actors themselves" (among other things) can, over time, produce a significant and unintended "gap" between the goals of the designers and the way institutions operate.[77]

Thus, against functionalist accounts that read the origins of institutions off their current functions,[78] a somewhat longer time frame is often necessary for us to see how institutions created for one set of purposes can be redirected to serve quite different ends. Alongside power-distributional accounts that stress how powerful actors design institutions to anchor their position,[79] we often need a longer time frame to see how institutions created by one coalition of interests can be "carried forward" on the shoulders of some other coalition entirely. And, beyond some cultural accounts that see institutions as reflecting shared cultural scripts,[80] a longer time frame may allow us to see more clearly how institutions can be constitutive and not just reflective of a particular social or cultural orientation. The point in each case is that the creation of an institution at one juncture can provoke significant shifts in the incentives, interests, and strategies of a range of actors—not just to conform but often in ways that inspire some further subsequent change.

Refuting accounts based on a "snapshot" view of institutions (Pierson) is often tricky because, if one were to take some slice of time out of the history I have just sketched out, one would find a system whose main features were broadly consistent with the expressed interests of the relevant and most powerful actors at the time. However, as Huber and Stephens have pointed out in another context, analyses based on such snapshots are likely to miss entirely the way in which past policy has shaped *who* the relevant actors are, *how* they define their interests, and *what strategies* are realistically available to them at any particular juncture.[81] In the case of German training, for example, the existence of a system for certifying skills in the handicraft sector was enormously important in causing skill-intensive industries to define and articulate their demands in a way that was consistent with the logic of a system not of their own making. This development was crucial to the defeat of an alternative (company-based) model of training that many prominent firms were actively pursuing in Germany in the late nineteenth and early twentieth centuries and that prevailed in many other countries. Even more striking is the impact of the handicraft system on the way that labor unions were constituted and especially the way in which they defined their interests with respect to skills and training. This leads me to a consideration of questions of institutional reproduction and change.

Institutional Reproduction

The case of German vocational-training institutions is also a good one for probing the limits of existing theories of institutional reproduction and change, for, as we have seen, core aspects of the system not only survived but sometimes experienced consolidation and reinforcement in the context of historic "breakpoints." Contrary to some accounts, it seems that political actors do not necessarily seize on these moments of relative "openness" to engage in creative experimentation but rather do just the opposite and cling (to the extent possible) to familiar institutional routines and organizational forms.

However, as we have also seen, institutional survival in the German case was not just a matter or inertia or even (more dynamically) increasing returns effects; rather, institutional survival required active political sponsorship, including assembling new coalitions to sustain these institutions as political and economic conditions changed. In fact, a central message of this chapter is that institutional reproduction is a much more problematic concept than is typically recognized.[82] "Inertia" and "stasis" are particularly misleading notions when it comes to explaining institutional stability, for what we find here is that, in order to survive, institutions can rarely just stand still. Their survival is guaranteed not by their "stickiness" but by their ongoing active adaptation to changes in the political and political-economic environment.[83]

The idea of conceptualizing institutional reproduction as a dynamic, not static, process is well developed in the literature on policy feedback.[84]

That literature has pointed to the ways in which in which the existence of institutions generates behaviors and strategies (within and beyond the boundaries of the institutions themselves) in ways that reinforce these institutions. For example, and as I have argued, the existence of the handi-craft system and the fact that social democratic unions organized large numbers of skilled workers certified under it stabilized that system in some ways—by encouraging labor to define its interests within the logic of the system (as opposed to against it). Employing Greif and Laitin's terms, this could be characterized as a situation in which the operation of these institutions produced behavioral effects that expanded the "quasi parame-ters" within which the institution was self-enforcing.[85]

However, saying that labor unions (or we could also make the argu-ment for the machine industry) came to frame their interests in relation to the existing system is not the same as saying that these groups were invested in those institutions *as originally constituted.* Here we leave the realm of positive feedback and most path-dependency arguments and enter the realm of institutional change. The question, in other words, becomes the extent to which the operation of these institutions themselves generate only positive feedback or whether these dynamics also generate contradictions or challenges that then complicate rather than contribute to the "*reliable* reproduction" of these arrangements.

Institutional Change

Thus, finally, the case of German vocational training sheds light on important sources and also modes of institutional change through cumu-lative, incremental adaptation, rather than breakdown and replacement (à la punctuated equilibrium). In terms of the sources of change, the present analysis underscores the insight of Clemens and others that actors "on the periphery" of a given set of institutions who are "aggrieved but not co-opted [can be] an important source of pressure for institutional change." In the present analysis, the most important initiators of change were pre-cisely those that were "outside" the vocational-training system as originally constituted (for the artisanal sector). This applies, above all, to skill-inten-sive industries (particularly the machine-building industry) and to orga-nized labor—both of whose strategies in some ways adapted to the logic of the existing system while in other ways forcing important changes in it.

The skill-intensive machine builders who despised the "unsystematic" training of the artisanal sector became obsessed with securing the right to certify skills, a right that the *Handwerk* sector monopolized and that these firms coveted. Through a process of what Schickler has called "institutional layering," they developed strategies and institutions *alongside* and in interaction with the preexisting artisanal system. As Schickler suggests, this kind of layering does not always push developments further along in the same direction (as in increasing returns arguments). In the case of Germany, such layering clearly altered the overall trajectory of vocational training, pulling it away from the decentralization and lack of systematic and uniform skill profiles characteristic of the *Handwerk* model and toward the high degree of standardization and uniformity that is now considered a hallmark and a defining feature of the system.

In the case of labor, we see a somewhat different mode of change, resulting in what we might call the institution's functional "conversion." Such a process can be set in motion by a shift in the environment that confronts actors with new problems that they address by using existing institutions in novel ways. Or, as in this case, it can be a consequence of the incorporation of new groups, previously on the margins, whose inclusion and participation in the institution's support coalition drives important changes in the functions these institutions serve or the role they perform. German unions' eventual full incorporation into the country's training system in effect turned it on its head, completing a process through which an originally deeply reactionary piece of legislation was transformed into a system that now reflects and also stabilizes labor's power in the political economy.

Neither of these modes of change—conversion or layering—sits well with the dominant punctuated-equilibrium model, because both of them combine elements of institutional innovation with institutional reproduction and because both of them capture change of a variety that is not abrupt and discontinuous but gradual though cumulatively transformative.[86] For both these same reasons, however, the modes of change documented here perhaps better reflect the more common way that institutions evolve in politics.

In sum, and taken as a whole, this analysis of German vocational-training institutions provides a powerful illustration of an alternative approach to institutional change. This new perspective is based less on a strong punctuated-equilibrium model that mostly looks for discontinuous change emanating from outside the institutions and relies instead on an analysis of changes in the political coalitions on which institutions themselves rest. Focusing attention on the coalitional base helps to explain why institutions are sometimes not as open to reconfiguration at historic "break points" as we might think. But, in addition, the political-coalitional approach elaborated here also suggests that, for institutions to survive major socioeconomic transformation (in the present case, industrialization, democratization, labor incorporation) or political disjuncture (regime change, conquest, occupation), the story of institutional reproduction will very likely be strongly laced with elements of adaptation and even transformation, as new or revised coalitions are mobilized to sustain them and carry them forward. In short, by tracking changes in the political coalitions on which institutions rest, this study illustrates the ways in which their form and functions can be gradually, cumulatively, incrementally, but ultimately radically, reconfigured over time.

NOTES

1. This chapter draws together material presented across several chapters of my book, Kathleen Thelen, *How Institutions Evolve: The Political Economy of Skills in Germany, Britain, the United States and Japan* (New York: Cambridge University Press, 2004). This material is reprinted here with the permission of Cambridge University Press. I wish to thank Peter Hall, whose comments on the book helped clarify my thinking at all stages.

2. Elisabeth S. Clemens and James M. Cook, "Politics and Institutionalism: Explaining Durability and Change," *Annual Review of Sociology* 25 (1999); Paul Pierson, *Politics in Time: History, Institutions, and Political Analysis* (Princeton: Princeton University Press, 2004); Avner Greif and David Laitin, "A Theory of Endogenous Institutional Change," *American Political Science Review* 98, no. 4 (2004).

3. Stephen D. Krasner, "Sovereignty: An Institutional Perspective," *Comparative Political Studies* 21, no. 1 (1988).

4. E. g., Ira Katznelson, "Periodization and Preferences: Reflections on Purposive Action in Comparative Historical Social Science," in *Comparative Historical Analysis in the Social Sciences,* ed. James Mahoney and Dietrich Rueschemeyer (New York: Cambridge University Press, 2003); Ann Swidler, "Culture in Action: Symbols and Strategies," *American Sociological Review* 51 (1986).

5. I owe this formulation to comments by Peter Hall.

6. There is a large literature by economists on these issues that I cannot go into here, but see Thelen, *How Institutions Evolve* for a discussion of these issues, as well as a full analysis of the German case with comparisons to Britain, the United States, and Japan.

7. Wolfgang Streeck, "Skills and the Limits of Neo-Liberalism," *Work, Employ-*

ment & Society 3 (1989); Wolfgang Streeck, "On the Institutional Conditions of Diversified Quality Production," in *Beyond Keynesianism,* ed. Egon Matzner and Wolfgang Streeck (Aldershot, UK: Edward Elgar, 1991); David Soskice, "Reconciling Markets and Institutions: The German Apprenticeship System," in *Training and the Private Sector: International Comparisons,* ed. Lisa M. Lynch (Chicago: University of Chicago Press, 1994); Peter A. Hall and David Soskice, eds., *Varieties of Capitalism: The Institutional Foundations of Comparative Advantage* (New York: Oxford University Press, 2001).

8. David Finegold and David Soskice, "The Failure of Training in Britain: Analysis and Prescription," *Oxford Review of Economic Policy* 4, no. 3 (1988).

9. John Gillingham, "The 'Deproletarization' of German Society: Vocational Training in the Third Reich," *Journal of Social History* 19 (1985).

10. Gerhard Lehmbruch, "The Rise and Change of Discourses on 'Embedded Capitalism' in Germany and Japan and Their Institutional Setting," in *The Origins of Nonliberal Capitalism: Germany and Japan,* ed. Wolfgang Streeck and Kozo Yamamura (Ithaca: Cornell University Press, 2001).

11. Paul Pierson, "When Effect Becomes Cause: Policy Feedback and Political Change," *World Politics* 45, no. 4 (1993); Greif and Laitin, "A Theory of Endogenous Institutional Change."

12. Eric Schickler, *Disjointed Pluralism: Institutional Innovation and the Development of the U.S. Congress* (Princeton: Princeton University Press, 2001).

13. But see Thelen, *How Institutions Evolve,* which does provide a comprehensive historical account of all of the events and developments that can only be sketched in broad brushstrokes here.

14. E. g., Pierson, "When Effect Becomes Cause."

15. The artisanate is actually a category that is explicitly defined in German law, but for present purposes it is important just to realize that artisans are small producers, self-employed, also often employers of others, and thus very different from "labor" or "organized labor," which constitutes another major actor in this case.

16. See, for example, Shulamit Volkov, *The Rise of Popular Antimodernism in Germany: The Urban Master Artisans, 1873–1896* (Princeton: Princeton University Press, 1978), ch. 7; and Heinrich August Winkler, "Der Rückversicherte Mittelstand: Die Interessenverbände Von Handwerk Und Kleinhandel Im Deutschen Kaiserreich," in *Zur Soziologischen Theorie Und Analyse Des 19. Jahrhunderts,* ed. Walter Rüegg and Otto Neuloh (Göttingen: Vandenhoeck and Ruprecht, 1971).

17. Heinrich Abel, *Das Berufsproblem Im Gewerblichen Ausbildungs- Und Schulwesen Deutschlands (Brd)* (Braunschweig, D: Georg Westermann Verlag, 1963), 35; Edwin G. Cooley, "Vocational Education in Europe" (Chicago: Report to the Commercial Club of Chicago, 1912), ch. 3; Jürgen Schriewer, "Intermediäre Instanzen, Selbstverwaltung Und Berufliche Ausbildungsstrukturen Im Historischen Vergleich," *Zeitschrift für Pädagogie* 32, no. 1 (1986): 83.

18. Hal Hansen, "Caps and Gowns," Ph.D. dissertation, University of Wisconsin-Madison, 1997, 329–330.

19. Ernst Hoffmann, *Zur Geschichte Der Berufsausbildung in Deutschland* (Bielefeld: W. Bertelsmann, 1962), 11–12; Wolfgang Muth, *Berufsausbildung in Der Weimarer Republik*, ed. Hans Pohl and Wilhelm Treue, vol. 41, *Zeitschrift Für Unternehmensgeschichte* (Stuttgart: Franz Steiner, 1985), 21; Heinrich Abel, "Zur Entwicklung Und Problematik Der Berufserziehung: Ein Bericht Über Die Zentralstelle Zur Erforschung Und Förderung Der Berufserziehung," in *Berufserziehung Und Beruflicher Bildungsweg*, ed. Karlwilhelm Stratmann (Georg Westermann Verlag, 1962), 35–36; Theo Wolsing, *Untersuchungen Zur Berufsausbildung Im Dritten Reich* (Kastellaun, D: A. Henn, 1977), 400–402.

20. See especially Hansen, "Caps and Gowns," 380–385.

21. William Knox, "British Apprenticeship, 1800–1914," Ph.D. dissertation, Edinburgh University, 1980; Michael J. Childs, "Boy Labour in Late Victorian and Edwardian England and the Remaking of the Working Class," *Journal of Social History* 23, no. 4 (1990).

22. Gertrud Tollkühn, *Die Planmäßige Ausbildung Des Gewerblichen Fabriklehrlings in Der Metall- Und Holzverarbeitenden Industrien* (Jena: D: Gustav Fischer, 1926), 13; see also Hansen, "Caps and Gowns," 310.; Gerhard Adelmann, "Die Berufliche Aus- Und Weiterbildung in Der Deutschen Wirtschaft 1871–1918," in *Berufliche Aus- Und Weiterbildung in Der Deutschen Wirtschaft Seit Dem 19. Jahrhundert*, ed. Hans Pohl (Wiesbaden: Franz Steiner Verlag, 1979), 12–13; Albert Kopsch, "Die Planmäbige Lehrlingserziehung in Der Industrie Und Die Gewerkschaften" (Philipps-Universität zu Marburg, 1928), 18–19.

23. Willy Albrecht, *Fachverein, Berufsgewerkschaft, Zentralverband: Organisationsprobleme Der Deutschen Gewerkschaften 1870–1890* (Bonn: Neue Gesellschaft, 1982).

24. Elisabeth Domansky-Davidsohn, "Arbeitskämpfe Und Arbeitskampfstrategien Des Deutschen Metallarbeiterverbandes, 1891–1914," Ph.D. dissertation, Ruhr-Universität, 1981, 32.

25. Ibid., ch. 1; James Mosher, "Labor Power and Wage Equality: The Politics of Supply-Side Equality" (University of Wisconsin-Madison, 2001), 291.

26. As we will see, some large industrial firms were also engaged in training. However, typically these firms were training workers that they intended to continue to employ. This was very different from the handicraft sector, where small firms mostly had no intention of keeping their apprentices after they achieved journeyman status.

27. Jürgen Kocka, "Problems of Working-Class Formation in Germany: The Early Years, 1800–1875," in *Working-Class Formation: Nineteenth-Century Patterns in Western Europe and the United States*, ed. Ira Katznelson and Aristide R. Zolberg (Princeton: Princeton University Press, 1986), 323–344; Friedrich Lenger,

Sozialgeschichte Der Deutschen Handwerker Seit 1800 (Frankfurt/M: Suhrkamp, 1988), 160–162; Adelmann, "Die Berufliche Aus- Und Weiterbildung in Der Deutschen Wirtschaft 1871–1918," 19.

28. Klaus Schönhoven, "Gewerkschaftliches Organisationsverhalten Im Wilhelminischen Deutschland," in *Arbeiter Im Industrialisierungsprozeß*, ed. Werner Conze and Ulrich Engelhardt (Stuttgart, D: Klett-Cotta, 1979), 411.

29. Domansky-Davidsohn, "Arbeitskämpfe Und Arbeitskampfstrategien Des Deutschen Metallarbeiterverbandes, 1891–1914," 30.

30. Hoffmann, *Zur Geschichte Der Berufsausbildung in Deutschland*, 95–97; Friedhelm Schütte, *Berufserziehung Zwischen Revolution Und Nationalsozialismus* (Weinheim: Deutscher Studien, 1992), 31–33; Roland Ebert, *Zur Entstehung Der Kategorie Facharbeiter Als Problem Der Erziehungswissenschaft* (Bielefeld: Kleine, 1984), 262.

31. Abel, *Das Berufsproblem Im Gewerblichen Ausbildungs- Und Schulwesen Deutschlands (Brd)*, 48.

32. M. E. Sadler, "Compulsory Attendance at Continuation Schools in Germany," in *Continuation Schools in England and Elsewhere*, ed. M. E. Sadler (Manchester: University of Manchester Press, 1908); Cooley, "Vocational Education in Europe."

33. Tollkühn, *Die Planmäßige Ausbildung Des Gewerblichen Fabriklehrlings in Der Metall- Und Holzverarbeitenden Industrien*, 4–5; Marhild von Behr, *Die Entstehung Der Industriellen Lehrwerkstatt* (Frankfurt/M: Campus, 1981), 44–45. In 1907, 46.5 percent of all youth in training were still in the smallest artisanal workshops (up to five workers) (Karin Wagner, "The German Apprenticeship System under Strain," in *The German Skills Machine: Sustaining Comparative Advantage in a Global Economy*, ed. Pepper D. Culpepper and David Finegold [New York: Berghahn Books, 1999], 23).

34. Peter Dehen, *Die Deutschen Industriewerkschulen* (München: A. Huber, 1928), 27–23; Tollkühn, *Die Planmäßige Ausbildung Des Gewerblichen Fabriklehrlings in Der Metall- Und Holzverarbeitenden Industrien*, 14–16; von Behr, *Die Entstehung Der Industriellen Lehrwerkstatt*, 60–61.

35. Von Behr, *Die Entstehung Der Industriellen Lehrwerkstatt*; Ekkehard Eichberg, *Die Lehrwerkstatt Im Industriebetrieb* (Weinheim/Bergstr.: Julius Beltz, 1965).

36. Dehen, *Die Deutschen Industriewerkschulen*, 15–16, 75–77.

37. Obviously, such an alternative training system supports a form of "social partnership" very different from and more employer-centered than the German version.

38. See especially Hansen, "Caps and Gowns", 380–391, on the importance of certification.

39. Ibid., 512; Günter Pätzold, "Berufsbildung: Handwerkliche, Industrielle Und Schulische Berufserziehung," in *Handbuch Der Deutschen Bildungsgeschichte. Die*

Weimarer Republik Und Die Nationalsozialistische Diktatur, ed. Dieter Langewi- esche and Heinz-Elmar Tenorth (München: C. H. Beck, 1989), 275; Schütte, *Beruf- serziehung Zwischen Revolution Und Nationalsozialismus,* 84.

40. Hansen, "Caps and Gowns," 510–511.

41. Ibid., 273–274; Gottlieb Matthias Lippart, "Einleitender Bericht Über Zukünftige Lehrlingsausbildung in Der Mechanischen Industrie," *Abhandlungen und Berichte über technisches Schulwesen* (1919), 7.

42. Lippart, "Einleitender Bericht Über Zukünftige Lehrlingsausbildung in Der Mechanischen Industrie," 7; R. Botsch, *Lehrlingsausbildung Und Gesellenprüfung in Der Metallverarbeitenden Industrie* (Berlin: Julius Beltz, 1933), 7–8; Fürer, "Förderung Der Facharbeiter—Ausbildung Durch Industrieverbände," *Der Arbeit- geber: Zeitschrift der Vereinigung der Deutschen Arbeitgeberverbände* (1927), 32–33; Fr. Frölich, "Die Gesellenprufung Der Industrielehrlinge," in *Abhandlungen Und Berichte Über Technisches Schulwesen,* ed. DATSCH (Berlin: DATSCH, 1919), 109–110; Frida Mack, "Fortschritte in Der Lehrlingsausbildung in Handwerk Und Industrie" (Ruprecht-Karls-Universität Heidelberg, 1927), 105–107. The pages of *Technische Erziehung* (Technical Education), a trade magazine directed toward training-intensive industries, contains accounts from this period of the problems that *Handwerk*-dominated certification posed for industry.

43. Mosher, "Labor Power and Wage Equality: The Politics of Supply-Side Equality", 256–258. Wage differentials recovered somewhat after 1922 but never again reached prewar levels.

44. For a general explanation of the economic logic see Daron Acemoglu and Jörn-Steffen Pischke, "Why Do Firms Train? Theory and Evidence," *Quarterly Journal of Economics* 113, no. 1 (1998), or Karl Ove Moene and Michael Wallerstein, "How Social Democracy Worked: Labor Market Institutions," *Politics & Society* 23, no. 2 (1995). For comparisons to other countries see Thelen, *How Institutions Evolve.*

45. Schütte, *Berufserziehung Zwischen Revolution Und Nationalsozialismus,* 131.

46. Ibid., 132.

47. Ibid., 131.

48. Gerald Feldman and Ulrich Nocken, "Trade Associations and Economic Power: Interest Group Development in the German Iron and Steel and Machine Building Industries, 1900–1933," *Business History Review* XLIX, no. 4 (1975): 422.

49. Muth, *Berufsausbildung in Der Weimarer Republik,* 348–352.

50. DATSCH, *Abhandlungen* (1910), 6.

51. Hella Schmedes, *Das Lehrlingswesen in Der Deutschen Eisen- Und Stahlin- dustrie* (Muenster: Verlag August Baader, 1931), 12; Tollkühn, *Die Planmäßige Aus- bildung Des Gewerblichen Fabriklehrlings in Der Metall- Und Holzverarbeitenden Industrien,* 40.

52. Hansen, "Caps and Gowns," 283.

53. Ibid., 607; Wolsing, *Untersuchungen Zur Berufsausbildung Im Dritten Reich,* 160; Michael Schneider, *Unterm Hakenkreuz: Arbeiter Und Arbeiterbewegung 1933 Bis 1939* (Bonn: Verlag J. H. W. Dietz, 1999), 370.

54. Pätzold, "Berufsbildung: Handwerkliche, Industrielle Und Schulische Berufserziehung," 276; Wolf-Dietrich Greinert, *The "German System" of Vocational Education: History, Organization, Prospects,* ed. Deutsche Gesellschaft für Technische Zusammenarbeit, vol. Band 6, *Studien Zur Vergleichenden Berufspädagogik* (Baden-Baden: Nomos Verlagsgesellschaft, 1994), 45.

55. Whereas in 1933 about 45 percent of industrial workers were skilled, after 1938 almost all (90 percent) of boys leaving grammar school were entering into apprenticeship training (Gillingham, "The "Deproletarization" of German Society: Vocational Training in the Third Reich," 428). The number of training workshops in place at the firm level increased between 1933 and 1940 from 167 to 3,304 (Martin Kipp and Gisela Miller-Kipp, *Erkundungen Im Halbdunkel: Fünfzehn Studien Zur Berufserziehung Und Pädagogik Im Nationalsozialistischen Deutschland* [Kassel, D: Gesamthochschul-Bibliothek, 1990], 34). Whereas in 1933 only 16,222 workers had received training in such workshops, the number rose to 244,250 by 1940 (Pätzold, "Berufsbildung: Handwerkliche, Industrielle Und Schulische Berufserziehung," 278).

56. Kipp and Miller-Kipp, *Erkundungen Im Halbdunkel: Fünfzehn Studien Zur Berufserziehung Und Pädagogik Im Nationalsozialistischen Deutschland,* 229; Joachim Münch, *Vocational Training in the Federal Republic of Germany,* 3rd ed. (Berlin: European Centre for the Development of Vocational Training, 1991), 34; Pätzold, "Berufsbildung: Handwerkliche, Industrielle Und Schulische Berufserziehung," 274–275; Abel, *Das Berufsproblem Im Gewerblichen Ausbildungs- Und Schulwesen Deutschlands (Brd),* 58–59; Karlwilhelm Stratmann and Manfred Schlösser, *Das Duale System Der Berufsbildung: Eine Historische Analyse Seiner Reformdebatten* (Frankfurt/Main: Verlag der Gesellschaft zur Förderung arbeitsorientierter Forschung und Bildung, 1990), 47–49.

57. DATSCH was also given greater responsibility for creating stronger links between the in-plant and school-based components of vocational training (Pätzold, "Berufsbildung: Handwerkliche, Industrielle Und Schulische Berufserziehung," 274). The trade school curricula were specifically organized around the trade profiles that DATSCH had worked out for in-plant training (Martin Kipp, "Perfektionierung Der Industriellen Berufsausbildung Im Dritten Reich," in *Erkundungen Im Halbdunkel: Fünfzehn Studien Zur Berufserziehung Und Pädagogik Im Nationalsozialistischen Deutschland,* ed. Martin Kipp and Gisela Miller-Kipp [Kassel, D: Gesamthochschul-Bibliothek, 1990], 228).

58. Pätzold, "Berufsbildung: Handwerkliche, Industrielle Und Schulische Berufserziehung," 278; Rolf Seubert, *Berufserziehung Und Nationalsozialismus* (Weinheim: Beltz, 1977), chs. 10, 11.

59. See, especially, Matthias Frese, *Betriebspolitik Im "Dritten Reich": Deutsche*

Arbeitsfront, Unternehmer Und Staatsbürokratie in Der Westdeutschen Grossindustrie 1933–1939 (Paderborn: Ferdinand Schöningh, 1991), 251–332; Wolsing, *Untersuchungen Zur Berufsausbildung Im Dritten Reich,* 234–396.

60. Frese, *Betriebspolitik Im "Dritten Reich": Deutsche Arbeitsfront, Unternehmer Und Staatsbürokratie in Der Westdeutschen Grossindustrie 1933–1939,* 272.

61. On the conflicts (not just on vocational training) that raged between the Economics Ministry (especially under Hjalmar Schacht) and DAF under Robert Ley, see especially ibid.; also Wolsing, *Untersuchungen Zur Berufsausbildung Im Dritten Reich.*

62. Bundesverband der Deutschen Industrie (BDI), "Der Präsident: An Die Industriellen Unternehmer Und Betriebsleiter," in *Quellen Und Dokumente Zur Geschichte Der Berufsbildung in Deutschland,* ed. Günter Pätzold (Köln: Böhlau Verlag, 1950); Reinhard Crusius, *Berufsbildungs- Und Jugendpolitik Der Gewerkschaft: Struktur Und Verlauf Bei Dgb Und Einigen Einzelgewerkschaften 1945–1981* (Frankfurt: Campus Verlag, 1982), 90–91; Günter Pätzold, ed., *Quellen Und Dokumente Zur Betrieblichen Berufsbildung* (Cologne: Böhlau Verlag, 1991), 2; Theodor Rohlfing, "Der Handwerkliche Lehrvertrag Und Das Verfahren in Lehrlingsstreitigkeiten" (Bremen-Horn: Industrie- und Handeslverlag Walter Dorn GMBH, 1949), 3–4.

63. Bundesministerium für Arbeit, ed., *Die Arbeiter Und Angestellten Nach Beruf Und Alter Sowie Die Lehrlingshaltung in Der Bundesrepublik Deutschland Am 31. Oktober 1950. Ergebnisse Einer Sondererhebung Der Arbeitsämter* (Bonn: Bundesministerium für Arbeit [Statistik], 1950), 30.

64. Abel, "Zur Entwicklung Und Problematik Der Berufserziehung: Ein Bericht Über Die Zentralstelle Zur Erforschung Und Förderung Der Berufserziehung," 32; Crusius, *Berufsbildungs- Und Jugendpolitik Der Gewerkschaft: Struktur Und Verlauf Bei Dgb Und Einigen Einzelgewerkschaften 1945–1981,* 89–91.

65. Gary Herrigel, "American Occupation, Market Order, and Democracy: Reconfiguring the Steel Industry in Japan and Germany after the Second World War," in *Americanization and Its Limits: Reworking U.S. Technology and Management in Post-War Europe and Japan,* ed. Jonathan Zeitlin and Gary Herrigel (New York: Oxford University Press, 2000), 377.

66. Adolf Kieslinger, "Berufsausbildung Am Scheideweg," in *Quellen Und Dokumente,* ed. Günter Pätzold (Cologne: Böhlau Verlag, 1950), 146.

67. The idea being that the state could intervene only when business and its self-government institutions were not fulfilling their tasks satisfactorily (Antonius Lipsmeier, "Berufsbildung," in *Handbuch Der Deutschen Bildungsgeschichte,* ed. Christoph Führ and Carl-Ludwig Furck [München: C. H. Beck, 1998], 450).

68. See especially Adolf Kieslinger, *20 Jahre Berufsausbildung in Der Bundesrepublik Deutschland, 1945–1965* (Bielefeld: W. Bertelsmann Verlag, 1966), 57–61; also Martin Baethge, *Ausbildung Und Herrschaft: Unternehmerinteressen in Der Bildungspolitik* (Frankfurt/M: Europäische Verlagsanstalt, 1970), 179–183.

69. Werner Crusius, "Kritik Der Berufsbildungsgesetzes," in *Zur Situation Der Berufsbildung,* ed. Deutscher Gewerkschaftsbund (Düsseldorf: DGB, 1970), 115, 27; Baethge, *Ausbildung Und Herrschaft: Unternehmerinteressen in Der Bildungspolitik,* 98–100.

70. Stratmann and Schlösser, *Das Duale System Der Berufsbildung: Eine Historische Analyse Seiner Reformdebatten,* 61–62.

71. Crusius, *Berufsbildungs- Und Jugendpolitik Der Gewerkschaft: Struktur Und Verlauf Bei Dgb Und Einigen Einzelgewerkschaften 1945–1981,* 89.

72. Stratmann and Schlösser, *Das Duale System Der Berufsbildung: Eine Historische Analyse Seiner Reformdebatten,* 64; George W. Ware, "Vocational Education and Apprenticeship Training in Germany" (Office of the U.S. High Commissioner for Germany, Office of Public Affairs, Division of Cultural Affairs, 1952), 45–47.

73. Stratmann and Schlösser, *Das Duale System Der Berufsbildung: Eine Historische Analyse Seiner Reformdebatten,* ch. 4; Heinrich Abel, *Berufserziehung Und Beruflicher Bildungsweg,* ed. Karlwilhelm Stratmann (Braunschweig: Georg Westermann Verlag, 1968), 21–23, 33; Baethge, *Ausbildung Und Herrschaft: Unternehmerinteressen in Der Bildungspolitik,* 170–173; Crusius, *Berufsbildungs- Und Jugendpolitik Der Gewerkschaft: Struktur Und Verlauf Bei Dgb Und Einigen Einzelgewerkschaften 1945–1981,* 91–93. Of course, the unions were calling for changes, but their demands for a vocational-training law and increased state oversight were pitched at the level of governance and regulation, not the core framework of plant-based training itself.

74. Crusius, *Berufsbildungs- Und Jugendpolitik Der Gewerkschaft: Struktur Und Verlauf Bei Dgb Und Einigen Einzelgewerkschaften 1945–1981,* 90.

75. Robert H. Bates, "Contra Contractarianism: Some Reflections on the New Institutionalism," *Politics & Society* 16, no. 2 (1988); Jack Knight, "Explaining the Rise of Neo-Liberalism: The Mechanisms of Institutional Change," in *The Rise of Neoliberalism and Institutional Analysis,* ed. John Campbell and Ove Pedersen (Princeton: Princeton University Press, 2001).

76. Although, as Schickler, Palier, Pierson, and others have pointed out, institutions also often represent compromises among groups with very different and even contradictory interests, too.

77. Pierson, *Politics in Time: History, Institutions, and Political Analysis,* 108–109.

78. E. g., Barry Weingast, "Rational-Choice Institutionalism," in *Political Science: The State of the Discipline,* ed. Ira Katznelson and Helen Milner (New York: Norton, 2002).

79. E. g., Moe, this volume.

80. E. g., J. W. Meyer and B. Rowan, "Institutionalized Organizations: Formal Structure as Myth and Ceremony," in *The New Institutionalism in Organizational Analysis,* ed. Walter W. Powell and P. DiMaggio (Chicago: University of Chicago Press, 1991).

81. Evelyne Huber and John D. Stephens, *Development and Crisis of the Welfare States: Parties and Policies in Global Markets* (Chicago: University of Chicago Press, 2001), 33; Jacob Hacker and Paul Pierson, "Business Power and Social Policy," *Politics & Society* 30, no. 2 (2002).

82. Kathleen Thelen, "Historical Institutionalism in Comparative Politics," *The Annual Review of Political Science* 2 (1999).

83. The reverse is true, as well. That is, institutions that are not updated and fitted to changes in the political and market environment can be subject to a process of erosion through what Jacob Hacker has called "drift" (Jacob Hacker, "Policy Drift: The Hidden Politics of Us Welfare State Retrenchment," in *Beyond Continuity: Institutional Change in Advanced Political Economies,* ed. Wolfgang Streeck and Kathleen Thelen [Oxford: Oxford University Press, 2005]). I don't have space to develop the point here, but it appears that the German vocational-training system is currently in just such a state of drift. What we now see is that, after surviving several massive historic breaks, the foundations of the system are being undermined through gradual long-term processes that affect the overall structure of the economy, which has diminished employers' interest in this system and compromised their capacity and willingness to collectively defend it.

84. E. g., Pierson, this volume.

85. Greif and Laitin, "A Theory of Endogenous Institutional Change."

86. For elaboration, see also Wolfgang Streeck and Kathleen Thelen, eds., *Beyond Continuity: Institutional Change in Advanced Political Economies* (Oxford: Oxford University Press, 2005), especially ch. 1.

REFERENCES

Abel, Heinrich. *Berufserziehung Und Beruflicher Bildungsweg.* Edited by Karlwilhelm Stratmann. Braunschweig: Georg Westermann Verlag, 1968.

———. *Das Berufsproblem Im Gewerblichen Ausbildungs- Und Schulwesen Deutschlands (Brd).* Braunschweig, D: Georg Westermann Verlag, 1963.

———. "Zur Entwicklung Und Problematik Der Berufserziehung: Ein Bericht Über Die Zentralstelle Zur Erforschung Und Förderung Der Berufserziehung." In *Berufserziehung Und Beruflicher Bildungsweg,* edited by Karlwilhelm Stratmann, 517–539: Georg Westermann Verlag, 1962.

Acemoglu, Daron, and Jörn-Steffen Pischke. "Why Do Firms Train? Theory and Evidence." *Quarterly Journal of Economics* 113, no. 1 (1998): 79–119.

Adelmann, Gerhard. "Die Berufliche Aus- Und Weiterbildung in Der Deutschen Wirtschaft 1871–1918." In *Berufliche Aus- Und Weiterbildung in Der Deutschen Wirtschaft Seit Dem 19. Jahrhundert,* edited by Hans Pohl, 9–52. Wiesbaden: Franz Steiner Verlag, 1979.

Albrecht, Willy. *Fachverein, Berufsgewerkschaft, Zentralverband: Organisationsprobleme Der Deutschen Gewerkschaften 1870–1890*. Bonn: Neue Gesellschaft, 1982.

Baethge, Martin. *Ausbildung Und Herrschaft: Unternehmerinteressen in Der Bildungspolitik*. Frankfurt/M: Europäische Verlagsanstalt, 1970.

Bates, Robert H. "Contra Contractarianism: Some Reflections on the New Institutionalism." *Politics & Society* 16, no. 2 (1988): 387–401.

Bundesverband der Deutschen Industrie (BDI). "Der Präsident: An Die Industriellen Unternehmer Und Betriebsleiter." In *Quellen Und Dokumente Zur Geschichte Der Berufsbildung in Deutschland*, edited by Günter Pätzold, 144–145. Köln: Böhlau Verlag, 1950.

Botsch, R. *Lehrlingsausbildung Und Gesellenprüfung in Der Metallverarbeitenden Industrie*. Berlin: Julius Beltz, 1933.

Bundesministerium für Arbeit, ed. *Die Arbeiter Und Angestellten Nach Beruf Und Alter Sowie Die Lehrlingshaltung in Der Bundesrepublik Deutschland Am 31. Oktober 1950. Ergebnisse Einer Sondererhebung Der Arbeitsämter*. Bonn: Bundesministerium für Arbeit (Statistik), 1950.

Childs, Michael J. "Boy Labour in Late Victorian and Edwardian England and the Remaking of the Working Class." *Journal of Social History* 23, no. 4 (1990): 783–802.

Clemens, Elisabeth S., and James M. Cook. "Politics and Institutionalism: Explaining Durability and Change." *Annual Review of Sociology* 25 (1999): 441–466.

Cooley, Edwin G. "Vocational Education in Europe." Chicago: Commercial Club of Chicago, 1912.

Crusius, Reinhard. *Berufsbildungs- Und Jugendpolitik Der Gewerkschaft: Struktur Und Verlauf Bei Dgb Und Einigen Einzelgewerkschaften 1945–1981*. Frankfurt: Campus Verlag, 1982.

Crusius, Werner. "Kritik Der Berufsbildungsgesetzes." In *Zur Situation Der Berufsbildung*, edited by Deutscher Gewerkschaftsbund. Düsseldorf: DGB, 1970.

DATSCH. *Abhandlungen*, 1910.

Dehen, Peter. *Die Deutschen Industriewerkschulen*. München: A. Huber, 1928.

Domansky-Davidsohn, Elisabeth. "Arbeitskämpfe Und Arbeitskampfstrategien Des Deutschen Metallarbeiterverbandes, 1891–1914." Ph.D. dissertation, Ruhr-Universität, 1981.

Ebert, Roland. *Zur Entstehung Der Kategorie Facharbeiter Als Problem Der Erziehungswissenschaft*. Bielefeld: Kleine, 1984.

Eichberg, Ekkehard. *Die Lehrwerkstatt Im Industriebetrieb*. Weinheim/ Bergstr.: Julius Beltz, 1965.

Feldman, Gerald, and Ulrich Nocken. "Trade Associations and Economic Power: Interest Group Development in the German Iron and Steel and Machine Building Industries, 1900–1933." *Business History Review* XLIX, no. 4 (1975): 413–445.

Finegold, David, and David Soskice. "The Failure of Training in Britain: Analysis and Prescription." *Oxford Review of Economic Policy* 4, no. 3 (1988): 21–53.

Frese, Matthias. *Betriebspolitik Im "Dritten Reich": Deutsche Arbeitsfront, Unternehmer Und Staatsbürokratie in Der Westdeutschen Grossindustrie 1933–1939*. Paderborn: Ferdinand Schöningh, 1991.

Frölich, Fr. "Die Gesellenprufung Der Industrielehrlinge." In *Abhandlungen Und Berichte Über Technisches Schulwesen*, edited by DATSCH, 108–112. Berlin: DATSCH, 1919.

Fürer. "Förderung Der Facharbeiter—Ausbildung Durch Industrieverbände." *Der Arbeitgeber: Zeitschrift der Vereinigung der Deutschen Arbeitgeberverbände* (1927).

Gillingham, John. "The 'Deproletarization' of German Society: Vocational Training in the Third Reich." *Journal of Social History* 19 (1985): 423–432.

Greif, Avner, and David Laitin. "A Theory of Endogenous Institutional Change." *American Political Science Review* 98, no. 4 (2004): 633–652.

Greinert, Wolf-Dietrich. *The "German System" of Vocational Education: History, Organization, Prospects*. Edited by Deutsche Gesellschaft für Technische Zusammenarbeit. Vol. Band 6, *Studien Zur Vergleichenden Berufspädagogik*. Baden-Baden: Nomos Verlagsgesellschaft, 1994.

Hacker, Jacob. "Policy Drift: The Hidden Politics of Us Welfare State Retrenchment." In *Beyond Continuity: Institutional Change in Advanced Political Economies*, edited by Wolfgang Streeck and Kathleen Thelen, 40–82. Oxford: Oxford University Press, 2005.

Hacker, Jacob, and Paul Pierson. "Business Power and Social Policy." *Politics & Society* 30, no. 2 (2002): 277–325.

Hall, Peter A., and David Soskice, eds. *Varieties of Capitalism: The Institutional Foundations of Comparative Advantage*. New York: Oxford University Press, 2001.

Hansen, Hal. "Caps and Gowns." Ph.D. dissertation, University of Wisconsin-Madison, 1997.

Herrigel, Gary. "American Occupation, Market Order, and Democracy: Reconfiguring the Steel Industry in Japan and Germany after the Second World War." In *Americanization and Its Limits: Reworking U.S. Technology and Management in Post-War Europe and Japan*, edited by Jonathan Zeitlin and Gary Herrigel, 340–399. New York: Oxford University Press, 2000.

Hoffmann, Ernst. *Zur Geschichte Der Berufsausbildung in Deutschland*. Bielefeld: W. Bertelsmann, 1962.

Huber, Evelyne, and John D. Stephens. *Development and Crisis of the Welfare States: Parties and Policies in Global Markets*. Chicago: University of Chicago Press, 2001.

Katznelson, Ira. "Periodization and Preferences: Reflections on Purposive Action in Comparative Historical Social Science." In *Comparative Historical Analysis in the Social Sciences*, edited by James Mahoney and Dietrich Rueschemeyer, 270–304. New York: Cambridge University Press, 2003.

Kieslinger, Adolf. *20 Jahre Berufsausbildung in Der Bundesrepublik Deutschland, 1945–1965.* Bielefeld: W. Bertelsmann Verlag, 1966.

———. "Berufsausbildung Am Scheideweg." In *Quellen Und Dokumente,* edited by Günter Pätzold, 146–148. Cologne: Böhlau Verlag, 1950.

Kipp, Martin. "Perfektionierung Der Industriellen Berufsausbildung Im Dritten Reich." In *Erkundungen Im Halbdunkel: Fünfzehn Studien Zur Berufserziehung Und Pädagogik Im Nationalsozialistischen Deutschland,* edited by Martin Kipp and Gisela Miller-Kipp, 218–271. Kassel, D: Gesamthochschul-Bibliothek, 1990.

Kipp, Martin, and Gisela Miller-Kipp. *Erkundungen Im Halbdunkel: Fünfzehn Studien Zur Berufserziehung Und Pädagogik Im Nationalsozialistischen Deutschland.* Kassel, D: Gesamthochschul-Bibliothek, 1990.

Knight, Jack. "Explaining the Rise of Neo-Liberalism: The Mechanisms of Institutional Change." In *The Rise of Neoliberalism and Institutional Analysis,* edited by John Campbell and Ove Pedersen, 27–50. Princeton: Princeton University Press, 2001.

Knox, William. "British Apprenticeship, 1800–1914." Ph.D. dissertation, Edinburgh University, 1980.

Kocka, Jürgen. "Problems of Working-Class Formation in Germany: The Early Years, 1800–1875." In *Working-Class Formation: Nineteenth-Century Patterns in Western Europe and the United States,* edited by Ira Katznelson and Aristide R. Zolberg. Princeton: Princeton University Press, 1986.

Kopsch, Albert. "Die Planmäbige Lehrlingserziehung in Der Industrie Und Die Gewerkschaften." Philipps-Universität zu Marburg, 1928.

Krasner, Stephen D. "Sovereignty: An Institutional Perspective." *Comparative Political Studies* 21, no. 1 (1988): 66–94.

Lehmbruch, Gerhard. "The Rise and Change of Discourses on 'Embedded Capitalism' in Germany and Japan and Their Institutional Setting." In *The Origins of Nonliberal Capitalism: Germany and Japan,* edited by Wolfgang Streeck and Kozo Yamamura. Ithaca: Cornell University Press, 2001.

Lenger, Friedrich. *Sozialgeschichte Der Deutschen Handwerker Seit 1800.* Frankfurt/M: Suhrkamp, 1988.

Lippart, Gottlieb Matthias. "Einleitender Bericht Über Zukünftige Lehrlingsausbildung in Der Mechanischen Industrie." *Abhandlungen und Berichte über technisches Schulwesen* (1919): 1–10.

Lipsmeier, Antonius. "Berufsbildung." In *Handbuch Der Deutschen Bildungsgeschichte,* edited by Christoph Führ and Carl-Ludwig Furck, 447–489. München: C. H. Beck, 1998.

Mack, Frida. "Fortschritte in Der Lehrlingsausbildung in Handwerk Und Industrie." Ruprecht-Karls-Universität Heidelberg, 1927.

Meyer, J. W. , and B. Rowan. "Institutionalized Organizations: Formal Structure as Myth and Ceremony." In *The New Institutionalism in Organizational Analysis,* edited by Walter W. Powell and P. DiMaggio, 41–62. Chicago: University of Chicago Press, 1991.

Moene, Karl Ove, and Michael Wallerstein. "How Social Democracy Worked: Labor Market Institutions." *Politics & Society* 23, no. 2 (1995): 185–211.

Mosher, James. "Labor Power and Wage Equality: The Politics of Supply-Side Equality." University of Wisconsin-Madison, 2001.

Münch, Joachim. *Vocational Training in the Federal Republic of Germany*, 3rd ed. Berlin: European Centre for the Development of Vocational Training, 1991.

Muth, Wolfgang. *Berufsausbildung in Der Weimarer Republik*. Edited by Hans Pohl and Wilhelm Treue. Vol. 41, *Zeitschrift Für Unternehmensgeschichte*. Stuttgart: Franz Steiner, 1985.

Pätzold, Günter. "Berufsbildung: Handwerkliche, Industrielle Und Schulische Berufserziehung." In *Handbuch Der Deutschen Bildungsgeschichte. Die Weimarer Republik Und Die Nationalsozialistische Diktatur*, edited by Dieter Langewiesche and Heinz-Elmar Tenorth, 259–288. München: C. H. Beck, 1989.

———, ed. *Quellen Und Dokumente Zur Betrieblichen Berufsbildung*. Cologne: Böhlau Verlag, 1991.

Pierson, Paul. *Politics in Time: History, Institutions, and Political Analysis*. Princeton: Princeton University Press, 2004.

———. "When Effect Becomes Cause: Policy Feedback and Political Change." *World Politics* 45, no. 4 (1993): 595–628.

Rohlfing, Theodor. "Der Handwerkliche Lehrvertrag Und Das Verfahren in Lehrlingsstreitigkeiten." 104. Bremen-Horn: Industrie- und Handeslverlag Walter Dorn GMBH, 1949.

Sadler, M. E. "Compulsory Attendance at Continuation Schools in Germany." In *Continuation Schools in England and Elsewhere*, edited by M. E. Sadler, 513–534. Manchester: University of Manchester Press, 1908.

Schickler, Eric. *Disjointed Pluralism: Institutional Innovation and the Development of the U.S. Congress*. Princeton: Princeton University Press, 2001.

Schmedes, Hella. *Das Lehrlingswesen in Der Deutschen Eisen- Und Stahlindustrie*. Muenster: Verlag August Baader, 1931.

Schneider, Michael. *Unterm Hakenkreuz: Arbeiter Und Arbeiterbewegung 1933 Bis 1939*. Bonn: Verlag J. H. W. Dietz, 1999.

Schönhoven, Klaus. "Gewerkschaftlisches Organisationsverhalten Im Wilhelminischen Deutschland." In *Arbeiter Im Industrialisierungsprozeß*, edited by Werner Conze and Ulrich Engelhardt, 403–421. Stuttgart, D: Klett-Cotta, 1979.

Schriewer, Jürgen. "Intermediäre Instanzen, Selbstverwaltung Und Berufliche Ausbildungsstrukturen Im Historischen Vergleich." *Zeitschrift für Pädagogie* 32, no. 1 (1986): 69–90.

Schütte, Friedhelm. *Berufserziehung Zwischen Revolution Und Nationalsozialismus*. Weinheim: Deutscher Studien, 1992.

Seubert, Rolf. *Berufserziehung Und Nationalsozialismus*. Weinheim: Beltz, 1977.

Soskice, David. "Reconciling Markets and Institutions: The German Apprenticeship System." In *Training and the Private Sector: International Comparisons*, edited by Lisa M. Lynch, 25–60. Chicago: University of Chicago Press, 1994.

Stratmann, Karlwilhelm, and Manfred Schlösser. *Das Duale System Der Berufsbildung: Eine Historische Analyse Seiner Reformdebatten*. Frankfurt/Main: Verlag der Gesellschaft zur Förderung arbeitsorientierter Forschung und Bildung, 1990.

Streeck, Wolfgang. "On the Institutional Conditions of Diversified Quality Production." In *Beyond Keynesianism*, edited by Egon Matzner and Wolfgang Streeck. Aldershot, UK: Edward Elgar, 1991.

———. "Skills and the Limits of Neo-Liberalism." *Work, Employment & Society* 3 (1989): 90–104.

Streeck, Wolfgang, and Kathleen Thelen, eds. *Beyond Continuity: Institutional Change in Advanced Political Economies*. Oxford: Oxford University Press, 2005.

Swidler, Ann. "Culture in Action: Symbols and Strategies." *American Sociological Review* 51 (1986): 273–286.

Thelen, Kathleen. "Historical Institutionalism in Comparative Politics." *The Annual Review of Political Science* 2 (1999).

———. *How Institutions Evolve: The Political Economy of Skills in Germany, Britain, the United States and Japan*. New York: Cambridge University Press, 2004.

Tollkühn, Gertrud. *Die Planmäßige Ausbildung Des Gewerblichen Fabriklehrlings in Der Metall- Und Holzverarbeitenden Industrien*. Jena, D: Gustav Fischer, 1926.

Volkov, Shulamit. *The Rise of Popular Antimodernism in Germany: The Urban Master Artisans, 1873–1896*. Princeton: Princeton University Press, 1978.

von Behr, Marhild. *Die Entstehung Der Industriellen Lehrwerkstatt*. Frankfurt/M: Campus, 1981.

Wagner, Karin. "The German Apprenticeship System under Strain." In *The German Skills Machine: Sustaining Comparative Advantage in a Global Economy*, edited by Pepper D. Culpepper and David Finegold, 37–76. New York: Berghahn Books, 1999.

Ware, George W. "Vocational Education and Apprenticeship Training in Germany." Office of the U.S. High Commissioner for Germany, Office of Public Affairs, Division of Cultural Affairs, 1952.

Weingast, Barry. "Rational-Choice Institutionalism." In *Political Science: The State of the Discipline*, edited by Ira Katznelson and Helen Milner, 660–692. New York: Norton, 2002.

Winkler, Heinrich August. "Der Rückversicherte Mittelstand: Die Interessenverbände Von Handwerk Und Kleinhandel Im Deutschen Kaiserreich." In *Zur Soziologischen Theorie Und Analyse Des 19. Jahrhunderts*, edited by Walter Rüegg and Otto Neuloh, 163–179. Göttingen: Vandenhoeck and Ruprecht, 1971.

Wolsing, Theo. *Untersuchungen Zur Berufsausbildung Im Dritten Reich*. Kastellaun, D: A. Henn, 1977.

7

When Does Politics Create Policy?

The Organizational Politics of Change

Margaret Weir

E. E. Schattschneider's observation that "new government policy creates new politics" has provided the inspiration for much of the most compelling work on policymaking.[1] In recent years, historical institutionalists concerned with explaining broad and enduring patterns of public policy have built on Schattschneider's implicitly historical and institutional perspective. Rather than treat each policy battle as one in which all alternatives are equally plausible, these accounts show that conflicts over policy are structured by the interests and institutions created by earlier decisions. This past confers advantages on some policies even as it rules others out of serious consideration. The historical institutional approach to policy is, as many have noted, especially useful in explaining broad patterns of continuity and in accounting for persistent variations across different political systems. It is less helpful when we seek to explain discontinuities because it offers few tools for analyzing how established policies lose support and how new policy directions take hold.

Historical institutionalists have addressed these problems in two main ways: by elaborating theories about institutional dissonance and by developing analyses of elite political strategies. In this chapter, I argue that what is missing in these approaches is attention to the organizational substructure of politics, particularly to processes of interest definition and coalition building among nonelite actors. In democratic political systems, institutional dissonance offers opportunities for social movements and policy entrepreneurs to promote change; likewise, elite political strategies require acceptance—or at least acquiescence—from below if they are to be successful. Explanations of policy persistence and change must account for the actions and inactions of nonelite actors.

The best way to do this, I argue, is to treat these actors as potentially complex organizational entities, themselves embedded in multiple institutional networks.[2] By recognizing that some actors are themselves organizations, this approach draws attention to the internal processes through which organizational actors define their policy interests. By recognizing that actors may define their interests in relation to multiple institutions, it shows how changes in the patterns or possibilities of support in any one policy arena may be conditional on developments in ostensibly distant domains. The first half of the chapter examines the problem of explaining policy change in historical institutionalism, showing how an actor-centered institutionalism contributes to understanding change. The second part of the essay illustrates these ideas by examining processes of interest definition and alliance building in two organizations whose support has been central to the defense of social welfare programs in the United States: the AARP, the organization dedicated to promoting the interests of the elderly, and the AFL-CIO, the central body of organized labor.

Policy Change in Historical Institutionalism

Historical institutionalist analyses of policy development have focused our attention on the forces that promote continuity in policymaking. Such concepts as policy legacies and path dependence provide a powerful correction to the implicit behavioralist assumption that each decision constitutes a new roll of the interest-group dice.[3] Instead, historical institutionalists argue, policies create new constituencies whose very existence transforms future politics. Further developments of this perspective posit connections among clusters of institutions. At their most coherent, such complementary institutions may constitute a regime. This picture of policymaking is much more structured by past decisions than a behavioral approach would suggest. As such, the historical institutional approach has considerably advanced our thinking about the forces that account for stable configurations of policy and the self-reinforcing cycles of change within those configurations.[4]

Historical institutionalism is less well equipped to explain policy changes that do not follow this reinforcing logic. The most common explanation for such changes points to critical junctures or crises in which normal constraints are lifted and new unexpected policy directions become possible. Yet, as Kathleen Thelen has argued, explanations that rely on critical junctures often overestimate the indeterminacy of crisis periods and underestimate the ongoing changes that occur in noncrisis periods.[5] Increasingly, as Paul Pierson has pointed out, analysts of public policy need to explain such endogenous incremental change, in part because the cumulative effects of such changes can have much broader repercussions.[6]

One of the central problems with critical-junctures explanations is that they fail to illuminate the mechanisms that keep institutions in place during noncrisis periods.[7] Instead, there is an implicit assumption that, once locked into place, institutions reproduce themselves. Yet, the normal course of socioeconomic changes poses ongoing challenges for all institutions. Gosta Esping-Andersen, for example, notes that socioeconomic change in the postwar decades confronted welfare states with the challenge of capturing the growing middle class whose needs were not met by existing programs.[8] Economic and demographic changes create possibilities for making new arguments about the suitability of existing policies and to make the case for alternatives. Only in a static world would policy be immune to such dynamics.

Historical institutionalists have taken two approaches to explaining different patterns of change, both of which seek to make room for agency in the context of institutional stickiness. The first, developed by Orren and Skowronek, points to institutional dissonance as a source of change. They argue that, "at any given time, institutions, both individually and collectively, juxtapose different logics of political order, each with their own temporal underpinnings." Instead of a single "political order," they portray a more disorderly politics in which institutions "abrade against each other and, in the process, drive further change."[9] In this analysis, institutions may operate relatively independently of one another and are less tightly linked than in the regime and path-dependence literature. Such abrasions create space in the political system for actors to promote change. Elisabeth Clemens presents a similar image of discordant elements coinciding in time, and she emphasizes the role that actors situated in different domains play in driving change. In her analysis, it is "the friction generated by actions that bridge domains organized on different principles . . . may disrupt routine processes of social reproduction and give rise to transformation."[10] Actors that do not fit neatly into prevailing structures are most likely to promote change as they seek to make politics address their interests.[11]

A second strand of historical institutionalism has sought to explain change by delineating the strategies of political elites. Building on Orren and Skowronek's idea of the coexistence of multiple institutions with different logics, Eric Schickler portrays congressional reform as a process of "layering" in which reformers do not abolish older institutions but rather place new institutions on top of the old.[12] This strategy effects change while avoiding the political challenge of dismantling existing institutions. Thelen extends this idea, showing how layering and conversion—using an old institution to serve new purposes—serve as mechanisms that powerful actors can use to transform old institutions to serve new purposes.[13] Her work shows how institutional persistence can be compatible with far-reaching change in the policies and practices that those institutions support. Likewise, by highlighting mechanisms of change, Thelen directs attention to strategies that agents can use to overcome institutional constraints.

Jacob Hacker takes a similar approach in his elaboration of strategies that political elites can use to roll back welfare-state policies.[14] Welfare-state policies, he notes, have been portrayed as particularly resistant to change because straightforward policy revision is too politically difficult, for all of the reasons historical institutionalists would predict, including entrenched constituencies. Instead, proponents of change use three less visible strategies to effect change: layering, conversion, and policy drift. Drift refers to the failure to adapt existing policies so that they can address new socioeconomic changes. Hacker stresses that drift, which is often viewed as an apolitical process, may be politically mediated: The decisions not to adapt policy so as to be more responsive can be traced to deliberate political intent. Hacker shows how each strategy is suited to particular political settings.

The emphasis on institutional dissonance and agency in this work illuminates how significant policy change can occur even when existing policies and institutions are exhibiting precisely the change-resistant effects that institutionalists would expect. Acknowledging that multiple forces with distinct trajectories are operating at any one time makes it easier to understand the emergence of new tensions and opportunities for policy change. The elaboration of strategies that eschew outright revision but that nonetheless effect dramatic changes on the ground shows how powerful actors can work around institutional barriers to change. Yet, the focus on elites illuminates only the one side of the coin; the success of elite strategies ultimately depends on the insulation from, acquiescence of, or defeat of opponents. As Hacker notes, in the more subterranean politics of drift, layering, and conversion, the activities and power of organized groups, such as unions, take on much more importance than in cases of established policies that enjoy strong support. To understand the prospects for policy change thus requires attention to the strategies of nonelites, as well as to those of elite actors.[15] How do such groups respond to challenges to policies that benefit their members? How do they attempt to build power to influence policy?

The Politics of Interests and Coalitions

Answering these questions requires the insights of institutionalism to analyze how organized interests define their policy preferences and how they identify alliance partners. A return to pluralist and behavioral strategies of explanation, in which actors' interests are whatever they say they are, simplifies the task of identifying actor interests but loses the insight that institutions—preexisting ties and commitments—help to pattern the definition of policy interests and allies. There are regularities and continuities not easily captured by pluralists.

These regularities are, however, far from immutable. In complex institutional environments, actors may have multiple identities, and they may define their interests in multiple ways.[16] On questions of public policy, preferences are especially malleable since there is much room for persuasion and reassessment about which policy truly matches a group's interest. Thus, established interest definitions and ties are subject to renegotiation. Such renegotiations are especially likely in political environments that challenge existing policies either directly or indirectly. When the actors are themselves organizations, it is crucial to open the black box of organizational structure and decision making to understand how groups define their interests and identify potential allies.

Conceiving of actors as potentially having multiple interests requires taking into account the organizational dynamics through which actor interests are defined and the multiple institutional networks in which actors are embedded. Actors define their policy interests in two distinct institutional settings: (1) internally, inside organizations where organizational actors contend over what policies best serve the interests of the organization; and (2) externally, at the intersection of the multiple institutional networks within which they are embedded. Both perspectives are necessary for understanding the possibilities for interest shifts among actors and, consequently, for understanding how coalition support for policy is built and how it may unravel.

The political dynamics that occur within organizations—the relationship of leaders to members and the possibilities for competing factions within the organization—may determine how organizations define the policy interests of their members. Proposed reforms can set off internal struggles over the true interests of the membership or the organization; conflict between the interests of the organization and the interests of the membership may also arise. Michels's iron law of oligarchy suggests that over time the interests of the leaders will inevitably become more conservative than those of the membership.[17] But other organizational dynamics may also promote change. Members may be more independent than Michels's perspective implies. Challengers internal to organizations may promote new perspectives on the organization's interest as part of their bid for power. They may also need to introduce new organizational structures to institutionalize their view of the organization's interest. When there are competing factions within an organization and the effects of policy are uncertain, particular perspectives may be championed because of the internal organizational advantages they confer rather than because of any rationally determined match with member interests.[18] Such internal dynamics are especially important for assessing the durability of policy change.

External ties are important because, as actors define their policy interests, they are also defining their relationship to other actors. Many policies persist because they are supported by "constellations of actors" that are brought together in specific institutional contexts.[19] When decisions about policy changes emerge, these actors are negotiating not only about policy but also about their power relationships with one another. Analyses of policy change must accordingly consider the power relationships among actors. How much do actors need one another to achieve their goals? Are there alternative alliances through which they can achieve their goals? How free are actors to leave an existing alliance? Shifts in actor relations may arise from new opportunities for alliances or from the diminished need for existing allies.

This organizational perspective recognizes that actor relationships are institutionally structured but maintains that they are structured not only by the institutions organizing a single policy area; they are shaped by relationships in multiple policy domains. For these reasons, it is important to recognize that actors may be embedded in multiple networks. As Peter Hall notes, " most people have multiple interests, often associated with the multiple roles they play in the world, some of which conflict with each other, and many of which are subject to multiple interpretations."[20] A strong alliance of interests in one policy area may not be matched by similarly shared perspectives in other areas. Such conflicting ties are the place to look for potential changes in preferences and for possibilities for new group alliances. Similarly, the rise of policy alternatives may pull groups away from a favored policy, just as the waning benefits of some alliances may provoke interest in alternatives.

Internal organizational dynamics and alliance conflicts that promote change are especially likely in environments where institutions are not tightly linked. When institutions exhibit diverse political logics, it is more likely that actors will be embedded in diverse networks and that competitors that seek to displace established policies will emerge. Likewise, when there is significant competition among policy alternatives, there is greater chance that existing constellations of support can become unstuck and that internal challengers will propose alternative definitions of organizational interests. In this way, policy shifts may emerge from changes that are peripheral to the policy in question.[21] By creating alternative policies, such changes create new possibilities that actors embedded in multiple networks will reevaluate their interest definitions. Just as the concept of regimes and the search for complementarities helps explain stability, institutional and policy diversity helps explain change.[22]

This approach suggests that our assessments of policy change must take into account the definition and redefinition of policy interests. Moreover, this process can occur internally within organizations and externally through relationships to other organizational actors. Interest redefinition may mean a reassessment of an actor's fundamental goals, but it can also be a less dramatic shift in judgment about which policies promote enduring goals. Critical junctures direct our attention to the rise of new interests or new actors, but such occasions when the slate is clear are rare. The approach outlined here offers insights into redefinitions of interest and recombinations of actors that promote policy change under less dramatic circumstances. As such, it puts political contestation within and between organizations at the center of institutional approaches to policy change.

Interests, Alliances, and Policy

These ideas can be illustrated by examining how the AARP and organized labor, two organizations central to the viability of liberal social policies in the United States, reacted to a political environment that challenged the foundation of the American welfare state. These cases demonstrate how organizations shape the way societal groups define their policy interests and show how calculations about alliances affect organizational policy positions.

Institutional Dissonance and the Effort to Overhaul Social Security

The effort to introduce private accounts and benefit cuts into Social Security, which took off after George W. Bush's reelection in 2004, illustrates how institutional dissonance made the direct effort at rolling back what was once called the "third rail of politics" politically plausible. The battle over Social Security shows how the availability and promotion of policy alternatives can threaten even the strongest of policies. As a long-established pension policy, the Social Security system was less vulnerable to challenge than newer pension policies.[23] The pay-as-you-go financing mechanism for the existing system also made a transition to private alternatives very expensive and hence difficult to achieve. Moreover, Social Security was the paradigmatic case of policy fostering new politics by creating new constituencies. Andrea Campbell has shown how Social Security not only built support among the elderly but also spurred them to become unusually politically active.[24]

Yet, even in this case, the potential for undermining support for Social Security was apparent. The creation of tax-subsidized individual retirement accounts in the 1970s and their dramatic growth in the 1990s created potential competition for Social Security.[25] The elderly and near-elderly who receive or expect to receive Social Security payments may also be stock market investors, benefitting from investments in their individual plans. As members of this alternative public-private policy network, these beneficiaries enjoyed an alternative source of information about the advantages of various retirement schemes. In the 1990s, the investment industry launched a concerted effort to undermine Social Security, issuing regular warnings about the unreliability of Social Security benefits and promising much greater security in a fully privatized system. The existence of private alternatives and the pressure for privatization created ominous new fissures in the once-solid support for Social Security among the elderly. The divisions fell along the class lines, with the affluent more likely to support privatization and low-income seniors most opposed.[26] Exaggerated warnings about the future insolvency of Social Security for more than a decade also created stronger support for private accounts among younger workers, providing another possible base of support for change.

As this case suggests, the existence of competing policy alternatives that fracture a base of solid support for existing policies or that mobilize new voices is a significant mechanism for promoting change. Such alternatives are most likely to appear in policy systems that exhibit multiple organizational logics. This is certainly true of the American welfare state, which has long been characterized by the existence of private systems of security designed to supplement public programs.[27] As Jennifer Klein shows in her history of the public-private benefit system in the United States, when the federal government embraced security as central public goal in the 1930s, businesses did not withdraw from providing private benefits. Rather, the insurance industry found new ways to supplement federal programs, continuing to make security a profit-making business for the private sector.[28]

Although the final chapter of this battle remains to be written, the AARP, the main advocacy group for the elderly, acted much as historical institutionalists would predict, challenging the effort to establish private accounts and joining in a broad coalition with other groups to defeat the Bush administration's proposals. Despite support from other groups claiming to represent the elderly—groups created by the advocates of private accounts—the voice of the elderly was expressed primarily as one opposed to the proposed changes. Moreover, the support of younger workers remained politically inert for the most part, since younger workers were not organized to inject their support into the debate. The most active group support for privatization came from business groups, most prominently the mutual fund industry, which owed much of its growth to 401(k)s and saw Social Security privatization as a means for further expansion. Whatever the outcome, the effort to restructure Social Security highlights the importance of competing alternatives as a tool for reshaping interests and pulling apart existing coalitions much as arguments about institutional dissonance would suggest. At the same time, it underscores the difficulty of launching a direct assault on an existing program with a broad constituency.

Medicare Reform: Constituency Interests versus Organizational Interests

The 2003 Medicare reform presents a very different picture, illustrating the pivotal role that organizations play in shaping definitions of policy interest. In this case, the AARP departed from its earlier resistence to change and supported a controversial reform whose benefits to seniors were sharply contested by the plan's Democratic opponents. Although the reform added a prescription drug benefit, it provided such limited coverage and imposed so many restrictions that its ultimate benefit to the elderly was doubtful. Moreover, the legislation authorized the creation of subsidized private health-care plans that defenders of Medicare charged would eventually hurt seniors by leading to the unraveling of the universal coverage.

The AARP's support for the 2003 reform can be explained only by delving into the internal processes through which the organization determined the policy interests of its members. As an officially nonpartisan organization that in 2002 derived more than 24 percent of its operating revenue from providing health insurance products to its members, the AARP had organizational prerogatives that were potentially in tension with the interests of its members.[29] Moreover, the organization's internal structure provided for very little member accountability. This distance from membership was reinforced in the late 1990s when new leadership centralized activities and eliminated the national delegate convention's role in selecting leadership.[30] Through a combined strategy of courtship and threat, congressional Republicans brought the AARP over to its side in the Medicare debate. The AARP actively campaigned for the legislation, sponsoring paid advertisements touting the plan's benefit to seniors.

In complex policy choices, such as that of reforming Medicare, organizational mediation of group interests takes on added significance. Medicare created a supportive constituency among its broad base of constituents, but organizations, not individuals, often play a key role in complex policy deliberations. The organizational interests and unaccountable internal structure of the AARP allowed it to break with former allies to support a reform of doubtful benefit to its members.

Organized Labor: Organizational Survival, Interests, and Alliances

While policy constituencies may play the decisive role in defending against headlong attacks on existing policies, the proactive power needed to combat retrenchment through policy drift must come from organized interests that have a broader stake in active government and that have the power to weigh in on a range of policy debates. The ability of such organizations to address major challenges is therefore another important area of inquiry for students of policy change. Major challenges may set off controversial efforts to remake organizations so that they can exercise power in the new setting that confronts them. Organizational capacity to challenge policy drift depends on the success of such restructuring.

Contending views about the true interests of an organization come to the fore when organizations are under external challenge, especially when challenges are serious enough to threaten their survival. At such moments, fundamental questions about the organization's interests and allies emerge: Is the organization's interest equivalent to the desires of its current members, or is it best defined as the organization's ability to grow and survive? Do organizational policy positions alienate it from potential allies needed to win strength? How organizations address these questions will determine whether major policy shifts, achieved by direct or indirect means such as drift, are successful. Organizations may rise to the challenge, or they may themselves drift into insignificance.

In the United States, organized labor, despite its comparative weakness cross-nationally, has been a central force in promoting public social-welfare policies. Yet, decades of organizational decline have left labor ill equipped to address the challenges not only to major social-welfare policies but also to labor's own organizational survival. The recent efforts to transform organized labor in the United States provide a compelling example of an organization in which a major effort at rebuilding power is under way. Organized labor's steady decline over several decades left it with 13 percent of the workforce during the 1990s (10 percent of the private workforce), down from a high of 35 percent in the 1950s. In the mid-1990s, this decline propelled to labor's top echelons a new leadership with innovative ideas about how to revive labor as an organization and a political force. John Sweeney's "New Voices" leadership took over the national AFL-CIO in 1995 with the explicit aims of increasing union density and building labor's power.[31]

As the new leadership has sought to rebuild labor, it has forced to the surface once-submerged debates about labor's true interests. For the previous two decades, union leaders and members equated the organization's interests with the interests of current members, both active and retired. As the number of unionized workers declined, however, the interests that labor represented grew ever more narrow. The defensive and narrow stance of labor in the 1970s and 1980s contrasted with its more ambitious and encompassing approach to politics and policy in earlier decades. Organized labor had once provided the political bulwark for New Deal liberalism. In federal politics, organized labor supported the emerging civil rights movement, and key elements within unions helped to fashion the War on Poverty.[32] In his study of labor politics in the 1950s and 1960s, David Greenstone argues that labor political activity reflected a social democratic impulse in American politics. Union political machinery was deployed toward "strengthening the Democratic Party in campaigns and pressuring for a welfare-state orientation."[33] Labor's federally organized Committee on Political Education (COPE) complemented and substituted for Democratic Party state and local mobilizing capacities, registering and turning out voters for liberal candidates. Moreover, to promote Democratic political success, unions not only organized union members but also mobilized nonunion minorities to take on active roles in the political process and backed social policies that would benefit these groups.

The new leadership of the AFL-CIO has sought to retrieve this broader vision, seeking to rebuild the organization's power and to recast it as an organization that represents all working people. But, because labor is an organizationally complex actor, redefining interests and allies is not a simple process. At the top of the federated union structure is the AFL-CIO central office, which pronounces on policy and lobbies on behalf of labor but which has limited ability to influence what its member unions do. The national leadership cannot on its own announce new policy objectives. Member unions themselves are decentralized, with a national (in union parlance, "international") leadership and union locals that enjoy significant autonomy. Paralleling the local-international structure is a separate federated structure meant to aggregate labor's voice on a territorial basis, representing labor in local and state politics, much as the AFL-CIO national leadership does in Washington. This territorial organizational structure is composed of central labor councils, which are usually county-level organizations, and state federations. Labor's complex organizational structure means that tracking efforts at change requires examining both the internal organizational channels through which new ideas are considered and the organization's external networks, which may either spur or restrain the efforts to alter existing patterns of policy support.

Internal complexity and diverse external networks can facilitate reinterpretation of organizational interests. Diverse views are more likely to emerge in complex organizations where different parts of the organization operate with some measure of autonomy. Likewise, members are likely to be exposed to more diverse sources of information than in more tightly controlled organizations where leadership controls access to information in order to enhance its freedom to maneuver.[34]

One way that labor has sought to rebuild its power is by building coalitions with low-wage workers and urban minorities, including immigrants. Labor's complex organizational structure facilitated a significant shift in its policy position on illegal immigration in 2000. An initially small group of immigrant-rights activists pressed the case for change, winning the support of top leadership by linking the rights of undocumented immigrants to the goal of promoting organizing. Showing that the failure to enforce the rights of undocumented immigrants was undermining organizing in the most active service sectors, these advocates cast their issue in terms of larger organizational goals.

Labor has also sought to shore up its alliances with urban minorities. The effort to build new alliances has meant identifying policy issues on which labor could unite with other actors with which it wanted to form a broader pro-activist government alliance. Many of these concerned labor's presence in metropolitan politics. In some cases, labor pressed for new policies, such as the living-wage effort, that enhanced the political connections between labor and community-based organizations representing low-income workers.[35] In other cases, it has meant shifting positions or becoming active on existing issues, as in labor's support for "smart growth," involving growth limitation efforts, increased support for public transit, and support for affordable housing. Packaged together, this cluster of issues connected labor with the interests of low-income residents, minority groups, and environmentalists.

Yet, new connections are not so easy to make. In many cases, they entail disentangling labor from other ties. For example, establishing closer ties to urban minorities may challenge longstanding alliances, such as those that have linked the building-trades unions and the construction industry in local politics. Moreover, the long history of mistrust and opposed identities between many unions and urban minorities means that these new coalitions are often fragile and vulnerable to efforts to break them apart.

Despite the creative efforts to promote change, these efforts have achieved only limited success, given the complex federated structure of the AFL-CIO. Indeed, deep internal fissures may ultimately lead to the breaking apart of the federation as the most activist factions of labor seek the freedom to rebuild along the lines they see as most effective.

Conclusion

Historical institutionalist explanations have powerfully improved our understanding of policymaking by showing how the political terrain changes after a policy is enacted. As constituencies that benefit from the policy form to support it, interests and actors are transformed. Yet, in these analyses, the main action is from the institution or policy to society, leaving little room for agency. Consequently, such accounts do not take us very far in understanding prospects for change, apart from extraordinary critical junctures when the floodgates open and significant change is possible.

I suggest that understanding evolutionary changes requires a more precise understanding of actors. I argue for a multidimensional perspective on actors that considers internal organizational politics, as well as the multiple external networks in which actors are embedded. These settings provide the context in which actors define their policy interests and consider alternatives. Thus, actor constellations are structured by existing policies but the institutional setting is complex and multiple. This multiple situating of actors opens increased possibilities for shifting interests and constellations of power and ultimately for policy changes.

NOTES

1. E. E. Schattschneider, *Politics, Pressures and the Tariff* (Hamden, CT: Archon Books, 1963); Theodore J. Lowi, "American Business, Public Policy, Case Studies, Political Theory," World Politics 16 (July 1964): 677–693.

2. Fritz W. Scharpf, *Games Real Actors Play: Actor-Centered Institutionalism in Policy Research* (Boulder, CO: Westview Press, 1997).

3. For representative discussions of these issues see Margaret Weir, *Politics and Jobs: The Boundaries of Employment Policy in the United States* (Princeton: Princeton University Press, 1992); Paul Pierson, *Dismantling the Welfare State? Reagan, Thatcher, and the Politics of Retrenchment* (New York: Cambridge University Press, 1996); Ira Katznelson, "Structure and Configuration in Comparative Politics," in *Comparative Politics: Rationality, Culture, and Structure,* ed. Mark Irving Lichbach and Alan S. Zukerman (Cambridge: Cambridge University Press, 1997), 81–112; Paul Pierson, "Increasing Returns, Path Dependence, and the Study of Politics,"

American Political Science Review 94 (June 2000): 251–267; Jacob S. Hacker, *The Divided Welfare State: The Battle over Public and Private Social Benefits in the United States* (Cambridge: Cambridge University Press, 2002).

4. For broader reviews of this literature see Kathleen Thelen, "Historical Institutionalism in Comparative Politics," *Annual Review of Political Science* (1999): 385–386; Paul Pierson and Theda Skocpol, "Historical Institutionalism in Political Science," in *Political Science: State of the Discipline*, ed. Ira Katznelson and Helen V. Milner (New York: Norton, 2002), 693–721.

5. Kathleen Thelen, *How Institutions Evolve: The Political Economy of Skills in Germany, Britain, the United States and Japan* (Cambridge: Cambridge University Press, 2004), ch. 1.

6. Paul E. Pierson, *Politics in Time* (Princeton: Princeton University Press, 2004).

7. Thelen, *How Institutions Evolve*, 292–296.

8. Gosta Esping-Andersen, *The Three Worlds of Welfare Capitalism* (Princeton: Princeton University Press, 1990).

9. Karen Orren and Stephen Skowronek, "Beyond the Iconography of Order: Notes for a 'New Institutionalism,'" in *The Dynamics of American Politics: Approaches and Interpretations*, ed. Lawrence C. Dodd and Calvin Jillson (Boulder, CO: Westview Press, 1994), 320–321; Karen Orren and Stephen Skowronek, *The Search for American Political Development* (Cambridge: Cambridge University Press, 2004), 182.

10. Elisabeth S. Clemens, "Continuity and Coherence: Periodization and the Problem of Institutional Change," in *Social Time and Social Change: Perspectives on Sociology and History*, ed. Fredrik Engelstad and Ragnvald Kalleberg (Oslo: Scandinavian University Press, 1999), 74.

11. See Elisabeth S. Clemens, *The People's Lobby* (Chicago: University of Chicago Press, 1997); see the discussion in Orren and Skowronek, *The Search for American Political Development*, 106–107.

12. Eric Schickler, *Disjointed Pluralism: Institutional Innovation and the Development of the U.S. Congress* (Princeton: Princeton University Press, 2001).

13. Thelen, *How Institutions Evolve*.

14. Jacob S. Hacker, "Privatizing Risk Without Privatizing the Welfare State: The Hidden Politics of Social Policy Retrenchment in the United States," *American Political Science Review* 98 (May 2004): 243–260.

15. For a similar emphasis on incorporating agency into institutionalist accounts, see Ira Katznelson, "Periodization and Preferences," in *Comparative Historical Analysis in the Social Sciences*, ed. James Mahoney and Dietrich Rueschemeyer (Cambridge: Cambridge University Press, 2003), 270–301.

16. Peter A. Hall, "The Role of Interests, Institutions, and Ideas in the Comparative Political Economy of the Industrialized Nations," in *Comparative Politics: Rationality, Culture, and Structure*, ed. Mark Irving Lichbach and Alan S. Zukerman (Cambridge: Cambridge University Press, 1997).

17. Robert Michels, *Political Parties: A Sociological Study of the Oligarchical Tendencies of Modern Democracy* (New York: Free Press; London: Collier-Macmillan Ltd., 1968).

18. Charles Sabel, "The Internal Politics of Trade Unions," in *Organizing Interests in Western Europe: Pluralism, Corporatism, and the Transformation of Politics,* ed. Suzanne D. Berger (Cambridge: Cambridge University Press, 1981).

19. Scharpf, *Games Real Actors Play;* Margarita Estevez-Abe, "Negotiating Welfare Reforms: Actors and Institutions in the Japanese Welfare State," in *Restructuring the Welfare State: Political Institutions and Policy Change,* ed. Bo Rothstein and Sven Steinmo (New York: Palgrave, MacMillan, 2002), 157–183.

20. Hall, "The Role of Interests."

21. Thelen, *How Institutions Evolve.*

22. Elisabeth S. Clemens and James M. Cook, "Politics and Institutionalism: Explaining Durability and Change," *Annual Review of Sociology* 25 (1999): 441–466.

23. John Myles and Paul Pierson, "The Comparative Political Economy of Pension Reform," in *The New Politics of the Welfare State,* ed. Paul Pierson (Oxford: Oxford University Press, 2001), 305–334.

24. Andrea Louise Campbell, *How Policies Make Citizens: Senior Political Activism and the American Welfare State* (Princeton: Princeton University Press, 2003).

25. Hacker, *The Divided Welfare State.*

26. Campbell, *How Policies Make Citizens.*

27. Hacker, *The Divided Welfare State;* Jennifer Klein, *For All These Rights: Business, Labor, and the Shaping of America's Public-Private Welfare State* (Princeton: Princeton University Press, 2003).

28. Klein, *For All These Rights.*

29. Theda Skocpol, "A Bad Senior Moment," The American Prospect Online, January 1, 2004, available at http://www.prospect.org/print/V15/1/skocpol-t.html; Barbara T. Dreyfuss, "The Seduction," The American Prospect Online, May 12, 2004, available at http://www.prospect.org/web/page.ww?section=root&name =ViewPrint&articleID=7702.

30. Dreyfuss, "The Seduction."

31. Margaret Levi, "Organizing Power: Prospects for the American Labor Movement," *Perspectives on Politics* 1 (March 2003): 45–68.

32. John C. Donovan, *The Politics of Poverty* (New York: Pegasus, 1967), 52; Alan Draper, *A Rope of Sand: The AFL-CIO Committee on Political Education, 1955–1967* (New York: Praeger, 1989); Graham Wilson, *Unions in American National Politics* (New York: St. Martin's Press, 1979).

33. David J. Greenstone, *Labor in American Politics* (New York: Knopf, 1969), 160.

34. Sabel, "The Internal Politics of Trade Unions."

35. Isaac Martin, "Dawn of the Living Wage: The Diffusion of a Redistributive Municipal Policy," *Urban Affairs Review* 36 (March 2001): 470.

8

Lineages of the Rube Goldberg State
Building and Blurring Public Programs, 1900–1940

Elisabeth S. Clemens

Against strong claims for the rational or functional design of institutions, historically inclined social scientists have treated the durable configurations of governance as legacies of the past, as projects informed by highly bounded rationalities and cultural scripts, by contingent conjunctures and available coalitions. To the extent that institutions appear to "work," it is because they have been made to work by being implicated in ongoing practices or projects, by the selective erosion and elaboration of time. Yet, even against this modest claim for the surface efficacy of political institutions, many aspects of American political institutions constitute a challenge. Our arrangements of governance appear infused not with the spirit of the Enlightenment but with the humor of Rube Goldberg; after releasing a marble that tips a lever that lifts a plug, a stream of water moves a pingpong ball from A to B. Unlike the clean geometry of checks and balances in constitutional design, the facts on the ground are an immensely complex tangle of indirect incentives, cross-cutting regulations, overlapping jurisdictions, delegated responsibility, and diffuse accountability. Simply put, the modern American state is a mess.

The theoretical implications of this tangle of governance are missed if we rely on a Weberian ideal type of bureaucracy, an analytic lens that frames this complexity as either historical residue or evidence of partisan corruption. Although it is tempting to cut through this tangle with an elegant piece of simplifying analysis, the disorderliness of American governance merits attention in its own right. One possible approach emphasizes the formal limits on the authority of different political institutions and actors: the reservation of some powers to the federal government and others to the states or the web of statutory regulation that constitutes types of organizational actors in the expectation that they will perform or refrain from particular activities. This complex differentiation of authority may be characteristic of any bureaucracy, and the fragmentation of the American polity has been a starting point for many comparative institutional studies.[1] But "fragmentation" orients us to governance in a distinctive manner: by establishing figure and ground, by highlighting separation among branches of government and between levels of government. This lens, too, obscures the cross-cutting ties, the pattern of government by indirection and delegation.

Consequently, it would be a mistake to treat the complex arrangement of American governance as a legacy of formal institutions alone. Political initiatives and policy decisions have increased fragmentation while also massively complicating relations of agency, fiscal dependency, and accountability that crosscut the boundaries of agencies and formal jurisdictions. Examples multiply: orphans first given to state-subsidized homes, then removed to private families that receive payments;[2] the creation of tax incentives to encourage individuals and firms to save or to purchase social insurance that might have been directly provided by state bureaucracies;[3] the use of revenue sharing to pressure state (or local) governments to follow the lead of federal (or state) policymakers.[4] Even the "legitimate monopoly of violence," taken by Weber to be the defining feature of states, may be delegated to private militias or "dollar-a-year men" or enacted through "private military contractors."[5] To the extent that relationships of funding and implementation crosscut an already fragmented institutional landscape, transparency and accountability are made into enormous challenges.

This tangle has typically been treated as the residue of the past, the sticky, less-than-rational predecessor of the modern bureaucratic state that remains at the center of many analyses of state-building in American political development. This Weberian imagery carries strong presumptions about the merits of this form of organization: "Experience tends universally to show that the purely bureaucratic type of administrative organization . . . is, from a purely technical point of view, capable of attaining the highest degree of efficiency and is in this sense formally the most rational known means of exercising authority over human beings."[6] As political actors, reformers have often celebrated this ideal type, casting themselves as proponents of professionalism, technical expertise, and nonpartisanship. In the same spirit, accounts of state-building have tended to foreground the visions and activities of reformers on the necessary—if not sufficient—presence of a career bureaucracy.[7] Resistance to the construction of efficient bureaucracies is explained by the desire of existing elites to defend the powers and benefits vested in prebureaucratic arrangements.[8]

To the extent that professionalism and the bureaucratic ideal have been equated with the project of modern state-building (as in Skowronek's path-breaking *Building a New American State*), self-interest and entrenched venality have been obvious candidates for explaining the recurrent pattern of indirect government in American political development. This explanation, however, obscures the many cases in which indirect governance has been celebrated as a method for raising standards nationally while respecting variation across states[9] or, in a more contemporary slogan, for "steering, not rowing," as the proper function of government.[10] Sometimes, it appears, delegated and indirect government is celebrated as the best of all possible arrangements, rather than the most corrupt and inefficient.

The challenge is to understand how, why, and with what consequences Americans have come to build such a complex, at times seemingly incomprehensible system of governance. Even the New Deal's foundational social insurance programs, the core elements of the nation's "laggard welfare state," were largely[11] organized through revenue-sharing programs with state governments rather than federally funded and federally delivered social services.[12] By exploring the first decades of the twentieth century, a period in which both state and federal governments increased the level and expanse of their activity, this essay seeks to illuminate at least some of the processes that have produced an institutional array for which few would aspire to claim authorship. From this vantage point, a different account of American state-building can be constructed in which professional reformers and champions of bureaucracy are decentered in order to illuminate how the twentieth-century state was constructed in a field already thickly populated by voluntary associations, political parties, and other organizational actors—a land already "full of governance," in the words of Karen Orren and Stephen Skowronek.[13]

In this essay, the problem of indirect or delegated governance is addressed from the vantage point of state governments during an era when many political actors favored construction of the "monocratic bureaucracies" analyzed by Weber and prized by so many reformers. While these ambitions called for the construction of explicitly public agencies fully funded by public revenues, more complex and hybridized arrangements often took hold. Why? First, legislatures and state officials faced an organizational field with many existing organizations, many of which were already embedded in collaborative arrangements with public agencies. Second, state governments were (and are) located within a federal system, complicating state-level governing arrangements with possibilities of delegation from or to federal institutions. So, while some political actors succeeded in constructing public bureaucracies in some policy domains, elsewhere the tangle of indirect governance prevailed. What features of policy and politics reproduced, extended, or transformed arrangements so apparently lacking in recognizable features of rational design?

Chronic Complexity: A Problem for Theories of the State

The kaleidoscopic opacity of the American state is both familiar and unfamiliar to contemporary political theory. This quality resonates with recent claims about the difficulty faced by constituents in tracing responsibility for program cuts and holding their representatives accountable.[14] Elected officials and opportunistic bureaucrats, it is argued, have incentives to choose forms of implementation that obscure chains of causation and responsibility; since virtually every policy hurts someone (or benefits some more than others), strategic political actors strive to avoid leaving fingerprints. This quality of policy, then, has implications for political mobilization. Citizens may make alliances that crosscut opposed economic interests because they do not accurately understand who pays taxes and who benefits; policies may multiply divergent interests, obscuring common grounds for grievances.[15] As one commentator of the 1920s observed, "For more than a century the March Hare and the Mad Hatter have been running things in Washington, and some hundred attempts to kick them out have resulted in nothing more fruitful than . . . confusion. Confidentially, politicians like their government scrambled, for that is the style in which it is least susceptible to critical analysis."[16]

In contrast to these befuddled citizens and befuddling politicians, theorists of the state often begin with images of unobstructed vision: Foucault's panopticon, Scott's high modernist state, which transforms the social and natural worlds so that they may be more easily surveyed.[17] Bureaucrats transform the complexity of the world into units that may be counted and connected in commensurable relationships that allow tradeoffs of guns and butter, of songbirds and power generation.[18] For those with a taste for parsimonious theory, the problem here is that both simplification and obfuscation are instruments of power, as well as products of the exercise of power. Thus, a purely instrumental argument, in which strategies of state-building are simply means to increase the power of particular actors—and rational bureaucracy is the central instrument of power—cannot adequately explain why some state-building results in institutionalized indirection and other efforts generate the exaggerated clarity of committed bureaucratization.

A parallel tension is evident when we move from the cognitive dilemmas of citizens and state officials to the patterns of relationships among political actors. Elegantly captured in Peter Evans's concept of "embedded autonomy,"[19] economic development is attributed to a balance between ties that crosscut the boundaries of formal political institutions and solidary ties within the formal bureaucracy of the state. Cooperation with, or delegation to, private actors is balanced by the Weberian ideal-type of bureaucracy, defined by "meritocratic recruitment and . . . predictable rewarding long-term careers."[20] For Evans, however, much of the puzzle for comparative politics involves explaining when and where the bureaucratic requisites for "embedded autonomy" have developed, in particular the career structures that discourage individually maximizing predation on the part of state officials. The implied question of when and why state actors rely on collaborators outside formal political institutions receives less attention.

How, then, might we explain the recurrent pattern of indirect or delegated governance in American political development? At least three distinct arguments can be advanced from theory alone. First, and most benign, relations between formal state institutions and nongovernmental actors (or between separate components of the state) may reflect an effort to "borrow" rather than build state capacity.[21] Lacking adequate public institutions in the late nineteenth century, state governments subsidized a range of benevolent institutions (including both charitable and proprietary or for-profit organizations) to provide for the welfare of orphans, the ill, and the aged (as well as women thought to be in need of refuge or moral reform). Given this line of argument, such episodes of collaborative or delegated governance should be expected whenever political projects seek to significantly increase the reach of government institutions. Thus, as federal funding for poverty programs expanded rapidly in the 1960s, state officials contracted out to nonprofit organizations (both as a means to rapidly implement program and to provide venues for the required "maximum feasible participation of the poor." Even that most *étatist* French welfare administration turned to nonprofit organizations when it was required to deal with new problems such as homelessness.[22] This argument suggests a kind of stage model in which states first rely on collaboration with private organizations to deliver publicly funded programs and then develop institutional capacity to deliver publicly funded programs through public institutions.[23] We should also expect persistent variation in arrangements across policy domains, with more contracting out in policy domains that require less standardized intervention and public bureaucracies in domains where uniform regulations or privileges are central. In these cases, the arrangements between state agencies and nonstate actors—and, by extension, among levels of government—are understood as flowing from the pragmatic requirements of delivering public services. Undesirable political consequences—corruption, patronage—are understood as avoidable problems that might be eliminated through a better-organized, more efficient system of administration.

Through an alternative lens, these relations of collaboration reappear in terms of dependence and predation. Why provide a subsidy to a charity? Perhaps to provide for the care of orphaned children with legitimate claims for public protection, but perhaps also to make the charity dependent on the goodwill of state legislators in control of the purse strings. During the early twentieth century, political reformers were sensitive to precisely this possibility, arguing that a legislative subsidy to an orphanage would coopt the upstanding members of the board of trustees, keeping these respectable citizens from joining up with the reform movements to which they otherwise would flock.[24] Party discipline could be enforced by leadership's control over appropriation, an arrangement that reached its pinnacle in turn-of-the-century Pennsylvania: "When an incorruptible member from an outlying county, who cannot be coaxed by any ordinary means to vote for legislation of which he does not approve, happens to want something for his home hospital, or desires to advance a piece of legislation he is pledged to by his constituents, he finds himself tied hand and foot."[25] But not in all periods at all times. Whereas a cynic might simply assert that the analysis of self-dealing should be placed front and center in the analysis of institutional development, the more telling questions concern when and where we find either public institutions effectively delivering public services or public-private collaborations that build capacity without engendering corruption. To the extent that this type of argument explains the recurrent complexity of American governance, we should expect either a pattern of oscillation between favored corporations or charities as politicians of different parties cycle in and out of power or, perhaps, an oscillation between moments of expansive delegation and recentralization to public agencies corresponding to the ascendance of either traditional party organizations or movements of reform.

In addition to the life-stage and the political-dependence explanations, a third line of argument flows from recognizing collaborative relationships as expressions of power, but in the form of the exercise of government within particular institutional arrangements, rather than the cooptation of supporters or strategic pursuit of some electoral logic. From this vantage point, the dense tangle of governance arrangements is a direct consequence of the delineation and the balancing of powers or jurisdictions that lie at the heart of constitutional design. Within an institutional framework that clearly divides and separates powers, those who would expand the reach of their influence must necessarily work by indirection. This tightrope performance appeared repeatedly in commentary on the expansion of federal activity during the 1920s: "The so-called fifty-fifty system of Federal Aid has been criticized as a wedge through which the Federal Government has invaded the reserved powers of the States. While this is in large measure true, such invasion is not of an arbitrary or despotic character, though it may be considered unwise and inappropriate. In each instance the State affected has voluntarily bartered some of its authority for a monetary consideration."[26] Here the sense is that federal bureaucrats might have preferred to build centralized bureaucracies but chose to move obliquely around the challenges to the legitimacy of such efforts as corrosive of constitutional arrangements.

In contrast to the languages of corruption as well as flexibility or responsiveness that inform debates over delegation from public agencies to private entities, the debates around delegation across levels of government prompted invocations of foundational issues in American politics. Envisioning a world of discrete state economies and interstate relationships, the Constitution created difficulties for any federal official who might seek to regulate the increasingly nationalized economy of an industrializing United States.[27] Within a political culture suspicious of governmental power, action through collaboration might well be less costly than the construction of explicitly public state capacity. Delegation from federal to state government might even remedy some of the problems of delegation from state government to private organizations. Advocates of expanded federal activity made precisely this argument, asserting that "whatever the method adopted, the effect of federal influence has been to provide more competent workers in the less progressive states. Federal aid has not eliminated state politics, but it has certainly mitigated the evils of partisan administration."[28] In this argument, the aims of antipartisan reformers could be advanced by extending relations of delegation and subsidy, rather than through the construction of classical bureaucracies.

This argument contrasts with accounts of state-building that foreground the projects of reformers in pursuit of a Weberian ideal. In *Building a New American State,* Stephen Skowronek portrayed a nineteenth-century system of governance—the "state of courts and parties"—that was inadequate to the demands of an expanding, industrializing economy.[29] His analysis focused on policy domains where this mismatch provoked midlevel officials and reformers to undertake projects of reform, specifically projects of constructing modern bureaucracies that approached the Weberian ideal more closely than had the agencies of the party state. But building bureaucracies was not the only imaginable, nor the only actual, response. In other policy domains, at other levels of government, new political projects entailed quite different structural rearrangements and innovations. Whether built around subsidies to nonstate organizations or financial grants between levels of government, these new models of policy implementation involved relations of dependence and collaboration, rather than "the forging of bureaucratic autonomy."[30]

These three lines of argument lead to divergent expectations about the pattern of delegated or indirect governance in American political development. From the first argument, highlighting delegation as a strategy of "borrowing capacity," we should expect to find indirect governance more frequently at earlier points in American political history (and subsequently superseded by public bureaucracies) or in those policy domains characterized by a requirement for heightened sensitivity to variation in implementation. From the second, we would conclude that indirect governance is a legacy of particularly venal and corrupt periods or locales in American politics, in which legislators and party bosses subvert public spending to provide particularistic benefits to constituents in return for political loyalty. The third identifies a quite different set of key actors, public bureaucrats who pursue expansive agendas in a context that constrains their legitimate exercise of power. Thus, complexity and interdependence should increase with projects of state-building.

These arguments begin to illuminate the lineages of the Rube Goldberg state. For politicians and political entrepreneurs with ambitious projects, state-building was both a means to specific improvement and an end in itself.[31] But not all were inspired by—or able to pursue—a vision of bureaucratic autonomy; in some policy domains, in some locales, other agendas prevailed. These dilemmas of state-building were particularly evident at the level of state governments, which were charged with responsibility for the activities most closely associated with the modern concept of "social welfare." In the states, would-be progressive reformers had to gain control of government in order to transform government; consequently, projects of state-building and party-building (or, for reformers, deconstructing) were undertaken in tandem.

This struggle was paralleled in federal politics with efforts to institute civil services and to weaken the hold of political patronage over government agencies. These party organizations had been an important source of cohesion within an inherently fragmented federal system: local, state, and federal offices were linked through careers of political achievements; diverse regions were joined in pragmatic electoral coalitions.[32] Yet, with the elaboration and expansion of federal policy ambitions (and governmental revenues), new ties across the components of the American state were developed.[33] The complex relations between state governments and private organizations, as well as across levels of government, exemplify the Rube Goldberg qualities of the modern American state.[34]

Although the early twentieth century has been understood as a critical episode of bureaucratic state-building (and it was), this was also a period when cross-cutting relationships and delegated governance were intensely contested political issues. By reversing the typical delineation of figure and ground that highlights the development of bureaucracy, the comparison of subsidy systems—both within states and between federal and state governments—illuminates the sources of the tangle of governance that characterizes much of American political development. Both cases suggest that the tangle is more than a residue or unintended consequence, but the contrasts between these episodes document that all tangles are not equally durable or prone to institutionalization.

Organizing Revenue and Spending in the States:
The Subsidy System

Across the industrializing nations of the nineteenth century, politicians and public officials were challenged with problems of social provision.[35] Early modern institutions—the almshouse, private benevolence— appeared increasingly inadequate to deal with what were understood as both new levels and new forms of need. With the mobilization of groups agitating for government responses to the "social problem" and the perception that the magnitude of the problems themselves had increased with industrialization and urbanization, state governments faced the challenges of both providing and financing expanded social provision.

States came to this debate with widely differing arrangements for the relief of poverty, illness, and old age indigence, as well as varying levels of resources. As of 1913, for example, per capita revenues to state government ranged from less than $2 in Mississippi, North Carolina, South Carolina, and Oklahoma to more than $10 in Nevada.[36] These variations in revenue were combined with differing levels of engagement with social provision. As Table 8.1 demonstrates,[37] charitable spending was a significant component of state spending from 1915 (when *Financial Statistics of the States* was first published) to 1930, but there were considerable fluctuations over time and across states. Even California, Massachusetts, and Wisconsin—three states with relatively strong, but varied, "progressive" movements— differed markedly in their financial commitment to social provision funded by public revenues. On average, however, fully one-quarter of state government spending in the United States was directed toward charity understood broadly as social provision for the needy. Consequently, the governance of social provision was a key site for establishing state-building projects.

TABLE 8.1.

Spending on Charity by State Governments as a Percentage of
All State Government Spending, 1915–1930.

	1915	1919	1925	1930
All States	23.5 %	24.7 %	16.3 %	24.7 %
California	21.0 %	24.2 %	13.1 %	24.2 %
Massachusetts	42.9 %	38.6 %	34.1 %	35.7 %
Wisconsin	17.5 %	19.2 %	15.5 %	19.2 %

Source: *Financial Statistics of the States* (Washington, DC: Government Printing Office, 1915, 1919, 1925, 1930).

Closer inspection of *how* public revenues were spent demonstrates that bureaucratization—public institutions funded by public revenues—was not the uncontested solution. An increase in the financial resources available to state governments did not automatically translate into the construction of a stronger—or more clearly delineated—system of public agencies. Public monies could also be spent through subsidies to private entities. To a considerable degree, public appropriations were a more important source of support for benevolent institutions in states whose governments had the lowest per capita revenues. With a few exceptions in the Northeast (Maine, Pennsylvania, and Ohio), benevolent institutions in states where public appropriations formed a large portion of their receipts also tended to be poorly funded benevolent institutions.[38] Well-funded benevolent institutions, by comparison, depended on a rich mix of public, philanthropic, and fee-based revenues. Here, again, increased capacity was associated with greater interdependence between public and private entities in social provision. During the late nineteenth and early twentieth centuries, much expansion of state capacity in the field of social provision took the form of collaboration, rather than the direct growth of public bureaucracies. Borrowing, rather than building, state capacity characterized much of this field of government activity.

This process of building state governments by borrowing organizational capacity was intertwined with the consolidation of distinctive types of polity. Beyond the variations in the level of support for benevolent institutions, states also displayed distinctive arrangements with respect to the networks among public, for-profit, and what we would now call "nonprofit" agencies (typically divided into private and ecclesiastical). In the child welfare sector, for example, more than 80 percent of private and religions organizations in California received some public funding as reported in studies done in 1904, 1910, and 1913.[39] Public funds were reported to account for 38 percent to 55 percent of the total budget of these nongovernmental agencies over this period. In Wisconsin, by contrast, less than 17 percent of private or religious organizations received public funding in 1904, a figure that rose to more than 31 percent by 1910. But, even at this later date, public subventions to private agencies in Wisconsin were minimal, accounting for only 2 percent of their budgets in 1910. Thus, in two states with reputations for progressive social policies, the systems of social provision established very different networks of ties among public agencies and private associations.[40] The dense ties among state agencies and private associations exemplified by California encouraged a pluralist politics of social spending in which associations active in the provision of care also became foci for political mobilization in support of expanded public subsidies for care. Here, then, were the conditions for one process of generating durable patterns of indirect governance: the mobilization of third parties with interests in government payments.[41]

The subsidy system, however, did not everywhere display the features that would be expected from the "lock-in" through sustained mobilization by third-party providers. With respect to collaboration, there were striking divergences across states and over time. Most state legislatures funded some delegated forms of publicly funded activity. Veterans were the most frequent target of these efforts, particularly through allocations to the Grand Army of the Republic to maintain its records or to monument societies.[42] Abandoned and needy children—not usually considered a key voting bloc—were the next most frequent target and often the most generously funded through indirect payments; orphanages, industrial schools, and societies for the prevention of cruelty to children all received public subsidies in at least some states.[43] But, in the early twentieth century, this was far from a uniform arrangement. Iowa, for example, approved subsidies for approximately half a dozen baby homes and women's refuges but, after 1906, rapidly reversed itself and rejected the subsidy system in favor of funding public institutions for the care of orphaned children and other dependents. Although some states, notably Wisconsin, hewed closely to a vision of publicly funded and publicly governed social services, overall the reliance of state governments on collaboration with private agencies grew steadily over the decades preceding the Great Depression. Thus in contrast to a stage model in which capacity-borrowing is supplanted by explicitly public capacity-building, expanded state funding of social provision in the early twentieth century generally increased the delegation of social provision to nonpublic institutions that received public payments. Across all states, government payments to institutions (both public and private) were increasingly directed to private institutions (charitable or ecclesiastical) during the first decades of the century, when important social policy precedents were established. On average, almost one-quarter of state government payments went to "other institutions" in 1915. The proportion increased steadily over the 1920s, pushing just past 50 percent in 1930.[44] Across states, over fifteen years, this pattern of increasing collaboration between government and nonpublic agencies in social provision captures something central to early-twentieth-century state-building, rather than the reaction to a sudden failure of state capacity in the face of the Depression.

These arrangements were not uncontroversial. The fiscal networks that had been established between some state governments[45] and private or religious charitable associations were challenged vociferously prior to World War I. The most explicit challenge came in the form of a debate within charitable and social work circles over the desirability of public subventions to private charities and the need for new methods of state supervision of private agencies. At least three distinct lines of criticism emerge from the literature. First, critics argued that the associations that received subsidies were often not authentic voluntary associations but what contemporary scholars would describe as "for-profits in disguise"; the façade of charitable enterprise, it was claimed, resulted in inmates being kept longer than necessary in institutions in order to maintain a revenue stream. One study reported that "The San Francisco dailies gave details in the spring of 1900 of a case where the children in a subsidized institution were found in a half-starved condition."[46] Although subsidy legislation typically contained provisions for mandatory state inspections, there was clearly a widespread concern among social reform advocates that state government's capacity for inspection was far exceeded by private motives for evasion. Second, subsidies were charged with distorting deliberations over the proper distribution of public resources insofar as they gave particular associations or factions special interests in increasing spending on certain activities at the expense of others: "The subsidized institutions can, however, bring such a pressure of political influence and such a persuasive lobby to their aid that the legislature votes all available funds before the pressing needs of the regular state institutions have been nearly provided for."[47] This concern took on heightened intensity when the institutions in question were religious benevolent organizations, particularly those linked to the Catholic Church.[48]

Finally, some commentators found virtue in public-voluntary collaboration but argued that these partnerships needed to be reconstructed. In one well-received article, the British reformer Sidney Webb argued for an "extension ladder" relationship in which voluntary action would be used "in the public service to be constantly raising the standard of civilized conduct and physical health above the comparatively low minimum which alone can be enforced by the public authority." Inspired by the Elberfeld system of poor relief, this model incorporated private citizens as "voluntary officials," extending the capacity of state agencies rather than as representatives of autonomous charitable associations that might claim some right to public subsidy.[49] This model promised to avoid the demobilizing effects of state centralization through the active incorporation of volunteers while at the same time preventing the corruption of civic life that reformers attributed to the subsidy system.

In the arguments mustered by advocates of social reform and good government, one finds both optimistic and cynical assessments of the delegation of public powers to private entities. Some commentators argued that such delegation invited corruption, not only by machine politicians but also by unprincipled private actors pursuing profit through the misuse of public revenues. Others, however, insisted that collaboration—especially with voluntary organizations guided by motives that were presumably more truly charitable—was necessary if the government was to sustain the kind of capacity for action needed to deal with complex, specific cases of social need and improvement. Thus, differences of opinion among social policy experts were a potential source of rapid shifts in policy, a situation that could easily be aggravated by conflicts between reform advocates and those more interested in harnessing public spending to party-building efforts. Policy reformers, party activists, and service-providing organizations were routinely at odds over the governance and financing of social provision. Not surprisingly, then, the pattern across states was characterized by variation and volatility, rather than the enduring lock-in that is often associated with the incorporation of third parties into systems of social provision.

In some respects, the history of the "subsidy system" at the state level lends support to both the "stages of development" and partisan corruption arguments. As state governments expanded their role in social provision, they "borrowed capacity" from private organizations. The pattern of these borrowings could be shaped by—and then reinforce—the logics of partisan loyalty and electoral support. Yet, even here there is some evidence of a quite different dynamic in which policy reformers were not irrevocably opposed to governance by delegation or collaboration. Foreshadowing calls for an "associative state," some reformers promoted alternatives to classical bureaucracy. This interplay of support and condemnation left the subsidy system as a volatile element of governance.

Federal-State Matching Grants

If the use of the subsidy system to "borrow" state capacity threatened to entangle social provision with party-building projects, the introduction of a seemingly mundane funding arrangement—federal-state matching grants—threatened a more thoroughgoing reorganization of the policy. To the extent that delegation from one public agency to another is shaped by the same considerations as delegation from public to private entities, we should expect these arrangements to generate ongoing volatility in American political development. A further challenge to the practice of public subsidy as an alternative to explicit public provision developed more indirectly, encouraged by the significant expansion of resources available to state governments through the invention of what was called the "federal-cooperative," "grant-in-aid," or "fifty-fifty" method. This federal program, through the provision of matching funds, encouraged state governments to expand the recognizably public capacity to provide public services.

Accounts of the "fifty-fifty" method typically begin with the 1857 proposal by U.S. Representative Justin S. Morrill, of Vermont, of "a bill providing that a portion of the public lands be granted to the several states, the proceeds from the sale of these lands to be used for the establishment and maintenance of colleges devoted to agriculture and the mechanic arts."[50] Although defeated by Southern resistance to federal intervention, after the Civil War there was extensive distribution of federal lands to state governments (for Morrill's original purpose) and continuing grants to local governments through the reservation of a portion of every township for public schooling, which had begun with the Ohio enabling act of 1802.

But the "fifty-fifty" method itself represented an important shift from these early land-distribution programs. Beginning with the Second Morrill Act of 1890, the Secretary of the Interior had been empowered "to ascertain whether the agricultural colleges were fulfilling the obligations imposed upon them by the federal government, and . . . to withhold the annual allotment to any institution in which he found conditions unsatisfactory, subject to an appeal by the state to Congress. Here at last was a weapon in the hands of a federal official with which he could force recalcitrant states into line and compel them to meet federal requirements. Here was a practical means of acquiring federal supervision over state activities."[51] Here the argument is not one of government "steering, not rowing," but rather of federal control exerted over state governments through the enticements of federal revenues. Delegation, when strengthened with fiscal dependence and organized supervision, had implications for state-building quite different from those inherent in the "borrowing" of capacity from private charitable organizations at the state-level.

First introduced in the context of agricultural extension work, this arrangement effectively circumvented the disjuncture of federal resources and state responsibilities represented by the Tenth Amendment insofar as the federal government did not directly "usurp" those powers reserved to the states but rather offered financial incentives for the states to exercise them in particular ways. Thus, a powerful financial incentive elicited an increasing "isomorphism" of both policy and institutional arrangements across the states,[52] while furthering the complexity and opacity of governance:

> All the recent subsidy laws have certain features in common. First, they provide for the payment of money from the Federal treasury to the states. Second, they make these grants to the states on the basis, generally speaking, of population. Third, the money paid from the Federal treasury is paid to the states conditionally. Certain stipulations must be met before the states are entitled to receive Federal funds. These conditions are: (1) acceptance of the act by the state legislature, which involves setting up within the state an adequate administrative agency; (2) the matching of Federal funds. Every state is required to put up a dollar of its own money for every dollar it receives from the Federal Government. This feature of Federal aid has led some to dub it the "fifty-fifty" system." (3) The state administering agency is required to submit detailed plans of its activities, which must be approved by the Federal bureau in charge. In each case the work is done in the state by state officials, but with a certain amount of Federal supervision.[53]

The invention and elaboration of the grants-in-aid system laid the foundation for the federalization of social provision during the 1920s and, increasingly rapidly, during the New Deal. Found constitutional in a 1923 Massachusetts challenge to the Sheppard-Towner Maternal and Child Health Act of 1921,[54] this policy tool rapidly enlisted state governments in new areas of activity. The pace at which states passed the legislation necessary to participate in these new federal programs was rapid and consistent; for most of the half-dozen initial matching programs, approximately 80 percent of the states had passed the necessary facilitating legislation within three years of congressional approval (Table 8.2).[55]

TABLE 8.2.
State Legislative Endorsement of Federal-State Matching Programs (cumulative).

	Smith-Lever 5/18/1914	Post Roads 7/11/1916	Smith-Hughes 2/23/1917	Chamberlain-Kahn 7/9/1918	Vocational Rehabilitation 6/2/1920	Sheppard-Towner 11/23/1921
1913	2 (2)	—	—	—	—	—
1914	4 (6)	—	—	—	—	—
1915	35 (41)	—	—	—	—	—
1916	2 (43)	2 (2)	1 (1)	—	—	—
1917	2 (45)	37 (39)	33 (34)	—	—	—
1918	1 (46)	4 (43)	4 (38)	3 (3)	—	—
1919	1 (47)	4 (47)	10 (48)	26 (29)	2 (2)	—
1920	—	—	—	1 (30)	5 (7)	—
1921	1 (48)	1 (48)	—	6 (36)	21 (28)	3 (3)
1922	—	—	—	—	4 (32)	4 (7)
1923	—	—	—	—	3 (35)	26 (33)
1924	—	—	—	—	—	2 (35)
1925	—	—	—	—	2 (37)	3 (38)
1926	—	—	—	—	—	—
1927	—	—	—	—	2 (39)	3 (41)
1928	—	—	—	—	—	—
1929	—	—	—	—	4 (43)	—

Source: Legislative Session volumes for all states.

The rapid and near-unanimous embrace of federal-state matching programs by state legislatures stands in contrast to the contested and divergent responses to the subsidy system within states. Although legislative maneuverings might produce variations in the generosity of the match (and thus the multiplier to any state appropriation), state legislatures were in general eager to endorse participation in this intergovernmental—specifically interbureaucratic—system of policy implementation. Through the use of carrots—or, perhaps, half-carrots if the spirit of the matching grant programs is to be respected—federal policy entrepreneurs could extend their reach across the divisions internal to the federal system without infringing on the power of state governments to endorse and, as important, to fund the matches.

Although some commentators attributed the eager endorsement of federal grant programs to fiscal shortfalls at the state level or to the greater ability of the federal tax system to reach wealth where it took taxable form in the commercial centers,[56] the overall result was that state revenues accounted for up to four-fifths of the spending under federal-state matching programs. Increases in federal grants brought increases in state spending along with expanded federal supervision of the states:

Since 1915 federal subsidies to the states have grown by leaps and bounds. In 1915 the total of federal payments was ten million dollars; by 1920 it was nearly thirty-six millions. The next year it mounted to ninety million dollars. . . . The 1927 federal-aid payments amounted to one hundred and thirty-six million dollars. Compared with the eight millions of 1912, the 1927 total seems large indeed. But far more significant than the amount is the fact that ninety-five per cent is given to the states with definite conditions attached. Ninety-five per cent is paid to the states only after state work has met the approval of federal inspectors.[57]

Not surprisingly, this expansion of federal engagement in policy domains considered the preserve of state government prompted considerable commentary and criticism. Arguments were raised in the name of "states' rights" and the original intentions embodied in the Constitution. In the words of a justice of the Supreme Court of Wisconsin, "If the tendency to centralization continues there is likely to be, as has been pointed out, a diminishing interest on the part of the people in governmental affairs, the Government will tend to grow more and more bureaucratic in its methods, State Governments will tend to become less and less efficient, and we shall thus ultimately bring upon ourselves the very evils which the framers of the Constitution sought to avoid."[58] Others worried that the acceptance of federal largesse was aided, and in turn intensified, a passive dependence by the citizens. Noting that Louis Napoleon had once praised the self-reliance of Americans in contrast to the tendency of the French to rely on government, Archibald Stevenson complained that "Our people no longer seem to cherish the reserved powers of the States. They have found it easier to lean upon the national government than to exert themselves to deal fearlessly with their own immediate problems. This attitude is the natural consequence of the effort of the individual to shirk his own responsibilities and to burden the State with them. The indifference of the majority of citizens towards their political and social duties has given rise to movements of reform by legislation. Such reforms have rarely proved effective."[59] Yet whereas the complaints of reformers and charges of corruption fueled volatility in the subsidy arrangements between state governments and private organizations, the federal-state matching grant programs became a central component of the fiscal infrastructure of American political development. How, then, to account for the durability of this particular form of complexity?

A part of the explanation lies in the processes through which policy creates politics. These new arrangements of funding and supervision were credited with changing patterns of political participation, at least according to contemporary commentators. Within states, it was argued, the establishment of a federal matching grant led to a distortion of political effort insofar as certain designated programs could be established at what was perceived as a 50 percent discount to the taxpayers of a particular state. Given federal subsidies for vocational rehabilitation, therefore, state legislators might be swayed to trim general education spending in favor of targeted spending that would bring in matching revenues.[60] These concerns were echoes of the complaints that subsidies to private charities would lead to the underfunding and erosion of core public programs.

As with the subsidy system, many of the complaints centered on the proper relationship of the organization of public provision to political participation. First, the elaboration of public programs elicited increasing political mobilization along the same lines of classification as policy domains: Vocational rehabilitation legislation encouraged the mobilization of associations interested in this topic rather than associations of those committed to education broadly construed. Second, the promise of federal funding altered the geography of political mobilization, encouraging local associations to form along lines of interest into federated associations and national associations to establish local groups in as many congressional districts as possible; these efforts produced the "new lobby" that was the object of much commentary and outrage in the 1920s.[61] As V. O. Key observed:

> Individual citizens, state-chartered corporations, and political subdivisions have been desirous of taking advantage of the benefits of the various Federal programs. These interests have brought their point of view to bear upon the state legislatures. To these pressures was added the persuasion of Federal administrative units. While it cannot be accurately said that the state legislatures were ground between the upper and nether millstones, they were under varying degrees of compulsion through the combination of pressures from above and below.[62]

At the local level, this interest-based, congressionally oriented style of political mobilization was perceived as disorganizing political communities: "in the heavily populated metropolitan centers, mayors and other officials look to the party in power in Washington for entering financial wedges. Governors, mayors, councilmen, and county officers no longer stay at home to enlist local aid during the period between their election and their assumption of office. Instead they are seen in the national capital, closeted with Federal officials and the officers of such groups as the United States Conference of Mayors."[63] As beneficiaries of these programs went directly to Washington, avoiding negotiations with state politicians who had served as brokers for publicly funded programs, the federal bureaucrats also worked steadily to erode the extent to which public programs supported systems of patronage politics at the state level:

> The representatives of the federal government are well aware of the extent to which partisan considerations determine the policies of certain states, and a great deal of their time is devoted to the task of improving conditions. They do not threaten to cut off all federal funds if state administration is not instantly withdrawn from the field of politics. Such a threat would be tantamount to an announcement of federal withdrawal from all further cooperative relationships, for no state could thus forcibly be led into the path of righteousness. . . . It is not federal policy to deal in personalities. A federal bureau chief will not demand the resignation of any person in the state service, but he may insist that someone better qualified be assigned to the cooperative work. . . . But whatever the method adopted, the effect of federal influence has been to produce more competent workers in the less progressive states. Federal aid has not eliminated state politics but it has certainly mitigated the evils of partisan administration.[64]

This, of course, was the assessment of one of the leading scholars and champions of the matching grant arrangement. One might well receive a different assessment from state-level party leaders, happy to add federal funds and a mandate for expanded constituency service to their portfolio of policy enticements. But, in many respects, this is the critical feature that distinguished the federal-state matching grants from the much contested subsidies to private charities. Federal bureaucrats, typically envisioned as champions of bureaucratic organization, could embrace government by delegation if this was the best method to extend federal power beyond the traditional boundaries of federal authority. This coincidence of motivations—notwithstanding the potential conflict over whether the programs eroded or sustained state-level party leaders—helped to cement the matching-grant into the structure of American government.

Finally, federal laws often required the construction of new kinds of agencies or associations at the state and local level; the label "matching grant" should not obscure the fact that these programs required institutional construction at the state level and, in the case of programs such as fire prevention grants under the Weeks bill, the mobilization of associations of private landowners in formal collaboration with state agencies.[65] Thus, each new policy could add new components to state and local governance, but components that were not directly and clearly accountable to those state and local governments. Here the efforts of federal legislators to shape policy at the state level received direct expression in the baroque multiplication of public agencies, linked through complex and often unclear lines of authority and financial dependence.

The institutionalization of this funding mechanism (and its legitimation by the courts) paved the way for increased interpenetration of federal funding and state spending. Starting in education and expanding across a range of policy domains, congressional decisions increasingly shaped state budget allocations (Table 8.3). Through the Great Depression, federal spending on highways subsidized work programs and, by the late 1930s, grants for public assistance and relief surpassed even the construction totals.[66] From then through 1970, federal revenue accounted for between 35 and 50 percent of state spending on welfare.[67] Overall, federal revenues accounted for an increasing proportion of state funds (Table 8.4), just as transfers to state and local governments constituted an increasing fraction of total federal expenditures.[68] Thus, central models of policy implementation furthered the opaque complexity of the American state, throwing up obstacles to any citizen—indeed, to any public official—who might seek to connect taxes paid to services rendered.

TABLE 8.3.
Federal Grants to the States, by Purpose: 1915–1939 (in thousands).

	Total	Highways	Education	Agricultural	Public Assistance and Relief	All Other
1915	5,357	—	2,757	—-	—-	2,600
1919	11,709	—	4,786	—-	—	6,923
1925	113,644	92,085	11,795	7,474	—-	2,293
1930	109,842	83,280	11,877	12,853	—-	1,852
1932	217,145	188,487	13,249	12,824	—	2,585
1937	564,807	317,409	24,844	21,801	155,061	45,692
1938	627,645	235,050	33,187	23,369	215,205	120,857
1939	644,863	207,767	49,520	24,346	248,900	114,330

Source: U.S. Census, *Financial Statistics of the States.*

TABLE 8.4.
Per Capita State Revenues: Total and from Grants: 1915–1939.

	Per Capita All Revenue	Per Capita Grant Revenue (as percent of total)
1915	$4.63	$0.05 (1.1 %)
1919	$6.39	$0.11 (1.7 %)
1925	$13.10	$1.08 (8.2 %)
1930	$18.24	$0.99 (5.4 %)
1932	$17.27	$1.84 (10.7 %)
1937	$31.90	$4.56 (14.3 %)
1938	$36.33	$5.08 (14.0 %)
1939	$36.54	$5.26 (14.4 %)

Source: U.S. Census, *Financial Statistics of the States.*

The expansion of federal-state matching grants represents a mutant form of "the forging of bureaucratic autonomy." Under such systems of governance, public funds may flow through public agencies staffed by career civil servants with professional identities, but the result is a system that is potentially opaque to citizens (as well as, perhaps, elected officials). Thus, even when funds flow entirely within public channels, the use of indirection and incentives to implement policies creates principal-agent dilemmas in politics. Elected officials at the federal level are challenged in overseeing programs that are actually implemented by state agencies yet may advocate the use of this indirect arrangement in order to extend federal intervention to policy domains understood as the reserve of state government; citizens lack an obvious connection between taxes paid to one government and services received from another.

The Rube Goldberg State

Through the lens of public finance, the geometry and balance of federalism as well as the clean boundaries of autonomous bureaucracies are overgrown by a tangle of cross-cutting relationships of collaboration and dependence. Consequently, analytic efforts to distill this complexity eliminate a pervasive feature of American governance. This is, of course, the cost of any analytic effort, but in this case the costs may be high to our understanding of American political development.

Why do the complexity and the institutionalized indirection matter? Above all, these arrangements encourage a misrecognition of public services as private, a misrecognition of federal funds as state government. As Hacker and Howard have argued with respect to the use of tax expenditures to encourage the expansion of employee benefits,[69] publicly subsidized benefits are understood as privately owned and privately earned. More locally provided services may also be understood as locally funded. Thus, this localizing and individualizing interpretation of the program undermines the capacity of social programs to facilitate redistribution in the interests of equity and the likelihood that policy entrepreneurs will be able to win widespread expansions of benefits.

Although studies of tax expenditures have emphasized the benefits of these publicly financed, privately implemented programs to third-party providers (insurance companies, real estate interests), dependence entails risk. This is perhaps more evident in policy domains that involve social services to the disadvantaged. As nonprofit providers found to their dismay in the 1980s, President Reagan's conviction that public welfare programs could be cut because charities would take care of the problem was based on a misrecognition that much "private" benevolent activity is extremely dependent on public sources of funds. Yet, in the implementation of programs and delivery of services, neither clients nor observant citizens may receive reminders that "your tax dollars are at work." Ironically, volunteerism and charity endanger the modern, bureaucratized systems of public social provision that was supposed to displace these less-efficient forms of support for dependent citizens.

Whereas recent theories have identified opacity and indirection as tools to protect elected officials,[70] the argument here suggests that the systemic complexity of the American state both has deeper institutional roots and sets in motion feedback processes that are more troubling than the reelection of less-than-candid candidates. Where policies are implemented largely through indirection and collaboration, we should expect public support for public funding to be fragile.[71] Thus, across diverse policy domains, the creation of public bureaucracies or the implementation of more variegated systems of contracting and collaboration has lasting political consequences. Rather than understanding these latter arrangements as simply failures of bureaucratic modernization, as historical residue or deviation from the Weberian ideal, scholarship in American political development should explore the diversity of the political projects that have combined to produce our oft-maligned tangle of governance.

NOTES

I am grateful to Jennifer Murdock for her help in collecting much of the data. Support for this project came from the Udall Center at the University of Arizona and from the National Science Foundation (SES-9911428).

1. E. g., Paul Pierson, *Dismantling the Welfare State? Reagan, Thatcher, and the Politics of Retrenchment* (New York: Cambridge University Press, 1994); Sven Steinmo, *Taxation and Democracy: Swedish, British, and American Approaches to Financing the Modern State* (New Haven: Yale University Press, 1993).

2. Matthew A. Crenson, *Building the Invisible Orphanage: A Prehistory of the American Welfare System* (Cambridge, MA: Harvard University Press, 1998).

3. Christopher Howard, *The Hidden Welfare State: Tax Expenditures and Social Policy in the United States* (Princeton: Princeton University Press, 1997); Jacob S. Hacker, *The Divided Welfare State: The Battle over Public and Private Social Benefits in the United States* (New York: Cambridge University Press, 2002).

4. Paul H. Douglas, "A System of Federal Grants-in-Aid I," *Political Science Quarterly* 35 (no. 2, 1920): 255–271, and Douglas, "A System of Federal Grants-in-Aid II," *Political Science Quarterly* 35 (no. 4, 1920): 522–544.

5. Jason Kaufman, *For the Common Good? American Civic Life and the Golden Age of Fraternity* (New York: Oxford University Press, 2002), ch. 6; P. W. Singer, *Corporate Warriors: The Rise of the Privatized Military Industry* (Ithaca: Cornell University Press, 2003).

6. Max Weber, *Economy and Society*, vol. I, edited by Guenther Roth and Claus Wittich (Berkeley: University of California Press, 1978), 223.

7. Daniel P. Carpenter, *The Forging of Bureaucratic Autonomy: Reputations, Networks and Policy Innovation in Executive Agencies, 1862–1928* (Princeton: Princeton University Press, 2001); Peter B. Evans and James E. Rauch, "Bureaucracy and Growth: A Cross-National Analysis of the Effects of 'Weberian' State Structures on Economic Growth," *American Sociological Review* 64 (no. 5, 1999): 748–765.

8. Stephen Skowronek, *Building a New American State: The Expansion of National Administrative Capacities, 1877–1920* (New York: Cambridge University Press, 1982). For a development of this argument, see Elisabeth S. Clemens, "Rereading Skowronek: A Precocious Theory of Institutional Change," *Social Science History* 27 (no. 3, 2003): 443–453. This asymmetrical treatment of reform visions and resisting interests contrasts with Wallace Stegner's narrative of John Wesley Powell and the establishment of government scientific bureaus. In his account, the opponents of rational bureaucratic management of the arid West were informed by their own substantive vision of how the settlement of the arid lands would produce riches. Wallace Stegner, *Beyond the Hundredth Meridian: John Wesley Powell and the Second Opening of the American West* (New York: Penguin 1992 [1954]).

9. Austin F. MacDonald, "Federal Aid to the States," Supplement to *National Municipal Review* 17, no. 10 (October 1928): 651–656.

10. David E. Osborne and Ted Gaebler, *Reinventing Government: How the Entrepreneurial Spirit Is Transforming the Public Sector* (Reading,MA: Addison-Wesley, 1992).

11. Social Security is the major exception here.

12. Ironically, even the social insurance program that most closely approximated the pure public bureaucracy had to be misrepresented to the public to make it comprehensible and legitimate. Proponents of Social Security deliberately drew on the model of the personal savings account—your payments in an account for your retirement—to mobilize support for what was actually a pay-as-you-go system of intergenerational transfers. Jerry Cates, *Insuring Inequality* (Ann Arbor: University of Michigan Press, 1983).

13. Karen Orren and Stephen Skowronek, *The Search for American Political Development* (New York: Cambridge University Press, 2004).

14. R. Douglas Arnold, *The Logic of Congressional Action* (New Haven: Yale University Press, 1990); Pierson, *Dismantling the Welfare State?*

15. Clarence Y. H. Lo, *Small Property versus Big Government: Social Origins of the Property Tax Revolt* (Berkeley: University of California Press, 1990); Edward J. McCaffery, *Taxing Women* (Chicago: University of Chicago Press, 1997).

16. George Creel, "Unscrambling Government," *Colliers* 67 (June 25, 1921): 5.

17. Michel Foucault, *Discipline or Punish: The Birth of the Prison* (New York: Vintage, 1977); James C. Scott, *Seeing Like a State: How Certain Schemes to Improve the Human Condition Have Failed* (New Haven: Yale University Press, 1996). In contrast to this emphasis on surveillance, it is possible to begin a list of what the modern American state has refused—or at least been reluctant—to see. Consider, for example, the demands for counts of traffic violations issued in the context of the "driving while black" controversy or the lack of appropriations to support tracking of former welfare recipients once they left the welfare rolls. More recently, information that might be relevant to political competition (e. g., data on jobs lost) has been removed from government Web sites.

18. Theodore M. Porter, *Trust in Numbers: The Pursuit of Objectivity in Science and Public Life* (Princeton: Princeton University Press, 1995); Wendy Nelson Espeland, *The Struggle for Water: Politics, Rationality, and Identity in the American Southwest* (Chicago: University of Chicago Press, 1998).

19. Peter B. Evans, *Embedded Autonomy: States and Industrial Transformations* (Princeton: Princeton University Press, 1995).

20. Evans and Rauch, "Bureaucracy and Growth," 749.

21. Elisabeth S. Clemens, Martin D. Hughes, Steven Nelson, and Wade Roberts, "The Politics of Benevolence: Building and Borrowing State Capacity, 1890–1920," manuscript, University of Chicago, 2002.

22. Steven Rathgeb Smith and Michael Lipsky, *Nonprofits for Hire: The Welfare State in the Age of Contracting* (Cambridge, MA: Harvard University Press, 1993); Claire F. Ullman, "Partners in Reform: Nonprofit Organizations and the Welfare State in France," in W. W. Powell and E. S. Clemens, eds., *Private Action and the Public Good* (New Haven: Yale University Press, 1998).

23. Note that, through these arrangements, state officials displace much of the risk of policy or budget changes onto nonstate organizations. When, for example, legislators turned from placing orphans in institutions to placing them in private families through fostering arrangements, charitable organizations and the Catholic Church were left with excess capacity and dwindling subsidies.

24. Charles Richmond Henderson, "Sidney Webb's 'Extension Ladder,'" *The Survey* 32 (May 23, 1914): 227; Florence L. Lattimore, "Prying up the Lid of the Subsidy System in Pennsylvania," *The Survey* 34 (April 10, 1915): 42–43.

25. "Wanted in Pennsylvania—A Man!" (by "A Pennsylvania Manufacturer"), *Outlook* 80 (June 10, 1905): 375. In an analysis of subsidies to private charitable organizations in Pennsylvania, we found that measures of socioeconomic development and ethnic conflict did not offer much explanation of the total amount of subsidies provided to benevolent institutions within each county. In our models, however, both the proportion of the vote given to the Republican gubernatorial candidate in 1910 and the number of county representatives on the appropriations committee were robustly associated with the benefits to the county. In this, admittedly one of the "most corrupt cases," the organization of public finance clearly followed a logic of party patronage. Clemens et al., "The Politics of Benevolence."

26. Archibald E. Stevenson, *States' Rights and National Prohibition* (New York: Clark Boardman, 1927), 89.

27. Albert W. Atwood, "Leaning on Uncle Sam," *The Saturday Evening Post* (January 10, 1931): 23.

28. MacDonald, "Federal Aid to the States," 656.

29. Skowronek, *Building a New American State;* see also Harry N. Scheiber, "Federalism and the American Economic Order, 1789–1910," *Law and Society Review* 10 (no. 1, 1975): 57–118.

30. Carpenter, *The Forging of Bureaucratic Autonomy.*

31. *Beyond the Hundredth Meridian,* Stegner's account of the life and work of John Wesley Powell, powerfully illustrates the entwinement of substantive policy projects and institutional reform. Aided by a tight network of co-adventurers from his expeditions down the Colorado River and throughout the surrounding regions of the arid West, Powell established the foundation for government science (arguably the site of some of the most autonomous bureaucracies of the late nineteenth century) and attempted to construct institutions that could regulate and direct the settlement of the regions east of the Mississippi and west of the Sierra. In this project, however, he was defeated by other political visions and strategies.

32. Joel H. Silbey, *The American Political Nation, 1838–1893* (Stanford: Stanford University Press, 1991).

33. Austin F. MacDonald, "Federal Subsidies to the States: A Study in American Administration," Ph.D. dissertation, University of Pennsylvania, 1923.

34. At the level of federal government, multiple forms of "policy by indirection" were developed. In particular, the use of incentives embedded in the tax code has received considerable attention as a central mechanism in the public/private American welfare state. See Howard, *The Hidden Welfare State*.

35. Although this discussion focuses on subsidy arrangements between state governments and private (charitable, ecclesiastical, or proprietary) organizations, collaborative arrangements were also used to expand, or substitute for, state capacity in other policy domains. On "regulation by association" in the insurance industry, for example, see Marc Schneiberg and Tim Bartley, "Regulating American Industries: Markets, Politics, and the Institutional Determinants of Fire Insurance Regulation," *American Journal of Sociology* 107 (no. 1, 2001): 101–146.

36. U.S. Bureau of the Census, *Wealth, Debt, and Taxation: 1913* (Washington, DC: Government Printing Office, 1915).

37. California, Massachusetts, and Wisconsin are simply convenient examples, demonstrating that considerable variation in financial arrangements existed even across relatively industrialized, relatively progressive states.

38. See also Frank A. Fetter, "The Subsidizing of Private Charities," *American Journal of Sociology* 7 (November 1901): 361–364.

39. William H. Slingerland, *Child Welfare Work in California: A Study of Agencies and Institutions* (New York: Russell Sage, 1915); U.S. Bureau of the Census, *Benevolent Institutions: 1904* (Washington, DC: Government Printing Office, 1905); U.S. Bureau of the Census, *Benevolent Institutions: 1910* (Washington, DC: Government Printing Office, 1913). See also Fetter, "The Subsidizing of Private Charities," 360; Alexander Fleisher, "State Money and Privately Managed Charities," *The Survey* 33 (October 31, 1914): 110–112.

40. For a more extensive discussion, see Elisabeth S. Clemens, *The People's Lobby: Organizational Innovation and the Rise of Interest Group Politics in the United States, 1890–1925* (Chicago: University of Chicago Press, 1997), ch. 7.

41. Hacker, *The Divided Welfare State*.

42. In a few cases, the GAR was designated as the agent to determine eligibility for state-funded military pensions. Here, state support might extend to paying both rent and payroll for the organization.

43. In some states, considerable policy powers were delegated to societies for the prevention of cruelty to animals (and sometimes to children), and fines might be designated as ongoing support for these organizations.

44. U.S. Census, *Financial Statistics of the States* (Washington, DC: Government Printing Office, 1915, 1919, 1925, 1930).

45. Arlien Johnson, *Public Policy and Private Charities: A Study of Legislation in*

the United States and of Administration in Illinois (Chicago: University of Chicago Press, 1931). Many state governments—twenty-six as of 1930—were constitutionally forbidden to make such payments, but these limits were not necessarily honored. In 1921, the Pennsylvania courts ended a three-decade history of subsidies to religious organizations by recognizing—albeit reluctantly—the longstanding constitutional requirement that "no appropriation, except for pensions or gratuities for military services, shall be made for charitable, educational or benevolent purposes to any person or community, nor any denominational or sectarian institution, corporation or association." The court refrained from endorsing the spirit of this restriction, concluding that "There can be no doubt that all the institutions at bar are worthy charities; but it is equally clear that they are within the inhibited class, as far as state aid is concerned. We did not write the constitution; but whether agreeing with, or dissenting from the rules of public policy there announced, our sworn duty is to enforce them. Those who adopted the restrictions against appropriating money to sectarian institutions must change the rule, if desired, either through an amendment to the present constitution or by making a new one; neither the legislature acting alone nor the courts have the power to do so." "Church and State," *The Survey* (July 16, 1921): 489–490.

46. Fetter, "The Subsidizing of Private Charities," 367.

47. Ibid., 371. In recommending principles for state aid to private agencies, one commentator complained that "Inadequate appropriations to the Mothers' Assistance Fund coupled with subsidies to children's institutions intent upon maintaining a clientele and 'operating in apparent ignorance of the security and protection offered to children' through mothers' assistance as well as 'other resources for family relief,' are patently absurd." Mary Clarke Burnett, "State Aid for Private Agencies," *The Survey* (August 1935): 234–235.

48. Crenson, *The Invisible Orphanage;* "Mixing Politics with Charity," *The Survey* (July 22, 1916): 427–428.

49. Sidney Webb, "The Extension Ladder Theory of the Relation Between Voluntary Philanthropy and *State* or *Municipal* Action," *The Survey* 31 (March 7, 1914): 703–707; Henderson, "Sidney Webb's 'Extension Ladder.'"

50. MacDonald, "Federal Subsidies to the States," 1.

51. Ibid., 11.

52. It is probably not irrelevant that the "Smith" of so much of the early federal-state matching legislation was Hoke Smith of Georgia. Smith had served as secretary of the interior under Cleveland (1893–1896), then became involved in state politics in Georgia and became governor in 1907. He was then elected to fill a seat in the U.S. Senate as of 1911. This path from one of the most powerful federal agencies through a state executive branch to the federal legislature provided Smith with an unusual perspective on the possibilities of federal-state cooperation. Dewey W. Grantham Jr., *Hoke Smith and the Politics of the New South* (Baton Rouge: Louisiana State University Press, 1958).

53. Austin F. MacDonald, "Federal Subsidies for Education," *Annals of the Academy of Political and Social Science* 129 (January 1927): 102.

54. Clemens, *The People's Lobby*, 313–314; MacDonald, "Federal Subsidies for Education," 103.

55. See also V. O. Key, "State Legislation Facilitative of Federal Action," *Annals of the Academy of Political and Social Science* 207 (January 1940): 7–13. During this period, many states had biennial legislatures with most of these meeting in odd-numbered years. In some cases, state legislatures anticipated congressional action and passed enabling legislation prior to passage of the federal statute.

56. Atwood, "Leaning on Uncle Sam."

57. MacDonald, "Federal Aid to the States," 622.

58. Marvin B. Rosenberry, "Development of the Federal Idea," *North American Review* 218 (August 1923): 166–167.

59. Stevenson, *States' Rights and National Prohibition*, 8–9.

60. Joseph P. Harris, "The Future of Federal Grants-in-Aid," *Annals of the Academy of Political and Social Science* 207 (January 1940): 18.

61. Clemens, *The People's Lobby*, ch. 8; John Mark Hansen, "Choosing Sides: The Creation of an Agricultural Policy Network in Congress, 1919–1932," *Studies in American Political Development* 2 (1987): 183–229; Pendleton Herring, *Group Representation Before Congress* (New York: Russell and Russell, 1929).

62. Key, "State Legislation Facilitative of Federal Action," 12.

63. G. Homer Durham, "Politics and Administration in Intergovernmental Relations," *Annals of the Academy of Political and Social Science* 207 (January 1940): 5.

64. MacDonald, "Federal Aid to the States, 656.

65. MacDonald, "Federal Subsidies to the States"; Key, "State Legislation Facilitative of Federal Action," 8–9.

66. Unfortunately, publication of these data was suspended during the early 1930s as a budget-cutting measure.

67. *Historical Statistics of the United States* (Series Y, Columns 750 and 754, p. 1131).

68. From a low of below 2 percent in 1902, this proportion peaked at approximately 16 percent in 1936 and then returned to near the turn-of-the-century low by the end of World War II. By 1970, this proportion had grown steadily to a level of just over 10 percent. *Historical Statistics of the United States* (Series Y, Columns 590 and 591, p. 1123).

69. Hacker, *The Divided Welfare State;* Howard, *The Hidden Welfare State.*

70. Arnold, *The Logic of Congressional Action;* Pierson, *Dismantling the Welfare State.*

71. Contrast the case of social welfare provision with the military. Here, as well, there is heavy reliance on contracting out, although typically to for-profit rather than nonprofit private organizations.

9

Government Institutions, Policy Cartels, and Policy Change

R. Kent Weaver

The renewal of interest in institutions in political analysis over the past twenty years has been accompanied by a broadening of the scope of what is defined as an institution. The "old" institutionalism focused primarily on the formal institutions of government (e.g., executives, legislatures, courts) and has been criticized for excessive emphasis on constitutional/legal structures rather than actual behavior and consequences, as well as for excessive normative emphases and for insufficient attention to cross-national theory building and testing.[1] Phenomena as broad as labor unions, party systems, the organization of labor markets, and even political ideas are now analyzed as institutions in North's broad sense of the term as "the humanly devised constraints that shape social interaction."[2] Indeed, Ellen Immergut has noted that it can be said of "new institutional" analysis, like the political behavior approach that preceded it as a dominant paradigm in political science, that the term "could encompass just about anything."[3]

As the scope of institutional analysis has broadened, relatively less attention has been devoted to what can be called "formal" governmental institutions, such as the structure of executive-legislative relations, federalism, bicameralism versus unicameralism, and electoral rules and procedures. But the total amount of research on governmental institutions has been quite robust. Governmental institutions have been analyzed as both independent and dependent variables, using a variety of approaches ranging from formal modeling to quantitative cross-national approaches to comparative and single-country case studies. And it has certainly transcended the "old" institutional paradigm of concentrating on formal rules and procedures to try to discern real patterns of behavior and impacts. For example, a lively debate exists on whether presidentialism and parliamentarism affect democratic performance in such areas as accountability, representation, and protection of minority rights.[4] Another substantial literature addresses the size and scope of government spending.[5] Hammond and Butler, using a formal modeling approach, argue that whether and how the arrangement of governmental institutions matters for policy choices depends as much on the distribution of public and policymaker preferences as on those arrangements themselves.[6]

The literature on welfare-state retrenchment suggests several arguments about how governmental institutions structure opportunities for policy change—especially changes that impose losses on domestic political groups with significant power resources. Perhaps the most obvious argument is that political systems that concentrate power in the executive, with few and relatively weak veto points where retrenchment initiatives can be blocked, are more likely to enact loss-imposing initiatives than those that lack these institutions. Thus, Westminster-style single-chamber legislatures with cohesive, executive-dominated single-party majorities and no requirement for a legislative supermajority or approval by subnational governments, for example, might be expected to exhibit higher loss-imposing capacity than systems with multiple veto points.

This chapter examines arguments about the effects of governmental institutions on governmental capacity for short- and medium-term loss imposition on politically salient constituencies, as well as their capacity to make "path-changing" shifts in the basic components of established "policy regimes" within a specific sector. The first section of the chapter provides an overview of what the existing political science literature suggests about the effects of governmental institutions, and in particular different executive-legislative arrangements, on governmental capacity to produce policy change. The second section of the chapter discusses several problems in analyzing institutional effects that make it unlikely that any effects of governmental institutions will be clear and consistent. The third section of the chapter looks very briefly at cross-national evidence on pension-retrenchment (short-term loss-imposition) and restructuring (regime-changing) initiatives in six countries: the United States, Canada, the United Kingdom, New Zealand, Sweden, and Germany. The concluding section revisits the arguments outlined in the first two sections in light of evidence from pension policymaking.

I. Political Institutions and Policy Change

Politicians are reluctant to take actions that impose concentrated losses on groups of voters, even if they produce offsetting gains for other voters, because voters tend to be more sensitive to losses they have suffered than to benefits provided. Indeed, politicians use a variety of strategies to avoid blame from disgruntled voters, including passing the buck to other decision makers, scapegoating, and delaying onset of losses until after an election.[7]

Political scientists have long argued that governing institutions that feature a great concentration of power and minimization of veto points should lead to higher capacity for loss imposition and policy innovation generally than occurs with governing institutions that lack these features. Ellen Immergut, for example, argues that the greater capacity of the Swedish government to impose policies opposed by the medical profession in Sweden than was the case in Switzerland or France does not reflect cross-national differences in the perceived self-interest or organizational strength of doctors. Instead, it reflects the fact that during the critical period of consolidation of government's role in health care, the Swedish Social Democrats could usually count on stable (single-party or coalition) support in both chambers of the Riksdag, while Swiss physicians enjoyed greater institutional leverage, notably the capacity to call referenda. French doctors enjoyed strong leverage in the unstable parliamentary regimes of the Fourth Republic but lost much of that leverage in the executive-dominated Fifth Republic.[8] Tsebelis frames the issue slightly differently, in terms of veto players. He argues that countries with multiple players (like the United States and Italy) and a larger distance between the preferences of those veto players are likely to have both a higher degree of policy stability and a larger policymaking role for nonelected officials (notably judges and bureaucrats) than those with fewer veto players.[9]

A particularly large literature has arisen on differences between Westminster-style parliamentary systems like that in the United Kingdom and the separation-of-powers system found in the United States, which features multiple veto points and a much greater diffusion of power. Minimal veto points are generally seen to produce not only greater capacity for loss imposition and policy change but also greater policy volatility—in particular, increased risk of policy reversal and "cycling" after elections lead to a change in party control of government. Parliamentary systems with proportional-representation electoral rules, which generally do not produce single-party majority governments, are presumably less likely than West-minster systems to produce major flip-flops in policy, especially when they are "anchored" by large centrist parties.

Other authors have questioned at least the magnitude and consistency of any effects of different political structures, however. Pierson and Weaver note that the advantages of concentrated power and minimal veto points may be at least partially offset by concentration of accountability in political systems.[10] Voters know that it is the governing party that is imposing losses, and those in power know that they know it and may therefore to be reluctant to undertake initiatives that are very likely to incur retribution at the next election. Moreover, even governing parties with extraordinarily strong formal powers may face pressures not to use them to maximize their own preferences because both they and direct stakeholders may view stability and predictability over time as more important than the governing party's maximizing its preferences in the short run.

Efforts to uncover consistent institutional effects on governmental capacity for loss imposition in other sectors have in fact been mixed. In concluding their eight-sector comparison of capacity for governmental loss imposition in the United States and Canada, for example, Pal and Weaver find modest and inconsistent institutional effects and argue that policy outcomes more frequently look similar within sectors across countries than they do within countries across sectors.[11]

II. Constraints on Institutional Explanations

Untangling relationships between governmental institutions and policy choices and outcomes is difficult for a number of reasons. Indeed, these analytical difficulties are common not just in the analysis of governmental institutions but in almost any type of institutional analysis.

Problem 1: Variation Based on Micro-Rules

Within the broad categories of institutional arrangements of separation of powers, Westminster parliamentarism, and proportional-representation-based parliamentarism, what can be called the "micro-rules" of how legislatures are selected and maintained in office, as well as procedural rules within the legislature, can have an important impact on capacity for policy change. For example, all other things being equal, we would expect that countries that have relatively short electoral cycles may find it particularly difficult to make changes that impose visible losses on political salient groups in the short term. Multiple electoral cycles (e.g., the differing electoral cycles for the president and legislature in France or for federal and provincial legislatures in Canada and Germany) may also inhibit governmental willingness and capacity to undertake loss-imposing actions if politicians at each of these levels are involved in decision making or feel that their electoral or policy objectives will be undercut if voters in those elections associate them with unpopular policies.[12]

Similarly, parliamentary systems that require a constructive vote of no confidence to bring down a government might have somewhat greater capacity to impose losses than systems in which a government can simply be turned out when it proposes unpopular legislation. Countries with a decentralized system of campaign finance and candidate-centered elections like the United States may be especially vulnerable to interest group influence and thus have poor capacity to impose losses at least on groups that have significant capacity for electoral mobilization. While the impact of specific institutional micro-rules may be small in most cases, variation is possible on a large number of dimensions, and their aggregate individual and interactive effects may overwhelm the effects of broad institutional arrangements.

Problem 2: Variation over Time

The capacity of governmental institutions to facilitate loss imposition and regime change may also vary over time on the basis of variations around any "modal tendency" in the way that those institutions operate. In general, we might expect a government in a parliamentary system to have greater capacity to impose losses (a) when a single party or durable coalition holds a majority of seats in the legislature than when there is a minority government, (b) when its legislative majority is large and (c) when opposition parties are very fragmented and do not, collectively or individually, form a credible alternative to the governing party or coalition. The situation of the British Labour Party under most of Margaret Thatcher's premiership in the United Kingdom is a good example of a weak opposition that may make a governing party more willing to risk loss-imposing actions. Similarly, we might expect the U.S. government to be more effective at imposing losses and innovating in policy when control of the executive and the legislative branches of government is united in the same party than when it is divided, although empirical findings in this regard have been mixed.[13] Echoes of this analysis can be found in Christopher Leman's well-known argument that multiple veto points in the United States have confined major periods of welfare-state expansion in the United States to times when progressive Democratic presidents enjoyed huge congressional majorities that rendered them less vulnerable to being watered down or rejected by entrenched conservative forces within Congress.[14] If the variation on these dimensions (e.g., in legislative majorities and in united versus divided governments under presidentialism) is large and their effects significant, the consequences of general institutional arrangements may be modest in effect, or simply harder to detect.

Problem 3: Venue Shifting

Scholars of the U.S. political system have long noted that groups that are unable to achieve their goals in their first-choice venue may seek to shift the locus of decision making to venues where they are more likely to get a decision that they prefer—for example, from legislatures to the courts. It is plausible that countries where legislative-executive arrangements are particularly prone to deadlock may also see venue shifting by government elites or others who seek to impose losses. Indeed, Pal and Weaver find that courts are more frequently used as a venue for loss imposition in the United States than they are in Canada. Federal judges do not have to be reelected in either country, but they may be more likely to be called upon for loss imposition in the United States both because of a long (but eroding) tradition of judicial deference in Canada and because the Canadian legislative process is less likely to result in deadlock.[15] Appointive regulatory commissions may also serve as a venue for decisions that elective politicians do not want to make.

Problem 4: Ad Hoc Institutional Arrangements

In addition to shifting conflicts to different institutional venues, systems with relatively weak capacity to impose losses may also develop ad hoc arrangements in specific policy sectors that allow politicians to overcome multiple veto points and avoid blame for unpopular actions by facilitating an agreement between key social and political actors. What these institutional arrangements, which can be labeled "policy cartels," have in common is that they have received at least tacit government recognition and acceptance as mechanisms to resolve policy conflict. But they can vary on a number of dimensions, including (1) the breadth of the interests they incorporate, (2) the degree to which they are sponsored by and formally are a part of government, (3) whether they operate within a single policy sector or multiple sectors, and (4) their actual and presumed perpetuity.

In the United States, for example, ad hoc commissions have been used to address politically sensitive issues like military base closings and Social Security reform, with varying degrees of success. In many European countries, bargaining between employers and trade unions, with government as a concerned (and sometimes guiding) third partner, is an important feature of the policymaking process. Myles and Quadagno have suggested that, because leaders of these "social partners" can reach binding agreements and allocate costs among their members, such arrangements may facilitate pension retrenchment and restructuring.[16] Karen Anderson has argued that labor unions that perceive welfare-state reforms as part of a broader effort at economic stabilization and that see themselves as essential partners in achieving that stability in collaboration with social democratic governments may be willing to make greater compromises than unions that are more marginalized in policymaking.[17] Nonpartisan "technocratic" governments in parliamentary systems are another form of policy cartel: Competing political parties agree to support a government that will make tough decisions with which supporting parties do not want to be directly associated.

If these policy cartel arrangements operate effectively over time in many policy sectors, they may significantly enhance the capacity of a political system to impose losses. If (as seems plausible) they are used disproportionately in political systems that have a weak capacity to impose losses through "normal" channels, the effects of broad governmental institutions may once again be offset or obscured.

Problem 5: Nongovernmental Variables That Swamp Institutional Effects

Particularly when comparisons are done using a small number of policy sectors and countries, there is a danger that institutional effects may be either obscured or overwhelmed by the effects of other variables. For example, Paul Pierson has highlighted what he calls the "politics of permanent austerity"—common but differentially felt pressures to reduce spending that are rooted in broad economic and demographic trends.[18]

These pressures may have a stronger impact on government's need and willingness to make painful spending cuts than whether governmental institutions concentrate power and accountability, potentially obscuring and/or overwhelming any effects of governmental institutions.

An equally important constraint on policy change—and especially a nonincremental shift in "policy regimes"—is also highlighted in Pierson's work: "policy feedbacks" from existing policies. Once in place, policy regimes tend to spawn supportive coalitions. Moreover, changes are likely to impose costs on politicians, program clientele, and implementers who have adapted their expectations and strategies to the current policy regime; thus, those policies are likely to at least be "sticky," if not "locked in."[19] Moreover, different policy regimes may provide very different opportunities for obscuring losses and avoiding blame that are unrelated to the overall set of governmental institutions in those countries. A focus on "path-dependent" policy regimes suggests that, once policy regimes have become deeply embedded, policy change should be primarily within the parameters of that regime.

Other nongovernmental factors may also lead outcomes that may cut across the lines predicted by an analysis of governing institutions. Participation in networks of policy learning and emulation within regions or under sponsorship of international financial institutions, for example, may affect the prospects that a country will introduce a major change in a particular policy regime.[20]

III. Pension Politics

Pension policy is a good area through which to examine governmental capacity for both short-term loss imposition and longer-term policy regime restructuring. All else being equal, we expect both short-term loss imposition and nonincremental policy regime change to be greater in Westminster systems than in the U.S. separation-of-powers system. Proportional-representation parliamentary systems should have lower capacity for policy change than Westminster systems, but the diversity of micro-rules in the PR parliamentary category should lead to highly diverse outcomes in that regime type. Countries with a large number of parties and fluid party alignments should have more difficulties in achieving policy change than countries with few parties and rigid party adherence. Because even strong governments are generally reluctant to

undertake visible cuts, especially during the lead-up to elections, differences in loss-imposing outcomes should be modest unless they are reinforced by other factors.

Other factors should also influence policy outcomes. Because public
pension systems are generally embedded in statute, venue shifting to other
government institutions should be limited in all regime types. But governing parties in all institutional regimes have incentives to use blame-diffusing "policy cartels," while opposition parties have incentives to reject them
or defect from them. Incentives for and customs of collaborating in such
mechanisms are likely to be highest in PR parliamentary systems.

Any effects of governmental institutions on loss imposition and
restructuring in pensions are also likely to be obscured by pressures for
change in existing retirement income systems that are common to all
industrialized countries but felt differentially across them. Most important
is the pressure of population aging, which is generally more severe in
Western Europe and in Japan than it is in Canada, the United States, Aus-
tralia, and New Zealand.

Politicians' common desire to avoid blame for unpopular action should
result in substantial similarities in policy choices across governmental
institution types in many aspects of pension reform, notably (1) delays
and long phase-in periods for changes in retirement ages, lowering of pension replacement rates, contribution rate increases, and other controversial changes, (2) grandfathering of current recipients to prevent them
from suffering highly visible losses, and (3) use of highly technical formula
changes to make retrenchment less visible. However, different policy
regimes provide distinctive opportunity structures for policy change
across countries. For example, poor targeting of universal flat-rate pensions may make them vulnerable both to benefit cutbacks at upper ranges
and to more fundamental restructuring initiatives, but universal pensions
make it harder to use "grandfathering" strategies to lower political resistance to cutbacks. Countries that require all pension expenditures to be
financed by current contributions and accrued surpluses may provide an
"action-forcing mechanism" for retrenchment or broader pension reform.

In the remainder of this section, thumbnail sketches are provided of
pension policymaking in one country with a separation-of-powers political system (the United States), three with Westminster-style parliamentary
systems (Canada, the United Kingdom, and New Zealand until 1996), and
three proportional-representation parliamentary systems (Sweden, Germany, and New Zealand after 1996). Each country discussion includes a

brief summary of the severity of the demographic challenges facing that country, the structure of government institutions, policy feedbacks from the existing pension system, and the record of pension-policy change over the past two decades.

The United States

Although the population of the United States is aging rapidly, its demographic challenge is in fact relatively modest relative to that facing most other industrialized countries in both the short and the long run. The United States relies overwhelmingly on a social insurance program (Social Security) with both contribution rates and benefits that are relatively modest by Western European standards. In addition, there is a very small means-tested tier (Supplemental Security Income) that pays very low benefits to very few seniors and a very large program of tax incentives for employer-provided and personal pensions.[21] A trust fund and strict limitations on the use of general revenues to finance Social Security benefits provides an action-forcing mechanism that can add pressure for benefit and eligibility retrenchment.

U.S. governmental institutions, however, make loss-imposing actions more difficult. Multiple veto points within the federal government have been strengthened by the existence of divided government for almost all of the years between 1981 and 2002, which further increased the potential for gridlock. Candidate-centered elections and weak party discipline make it more difficult for politicians to avoid blame for unpopular votes in favor of Social Security retrenchment or restructuring.

The experience of Social Security reform over the past thirty years reflects this combination of policy feedbacks and institutional constraints. Major funding crises that threatened imminent inability to pay out benefits served as an action-forming mechanism for two major rounds of retrenchment in 1977 and 1983, including a long-term reduction in replacement rates in 1977 and introduction of benefit taxation for upper-income recipients and a delayed and very gradual increase in standard retirement age from sixty-five to sixty-seven (with a simultaneous increase in penalties for early retirement) in 1983. Ad hoc indexation cuts were also made in 1983, but the indexation principle remained intact. Those changes restored a positive cash flow to Social Security that will last until around 2017, making restrictive changes politically much more difficult. Indeed, the United States stands out from other industrialized countries in experiencing virtually no retrenchment since 1983, except for an increase in taxation of Social Security benefits for upper-income recipients in 1993.

A very broad range of restructuring options for Social Security has been discussed over the past decade. The Clinton administration proposed allowing investment of Social Security surpluses in equities markets to increase returns, in addition to a system of supplemental individual retirement savings accounts. At the beginning of his second term, George W. Bush proposed a major initiative to allow individuals to partially opt out of Social Security into a system of funded individual accounts. Even though Bush has significant majorities both chambers of Congress, the political sensitivity of Social Security and the absence of an immediate funding crisis make passage of a major reform package very much an uphill battle.

Canada

Like the United States, Canada confronts a demographic challenge that is more modest than that in most other industrialized countries. However, Canada also confronted severe fiscal pressures in the 1980s through the mid-1990s that made social spending politically vulnerable. Canada's public pension system is multitiered, with a quasi-universal (phased out at high incomes) flat-rate Old Age Security program and an income-tested Guaranteed Income Supplement, both financed by general revenues. In addition, there is a contributory, earnings-related Canada Pension Plan (Quebec operates a parallel and integrated Quebec Pension Plan) on top of OAS that is financed entirely by payroll taxes.

In general, Canada's Westminster-style parliamentary system facilitates making politically contentious decisions because there is no separation of executive and legislative power and the second legislative chamber (the appointive Senate) is very weak. Moreover, Canada had uninterrupted single-part majority government from 1980 until 2004 and has had weak and divided opposition parties since 1993. However, the structure of the CPP/QPP inhibits policy change because revisions must be approved by the federal government and a supermajority of provinces.

Pension-policy change in Canada, as in the United States, has been limited. A benefit "clawback" for upper-income recipients of Old Age Security was introduced by a Conservative government in 1988, using procedurally privileged budget legislation that is almost impossible for opposition parties to block or amend so long as the government has a majority, but only after the same government backed down from a 1985 initiative to partially de-index OAS benefits. And Canada has experienced only very modest restructuring of its public pensions in recent years. In the mid-1990s, the Chretien government announced plans to merge the quasi-universal OAS program and the income-tested GIS in a way that would further reduce benefits for upper-income recipients. But the plan was repeatedly delayed because of its political sensitivity, and it was eventually shelved when emerging federal budget surpluses made cutting public pensions seem like a political nonstarter.

For the payroll-tax-financed Canada Pension Plan, efforts to address growing deficits in the program were initially delayed by the difficulty of securing the broad federal-provincial agreement needed to revise the program. But, once Ottawa and most provincial governments reached an agreement in 1997, there was little that opponents could do to block or revise it. The outcome was a major contribution-rate increase enacted in 1997, but only modest (and hard-to-see because of their technical nature) cutbacks in benefits.[22] But a broader restructuring toward individual accounts as a mandatory component of or opt-out from the CPP made even less headway than in the United States; the major opposition party favored such a shift but was powerless to get it on the agenda in a political system where the governing party has a virtual monopoly on the policy agenda.

United Kingdom

A quasi-universal flat-rate basic pension has long been the anchor of the United Kingdom's public pension system. A prolonged stalemate between Labour and the Conservatives delayed adoption of a State Earnings Related Pension Scheme (SERPS) until 1975. Because many workers were already covered by occupational pension schemes by this point, SERPS included an opt-out for approved occupational schemes rather than keeping them as an add-on to the state scheme. The United Kingdom also relies heavily on income-tested benefit programs for the elderly.

Several aspects of U.K. political institutions facilitate both short-term loss imposition and policy regime change: the lack of separation of executive and legislative power, single-party majority government since the 1979 election (frequently with very large majorities in the House of Commons), and extremely weak bicameralism.

Policy outcomes in the U.K retirement-income system reflect this concentration of power; there has been major restructuring as well as frequent tinkering. Under Margaret Thatcher, indexing of the Basic State Pension shifted to prices from the higher of wages and prices, resulting in very large long-term cuts in benefits. The Thatcher government also marginalized SERPS by lowering benefits and creating additional incentives to opt-out into portable "personal pensions." Not surprisingly, this restructuring was enacted by a government that enjoyed strong formal powers, a clear majority in the House of Commons, and an exceptionally weak and divided Labour opposition. Even the Thatcher government was not omnipotent, however; it had to back away from its initial 1985 proposal to abolish SERPS entirely in the face of widespread criticism from its usual allies (employers and pension providers) and a pledge from Labour Party leader Neil Kinnock to reverse the change when Labour came back into power.[23]

Additional, generally incremental changes have been made under Tony Blair's New Labour. SERPS has been converted to the State Second Pension (S2P), which will increase benefits for low lifetime earners but is also intended to lower replacement rates for high earners in the long run. Other changes under Blair have generally been modestly expansionary, while addressing problems in Britain's unusual public-private pension mix. These include a series of ad hoc increases in the Basic Pension, the introduction of "stakeholder" pensions to provide an alternative to high and opaque personal pension fees, a new Pension Credit to give low earners greater incentives to save for retirement, and recent proposals for pension insurance for private pensions.

New Zealand

Like the United States and Canada, New Zealand faces a less severe aging crisis than most European countries in the short and medium terms. But New Zealand has also encountered relative economic decline and repeated budgetary and economic crises over the past thirty years.

Policy feedbacks have also heavily influenced policy choices. At the beginning of the 1970s, New Zealand relied on a combination of a universal flat-rate pension payable at age 65 and a means-tested pension, payable at age 60, both paid from general revenues. The 1972–1975 Labour government sought to add a payroll-tax-financed earnings-related pension tier, but the National government elected in 1975 quickly abolished it and substituted a more generous universal pension financed by general revenues. The absence of a trust-fund device has meant that there is no action-forcing and legitimizing mechanism for pension retrenchment, while flat-rate pensions paid to all have made it more difficult to impose retrenchment gradually by "grandfathering" current recipients and cutting benefits for later ones.

New Zealand's political institutions have had complex and ambiguous impacts. Until 1996, New Zealand's unicameral legislature was elected in single-member constituencies, leading to consistent single-party majority governments—although not always the party that won a plurality of the popular vote. Since the adoption of Mixed-Member Proportional (MMP) electoral rules in 1996, New Zealand has consistently had coalition governments. But continuation of some Westminster traditions (including quick passage of legislation through use of "urgency" procedures) even after onset of MMP in 1996 continue to concentrate both governmental power and governmental accountability. Moreover, the combination of short electoral cycles (generally three years) and close electoral competition gives politicians strong incentives to act quickly and with minimal consultation to try to embed policy and allow long-term gain to emerge from short-term pain before next election. But short electoral cycles also make it likely neither that policies will be embedded nor losses forgiven by next election.

Changes in public pension policy in New Zealand over the past two decades reflect these patterns. A National Party government was able to enact and implement a rapid increase in the age of eligibility for New Zealand Superannuation in the early 1990s, but efforts to make substantial short-term cuts in Superannuation benefits relative to the average wage and to income-test benefits for upper-income recipients proved more difficult to sustain. Efforts to limit politicking over pensions through a multiparty accord in the early 1990s failed to survive the move to MMP in 1996, when a new "swing" party, New Zealand First, condemned the accord and called for a restoration of many of the cuts made in the first part of the decade. As a junior coalition partner in the 1996–99 government, NZ First also insisted on a referendum on a complex new individual-account pension scheme. New Zealand voters overwhelmingly rejected this pension restructuring in 1997, leaving New Zealand with its existing system of flat-rate universal benefits.

Sweden

Sweden currently is among the oldest countries in the world in terms of its population over age 65. Sweden's generous public pension system—until the late 1990s a universal pension with earnings-related pension on top and an income-tested pension supplement for those with low-earnings histories—was very effective at poverty reduction, but also very expensive.

Swedish political institutions offer limited opportunities for imposing unpopular policy changes. The Social Democratic Party has been the dominant party in Sweden's single-chamber (since 1970) legislature over the past half-century, holding power for all but nine years. But a long decline in the Social Democrats' vote share, persistent minority governments, and short electoral cycles (three years between 1970 and 1994, after which the cycles returned to four years) all make loss imposition difficult.

Sweden experienced an extremely severe fiscal and economic crisis in the early 1990s, with both unemployment and budget deficits soaring to unprecedented levels. Because both payroll taxes and the overall tax burden were very high, increasing taxes was not seen as a viable option. Instead, Sweden turned to multiple rounds of incremental retrenchment in pension policy. At the same time, however, the nonsocialist government elected in Sweden in 1991 began a multiparty negotiating process for a comprehensive reform that was continued by the Social Democrats when they returned to power in 1994. This process was notable in several respects: It included most of the "coalitionable" (i.e., likely to serve in government) parties on both sides of the left/right divide; it was dominated by pragmatists on both sides; employer and union "social partners" were excluded from direct participation; and participating parties agreed to stick to the principles of agreement. Use of a multiparty working group helped to shield any particular party or set of parties from blame. The Riksdag endorsed the working-group principles in the summer of 1994, but a final agreement was not enacted until 1998, in large part because of opposition at the grassroots of the Social Democratic Party and the blue-collar labor union confederation.[24]

The new Swedish pension system is a major change in concept from the old one, although its impact is being phased in gradually. The universal pension tier is being phased out, and a new earnings-related pension will be less generous than its predecessor. The new pension system is based on what Swedes call "notional defined contribution" principles: Benefits are paid out based on the entire lifetime of contributions, with contribution rates stabilized permanently. The new system also includes a parallel system of individual accounts. The risks of poor economic performance and increased longevity have been shifted from the state to workers through a system of "automatic balancing mechanisms" that will insulate politicians from political blame and to the state budget through an expanded income-tested pension.

Germany

Germany faces a very serious challenge in the near term because of the aging of its population and an even greater challenge in the longer term, exacerbated by very low fertility rates. Germany relies overwhelming on a single pay-as-you-go social-insurance pension tier with generous provision for early retirement. The task of financing public pensions was further exacerbated by the post-1989 decision to use the pension system to help finance the costs of German reunification by promoting early labor-market exit in the former East Germany. With pension payroll tax rates already approaching 20 percent by the late 1980s (with additional subsidies from general revenues), pressures for retrenchment were enormous.

Germany's MMP electoral system has resulted in consistent coalition governments in recent years in the Bundestag. But the nature of coalition politics has changed as the party system has grown more fragmented in recent years and a two-block (Christian Democrat/Christian Social Union/Liberal versus Social Democrats and Greens) party system has emerged. The fact that the second chamber (Bundesrat) has veto power on some issues and is sometimes controlled by opposition parties further complicates pension reform efforts. Equally important, however, is the breakdown in the 1990s of a longstanding cross-party "pension consensus" mechanism that had incorporated employers and unions as well as the major political parties and helped to keep pension issues out of electoral politics.

Rising costs and payroll taxes have contributed to multiple rounds of pension retrenchment, including reductions in the generosity of early-retirement benefits (although still less-than-complete actuarial reductions), enactment (and later revocation when a new Social Democratic/Green coalition came to power) of a "demographic factor" that would have automatically lowered benefits as life expectancy rises, additional reductions over time in replacement rates, and a closer linkage between contributions and benefits. Targets were also set for both near-term and longer-term caps on payroll tax rates.

Change has continued under the Social Democratic/Green coalition. After a prolonged debate, a new quasi-mandatory tax-advantaged individual account tier was enacted in 2001 to compensate for planned future declines in public system replacement rates. And the coalition has re-enacted under a new label most of the features of the "demographic factor" it initially revoked after coming to power. Thus, while Germany has not moved as far in restructuring its pension system as Sweden, fundamental restructuring has begun and is likely to continue in the future.

Conclusion

The cases examined here suggest some mixed conclusions about the impact of governmental institutions on short-term loss-imposition and nonincremental policy restructuring. A number of common patterns in pension reform are visible across all types of governmental arrangements, notably a strong tendency for governments to use long lead times and "grandfathering" to avoid blame. Also striking is the frequency with which a variety of nonstandard legislative procedures was used to enact politically risky pension reforms. These include procedurally privileged budget procedures (Canada, United States, New Zealand) and legislation under Urgency rules (New Zealand). Nonstandard legislative procedures can also be seen in other countries' pension reforms, such as the use of executive decree authority in Italy. Overall, policy feedbacks appear to be more important and predictable determinants of outcomes than governmental institutions.

Some significant institution-specific patterns are also visible, however. With respect to the U.S. separation-of-powers system, multiple veto points clearly contributed to the extreme outlier status of the United States in not enacting any major policy change in Social Security since 1983. The structure of U.S. institutions can also help to explain why the pension reform agenda has remained relatively broad (agenda control is not monopolized by political executives), and why presidents and legislative leaders do not press very hard for restructuring reforms that are unlikely to get enacted, as with Social Security privatization proposals in the first term of George W. Bush.

The pension reform records of Westminster-style parliamentary systems, on the other hand, vary greatly, ranging from a major restructuring and cutbacks in the United Kingdom under Thatcher, to frequent tinkering in that country under Blair, to modest and intermittent change in Canada, to highly volatile short-term retrenchment as well as one major restructuring enacted and immediately reversed in New Zealand. The New

Zealand case in particular suggests that, even where short-term losses are imposed in Westminster systems, they may not be sustainable over time. The United Kingdom under Thatcher was an outlier, even among Westminster systems, in its capacity to impose both short-term losses and a shift in policy regimes. Westminster institutions were a necessary but insufficient cause: long electoral cycles, favorable policy inheritances, divisions among the political opposition, and a political leader willing to take risks were all important contributing causes to the Thatcher government's success at pension reform.

Proportional representation-based parliamentary systems also show very high variation on loss-imposing capacity. For example, Sweden was able to enact a major restructuring of its public pension system, whereas Germany enacted a less fundamental reform and New Zealand voters rejected a major reform proposal in a 1997 referendum.

The countries examined here also suggest that ad hoc mechanisms may act as functional substitutes for concentrating power and/or diffusing blame. In particular, there is a recurring pattern of blame-diffusing arrangements between major political actors that is used in pension policy. These arrangements, which might be called "policy cartels," take different forms: a multiparty pension working group in Sweden, a bipartisan Social Security Reform Commission in the United States from 1981 to 1983, a multiparty pension consensus in Germany, a Multi-party Pensions Accord in New Zealand, and closed-door negotiations between federal and provincial finance ministers on Canada Pension Plan reform. Technocratic governments in countries like Italy can also be considered to be a form of multisector policy cartel, since they are tolerated by multiple political parties but insulate those parties from political blame for tough decisions taken.

Why do governments use policy cartels and other ad hoc mechanisms relatively frequently rather than simply change the structure of governmental institutions? One obvious reason is that governmental institutions are hard to change: They are frequently embedded in constitutions and/or can be changed only by the vote of a supermajority. Moreover, existing formal institutions are also likely to be beneficial to participants in other sectors or for other purposes. Moreover, change in governing institutions creates unpredictable risks. Policy cartels can serve as a sector-specific adaptation to shortcomings in overall governmental institutions that achieve acceptable outcomes without the costs and uncertainty of broader governmental reforms.

The cases considered here also suggest, however, that there are significant cross-national differences in attempts at and success in cartelization. Policymaking cartels in pension policy have been largely absent in the United Kingdom, rare and unsustained in the United States and New Zealand, sustained but eventually collapsing in Germany, sustained in Sweden, and intermittent but hard to classify (since it involved federal-provincial negotiations rather than negotiations with social actors) in Canada. These arrangements are inherently hard to predict in a general analysis of governmental institutions, since they are by nature ad hoc. But they can be understood as arising from the desire of policymakers to "venue shift" from governmental arrangements that (1) have high political costs and/or (2) are unlikely to produce acceptable outcomes in a high-profile policy sector.

The cases suggest several conditions that are likely to make a pension policy cartel more successful and sustainable. A first condition is the existence of established patterns of cross-party/bloc policy cooperation on multiple issues, which helps to establish trust and mutual dependence. This is probably more likely to occur in PR systems than in Westminster ones, but, as Tsebelis argues, the distribution of participants' preferences as well as structure of institutions is a critical determinant of policy change.[25] Second, policy cartels are more likely to be sustainable when action-forcing mechanisms threaten large and unpredictable political costs if there is no cooperation, as in the case of the 1981–83 Social Security reform commission in the United States. Third, policy cartels may succeed when an opposition party or parties thinks that it is likely to win the next election in any event and doesn't want to deal with the issue in government. Also helpful are the presence of a labor-oriented party that is perceived by other parties to have a high capacity to prevent grassroots labor mobilization to overturn any agreement and make it an election issue and the availability of credible sanctions to prevent defection from the cartel. A pension policy cartel is less likely to be sustainable and successful in promoting controversial policy changes when there are veto points that are not controlled by members of the policy cartel, when party discipline is weak, when electoral cycles are short, and when parties negotiating an accord have weak credibility with voters.

The effects of governmental institutions on capacity for policy change are, in short, uneven and heavily contingent on micro-rules and interaction with other causal forces. Indeed, institutional effects are probably best conceptualized as interaction terms with those other forces (e. g., separation of powers *and* divided government, Westminster systems *and* short electoral cycles), rather than as separate variables. But this pattern is by no means unique to governmental institutions, and the conclusion that social scientists should draw is not that we should give up studying the impact of these institutions. It is rather that we should proceed cautiously both in the research that we do and in the conclusions that we draw from our research. More specifically, in designing research on the effects of institutions, it is important to:

- Consider multiple alternative hypotheses and causal chains
- Test our hypotheses about impacts across countries, time periods, and policy sectors to try to increase their robustness, and to find out where they need to be qualified
- Look for institutional adaptations such as policy cartels that fall outside the main categorizations used in institutional analysis and for "venue-shifting" that counteracts "normal" institutional characteristics
- Generalize cautiously and sparingly
- Draw conditional conclusions.

Clearly, these cautions apply not only to the study of governmental institutions but to the study of labor market institutions, political parties, and indeed any set of institutional arrangements.

NOTES

1. Kathleen Thelen and Sven Steinmo, "Historical Institutionalism in Comparative Politics," pp. 1–31 in Sven Steinmo, Kathleen Thelen, and Frank Longstreth, eds., *Structuring Politics: Historical Institutionalism in Comparative Politics* (Cambridge: Cambridge University Press, 1992).

2. Douglass C. North, *Institutions, Institutional Change, and Economic Performance* (Cambridge: Cambridge University Press, 1990), 3.

3. Ellen Immergut, "The Theoretical Core of the New Institutionalism," *Politics and Society* 26, 1 (1998), 5–34, at p. 5.

4. Joe Foweraker and Todd Landman, "Constitutional Design and Democratic Performance," *Democratization* 9 (Summer 2002), 43–66.

5. Torsten Persson and Guido Tabellini, *The Economic Effects of Constitutions* (Cambridge, Mass.: MIT Press, 2003).

6. Thomas H. Hammond and Christopher K. Butler, "Some Complex Answers

to the Simple Question 'Do Institutions Matter?': Policy Choice and Policy Change in Presidential and Parliamentary Systems," *Journal of Theoretical Politics* 15, 2 (April 2003), 145–200.

7. R. Kent Weaver, "The Politics of Blame Avoidance," *Journal of Public Policy* 6, 4 (1986), 371–398, and Paul D. Pierson, *Dismantling the Welfare State?: Reagan, Thatcher, and the Politics of Retrenchment* (Cambridge: Cambridge University Press, 1994).

8. Ellen Immergut, "Institutions, Veto Points, and Policy Results: A Comparative Analysis of Health Care," *Journal of Public Policy* 10, 4 (1990), 391–416.

9. George Tsebelis, *Veto Players: How Political Institutions Work* (Princeton: Princeton University Press, 2002).

10. Paul D. Pierson and R. Kent Weaver, "Imposing Losses in Pension Policy," pp. 110–150 in R. Kent Weaver and Bert A. Rockman, eds., *Do Institutions Matter?: Government Capabilities in the U.S. and Abroad* (Washington, D.C.: Brookings Institution, 1993).

11. Leslie Pal and R. Kent Weaver, *The Government Taketh Away: The Politics of Pain in the United States and Canada* (Washington, D.C.: Georgetown University Press, 2003), 297–299.

12. See Giuliano Bonoli, *The Politics of Pension Reform* (Cambridge: Cambridge University Press, 2000); Pal and Weaver, *The Government Taketh Away.*

13. See for example David Mayhew, *Divided We Govern* (New Haven: Yale University Press, 1991); Sarah A. Binder, *Stalemate: Causes and Consequences of Legislative Gridlock* (Washington, D.C.: Brookings Institution, 2003).

14. Christopher Leman, "Patterns of Policy Development: Social Security in the United States and Canada," *Public Policy* 25, 2 (1977), 261–291. For a contrasting view, see Paul D. Pierson, "The Creeping Nationalization of Income Transfers in the United States, 1935–94," pp. 301–328 in Stephan Leibfried and Paul Pierson, eds., *European Social Policy: Between Fragmentation and Integration* (Washington, D.C.: Brookings Institution, 1995).

15. Pal and Weaver, *The Government Taketh Away.*

16. See John Myles and Jill Quadagno, "Recent Trends in Public Pension Reform: A Comparative View," pp. 247–271 in Keith G. Banting and Robin Boadway, eds., *Reform of Retirement Income Policy: International and Canadian Perspectives* (Kingston, Ontario: Queens University School of Policy Studies, 1997); and John Myles and Paul Pierson, "The Comparative Political Economy of Pension Reform," pp. 305–333 in Paul Pierson, ed., *The New Politics of the Welfare State* (Oxford: Oxford University Press, 2001).

17. Karen M. Anderson, "The Politics of Retrenchment in a Social Democratic Welfare State: Retrenchment of Swedish Pensions and Unemployment Insurance," *Comparative Political Studies* 34 (November 2001), 1063–1091.

18. Paul D. Pierson, "Coping with Permanent Austerity: Welfare State Restruc-

turing in Affluent Democracies," pp. 410–456 in Pierson, ed., *The New Politics of the Welfare State* (Oxford: Oxford University Press, 2001).

19. See for example Paul D. Pierson, "Increasing Returns, Path Dependence, and the Study of Politics," *American Political Science Review* 94, 2 (2000), 251–267; Kathleen Thelen, "Historical Institutionalism in Comparative Politics," *Annual Review of Political Science* 2 (1999), 369–404.

20. See for example Kurt Weyland, ed., *Learning from Foreign Models in Latin American Policy Reform* (Washington, D.C., and Baltimore: Woodrow Wilson Press and Johns Hopkins University Press, 2004).

21. Jacob Hacker, *The Divided Welfare State* (Princeton: Princeton University Press, 2002).

22. The range of investment vehicles allowed for the CPP trust fund was also broadened to include equities and other securities in addition to the traditional portfolio of provincial bonds.

23. Pierson, *Dismantling the Welfare State?* ch. 3.

24. See in particular Urban Lundberg, *Juvelen i kronan: Socialdemokraterna och den allmänna pensionen* (Stockholm: Hjalmarson and Högberg, 2003).

25. Tsebelis, *Veto Players*.

Part III

Institutions and Democracy

10

Institutions for Implementing Constitutional Law

Mark Tushnet

This chapter considers institutions for implementing constitutional law understood as political law. After a brief discussion of what it means to describe constitutional law as political law, the chapter examines the ways in which institutions can be designed to respond to different "proportions" of politics and law in one's understanding of constitutional law. The aim is primarily to map understandings of constitutional law onto institutional designs in a way that illuminates the observable variations in institutions actually used to implement constitutional law.

Larry Kramer has recently brought to the attention of U.S. constitutionalists an understanding of constitutional law that had been lost from view for a while in the United States, although it has remained close to the forefront of discussions of constitutional law elsewhere in the world.[1] On that understanding, constitutional law is political law. Both terms on the right side of the equation matter. Constitutional law is political in a sense to be described shortly, but it is also law in the usual sense. Law is a set of normative rules and principles designed to guide decision in particular cases pursuant to a disinterested ("neutral," to use a term familiar from U.S. constitutional discussions) application of the rules and principles to the facts at hand. In addition, the guidance law provides is reasonably well defined; no doubt, there is a range of choices available to sincere interpreters, but that range is reasonably small.[2] Finally, law's rules and principles are embodied in "texts" that exist prior to the time when someone engaging in the practice of law makes a decision that consists of interpreting the texts. The term "text" must be understood in an extended sense. It refers to written material such as constitutions, statutes, and prior judicial decisions, but it also may refer to unwritten material, such as conventions and cultural understandings about the behavior appropriate to particular social actors.

Constitutional law could be understood to be ordinary albeit supreme law. *Marbury v. Madison* exemplifies that understanding. The view that constitutional law is political law is different: "Political" does not mean (merely) supreme. Rather, constitutional law is political law for several other reasons. Consider first a standard distinction between law and politics. Political actors empowered to adopt statutes and regulations exercise a discretion that is not tightly constrained by legal texts. They are charged with enacting statutes that advance the general welfare, for example, or that are compatible with an expansively understood police power. They may be constrained, again loosely, by unwritten conventions that direct them to advert to the public interest in legislating prospectively. One can treat their decisions as interpreting constitutional and conventional norms by means of specifying the methods by which those norms are to be advanced in statutes, but the interpretations are typically—though not always—more implicit than the interpretations that decision makers engaged in the practice of law offer.

Constitutional law is political, in part, because the range of interpretive discretion with respect to constitutional rules and principles is closer (in size) to the range of discretionary action that legislators have than to the range of discretion that exists with respect to ordinary law. In this sense, as continental legal theorists emphasize, a constitutional interpreter is a special type of legislator.[3]

In addition, constitutional law is political law because important parts of constitutional law deal with what Frank Michelman calls the laws of law making.[4] These are the rules that govern the processes by which ordinary laws are made. Democratic participation in making the laws of law making is particularly important because the resolution of disagreement about what those laws should be has strong implications for the ordinary laws that are then generated. The point is obvious with respect to free expression. If the laws of law making are interpreted to allow the government to prohibit advocacy of particular policy positions, it will surely be more difficult to enact those policies than if the laws of law making barred the government from enacting such a prohibition. Similarly, a law of law making that forecloses some systems of financing election campaigns will also foreclose—or at least make it more difficult to enact—some substantive laws that could be more easily enacted were one of the prohibited campaign finance systems in place.

In an important and interesting sense, all law, not merely constitutional law, is political. But the sense in which ordinary law is political actually emphasizes what is distinctive about constitutional law understood to be political law. Ordinary law—the law of accidents or contracts, for example—is political because the choices made among different regimes of accident or contract law reflect and help create large-scale ideologies about the normatively desirable relations among people. But, the rules and principles of ordinary law do not usually advert directly to those ideologies, except occasionally, and then typically only by the invocation of quite high-level abstractions. Those ideologies and, more important, abstractions are precisely the subject of constitutional law expressly. Rules of contract law reflect and help create ideals of distributive justice, for example, whereas constitutional doctrines dealing with equality are overtly about those ideals.

Still, I must concede that the distinction between law and politics that undergirds this chapter is not a sharp one. Much critical legal scholarship has been devoted to showing how law *is* politics. I note as well that politics is sometimes law-like if law is understood as involving constrained, textual interpretation. Legislatures that enact civil rights statutes, for example, are implementing shared constitutional values and thereby interpreting text-equivalents (analogous to constitutional background understandings that shape what constitutional courts do). Further, alternative versions of civil rights statutes—defeated amendments to proposed legislation, for example—often show the constrained range of choices made available to legislators.

Constitutional law is political, then, for several reasons. It is more discretionary than ordinary law, it deals with fundamental questions about law making, and it is *expressly* about choices among competing ideologies.[5] It is law, though, because it is not quite as discretionary as other law-making processes, and because it involves more obvious forms of interpretation of preexisting texts. Note that nothing in my exposition requires one to assume that those engaged in the practice of constitutional law are not attempting to implement their own values and preferences. The only assumption is that they do so within a range somewhat smaller than that within which those engaged in nonconstitutional politics operate.

Clearly, constitutional law can have its political and legal components in any number of combinations. Written texts may play a larger or a smaller role; the written texts may be relatively specific, thereby constraining interpretation, or relative abstract, thereby placing the interpreters under constraints nearly as loose as those that constrain political actors.

For convenience in this chapter's mapping exercise, I divide the possibilities into two types and then the latter type into two groups. The two types are (A) institutions of constitutional change through (i) permanent amendment and (ii) one-time or *pro tanto* amendment, and (B) institutions for the consideration and application of existing fundamental law. Within the latter type, which includes, importantly, systems of judicial review for constitutionality, the political component of constitutional law has the larger role in the first group I consider—roughly (i) systems of parliamentary supremacy—while the legal one has the larger role in the second, again roughly (ii) systems of judicial review.[6]

(A) Written constitutions can be easy to amend or hard to amend, and amendment can occur through permanent changes in the formal, written document that is called *the constitution* or through changes in that document or in unwritten conventions in connection with particular controversies.

(i) Consider first a written constitution that is quite easy to amend—in the limit, of course, by a simple majority vote of the usual legislative quorum.[7] Such a constitution is simultaneously entirely legal and entirely political. Its legal component is expressed when it is applied, its political component when it is amended, perhaps in response to an unexpected or disfavored application. As the difficulty of amendment increases, so does the legal component of constitutional law. Politics will still play a large role in determining fundamental law when a constitution can be amended by a qualified majority of a sitting legislature (a majority of the house rather than a majority of a quorum, or a supermajority of the house), and even when it can be amended by majority action in successive parliamentary sessions.

Beyond those forms, though, the legal component begins to play the predominant role. There are, I think, two reasons for making written constitutions difficult to amend formally. The first is a desire for stability in fundamental law. And yet, it is not immediately apparent why stability in fundamental law needs to be secured by provisions that make the constitution difficult to amend. After all, legislators able to amend the constitution easily could nonetheless recognize on their own the importance of stability in fundamental law. And, to the extent that legislators have incentives to try to guarantee their own reelection, they have an interest in stability, or at least an interest in stability unless change improves their chances of reelection. Such legislators would amend the constitution only when they thought the benefits of change exceeded the costs of instability.[8]

Perhaps the idea is that legislators will perceive short-run benefits from amending the constitution and undervalue the long-run costs in instability from doing so. Yet, the idea of instability as only a long-run phenomenon sits uneasily with the obvious fact that society and its laws change without anyone being concerned that such change evidences instability. That is, distinguishing between undesirable long-term instability and acceptable long-term social change seems quite difficult.

The second reason for making constitutions difficult to amend is precisely that a difficult amendment process is a way of demonstrating that the constitution is more legal than political. In the United States, for example, there is a rhetoric that opposes constitutional amendment in principle, resting on the assertion that getting into the habit of amending the Constitution would lead the people to think of the Constitution less as law and more as a mere instrument of politics, not on the ground that particular proposed amendments are bad ideas.[9] (See, for example, Sullivan 1995.)

(ii) Constitutional amendments change the constitution permanently. There are devices for changing it *pro tanto*, with respect to a particular proposal at hand. These devices too respond to different conceptions of the role of the political (that is, the nontextual and more discretionary) in constitutional law and can be organized by identifying the triggering event that leads to displacing the existing constitutional rule. The most modest event is a sense arising from the culture of constitutionalism that the proposal is inconsistent with the constitution. Legislators can respond to that sense by denying the existence of an inconsistency, by modifying the proposal, or by acknowledging the inconsistency and concluding that present exigencies justify a one-time departure from the constitution.[10] In these ways, legislators take constitutional values to be relevant to their decisions, though not dispositive. Or, put another way, the ordinary political process contains a legal component as well, to the extent that legislators are loosely constrained by high-level abstractions embodied in written constitutions or unwritten conventions.

In one of its uses, Section 33 of the Canadian Charter of Rights serves this function. Section 33 authorizes legislatures to make legislation effective (for no longer than five years) notwithstanding its inconsistency with some of the rights guaranteed by the Charter. The Canadian Supreme Court has held that Section 33 can be used prospectively, that is, before any court has actually found such an inconsistency. Prospective uses of Section 33 are rare and in the Canadian constitutional culture seem likely to occur only when the legislation's proponents believe that the courts would find the legislation, if enacted, to violate Charter rights.[11] Section 33, used prospectively, displaces the otherwise applicable constitutional law in the service of politics.

There are other institutions that can be used to trigger that sort of reconsideration. A legislature might have a committee on constitutional matters charged with vetting legislative proposals for constitutionality. Having concluded that a proposal is inconsistent with the constitution, the committee would notify the legislature, which again would have the opportunity to respond in the ways I have mentioned: denial of inconsistency, modification of the proposal, or *pro tanto* change in fundamental law. The British Parliamentary Joint Committee on Human Rights is an example of a legislative committee on constitutional matters. The Committee consists of members from the House of Commons and the House of Lords.[12] It is charged with "examining matters relating to human rights in the United Kingdom" and has taken a fairly active role in vetting proposed legislation. Although it is a relatively recent innovation, it appears to have worked reasonably well in bringing constitutional problems with proposed legislation to the attention of members of Parliament.

Legislative committees on constitutional matters are of course composed of members of a government's political branches and so are likely to give the political component of constitutional law a large role in their deliberations. Yet, as studies of committee composition in the United States suggest[13] (see, for example, Krehbiel 1992), the members chosen to serve on such committees and willing to do so are likely to think that the constitution has a substantial legal component as well. And, a legislature that sets up such a committee is, by that very fact, indicating its view that the legal component of constitutional law deserves more attention than the legislature would give it in the ordinary course.

One can increase the legal component even more by charging a court with the responsibility to determine whether legislation is consistent with the constitution and then giving the legislature an opportunity to respond to the court's action.[14] The British Human Rights Act of 1998 is an example. Under the Act, courts have the power to declare statutes incompatible with the European Convention on Human Rights. Such declarations (of which only a handful have been made so far) have no immediate legal effect on any ordinary person's rights. Rather, the declaration is a trigger for reconsideration of the legislation. The minister responsible for the legislation can do nothing in response, of course, or may introduce amendatory legislation in the ordinary course. In addition, the minister has the power to introduce such legislation and automatically place it on a fast track for adoption and even to amend the legislation himself or herself if doing so is urgently necessary, subject to parliamentary ratification.[15]

In all these settings, we can conceptualize the "do-nothing" response in two ways. Doing nothing might reflect a judgment that the statute or proposal is indeed compatible with fundamental law, notwithstanding what some other decision maker says. Or, it might reflect agreement with the other decision maker about compatibility and a further judgment that a one-time revision of fundamental law is desirable.

The judgment of a political body controls the outcome in all these institutional designs. But, different designs embody different visions of the relative role of the political and the legal in constitutional law. Sometimes the political body confronts a relative nonlegalized judgment of what constitutional law requires and so can displace that judgment without considering the extent to which constitutional law is law. In the more interesting designs, the political body faces a relatively more legalized judgment, and, though it has the *power* to displace that judgment, it can do so only by considering the higher-level question of the degree to which constitutional law is law.

(B) I turn now to the second type of institution concerned with constitutional law as political law. Here the choice of institution design is between parliamentary supremacy and judicial review.

(i) Systems of parliamentary supremacy obviously give the political component of constitutional law a very large role. Indeed, one might wonder whether such systems treat constitutional law as law at all. The answer, though, is that they do—or at least that they can. First, a culture of constitutionalism places some limits on what legislators in such a system believe they can properly do. The difficulty is that such a culture is a form of long-term politics, and legislators may succumb to the pressures of short-term politics and treat constitutional fundamentals in the same way they treat ordinary issues of public policy. Or, put another way, a culture of constitutionalism may not count as an *institution* for implementing constitutional law.

Still, culture may matter at least sometimes. The political-questions doctrine of U.S. constitutional law, when understood in a particular way, provides an example of how a constitutionalist culture operating through politics can constrain action and thereby enhance the effective role of the legal component of constitutional law in a system that treats legislative/executive action as final. Political questions are questions of constitutional interpretation, fairly open to disagreement, where the political branches' interpretation is final. The problem for the political questions doctrine has always been to identify the criteria for determining when a constitutional question is a political question. The best answer to that problem, I believe, is that political questions are those where there is good reason to believe that the political branches have strong incentives to interpret the Constitution in a reasonably disinterested way[16] (Tushnet 2002).

Some hints of this answer come in the opinion of Justice John Paul Stevens in *Walter Nixon v. United States*.[17] That case involved an impeachment of a federal judge. After the House impeached the judge, the Senate convened a committee to hear live testimony. That committee prepared a report, which provided the basis for a vote on conviction or acquittal by the entire Senate. Judge Nixon argued that this procedure did not give him the "trial" to which he was entitled by the Constitution. The Court held that the question of whether Judge Nixon received a trial within the meaning of the impeachment clauses presented a political question. In doing so, the Court necessarily held that Judge Nixon could not challenge in court a "trial" that consisted of a coin toss. In response to that conclusion, Justice Stevens wrote, "Respect for a coordinate Branch of the Government forecloses any assumption that improbable hypotheticals . . . will ever occur. . . "[18] Justice Stevens's thought here is that senators will be constrained by *something* to provide basic fairness in their procedures. The best candidate is a sense of constitutional responsibility, that is, a sense that, with respect to constitutional fundamentals, the Senate should treat the Constitution as having a significant legal component. That sense is induced by electoral considerations: Senators reasonably fear that their constituents will retaliate against them at election time unless the senators take their constitutional responsibilities seriously[19] (for discussions of actual practice, see Tushnet 2001; Tushnet 2003).

Second, and perhaps more important, in the present context, "parliamentary supremacy" should not be taken to refer exclusively to systems in which executive and legislative power are combined, as they are in Great Britain. Rather, it refers to a system in which decisions about constitutional matters taken by ordinary political actors—not by judges—are final. So, a separation-of-powers system can give a very large role to the political element of constitutional law. One aspect of *The Federalist*'s argument for a separation of powers system deserves note here. Separation of powers worked to secure constitutionalism, according to *The Federalist*, because it set ambition against ambition and linked the political interests of particular powerholders to the interests of the institution in which they held power. The libertarian-leaning interpretation of this argument is that separation of powers makes it hard to get the government to do anything, which itself preserves liberty. There is another interpretation, though, more resonant with the interests of this chapter. The purely self- or constituency-oriented interests of particular powerholders cancel each other out when ambition is set against ambition. Yet, ambition means that powerholders want to get *something* done. In the absence of self-interest or constituency interest, all that powerholders can do is enact laws that advance the public interest—or, in the terms I have been using, promote fundamental constitutional values.

A constitutionalist culture and separation of powers, then, are two institutions that fit reasonably well the conception of constitutional law as law that is primarily political. Other possibilities deserve mention, as well. The previously mentioned legislative standing committee on constitutional matters is one. Another is an office in the executive branch whose charge is to vet executive proposals and about-to-be-enacted legislation for constitutionality.[20] And, finally, a "court" understood as largely political might be given power to determine—either provisionally or finally—that legislation is unconstitutional. These institutions give the legal component of political law a slightly larger role than pure parliamentary supremacy does.

These agencies specialize in constitutional matters and therefore are likely to think of their "mission" as taking constitutional fundamentals more seriously than do the generalist politicians elsewhere in the government. Their staffs are likely to have a large number of lawyers and may develop an institutional culture in which responsibility to the legal aspects of constitutional law plays a significant role. Of course the nonjudicial versions consist of members of the government (or employees of the government) and so are not likely to treat constitutional law as law only. Further, committees and specialized offices report to ordinary politicians, and their reports will be acted on, or not, with an eye to the political dimension of constitutional law.[21] This is to say only that these institutions still fall within the category of institutions in which the political component of constitutional law plays a larger role than the legal one.

Also in this category but moving toward the "more law-like" end of the spectrum are constitutional courts on the Kelsenian model. According to Kelsen, the political component of constitutional law meant that the ordinary courts could not properly be involved in "judicial" review. Instead, a court that specializes in constitutional law should exercise that power. Specialization and the concomitant removal from the administration of ordinary law would make such a court sensitive to the political component of constitutional law. Further, Kelsen thought, the constitutional court should be removed from case-specific adjudication, where individual claimants would assert that they had constitutional rights to be determined according to law. Individual claims, that is, would induce reviewing courts to reduce the political component of constitutional law and favor the legal component more than they should. Finally, the decision makers who compose a Kelsenian constitutional court should be selected with an explicit concern for their sensitivity to the political component of constitutional law.

Of the modern systems of constitutional review, probably only France's fits the Kelsenian model reasonably well.[22] French legal theorists conceptualize the *Conseil Constitutionel* as an extension of the legislative process, thereby emphasizing the political over the legal. It exercises review before legislation goes into effect, entirely divorced from case-specific adjudication. Politics of the ordinary sort plays an explicit role in selecting members of the *Conseil Constitutionel,* as is symbolized by the entitlement of former presidents of the Republic to sit on the *Conseil.*[23]

Contemporary international courts provide an example of another institutional arrangement that responds to the dual components of constitutional law, although of course they do not enforce constitutional law in the usual sense. The most obvious recognition of the political in international tribunals is their composition: Representatives of the states whose actions are in question are entitled to sit on the tribunal considering the complaint. At present, for example, each member-state of the European Union appoints a judge to the European Court of Justice.[24] In other tribunals, a temporary judge is appointed when the court does not have a judge from a state whose action is at issue.

In addition, the European Court of Human Rights uses a legal doctrine that recognizes the political component of the law it administers. This is the "margin of appreciation" doctrine, which seems likely to be increasingly emulated in international tribunals. According to that doctrine, each nation is to be given some leeway in its application and interpretation of fundamental human rights, because nations face different arrays of social, economic, and political problems, such that what is acceptable *as an interpretation of fundamental law* in one nation (perhaps one experiencing high and persistent levels of crime) would not be acceptable in another. At the same time, the actual adjudications of international tribunals tend to be highly legalized.

(ii) With the introduction of (real) courts into the institutional mix, I can turn to the second group of institutional arrangements I mentioned earlier. These are arrangements that emphasize the legal component of constitutional law over the political component, essentially by giving courts a large role in implementing the constitution.[25] Earlier I discussed prospective uses of Canada's Section 33 procedure, but more commonly Section 33 is seen as providing opportunities for legislators to respond to judicial rulings[26] (see Hogg & Bushell 1997; Manfredi & Kelly 1999). The idea is that the Canadian courts can approach constitutional interpretation in a relatively legalized way, knowing that if they undervalue the political component of constitutional law the political branches can readjust the balance by overriding the courts' interpretation. Constitutional law as a whole, then, consists of judicial interpretations, which treat constitutional law as mainly ordinary law, and legislative decisions to override or not, which treat constitutional law as mainly political.

That way of understanding the power to override allocates the different components of constitutional law to different institutions. Section 33 says that legislatures can declare legislation effective notwithstanding Charter provisions (rather than notwithstanding judicial interpretations of the Charter). This suggests that the legislature is insisting on implementing the statute despite its inconsistency with the Charter because it regards the statute's policy as more important than the Charter's law. Section 33 treats constitutional law as articulated by the courts as almost entirely legal, but constitutional law as articulated by the Canadian government taken as a whole inserts a political element through the possibility of the legislative override for policy or political reasons. One who believes that constitutional law is political law might be concerned with the incentives Section 33 provides courts and legislatures on this conceptualization.

There is, however, an alternative conceptualization that uses Section 33 to show that constitutional law is political law through and through and that its different components need not be allocated to different institutions. On the alternative conceptualization, a legislature's override is not a (mere) policy judgment that inserts political considerations into an otherwise legalized constitution. Rather, it is an expression of disagreement with the courts' interpretation of the constitution. That is, a legislature that uses Section 33 is not necessarily making a statute effective notwithstanding the Charter but is making it effective notwithstanding an erroneous Charter interpretation provided by the courts. The legislature's action is just as legalized as the courts'.

This alternative conceptualization is a useful corrective to the final mapping of constitutional law as political law on to institutional forms. That mapping is, of course, the U.S. system of judicial review, which I call strong-form review (Tushnet 2003). In strong-form review, courts' interpretations of the constitution are final and binding—in terms of political morality if not in terms of enforceable law—on all political actors.

The U.S. Supreme Court's recent decision invalidating the Religious Freedom Restoration Act exemplifies strong-form review.[27] There the Court insisted that Congress lacked the power to specify the content of constitutional norms differently from the way the Court itself did even where Congress's specification could not be dismissed as entirely unreasonable. The tradition of strong-form review goes back a long way, though. One can find it in what is perhaps the easiest reading of the passage in *Marbury v. Madison* that has been taken to articulate the political questions doctrine. Chief Justice Marshall wrote:

> The province of the court is, solely, to decide on the rights of individuals, not to inquire how the executive, or executive officers, perform duties in which they have a discretion. Questions in their nature political, or which are, by the constitution and laws, submitted to the executive, can never be made in this court.[28]

The most straightforward reading of this passage has Marshall distinguishing between questions of law, which implicate individual rights, and political questions, which do not.[29] The Constitution, that is, is a legal document remitted to the ordinary courts for ordinary interpretation when individuals raise claims that their rights have been violated. Constitutional law has no political component at all; politics is the realm of the discretion conferred by the Constitution on the political branches.

If, however, constitutional law is (by definition) political law, strong-form review might cause some problems unless it is tempered with some other institutional devices. Strong-form review allocates the political and legal components of constitutional law to different institutions. As noted in connection with the first understanding of the Section 33 override procedure described above, doing so may create incentives that lead constitutional law to be overlegalized and underpoliticized.

The United States lacks a Section 33 procedure that tempers strong-form review, but it contains some institutional devices aimed at ensuring that the courts have some incentives to treat constitutional law as at least in part political. Some of the mechanisms are primarily backward-looking. Such mechanisms allow the political branches to respond to decisions they disagree with. The backward-looking mechanisms are often enumerated as involving political *control* of the courts: Congress's power to regulate the jurisdiction of the federal courts and the impeachment power. These mechanisms may be somewhat forward-looking, to the extent that their use has effects on the incentives of judges. The power of nomination and confirmation, in contrast, is fully forward-looking.

The backward-looking mechanisms are primarily methods of retrospective control, or responses to decisions by the courts, and in that they seem to resemble the retrospective uses of the Section 33 power. But, there is an important difference. An override used to correct an erroneous judicial decision need not affect the justices who made that decision in the slightest; they need not even be embarrassed by the override to the extent that they take it to express only disagreement on a matter about which reasonable people can disagree. The existence of a power to override judicial decisions retrospectively, that is, need have no incentive effects on judges as they consider what to do next. The impeachment power is obviously different, because it gives the legislature a power to place a judge's continuation in office in question. The power to control jurisdiction has some incentive effects as well, albeit more modest ones: The threat of losing work may be significant to a judge who has taken the position to do something.[30]

The retrospective mechanisms do have some forward-looking effects. But, in the United States, those mechanisms have fallen into disuse to the point that a rational judge looking forward should not give any more weight to them than he or she does to the possibility that a legislator dismayed at a ruling would hire an assassin to kill the judge.[31]

The problem with the powers over nomination and confirmation is somewhat different. These powers operate as screening devices at the point of entry to the judicial role. They can be used to ensure the selection of judges who understand constitutional law to have a political component as well as a legal one. They cannot influence the behavior of judges once seated. For judges to treat the political component of constitutional law with appropriate seriousness, then, the president and Congress must insist on choosing judges who already have, and are likely to continue to have, the appropriate understanding of constitutional law. With respect to the latter, one might think that something like a minimum-age qualification would be desirable. The theory would be two-fold: An older nominee has a longer track record on which the president and Congress can base their judgment about the candidate's understanding of constitutional law, and, probably more important, an older nominee's views are less likely to change because of the conservatism associated with age.

We might return to Kelsen's views in addressing the concern that nominees have the right understanding of constitutional law. Working within a civil-law tradition in which judges were members of a certain kind of bureaucracy, Kelsen thought that judges on a constitutional court ought to be drawn from *outside* the judiciary precisely to ensure that such judges take seriously constitutional law's political component. Kelsen's position, in its strongest form, seems inappropriate for a system of strong-form review like that of the United States, particularly where, as in the United States, the constitutional court is also a generalist court. Both the generalist character of the court and, perhaps more important, the system's commitment to a strong-form system of judicial review suggest that the judges on such a court should treat the legal component of constitutional law as the predominant one. What can be said, though, is that these commitments must be tempered a bit to ensure that the judges also understand that constitutional law is political law. Probably the best that can be done is to develop a norm for nominations and confirmations that judicial experience is *not* a prerequisite for service on a court with substantial responsibility for constitutional law and that the desirability of judicial experience in a nominee will vary depending on the composition of the court already in place.

Yet, this set of institutions seems incomplete. It gives courts some incentives to treat constitutional law as political. It does not, however, contain arrangements that give the legislature incentives to treat constitutional law as law. Perhaps, though, we might return to points made earlier about systems of parliamentary supremacy. A culture of constitutionalism and the institutions of separated powers may give political actors the appropriate incentives.

It would be convenient were I able to conclude by arguing that some particular mix of the legal and the political in constitutional law was normatively desirable, but I cannot. Instead, in the spirit of the descriptive effort I have made, I end with three observations.

First, I find that different constitutional systems appear to reflect commitments to different mixes at any one time. A few weak normative conclusions may flow from that observation. First, institution designers probably should attempt to ensure that the institutions of constitutional review correspond to the mix that their political-legal culture deems correct. Institution designers who come from within the political-legal culture itself will almost inevitably do so. Designers who come from the outside to offer advice might not.

Second, it seems likely that, within any constitutional system, the mix that seems desirable may change from time to time. Institution designers can respond to the possibility of change in several ways. They might make it relatively easy to change the institutions of constitutional review.[32] Alternatively, they might be attentive to the ways in which the political-legal culture affects the way in which the institutions they put in place are likely to operate in fact. But, as noted earlier, such cultural factors may be particularly difficult to build into relatively stable institutional designs. In the end, then, we may face a situation in which the institutions of constitutional review recurrently come into tension with the political-legal culture within which those institutions operate.

Finally: The map of institutional-design possibilities that I have sketched makes it possible to examine the political reasons institution designers have for choosing one design over another. The Human Rights Act of 1998, for example, is usually described as the result of the Labour Party's disenchantment with parliamentary supremacy as it existed under Margaret Thatcher. That seems superficial. With victory in hand, why would the Labour Party disempower itself in the present out of fear of some future Thatcher, rather than simply enact substantive programs that would strengthen the party's long-term electoral prospects? Or, alternatively, why adopt the limited Human Rights Act version of judicial review rather than a stronger-form version? I suspect that a more complete political analysis would require some treatment of Tony Blair's political circumstances within the Labour Party, and certainly much more. More generally, the map I have sketched opens up the possibility of examining what political interests are served by institutional designs giving different proportions to the legal and the political in constitutional law. Although I am not qualified to engage in such examinations, I am sure that they would be quite informative.

NOTES

1. Larry Kramer, *The People Themselves: Popular Constitutionalism and Judicial Review* (New York: Oxford University Press, 2004).

2. I do not have a metric for determining the size of the range of choice, though.

3. I believe that there is something to the idea that constitutional interpreters are legislators because they have a relatively wide range of discretion in interpretation, whereas interpreters of ordinary (nonpolitical) law have a smaller range of discretion. I also believe, though, that this idea should not carry a great deal of weight because the range available to interpreters of ordinary law is wider than continental legal theorists believe it to be.

4. Frank Michelman, *Brennan and Democracy* (Princeton: Princeton University Press, 1999), p. 6.

5. One standard distinction between law and politics is, however, ruled out by treating constitutional law as political law. That distinction treats politics as a forum for (mere) preference aggregation and law as a location of deliberations that include some elements other than preference aggregation (and that, on what is probably the prevailing view, excludes preference aggregation altogether). Treating constitutional law as political law strongly suggests that the political component of constitutional law is different from preference aggregation, although perhaps the political component could be understood to be that portion of law, if there be one, that does implicate mere preference aggregation. Combining the latter view with standard notions that bar judges from implementing their preferences suggests that constitutional law as political law should not be implemented by judges. Alternatively, the law practice could be treated as preference aggregating if the term "preferences" referred to a decision maker's desire to promote his or her preferred understanding of the role of judges and other actors in the law practice. Doing so, I believe, deprives the preference-aggregation view of much of what makes it analytically distinctive (and of much of what makes it interesting).

6. My examples of how different conceptions of constitutional law map on to different institutional forms are quite stylized. For example, in discussing parliamentary supremacy, I ignore the complications introduced by the effects in Great Britain of the Human Rights Act of 1998 and Great Britain's agreement to be bound by the decisions of the European Court of Human Rights.

7. At this limiting point, the sense in which constitutional law is fundamental or higher than ordinary becomes rather obscure, and I mention the limit simply to identify the point at which constitutional rules collapse into ordinary political ones.

8. Note that the interest in stability is different from, and independent of, an interest in making the right decision. With an easily amendable constitution, unwise amendments might be adopted easily, but they could be undone just as easily. Fear of unwise amendments cannot explain the decision to make amendment difficult in the absence of an account of why people would adopt unwise amendments and then fail to see their unwisdom.

9. See, for example, Kathleen Sullivan, "Constitutional Amendmentitis," *The American Prospect* 6, 23 (September 21, 1995).

10. The British antiterrorism legislation adopted in 2001 illustrates this possibility, with the peculiar twist that the constitutional norms applied are external to the British legal system. The Human Rights Act of 1998 directs British courts to construe legislation to be consistent with the European Convention on Human Rights where such a construction is fairly possible and to make a declaration that legislation is incompatible with the Convention when it cannot be so construed (and is, in the court's judgment, incompatible with the Convention). One provision of the proposed antiterrorism legislation was clearly incompatible with the Convention. Pursuant to Convention provisions, the British government issued a declaration derogating from the relevant Convention provision with respect to the legislative proposal (that is, declaring that the Convention provision was inapplicable). For a brief discussion, see Mark Tushnet, "Non-Judicial Review," *Harvard Journal on Legislation* 40, 2 (Summer 2003): 453–492. In December 2004, the House of Lords held that the derogation was not authorized by the applicable law and issued a declaration of incompatibility with respect to the provision.

11. For example, Section 33 was invoked prospectively by the government of Alberta to insulate its statutes that limit marriage to heterosexuals from a Charter challenge that Canadian constitutionalists fully expected to succeed within a few years with respect to some other province's marriage statute. See Janet Hiebert, *Charter Conflicts: What Is Parliament's Role?* (Montreal: McGill Queen's University Press, 2002), 198.

12. At present, six Committee members are from the Labour Party, two are Liberal Democrats, three are Conservatives, and one is a "cross-bench" member.

13. See Keith Krehbiel, *Information and Legislative Organization* (Ann Arbor: University of Michigan Press, 1992).

14. Obviously, the legal component is high here because of the general view that court decisions have as large a legal component as one can ensure in institutional design.

15. Finally, it is worth noting that we can make a legislature's power to override existing constitutional provisions *pro tanto* less or more difficult to exercise. As

noted, Section 33 has an automatic sunset provision, unlike all other legislation. One could require that legislative overrides of constitutional provisions be adopted by supermajorities or by ordinary majorities in successive parliamentary sessions or by any of the other devices that are used to make permanent amendments difficult to adopt.

16. For a discussion, see Mark Tushnet, "Law and Prudence in the Law of Justiciability: The Transformation and Disappearance of the Political Question Doctrine," *North Carolina Law Review* 80, 4 (May 2002): 1203–1235.

17. 506 U.S. 224 (1993).

18. *Id.* at 238.

19. For discussions of actual practice, see Mark Tushnet, "Evaluating Congressional Constitutional Interpretation: Some Criteria and Two Informal Case Studies," *Duke Law Journal* 50, 5 (March 2001): 1396–1425; Tushnet, "Non-Judicial Review."

20. The Office of Legal Counsel in the U.S. Department of Justice is an example of an executive branch agency with similar responsibilities.

21. Political circumstances might be such that the government would not be embarrassed by a report from one of these agencies that a legislative proposal violates constitutional principles, or it might be willing to acknowledge the violation but enact the law that excepts the statute from ordinarily applicable constitutional principles.

22. Other post–World War II constitutional courts depart in varying degrees from the Kelsenian model. In particular, most such courts have some mechanism for consideration of individual complaints, either by reference from the ordinary courts when a constitutional question arises in connection with a pending case or by direct consideration of applications from aggrieved individuals. In such courts, the balance between the political and the legal components of constitutional law begins to tip in favor of the legal.

23. The point is symbolic because the entitlement has gone largely unexercised.

24. That may change as the Union's membership expands, although my understanding is that those responsible for institutional design in the Union expect the ECJ to grow.

25. These courts could be specialized constitutional courts or generalist courts. For reasons suggested earlier, generalist courts are likely to give the legal component of constitutional law a larger role than they give the political component.

26. *See* Peter W. Hogg and Allison A. Bushell, "The *Charter* Dialogue Between Courts and Legislatures (or Maybe the Charter of Rights and Freedoms Isn't Such a Bad Thing After All)," *Osgoode Hall Law Journal* 35, 2 (Spring 1997): 75–124; Christopher P. Manfredi and James B. Kelly, "Six Degrees of Dialogue: A Response to Hogg and Bushell," *Osgoode Hall Law Journal* 37, 3 (Fall 1999): 513–527.

27. City of Boerne v. Flores, 521 U.S. 507 (1997).

28. 5 U.S. (1 Cranch) 137, 170 (1803).

29. On this reading, the reference to questions that are submitted to the executive by the constitution is equivalent to a statement that the executive's action in resolving such a question implicates no legal rights.

30. Recall the interpretation of *The Federalist* offered earlier.

31. Disgruntled litigants have assassinated federal judges on the lower courts, but the scenario I describe in the text has not yet come to pass.

32. That course seems acceptable only if their political-legal culture accepts the view that, whatever is true about *other* matters, the institutions of constitutional review are almost entirely political in nature.

11

Beyond Rational Self-Interest
Authors and Actors in French Constitution-Making

Jon Elster

I. Introduction

Occasionally, constitutions are written by individuals who do not anticipate to play a role in postconstitutional politics. Thus, after Solon had
enacted his laws, in the early sixth century B.C., he reportedly left Athens
for ten years because he did no want to be involved in their day-to-day
operation. This case is not typical. More frequently, constitution-makers
expect to be actors in the play they are writing. When the Federal Convention, presided over by George Washington, debated the powers that were
to devolve on the presidency in the Constitution, it was common knowledge that he would be the first occupant of that office. Given his cult of
disinterestedness,[1] it is unlikely that this would provide him with a reason
for trying to enhance its prerogatives or the economic perks that might
come with it. This case may not be typical either, however. Political scientists routinely take it for granted that we can explain the behavior of
politicians by the parsimonious assumption that they are pursuing their
rational self-interest. Applied to the case of constitution-making, we
would expect the politicians who are in a position to influence the content
of the document to bias it in favor of their economic or political interest.

In this chapter, I confront the rational-self-interest approach to politics
with four French episodes of constitution-making: 1789–1791, 1814, 1848,
and 1958. In each of them, both legislature and executive (or candidates for
that position) were in a position to shape the rules that would, among
other things, regulate relations between the legislative and the executive
powers. In each episode, the document was also shaped by extrainstitu-

tional forces. In 1789, the *constituants* were suspended between the king's soldiers and the crowds in Paris. In 1814, the impetus to the new constitution came from the victorious Allied powers. In 1848, the behavior of the crowds in Paris had the effect first of radicalizing and then of deradicalizing the constitution-making process. In 1958, the parliamentarians of the Fourth Republic would not have delegated the constitution-making power to de Gaulle had it not been for the actions of the generals in Algiers.

My discussion of these moments is inevitably selective and summary. Rather than trying to offer a positive account of these processes and their outcomes, I set myself the negative task of challenging the rational-self-interest explanation. I try to show that in some of these episodes many crucial actors were not rational and that in others they were not moved by their self-interest. I do not exclude that the rational-self-interest explanation may offer powerful explanations in other constitution-making episodes. In the making of the French constitution of 1799, for instance, Napoleon ruthlessly modified the draft presented by Sieyes so that as First Consul he would have a firm hold on the levers of power. Nor do I deny—in fact I argue—that, in the episodes I consider, some actors may have been swayed by their rational self-interest. I am merely trying to show that we cannot understand the outcome of these particular episodes on the bare assumption of rational self-interest as the motivation of all actors.

II. The Constitution of 1791

When the first French constitution was adopted, in September 1791, the king's flight to Varennes in June of that year had already made it a dead letter. If it had not been for that event, and for three fateful votes to be discussed shortly, constitutional monarchy might have been a viable option. Although some have claimed that the monarchy was doomed by October 6, by July 14, or by June 27, three occasions on which the king was forced to back down under popular pressure, there were plenty of precedents in French history for allegedly all-powerful kings making tactical retreats of this kind.

The Estates-General had been called by the king and then transformed themselves, by an act of constitutional bootstrapping, into a constituent assembly. From my perspective here, two issues stand out: the king's veto *in* the constitution (over ordinary legislation) and his veto *over* the constitution itself. Most delegates to the Estates-General took it for granted that

the king would have some kind of legislative veto, either absolute or suspensive, but it was much more controversial whether he should also have a
veto over the constitution. Mounier, the leader of the constitutional
monarchists, argued that since "the power of the king who convened the
assembly existed before it came into being," he could hardly lose it once it
was created. Moreover, "if the assembly had the right to adopt the constitution without the king having any part in it, it would follow that it also
has the right to dispose as it deems fit of all the prerogatives of the
Crown."[2] The king's veto in the constitution could not be ensured unless
he also had a veto over it. On the other side, the radical deputy Target
argued that everything "would be put into question if the constituent
power could act only with the permission of the constituted power [i. e.,
the king]."[3]

A further issue was whether the Constituent Assembly, having transformed itself from tricameral into unicameral, would adopt a unicameral
or bicameral constitution. Mounier argued that "The present Assembly . . .
had to be formed as a single body, to have greater strength and swiftness;
but this same degree of strength, if it were to be retained after the constitution, would end up destroying everything."[4] Combining Target's view on
the veto with Mounier's position on bicameralism, another monarchist,
Clermont-Tonnerre, observed that the "three-headed hydra"—king, first
chamber, and second chamber—to be created by the constitution could
not itself create one.[5] For him, the privileged character of the Constituent
Assembly, by virtue of which it could be a law unto itself, derived from the
extraordinary circumstances in which it operated. "Anarchy is a frighten-
ing but necessary transitional stage; the only moment in which a new
order of things can be created. It is not in calm times that one can take
uniform measures."[6]

The outcome of these debates was a suspensive veto for the king in the
constitution, no veto over the constitution, and a unicameral parliament.
A large part of the explanation is to be found in the extrainstitutional
forces that the actors could mobilize. The unicameral assembly was
obtained, in part, because some of the moderates feared for their lives if
they voted for bicameralism. The king had to renounce a veto over the
constitution when, having reneged on an earlier bargain struck with the
Assembly, he called in a company of soldiers from Flanders for a show of
force but had to back down before the crowds from Paris. The outcome
also owed much to the internal dynamics of the Assembly. Some of the
reactionary nobles, acting as "constitution-wreckers" rather than constitu-

tion-makers, voted for unicameralism because they thought it would destabilize the system.[7] Among the radicals, some voted against an upper house because they thought it would reintroduce the system of orders that they had just abolished.[8] Others voted against the cooling-down mechanism of an upper house because in the heat of passion they could not imagine that the future legislature would need to be protected against the heat of passion.[9]

The Constituent Assembly also acted as an ordinary legislature. According to the rational self-interest hypothesis, one would expect the *constituants* to try to write a large place for the legislature into the constitution. Given the extrainstitutional forces they could mobilize, we would also expect them to succeed. Since unicameralism strengthened the legislature and a suspensive rather than absolute veto weakened the executive, we may conclude that they did in fact succeed. We have to ask, however, about the exact mechanism by which the effect was produced. First, there is what one might call "institutional patriotism," the result of a natural tendency to believe that an institution to which one belongs must be an important one.[10] Second, there is ordinary self-interest: If the members of the Constituent Assembly expected to be elected to the first ordinary legislature, they had a clear incentive to grant extensive powers to themselves. There is no doubt that in the Constituent Assembly, the first mechanism operated in abundance. The second, by contrast, did not. On three occasions, the deputies deliberately excluded themselves from any personal benefits, including power and positions, they might have derived from the new constitution.

On November 7, 1789, the Assembly voted that "No member of the National Assembly shall be eligible as minister during the current session." By this self-denying ordinance, the deputies refused themselves the opportunity to become ministers. In reality, the motion was directed against Mirabeau, who was at the time both arguing for the permission of the ministers to speak before the assembly and positioning himself as a future minister. His ironic self-denying amendment to the motion, according to which "the required exclusion would be limited to M. de Mirabeau, deputy of the third estate from Aix," was rejected. The spiteful desire to keep Mirabeau out of power blocked the adoption of a genuine parliamentary system which might (or might not) have saved the Revolution from its later excesses.[11]

On April 7, 1791, Robespierre made a motion that members of the Assembly should be pronounced ineligible to become ministers for four

years *after* the end of a session. In his explanation of the need for the measure, he cited a "philosopher whose memory you honor" to the effect that
"To inspire more confidence and respect for the laws, the legislator must
in some way isolate himself from his work and liberate himself from all
the personal relations [*rapports*] which might link him to the great issues
[*intérêts*] he has to decide."[12] The motion, which mediates between that of
November 7, 1789, and that of May 16, 1791, was passed in a "spirit of
quixotism,"[13] together with an amendment that extended the prohibition
to future legislatures. It was in all likelihood directed against Robespierre's
rivals in the Assembly, the "triumvirs" Barnave, Duport, and Alexandre
Lameth.

An even more fateful self-denying ordinance, which made members of
the current legislature ineligible for membership in the next one, was
adopted on May 16, 1791, again on Robespierre's initiative. In explaining
his motivation for making the proposal, he repeated the idea that "before
deciding on the functions and powers of the legislature, and the mode of
election to it, it would seem appropriate and useful that the legislator
made sure he had no interest [*se désintéressât*] in this great question." The
motives of the deputies in their unanimous adoption of the proposal were
complex.[14] As in the previous vote, Robespierre's motives, although
shrouded in the hypocritical and intimidating appeal to the public interest
of which he was a master, were purely tactical. Others may have been genuinely "drunk with disinterestedness," in the words of the biographer of
the deputy Thouret, who unsuccessfully tried to stem the tide of enthusiasm.[15] Still others voted for the motion because they feared to be stigma-
tized as self-interested and perhaps persecuted if they opposed it. Using a
routine tactic of the left, one deputy called for a roll-call vote: "in this
manner we shall learn who wants to be reelected."[16] Finally, as in the vote
over bicameralism, many right-wing deputies voted for the measure
because they thought it would destabilize the regime by ensuring that the
new legislature would be made up of inexperienced novices.[17]

The self-interest model of politics breaks down here, at least if offered
as a complete explanation. Robespierre and his allies saw their interest in a
weak legislature because this would remove their political enemies from
power and allow the Jacobin clubs to dominate. The far right shared this
policy preference because it wanted an assembly too weak to resist the
counterrevolution that would be triggered by the king's impending flight,
which at that time "was no longer a secret for anyone."[18] The bulk of the

deputies, however, were dominated by sincere disinterestedness, mixed (in proportions that are impossible to determine) with the fear of appearing to be insufficiently disinterested. To reduce their behavior to rational self-interest, one would have to show that the fear (i) completely dominated sincere enthusiasm and (ii) was prudential rather than visceral. Neither claim seems plausible.

III. The Charter of 1814

The constitution or "Charter" that was adopted after the fall of Napoleon and the restoration of the Bourbon monarchy in 1814 was the result of a complex bargaining process. It involved the leaders of the victorious allied forces, notably Tsar Alexander; Talleyrand, who had fallen out of Napoleon's graces and was intriguing to create a new regime in which, by virtue of his efforts, he would have a central role; Napoleon's senate, which under the terms of the constitution of 1804 was the dominant political body; the Comte d'Artois, later Charles X; and his older brother, Pretendant to the throne, later Louis XVIII. Many of the complexities are irrelevant for my purposes here, and I will ignore them, focusing instead mainly on the bargaining between the senate and the king.

In March 1814, when Napoleon's downfall began to seem certain, the question of the successor regime arose naturally. None of the Allies had a strong preference for the return of the Bourbons, and Alexander was initially strongly against this option. Talleyrand was won for this cause, however, when he was shown a letter to the Pretendant stating that he would never arrive at the throne without the assistance of Talleyrand.[19] In a dramatic meeting with Alexander on March 31, Talleyrand argued that the return of the Bourbons was the only stable or focal-point solution. When Alexander asked him, "How can I know that France desires the House of Bourbon?," Talleyrand answered, "By a motion that I take upon me to have adopted by the senate," of which, in the absence of Napoleon and his brother Joseph, he was the leader.[20] Over the next days, the senators virulently denounced Napoleon, whose unconditional creatures they had been, and sketched their terms for accepting the restoration of the Bourbon dynasty.

The first senatorial draft of the charter was proposed on April 6. On three crucial points, it was heavily biased in favor of the existing senate.

First, by the clause asserting that "The French people freely calls Louis-Stanislas-Xavier of France, brother of the last king, to the throne," the senate explicitly cast itself as kingmaker. For Louis XVIII, this formula was absurd. The way he saw it, he became king at the moment of the death of his nephew, Louis XVII. This was not a purely symbolic disagreement. Referring to an episode from the reign of Henri III, the Abbé de Montesquieu, Louis XVIII's representative in the constitutional bargaining, asked "how one could imagine recognizing an hereditary throne while removing the advantages of heredity by pretending to offer the crown. This would be like the throne of M. de Mayenne about which The Sixteen said: whoever could make it could also unmake it."[21]

Second, although the draft allowed the king to name the senators, their number was not to exceed two hundred. The draft also stated that all the 140 current members of the senate were to retain their places and that laws and budgets would need their approval, together with that of the king and the lower house. Thus, if the draft had been adopted, Napoleon's senate would have transformed itself from a passive appendage to its master into one of the most powerful organs of the state. The upper limit on the number of senators was crucial. Without this condition, the king could simply have appointed new senators until he had the majority he needed. In the constitution of 1804, Napoleon had in fact removed the *numerus clausus* for the senate, leaving him free to appoint or threaten to appoint "batches of senators" if the institution showed signs of independence, which for that reason (among others) it never did.[22] Similarly, the Abbé de Montesquieu insisted on the king's freedom to appoint an unlimited number of senators: "In this kind of government it is the upper house that makes the difference between a democracy and a monarchy; it should always have the same interest as the king; the majority of this house must therefore always be on his side: and how can it be . . . if the king cannot at will destroy any bad majority that might emerge there?"[23]

Third, in an extraordinary show of egoism, the senators insisted on retaining their economic situation. One of the means Napoleon had used to tame his senators was to endow each of them with a "sénatorerie," a substantial property taken from "biens nationaux" that had been confiscated from the Church and from émigré nobles. At the same time that the senators were trying to gain political power, they wanted to retain the economic privileges that had been the price of their political impotence. The draft article deserves to be cited in full:

There are at last one hundred and fifty senators and at most two hundred. Their dignity is inamovable and hereditary in the male line, by primogeniture. They are named by the king.

The existing senators, except for those who might give up their French citizenship, are maintained in their office and are included in this number. The existing endowment of the senate and the "sénatoreries" belong to them. The revenues derived therefrom are divided equally among them, and are passed on to their successors. If a senator should die without leaving a male descendant, his share returns to the Treasury. Senators to be named in the future will not share in this endowment.[24]

By displaying their egoism and even malice (toward the new senators) in this blatant form, the senators shot themselves in the foot. Public opinion reacted strongly and unanimously, thus undermining the bargaining position of the senators.[25] It took a while, however, for the full consequences of this faux pas to emerge. Louis XVIII had still not returned from his exile in England, and Alexander was firmly committed to imposing the senatorial constitution. When Talleyrand expressed his concern over crowds in Paris shouting "Down with the senate!," Alexander allegedly answered, "I will give you thirty thousand men to arrest the king as soon as he sets foot on French soil; and you will not let him go until he agrees to do all that is necessary."[26] When the king did arrive, at the end of April, Alexander immediately went to see him in Compiègne, north of Paris, to persuade him to accept the first point of the senatorial constitution. The king responded that he would rather go back into exile than receive as a gift the crown that was his as of right. In these negotiations, the king's assets, which lent credibility to his threat, were moral rather than physical. "The roles were inverted. Through the ascendancy conferred by moral force and the conscience of right, Louis XVIII dominated the emperor of Russia and already seemed to speak from the throne to which Alexander, in the name of the senate, tried to block his way."[27]

The outcome was a declaration, on May 3, in which the king asserted that, although the bases of the senatorial draft were good, it needed to be revised on a number of points. He announced that on June 10 he would present to the upper and lower houses a constitution that he would elaborate in collaboration with a commission chosen from these two bodies. The commission would be strictly consultative, and care was taken to prevent its appearing as a constituent body.[28] The declaration also asserted that the constitution would have a bicameral legislature, respect individual freedoms and the rights of property (including the inviolability of the "biens nationaux"), and promote a general amnesty for opinions and votes expressed in the past. It was stated in brief and general terms, and neither the second nor the third of the senatorial demands was mentioned.

Over the next weeks, successive drafts of the Charter took away most of the prerogatives the existing senators had given themselves. In the first draft, the king was granted the right to create an unlimited number of senators and to decide whether the offices should be hereditary or for life. At least ninety of the existing senators would join the new senate. Economic guarantees for the existing senators were maintained. In the second draft, the number of existing senators who would join the new institution was reduced to fifty, while the economic guarantees were maintained. In the third draft, and in the Charter itself, there is no mention of the existing senators, except that the third draft asserts that they will retain their emoluments. All was done to prevent the Charter from appearing to be the outcome of bargaining between the senate and the king.[29] At the same time, the king had an interest in not alienating the losers. After the Charter was announced, he named 154 senators, of whom 87 came from the imperial senate. (The 51 former senators who were not reappointed received generous pensions.) Because there was no limit on their number, the presence of imperial senators was no threat to the king, who could and did make new appointments if the upper house became too unruly.[30]

In the first draft, the mode of election to the lower house was not indicated. In a comment on that draft, some of the king's advisers proposed the maintenance of the imperial system of election to the lower house, according to which members were chosen by the senate from a list established by local electoral colleges. Since the upper house would be controlled by the king, this system would also enable him, at one remove, to control the lower house. In the second draft, the indirect control was replaced by a direct one: The king would choose deputies from lists presented by the départements. The king and his advisers may have been dizzy with success, but this was going too far. The "representative government" that was asserted in the declaration of May 3 would be a travesty if the upper and lower house were both essentially royal commissions.[31] In the third draft and in the Charter itself, deputies to the lower house were to be elected locally without any interference by senate or king.

Ultimately, Talleyrand was the kingmaker in 1814, and the senate was merely the instrument for furthering his aims. Unlike the senate, however, he could not aim at writing any prerogatives for himself into the constitution. The senators, when pushed into the role of proximate kingmaker, thought they could use Alexander's soldiers to obtain constitutional guarantees for new political power in addition to preserving their old economic privileges. Had they asked for less, they might have obtained more. Their public display of self-interest, in other words, was self-defeating. In this sense, their behavior was clearly lacking in rationality.

IV. The Constitution of 1848

The constitution of 1848, like that of 1791, was written in a force field defined by government troops and the people of Paris. In 1848, however, the movement was in the opposite direction. After the initial victory of the revolutionary forces, in February 1848, the defeat of the June insurrection ushered in the counterrevolutionary movement that eventually brought Louis Napoleon into power. As in 1789, the making of the constitution was heavily shaped by extraparliamentary events. As Tocqueville wrote, "if the Committee had met on the 27th June instead of the 16th May, its work would have turned out to be entirely different."[32]

The Constituent Assembly was elected on April 23 and met in Paris on May 4. Between May 12 and May 17, the Assembly discussed the procedure for electing the constitutional committee. In the middle of these deliberations, on May 15, a large crowd invaded the assembly to demand support for Polish independence, throwing a scare into many of the deputies. The eighteen members of the constitutional committee, whose composition may have owed something to the events of May 15, began their work on May 19 and delivered a first draft on June 19.[33] In the meantime, Louis Napoleon had been elected deputy by four districts in the by-elections that took place on June 4. The Assembly, having first upheld the 1832 law barring members of former dynasties from entering France, then voted the next day (June 13) to allow Louis Napoleon to enter the country. On June 23, the government announced the closing of the national workshops, thus provoking an insurrection that was repressed after four days of bloody struggle. In July and August the *bureaux* of the Assembly deliberated on the project and submitted their comments to the committee, which delivered its final draft to the Assembly on August 30. In September and October, the Assembly discussed the draft, which was adopted, with only one significant change, on November 4.

The two drafts were clearly written under the shadows of, respectively, the February and June insurrections. The first draft included not only a general proclamation of the right to work but also institutional guarantees for the exercise of this right. It prohibited the practice of buying replacements for military service and opened the doors for progressive taxation. The second draft abolished the right to work and constitutionalized proportional taxation. The ban on replacement was maintained but was dropped in the final version that was adopted by parliament. By contrast, the clauses in the first draft were essentially retained in the second draft and in the final version. The basic principles were unicameralism and direct election of the president. These ideas were not necessarily the first choices of the members of the commission, but, on these topics, as in the matter of the right to work and the ban on replacement, they gave into the pressure of public opinion.[34]

On the afternoon of May 27 and then again on June 14–15, the constitutional committee discussed the mode of electing the president. On the first occasion, it decided to have the president elected by universal suffrage and a relative majority, with a minimum of 2 million votes being required. (The electorate was about 9.3 million.) Nobody at this time advocated election of the president by the Assembly. On the second occasion, a number of modifications were proposed, and one of them adopted. Although the *procès-verbal* of the debates in the commission makes no reference to the emergence of Louis Napoleon as a plausible presidential contender, in his *Recollections*, Tocqueville makes it clear that the new proposals were motivated by fear of his candidacy.[35]

Victor Considérant, the only socialist member of the committee, may have lost some of his trust in the people by the success of Louis Napoleon in the June by-elections. This is, I think, the most plausible explanation for his statement in the committee: "M. Considérant requested that [the president] be elected by the national assembly. True principles, he said, would require the president to be elected by the entire people. But the people's education has not been achieved; it cannot exercise its rights until it has learned better to appreciate them."[36] On May 27, his only observation on this point had been to speak out against a proposal to have the people choose the president among five candidates selected by the assembly: "M. Considérant said that this necessity for the people to limit its choice to certain candidates was an attack on the national sovereignty."[37] Clearly, something had happened in the meantime to make him change his mind.

Although two other members of the committee spoke out for election of the president by the assembly, the proposal got only two votes.

Tocqueville proposed two changes: indirect elections by an electoral college (as in the United States) and requirement of an absolute majority of votes.[38] From his *Recollections,* it appears that at this time his initial preference was for an election by the assembly. In the debates on May 27, he says,

> I was much more concerned with putting a powerful leader quickly at the head of the Republic than with drafting a perfect republican constitution. At that time we were under the divided, vacillating rule of the Executive Committee, socialism was at our doors, and we were drawing near to the [insurrectional] days of June. . . . Later on, after those days, I energetically supported in the Assembly election of the president by the people and to some extent helped to get this accepted. The main reason I gave was that, having announced to the nation that this ardently desired right would be granted, it was no longer possible to refuse it.[39]

This argument against election by the Assembly refers only to public opinion, suggesting that he would otherwise have preferred this system, presumably because it would have prevented the election of Louis Napoleon. It is reasonable to infer, then, that he thought the chances of a victory by Louis Napoleon would be reduced by the modifications he proposed. Perhaps a system of two-step elections might in fact have prevented his election. This part of Tocqueville's proposal was rejected by four votes. The requirement of an absolute majority, which was adopted, did not block Louis Napoleon, who got more than five million votes in the elections on December 10. A fortiori, his election was not blocked by the constitutional provision that unless a candidate chosen by a majority of voters received at least two million votes, the choice would be delegated to the assembly. The originator of this provision, Person, explicitly explained it (on October 9) by saying that, "given the lack of eagerness of voters to participate in the elections, it would be a means of bringing the choice of president back to the assembly." More accurately, it would be a means of blocking the election of Louis Bonaparte without appearing to do so.

Although the Assembly had decided to let Louis Napoleon enter France and take his seat as deputy, he might still be declared ineligible to the presidency. On June 15, "M. Pagès proposed the adoption of an article which excluded members of families which have reigned in France from the presidency," but it was rejected by nine votes against seven.[40] It is not clear what arguments were offered against this proposal. Later, when the fifteen *bureaux* offered their comments on the first draft, several made it clear that they had entertained the idea of excluding members of dynastic families but had rejected it as "undignified."[41] Some of the *bureaux* did, however, express their support for the idea.

One bureau "adopted an amendment in which it expressed the view that the first time the president would be elected by the assembly, but later by the nation."[42] In its deliberation on the comments and the preparation of the final draft, the committee returned to this idea, which was manifestly intended as yet another device to exclude Louis Napoleon. "A long discussion was engaged on this subject, the majority was in favor of maintaining the article, but it was agreed that this decision was only provisional and that one would revisit the issue later, especially after listening to the head of the executive power." On August 12, in fact, the committee decided to hear the provisional head of state, General Cavaignac, who explicitly supported election of the president by the people:[43] "Was this opinion sincere or dictated by personal scruples which prevented the general from favoring a mode of election which everybody knew would work in his favor-the election by an assembly whose bound servant [*homme lige*] he was. The second hypothesis is the most plausible, although conversely Cavaignac's enemies have claimed that he spoke out for popular election because he was confident that he would be chosen."[44]In other words, was Cavaignac guided by sincerity, modesty, or self-interest? We do not know.

A similar question arises with regard to Lamartine's "decisive intervention" in the assembly on October 6, in which he made an impassioned, thoroughly confused, and apparently persuasive argument for direct elections.[45] His speech poses two puzzles. Was he, as may have been the case with Cavaignac, motivated by the hope that when no candidate received an absolute majority, the choice of the Assembly would fall on him? Probably not; "Lamartine was vain rather than cunning."[46] Second, how could the Assembly be swayed by his argument that if the people betrayed their trust and "let itself be blinded by the splendor of past glories . . . so much the worse for the people" and that, "Regardless of what happens, it will be a beautiful part of history to have attempted the Republic"? Unlike Considérant, Lamartine thought the freedom of the republic was worth nothing if the people were prevented from using it to destroy the republic. The puzzle is why the Assembly did not see that, with direct elections of the president, the victory of Louis Napoleon was not a mere possibility, a risk worth taking for the sake of proving the viability of democracy, but an overwhelming probability. Maybe the members put their hopes in the two-million-vote threshold.

The Assembly rejected the proposal to exclude Louis Napoleon on the grounds of his dynastic past. As noted earlier, many of the *bureaux* found it "undignified" to exclude members of earlier dynasties. The same concern came up when the Assembly debated this issue on October 9. Coquerel said that "You are being asked to adopt a law against a man. A law against a man is not worthy of a great assembly, a great nation." There was in fact an obvious tension between trusting the people enough to have the president elected by universal suffrage and not trusting them to choose the right person. Woirhaye asserted that "We are certain that the people will not search among the former princes for the one to whom it wants to entrust its fate."[47] In closed deliberations, even a socialist such as Considérant might assert a less positive view of the people's ability to discern, but this was hardly an argument that could be made in public debate, even after the June days. It was apparently acceptable to say that the people were uninterested in politics but not to claim that, in their zeal, they might make a bad choice.

We may discern three motives in the deputies. The large majority wanted to write a constitution that would prevent the election of Louis Napoleon as president. Their goal was not so much to write a play in which they would have the leading roles as to prevent a dangerous adventurer from usurping power. To do so, they had to adopt means that would also detract from the power and prestige of the presidency, that is, election by the Assembly rather than by universal suffrage, but that outcome was not the goal of their efforts. The situation differed, therefore, from that of Poland in 1921 or France in 1946, where a prestigious candidate was seen as a certain winner of the presidential elections and all the efforts were concentrated on reducing the power of the presidency. (The two generals refused to stand for the emaciated office but came back with a vengeance.) Some of the leading politicians may also have had wanted to write the constitution to enhance their own chances of being elected, even if to a less powerful office. Finally, Louis Napoleon and his followers in the Assembly wanted direct elections both to ensure that he would be chosen and to increase the power of the office. They succeeded because of the romanticism, wishful thinking, and lack of nerve in the majority.

V. The Constitution of 1958

The constitution of the Fifth French Republic was put together between June 3 and September 3, 1958, and adopted in referendum by an 80 percent majority of a turnout of 85 percent on September 28, 1958. The intellectual genesis of the 1958 constitution dates from 1946. On January 20 of that year, de Gaulle resigned as head of government. According to the (contested) version of Jules Moch, he explained his decision in the following terms: "The exclusive rule by the political parties has reappeared. I disapprove. But short of establishing by force a dictatorship I do not want and that no doubt would end badly, I do not have the means to prevent this development. I am thus forced to step down."[48]

On May 5, 1946, the National Assembly presented for referendum a constitutional project that would have created a unicameral parliamentary regime. In a rare example of a constitutional proposal turned down by referendum, it was rejected by the voters, arguably because the Communist members of the constitutional commission, like the senators in 1814, showed their power-grabbing intentions too clearly.[49] Elections to a new constituent assembly were then held on June 2. Before it began to prepare a new constitution, de Gaulle set out his own constitutional conceptions in a speech in Bayeux on June 16. The leading ideas, all of which are found in the 1958 constitution, are bicameralism and, most crucially, a strong executive. Although the new Assembly made some concessions to these ideas, it vested great powers in parliament and, fearing de Gaulle's return to power, very few in the presidency. Combined with a proportional electoral system, the new constitution (adopted by referendum on October 13, 1946) was at the root of the governmental instability of the Fourth Republic.

The Algerian crisis of May 1958 offered de Gaulle a chance to implement his ideas. On May 13, when a new government was scheduled to present its program to parliament, activist groups supported by the army took power in Alger. On May 15, de Gaulle announced that he was willing to take power if called upon. After weeks of negotiations, interspersed with threats by the Algerian rebels, the political elite decided, reluctantly, that only de Gaulle could save the country from an army coup and possibly a civil war. In de Gaulle's own, inimitable words, "In 1958 I had a problem of conscience. I could just let things take their course: the paratroopers in Paris, the parliamentarians in the Seine, the general strike, the government of the Americans: it was written on the wall. Finally a moment would have come when everybody would have come looking for de Gaulle, but at what price? Thus I decided to intervene in time to prevent the drama."[50]

On June 1, parliament passed a vote of confidence in de Gaulle, with 329 votes against 224. On June 3, the deputies voted to give de Gaulle full powers for six months. On the same day, they voted a revision of the article in the 1946 constitution that regulated revisions of the constitution, thus allowing de Gaulle to proceed within the framework of formal legality. De facto, however, the whole enterprise lacked democratic legitimacy, because conducted under the threat from Alger. Pierre Mendès-France characterized the vote on June 1 as a form of blackmail, rather than free consent.[51] As Paul Reynaud, president of the Comité Consultatif (consultative committee) said that France was in a "quasi-revolutionary state."[52]

Before the vote of June 3, parliament had insisted that a draft of the constitution be submitted to a consultative constitutional committee (CCC), of which two-thirds of the members would be deputies or senators. Also, parliament voted on the broad outlines of the revision that the government was about to undertake. Although this was "the first time in [French] history that the constituent power had not been invested with an unconditional competence," the constraints did not really matter.[53] The only solution excluded by the outlines—specifically by the clause "the Government must be responsible before Parliament"—was an American-style presidential regime, which de Gaulle had never desired.

In the elaboration of the constitution, Gaulle's main political adviser was Michel Debré, who also served as Garde des Sceaux (Minister of Justice) in his government. In addition, he had coopted two central political actors from the Fourth Republic, Guy Mollet and Pierre Pflimlin. Their intended function was to add democratic legitimacy to the project; in addition, they suggested important modifications on specific points. The project thus elaborated was then presented to the CCC, which proposed a number of changes, almost none of which were retained by the government. A revised governmental draft was then passed on to the *Conseil d'E-tat,* a judicial body that reviews administrative decisions issued by the government. It made a number of minor modifications, many of which were accepted by the government.

From the debates in the CCC, two remarks may be excerpted: first, "We are not making the constitution for one man nor for a specific set of circumstances,"[54] and second, "a good constitution is one that is not 'tailor-made' but a constitution made 'ready to wear' because it is intended to last for a long time."[55] These remarks, by Bour and by Teitgen, may appear naive. Among modern constitutions, none seems to be as tailor-made—in fact, made by the tailor for himself—as that of the Fifth French Republic. The author was writing a play in which he would have the only starring role. Yet, some remarks by de Gaulle to Alain Peyrefitte cast a different light on de Gaulle's thinking. Although they relate to events of 1962–1964, I believe they also illuminate his constitutional philosophy.

In 1962, de Gaulle decided to change the constitution so that the president would be elected directly, rather than, as in the 1958 document, indirectly. He chose, moreover, to do in a way that was a "flagrant violation of the Constitution," by popular referendum rather than by the more complex procedures laid down in the constitution itself.[56] Consciously or unconsciously, he must have thought that, "As the author of the play in which I am starring, I am free to change the lines as needed." The purpose of the move, however, was to bind those who would appear in later performances of the revised play. When Peyrefitte asked him whether he was going to apply this reform to himself, he answered:

Of course not! I have no need for election by universal suffrage for myself. It is for my successors. They have to be able to stay the course [tenir la charge] outside and above the political parties. Do you understand, they have to be obliged [obligés] to stay the course. If my successor receives the anointing of universal suffrage, he will not be able to evade his responsibilities.[57]

In 1963, when de Gaulle was seriously thinking about Jacques Rueff's proposal to go back to the gold standard, he explained his reasoning as follows:

As long as I am here, I can force the government to fight against the deficit budget and inflation, and to hold up the franc. But you will see that when I am no longer there, the facile solutions will come back. The franc could resist, however, if like other currencies it was linked to gold, as that would oblige the governments to be reasonable, the American government as well as the others.

The popular election of the President is not made for me, but so that after me, the State and the country have a head. In the same way, one has to create a situation in which the political and monetary authorities are obliged to assume their responsibilities.[58]

To put it simply, one does not need a strong presidency if the president is strong. The strong powers of the office are needed to bolster the will of more ordinary individuals, who cannot change the lines of the play as de Gaulle did. The actor-playwright wrote the script with later performers in mind, who would not be capable of rewriting the text as needed. In this perspective, we can also understand de Gaulle's response when he was encouraged, during the presidential campaign of 1965, to use the incriminating past of his opponent, François Mitterrand, against him. In spite of his personal animosity toward Mitterrand, de Gaulle refused to use these tactics. "One must not do anything that would damage the presidency, if he should one day come to occupy it.[59]

With respect to other issues, however, de Gaulle was reluctant to bind his successors too much. He thought it would be dangerous to constitutionalize the electoral law, which could be a crucial control instrument in a national emergency. "In 1945, the Communists represented one voter out of three, and the two other thirds were dispersed among numerous parties. If I had adopted majoritarian voting, the Chamber would have been made up of three quarters Communists. One could only avoid that outcome by proportional voting."[60] The following exchange is also relevant:

> Alain Peyrefitte: Michel Debré wanted the principle of majority vote to be laid down in the constitution. Ought that not to be done?
>
> De Gaulle: No. Debré is right in saying that majority voting is the best means to assure the stability of institutions. But one never knows what might happen. There might be, one day, once again, reasons to revert to proportional voting for the sake of the national interest, as in '45. We should not tie our hands. What one could do is to impose severe conditions for changing the mode of voting, so as not to allow a majority to manipulate the elections at the last moment, by changing the system to adopt one that would be more favorable to its interest."[61]

For a while, de Gaulle was in favor of constitutionalizing a balanced budget. He observed, in June 1964, that, in former budgets, "the idea of voting expenses that were not covered by real revenues would never have appeared. It did so only when inflation became the rule and was used to close the books."[62] Constitutionalizing the balanced budget, together with a return to the gold standard, would impose rigor and make facile solutions impossible. Yet, when his finance minister, Valéry Giscard d'Estaing, proposed the same idea in August of the same year, de Gaulle had changed his mind:

> The principle is good, but you should not be more royalist than the king. Giscard showed that you cannot establish a budget without deadlock, and now he wants us to oblige ourselves to do so by the constitution. We need to have our hands free. Suppose there is a war or an economic depression from which one can escape only by taking up a loan. One can never know. Life is unpredictable. We have to set rules for ourselves, but not impose them artificially for a future period about which we know nothing.[63]

These remarks illustrate what I have come to believe is the most appropriate view of political constraint mechanisms: In politics, people try never to bind themselves, only to bind others.[64] As actor-playwright, de Gaulle was concerned with constraining those who would succeed him in the lead role, not with limiting his own freedom of action.

De Gaulle was not a self-interested actor, but he was conspicuously rational and very successful. The politicians of the Fourth Republic who abdicated in his favor were largely moved by fear—whether prudential or visceral is hard to tell. To the extent that their fear was visceral, as suggested by the scenario of "the parliamentarians in the Seine," they may not have been rational, given the ability of this emotion to distort judgment. The generals who forced them to abdicate may also have been deficient in cognitive rationality. Just as de Gaulle in 1945 ruthlessly disarmed the resistance movement that had brought him to power, he was able to outwit the kingmakers in 1958. They ought to have been suspicious of him.

VI. Conclusion

Each of the four constitution-making episodes was, in one way or another, a failure. Those who voted for the self-denying ordinance in 1791 made the constitution unworkable while believing they were consolidating it. The senators in 1814 had power within their reach, but it slipped from them when they also insisted on retaining their economic privileges. The *constituants* of 1848 were led by Lamartine's rhetoric and their own self-deception into voting for a constitution that predictably led to their ruin. While the generals in 1958 may have believed, with some of the parliamentarians, that de Gaulle would be the creature of the kingmakers, they were in fact merely a ladder beneath him that he would kick away once his position was assured.[65]

Now, failure does not by itself prove irrationality. A calculated gamble may end badly, even if the actor's choice was the best he could have made under the circumstances. We have to ask, then, whether the actors in these four episodes did in fact conceptualize the situation as one of making decisions under risk, making rational assessments of the relevant probabilities, and choosing the option with the greatest expected value. I have not seen any evidence in the historical record to suggest that they consciously thought of the situation in this way, and their behavior strongly suggests that they did not. In the case of the generals who brought de Gaulle to power, their violent reaction to what they perceived as his betrayal suggests that it came as a total surprise, rather than as the realization of a low-probability outcome. The *constituants* of 1848 may have known that they were taking a risk when establishing direct election of the president, but because of their "motivated irrationality" they vastly underestimated the likelihood of the worst-case scenario. In 1814, the senators were so blinded by greed and ambition that they failed to take account of public opinion. In 1791, the bulk of the *constituants* failed to perceive what was obvious to Robespierre—that an assembly of new and inexperienced deputies would lead to the domination of the radical clubs.

In the first and the last of the four episodes, we also observe non-self-interested motivations. The case of de Gaulle is uncontroversial. That of the framers of 1791 is more ambiguous. As Tocqueville writes about a similar episode (the night of August 4, 1789), the self-denying ordinance "was the combined result, in doses that are impossible to determine, of fear and enthusiasm."[66] In the vast literature on the episode, however, I have not come across a single suggestion that the behavior could be reduced *completely* to prudential fear (based on rational assessment of probabilities) that a negative vote might place the deputies in physical danger. In the late eighteenth century, in France as well as in the United States, there was a cult of disinterestedness that had genuine causal efficacy.

In arguing against rational self-interest as the master hypothesis in political science, I am not advocating the alternative of "pure" narrative, simply because there is no such thing. Rather, I am proposing what might be called "conceptual narratives" that rely on a small and manageable number of motivational and cognitive mechanisms. In fact, it is the *interplay* of motivation and cognition—that is, the distorting impact of hope and fear on belief formation—that is at the core of many political sea changes. The basic premise of rational-choice theory—that beliefs are causally shielded from values—is hopelessly wrong. Thus, in 1791, either the extreme left or the extreme right *must* have been irrational: From their shared evidence, it cannot be inferred both that the self-denying ordinance would have promoted the revolution and that it would have undermined it.

NOTES

1. Gordon Wood, "Interest and Disinterestedness in the Making of the Constitution," in Richard Beeman, Stephen Botein, and Edward C. Carter II, eds., *Beyond Confederation: Origins of the Constitution and American National Identity* (Chapel Hill: North Carolina Press, 1987), 69–109.

2. *Archives Parlementaires. Série I: 1789–1799*, Paris 1875–1888. Vol. 8, p. 587.

3. Ibid., 603.

4. Ibid., 556.

5. Ibid., 574.

6. *Archives Parlementaires. Série I: 1789–1799*, Paris 1875–1888. Vol. 9, p. 461.

7. Charles Élie, marquis de Ferrières, *Mémoires*, in M. de Lescure, ed., *Bibliothèque des mémoires*, t. XXXV (Paris: Firmin-Didot, 1880).

8. Jean Egret, *Necker, Ministre de Louis XVI* (Paris: Champion, 1975), 352.

9. Adrien Duquesnoy, *Journal sur l'Assemblée Constituante 3 mai 1789–3 avril 1790* I (Paris: Alphonse Picard, 1894), 324.

10. See for instance Donald R. Matthews, *U.S. Senators and Their World* (New York: Norton 1973), 101–102.

11. R. K. Gooch, *Parliamentary Government in France: Revolutionary Origins 1789–1791* (Ithaca: Cornell University Press, 1960),127–129.

12. *Archives Parlementaires. Série I: 1789–1799*, Paris 1875–1888. Vol. 24, p. 621. Although "the philosopher" Rousseau, did not use these very terms, the discussion of the legislator in *Le Contrat social* (Book II, Ch. VII) makes essentially the same point.

13. Eiza Dorothy Bradby, *The Life of Barnave* II (Oxford: Oxford University Press, 1915), 84.

14. Barry M. Shapiro, "Self-sacrifice, Self-interest, or Self-defense? The Constituent Assembly and the 'Self-denying Ordinance' of May 1791," *French Historical Studies* 25, 625–656.

15. Ernest Lebègue, *Thouret* (Paris: Felix Alcan, 1910), 261.

16. *Archives Parlementaires. Série I: 1789–1799*, Paris 1875–1888. Vol. 26, p. 112.

17. Charles Élie, marquis de Ferrières, *Correspondance Inédite* (Paris: Armand Colin 1932), 344.

18. Gérard Walter, *Maximilien de Robespierre* (Paris: Gallimard, 1989), 111.

19. Georges Lacour-Gayet, *Talleyrand* (Paris: Payot 1990), 737.

20. Charles Maurice de Talleyrand, *Mémoires* II (Paris: Jean Bonnot, 1967), 164.

21. Pierre Rosanvallon, *La Monarchie impossible: Les Chartes de 1814 et de 1830* (Paris: Fayard 1994), 202.

22. Jacques Leon Godechot, *Les Institutions de la France sous la Révolution et l'Empire* (Paris: Presses Universitaires de France 1998), 584–585.

23. Pierre Rosanvallon, *La Monarchie impossible*, 203.

24. Ibid., 194.

25. Guillaume Bertier de Sauvigny, *La Restauration* (Paris: Flammarion 1999), 46.

26. Alfred Nettement, *Histoire de la Restauration* I (Paris: Jacques Lecoffre 1860), n.315.

27. Ibid., 317.

28. Pierre Rosanvallon, *La Monarchie impossible*, 36.

29. Ibid., 37.

30. Guillaume Bertier de Sauvigny, *La Restauration*, 288–289.

31. Pierre Rosanvallon, *La Monarchie impossible*, 41; Alfred Nettement, *Histoire de la Restauration* I, 419–420.

32. Alexis de Tocqueville, *Recollections* (New Brunswick, N.J.: Transaction Books, 1995), 169.

33. Jacques Cohen, *La Préparation de la Constitution de 1848 (pouvoirs législatif et exécutif)* (Paris: Jouve, 1935), 49.

34. Piero Craveri, *Genesi di una Costituzione* (Naples: Guida Editori, 1985), 120, 131, 135, 199, 205. This volume contains the complete transcripts, in French, of the *procès-verbal* of the constitutional committee of 1848.

35. Alexis de Tocqueville, *Recollections*, 177.

36. Piero Craveri, *Genesi di una Costituzione*, 198.

37. Ibid., 147.

38. Ibid., 198.

39. Alexis de Tocqueville, *Recollections*, 178.

40. Piero Craveri, *Genesi di una Costituzione*, 201.

41. Ibid., 262.

42. Ibid., 262–263.

43. Ibid., 296.

44. Paul Bastid, *Doctrines et institutions politiques de la Seconde République* II (Paris: Hachette, 1945), 53.

45. Ibid., 111.

46. Ibid., 113.

47. Ibid., 117.

48. Jean Lacouture, *De Gaulle* II (Paris: Seuil, 1990), 239.

49. Philippe Buton, *Les Lendemains qui déchantent: le Parti Communiste Français à la Libération* (Paris: Presses de la Fondation Nationale des Sciences Politiques, 1993), 226.

50. Alain Peyrefitte, *C'était de Gaulle* I (Paris: Fayard, 1994), 262.

51. *Documents pour servir à l'histoire de l'élaboration de la constitution du 4 octobre 1958* I–III (Paris: La Documentation Française, 1987, 1988, 1991), I:108.

52. Ibid., II:276, 303.

53. Georges Burdeau, Francis Hamon, and Michel Troper, *Droit Constitutionnel*, 22ᵉ édition (Paris: Librairie Générale de Droit et de Jurisprudence, 1991), 449.

54. *Documents pour servir à l'histoire de l'élaboration de la constitution du 4 octobre 1958*, II:89.

55. Ibid., 218.

56. Eric Roussel, *De Gaulle* (Paris: Gallimard, 2002), 736.

57. Alain Peyrefitte, *C'était de Gaulle* I, 178.

58. Alain Peyrefitte, *C'était de Gaulle* II (Paris: Fayard, 1997), 75.

59. Ibid., 602.

60. Alain Peyrefitte, *C'était de Gaulle* I, 451.

61. Ibid., 452.

62. Alain Peyrefitte, *C'était de Gaulle* II, 343–344.

63. Ibid., 344.

64. Jon Elster, *Ulysses Unbound* (Cambridge: Cambridge University Press, 2000).

65. *Documents pour servir à l'histoire de l'élaboration de la constitution du 4 octobre 1958*, I:125.

66. Alexis de Tocqueville, *L'Ancien régime et la Révolution* II (Paris: Gallimard, 1953), 214.

12

Preserving the "Dignity and Influence of the Court"

Political Supports for Judicial Review in the United States

Keith E. Whittington

The power of the courts to strike down laws as unconstitutional has been the subject of substantial political controversy over the course of American history. The power of judicial review is of abstract and scholarly interest, but it becomes politically salient and controversial primarily in connection with particular constitutional decisions of the courts. Often, political controversy focuses on the substantive merits of those individual decisions, and the courts come in for the criticism that they have made some constitutional mistake and reached the wrong outcome in those cases. Such criticism can be quite harsh and sometimes can lead to proposals for fairly dramatic remedies, including constitutional amendments and statutory efforts to check the courts. Nonetheless, the substantive criticism of particular cases still accepts the legitimacy of judicial review more generally.

The power of judicial review itself can also be called into question. Such questioning has characteristically been posed in the twentieth century in the form of what Alexander Bickel influentially called the "countermajoritarian difficulty." Bickel launched his own normative study of the use of judicial review with a critique of Chief Justice John Marshall's opinion justifying judicial review in *Marbury v. Madison* and the following claim:

> The root difficulty is that judicial review is a counter-majoritarian force in our system . . . the reality [is] that when the Supreme Court declares uncon-

stitutional a legislative act or the action of an elected executive, it thwarts the will of representatives of the actual people of the here and now; it exercises control, not in behalf of the prevailing majority, but against it. That, without the mystical overtones, is what actually happens . . . it is the reason the charge can be made that judicial review is undemocratic.[1]

Bickel had come not to bury judicial review but to praise it. The task he had set for himself, and for generations of constitutional scholars, was to justify active use of the power of judicial review by the Supreme Court, despite the countermajoritarian difficulty that inhered in that power.

Here, I examine why judicial review has been so durable, given this background assumption that it is so hostile to democratic forces. I begin by reviewing the origins of the countermajoritarian critique of the Court in the Populist and Progressive movements of the early twentieth century. I then contrast the Progressive analysis of judicial review with Robert Dahl's argument that the Court will be deferential to legislative majorities. I then review a number of political supports for the active exercise of judicial review that have been available over the course of American history, before looking more closely at the successful public campaign on behalf of judicial power mounted by conservative politicians in the early twentieth century and the eventual acquiescence of liberals to judicial review.

The Populist Critique of Judicial Review

Though it now seems commonplace and intuitive, the charge that the Court is inherently undemocratic is largely a twentieth-century phenomenon. In 1803, when the Court decided *Marbury* and for the first time formally struck down a federal statute in the name of the sovereign people, the judiciary's claim to enforce the people's Constitution against the people's legislative agents seemed consonant with contemporary republican theory and recent experience. The 1819 case *McCulloch v. Maryland* was more representative of the main business of judicial review in the nineteenth century, however. In *McCulloch,* the Court upheld the federal incorporation of the Bank of the United States, while striking down a state law that interfered with the operation of the Bank. In ruling against the state of Maryland, Marshall emphasized the difference between the will of the national, whole people and that of a state or part. The former was supreme to the latter in the constitutional scheme. Although the federal judiciary's invalidations of state laws in the early nineteenth century were often controversial, the complaint was that the Supreme Court was nationalistic, not that it was antidemocratic. Although the *Dred Scott* decision provoked Abraham Lincoln to proclaim that democracy would be lost "if the policy of the government, upon vital questions affecting the whole people, is to be irrevocably fixed by decisions of the Supreme Court," his point was precisely that the Court, acting on behalf of the Democratic majorities that had controlled the antebellum government, could not entrench slave policies against future political revision.[2] Neither the controversies that engaged the Court nor the contemporary conceptions of democracy and constitutionalism gave much support to countermajoritarian complaints during much of the nineteenth century.[3] Judicial review and popular government were not regularly perceived to be at odds with each other.

Things changed in the twentieth century. The cases concerned with the government's response to industrialization and economic upheavals that reached the Court beginning in the late nineteenth century proved particularly salient and enduring. The Court found itself routinely operating in the midst of, and taking sides in, the central political controversies of the period. At the same time, judicial decisions were understood to fix, perhaps "irrevocably," the relevant law. With an expanded federal court system, a professional bar and a pool of active litigants, and recurring legal disputes, a precedent-setting Supreme Court decision had substantial ripple effects and policy consequences. At the same time, the perceived requirements of republican government were taking on a distinctly more populist cast in the broader political culture. These were the ingredients for more fundamental challenges to judicial authority in the United States.

The Supreme Court truly burst onto the political scene in the last decade of the nineteenth century. The Court had been far more active in invalidating state and federal laws after the Civil War than it had been before the war. In the three decades after Lincoln's election, the Court struck down, on average, more than three state laws per year, compared to an average closer to one law every two years in the prior three decades. The rate of judicial activity did not notably increase in the 1890s, but the political significance of the Court's constitutional decisions did.

In 1890, the Court effectively overturned its precedents in the Granger cases of thirteen years earlier and imposed new constitutional restrictions on the authority of the states to regulate railroad rates, the leading edge of progressive economic regulations in the late nineteenth century. In

Chicago, Milwaukee and St. Paul Railway Company v. Minnesota, the Court held that, though the states could establish a commission with the power to set railroad rates, they could not, consistent with the due process guarantees of the Fourteenth Amendment, shield the commission's decisions from judicial scrutiny. The Minnesota statute allowed railroads to charge only "reasonable" rates, and the "question of the reasonableness of a rate of charge for transportation by a railroad company, involving as it does the element of reasonableness both as regards the company and as regards the public, is eminently a question for judicial investigation, requiring due process of law for its determination."[4] Justice Joseph Bradley complained in dissent, "by the decision now made we declare, in effect, that the judiciary, and not the legislature, is the final arbiter in the regulation of fares and freights of railroads and the charges of other public accommodations." Bradley argued that this represented an "assumption of authority on the part of the judiciary which . . . it has no right to make."[5]

In 1895, the Supreme Court issued three important decisions with constitutional implications. The Court upheld the broad power of federal judges to issue injunctions to prevent labor unrest from disrupting interstate commerce and the jailing of the socialist leader Eugene V. Debs for violating such an injunction during a railway worker strike.[6] A few months earlier, however, the Court had allowed, over the government's objections, a merger that would give a single company control of 98 percent of the national market in refined sugar, ruling that federal regulatory power did not extend over manufacturing and sharply limiting the scope of the 1890 Sherman Antitrust Act.[7] Responding to an appellant lawyer's charge that the 1894 income tax was "communistic in its purposes and tendencies," the Court also narrowly struck down most of that law as beyond the taxing power granted to Congress, noting that the Constitution was designed "to prevent an attack upon accumulated property by mere force of numbers."[8]

The political response to these decisions was immediate and substantively striking. In his manifesto supporting his 1892 presidential run, the Populist James Weaver expressed amazement that the judges would assume the responsibility for evaluating the reasonableness of railroad rates, given that they were "speaking beyond the reach of the ballot box."[9] He pointedly recalled that when "judges [who] are not subject to popular control" had allied themselves with the slave power, "there was no alternative but the sword."[10] In 1896, William Jennings Bryan and his populist allies wrested control of the Democratic Party from the incumbent conservatives and continued the attack. Denunciations of a "judicial oligarchy" were common. Illinois governor John Altgeld declared, "The Supreme Court cannot by mere decision upon a constitutional question rob the people of the powers of self-government."[11] Such concerns drove new calls for subjecting federal judges to elections. The District of Columbia's *Evening Star* fretted, "the Supreme Court as at present constituted does not spring from the people, and therefore does not properly represent the people."[12] The popular North Carolina state judge Walter Clark, in a prominent law review, called for federal judicial elections, arguing that the "most dangerous, the most undemocratic and unrepublican feature of the constitution, and the one most subject to abuse, is the [current] mode of selecting the Federal judges."[13] The former Republican congressman James M. Ashley declared the Court a "menace to democratic government" and proposed reforms to limit the power of judicial review and allow Congress to override judicial invalidations.[14]

The debate over the potentially antidemocratic character of the federal judiciary only picked up steam in the first decades of the twentieth century as the Court continued to strike down progressive economic reforms. Most famously, in his dissent from the *Lochner* case that struck down a New York maximum-working-hours regulation for bakers as "an unreasonable, unnecessary, and arbitrary interference with the right of the individual to his personal liberty, or to enter into those contracts in relation to labor which may seem to him appropriate or necessary for the support of himself and his family," Justice Oliver Wendell Holmes denounced the majority for interfering with the democratic process.[15] The Constitution "is made for people of fundamentally differing views," and the Court should not attempt to prevent "the natural outcome of a dominant opinion," no matter how "injudicious, or if you like as tyrannical" it might seem.[16]

Off the bench, a lively scholarly debate had developed over the origins and proper scope of the power of judicial review. Some progressive scholars argued that the very foundation of judicial review was "a dangerous innovation" contrary to the constitutional scheme, while others found it in keeping with the counterrevolutionary nature of the Constitution itself, and still others contended that the growth of judicial review at the turn of the century was what was "revolutionary."[17] Certainly, something had changed at the turn of the century. It was not until the twentieth century that a particular term, judicial review, was coined to refer to the judicial power to set aside legislation as unconstitutional.[18] The power of judicial review had long been recognized and occasionally exercised, but it was not until the turn of the century that the Court routinely played this role and seemed to review the actions of the coordinate legislative branch as if it were a mere administrative agency or subordinate court.[19] Tracing the rise of the "American Doctrine of Judicial Supremacy" in 1914, Charles Grove Haines observed that, through the power of judicial review, "the judiciary, a coordinate branch of government, becomes the particular guardian of the terms of the written constitution." For "most practical purposes the judiciary exercises supreme power in the United States" by possessing the "sole right to place an authoritative interpretation upon the fundamental written law."[20] The power of judicial review had become too important to ignore or to relegate to a mere background feature of the American constitutional system, but it was increasingly understood as antidemocratic in character.

The debate over judicial review was prominent in early-twentieth-century presidential politics, as well. Judicial reform was one of the issues that former president Theodore Roosevelt used to propel himself back onto the public stage and to set up his independent run for the White House. By the end of his presidency, Roosevelt was already pondering the problem. Writing to one of the dissenting justices after the *Lochner* decision, Roosevelt expressed the conviction that if the "spirit" of that decision became pervasive in the judiciary, then "we should not only have a revolution, but it would be absolutely necessary to have a revolution."[21] The sitting president was still looking for "some satisfactory scheme" by which he could raise a protest "without impairment of that respect for the law which must go hand in hand with respect for the courts," but he ended his term of office worried that "there is altogether too much power in the bench."[22] A few years later, he believed that action was needed. In the very 1911 speech in which he announced his new campaign for the presidency, Roosevelt declared that judicial rulings that invalidated laws on constitutional grounds "should be subject to revision by the people themselves" through a "right to recall" individual judicial decisions. Asserting that "I believe in pure democracy," Roosevelt argued, "If the courts have the final say-so on all legislative acts, and if no appeal can lie from them to the people, then they are the irresponsible masters of the people."[23] In a 1912 campaign address, Roosevelt called the "right of the people to rule" the "first essential in the Progressive programme," and that commitment was in clear tension with active judicial review.[24] Roosevelt's Progressive Party platform in 1912 demanded "such restrictions on the power of the courts as shall leave to the people the ultimate authority to determine fundamental questions of social welfare and public policy."[25] The Socialist Party, led by Eugene Debs, called for the "abolition" of the "usurped" power of judicial review.[26] Robert La Follette picked up the banner again in his 1924 presidential campaign as the Progressive Party nominee. He declared to a New York audience, "If the court is the final and conclusive authority to determine what laws Congress may pass, then, obviously, the court is the real ruler of the country, exactly the same as the most absolute king would be."[27]

In his extended "history of the countermajoritarian difficulty," Barry Friedman has argued that countermajoritarian concerns were less prominent in the New Deal than they had been in the earlier Populist and Progressive eras.[28] In first place was a new theme of criticizing the justices for being too old and out of touch with the requirements of the present crisis and the new age. President Franklin Roosevelt's most memorable line in criticism of the Court during his first term was that it had pitched the country back to the "horse-and-buggy age" by neglecting to interpret "the Constitution in light of these new things that have come to the country."[29] Similarly, when defending his Court-packing plan, Roosevelt focused on the problem of individual justices who had failed to "bring the Court to a present-day sense of the Constitution."[30] The president found his anchor in "democracy—and more democracy," but he needed the justices to fall in line.[31] Assistant Attorney General, and later Associate Justice, Robert Jackson was among those, however, who framed the problem in countermajoritarian terms after the judicial battles were over and the Court had capitulated. Jackson told an audience at the University of North Carolina, "Either democracy must surrender to the judges or the judges must yield to democracy."[32] Other prominent jurisprudential figures such as Judge Learned Hand and Justice Felix Frankfurter helped carry the countermajoritarian reading of the New Deal experience into the postwar period, and the dilemma posed by the supposedly antidemocratic character of judicial review helped frame the scholarly reaction to *Brown v. Board of Education.*

Expecting Judicial Deference

Despite these persistent doubts about the propriety of the exercise of the power of judicial review in a democracy, judicial review flourished. The political persistence of judicial review may also pose an empirical puzzle.

Robert Dahl influentially argued that the Supreme Court would not behave in a countermajoritarian fashion for any extended period of time. Political scientists at Yale held that the faculty at the Yale Law School was obsessing over an empirical improbability. Bickel, Dahl might have explained, was constructing constitutional theory on the basis of an imagined form of democratic politics (majoritarianism) and judicial politics (countermajoritarianism) that did not exist.

Writing in 1957, in a law review symposium called to consider the political role of the Court as it entered a new period of controversy and a seemingly new commitment "to erect protections for the individual against monolithic government," Dahl argued that the Supreme Court was unavoidably a "political institution" but not one that was likely to stand against the government.[33] Dahl recognized the normative concern that "no amount of tampering with democratic theory can conceal the fact that a system in which the policy preferences of minorities prevail over majorities is at odds with the traditional criteria for distinguishing a democracy from other political systems," but his focus was on the problems of "fact and logic" that he thought beset any notion of "the Court as a protector of the liberties of minorities against the tyranny of majorities."[34] A Court that acted in a consistently countermajoritarian fashion "would be an extremely anomalous institution" in a generally democratic political system.[35] Instead, because of the regular workings of the judicial appointment process, Dahl concluded, "the policy views dominant on the Court are never for long out of line with the policy views dominant among the lawmaking majorities of the United States." It would be "unrealistic" and contrary to historical experience, he argued, "to suppose that the Court would, for more than a few years at most, stand against any major alternatives sought by a lawmaking majority."[36] Laying aside the "ticklish question of federalism" and judicial review of state legislation, which he did not address, Dahl found little reason to believe that judicial review was important to American politics.[37]

Dahl was most directly interested in explaining the incidence of constitutional invalidations by the Supreme Court. Though his empirical findings have been complicated somewhat by subsequent research, his basic perspective on the Court is reasonable and consistent with a range of recent studies.[38] For present purposes, what is interesting about Dahl's argument is the assumption it makes about the orientation of elected officials toward the Court and judicial review. For Dahl, as for Bickel, judges and legislators stand in a fundamentally antagonistic relationship.

The two scholars differ only in how they expect the Court to behave in such circumstances.

Dahl's approach would suggest little political support for judicial review. Elected officials have an interest in a quiescent Court, and that is all. Bringing the judiciary into line with legislative majorities through the appointment process means eliminating the potential obstruction of judicial review from the policymaking process. It is perhaps unsurprising, therefore, to find a late student of Dahl's concluding that "the hypothesis of judicial independence is wrong" and that the Court quickly becomes "subservient" in the face of political criticism.[39] The surprise, from this perspective, would be to find any political supports for judicial review at all, or to find a regular practice of judicial invalidation of legislation.

Political Supports for Judicial Review

But the Court, and the power of judicial review, does have political supports. The Court has proven able to enter and weather heavy political controversy, and judicial review has emerged as a regular, even routine, feature of the American political system. Elected officials have proved less antagonistic to the power of judicial review than Dahl seems to have assumed.

Indeed, aggressive defenders of judicial review emerged at the same time that populists were developing the countermajoritarian critique. Our image of the *Lochner* Court has been decisively shaped by the ultimate electoral, legislative, and (finally) judicial victory of its opponents. We now tend to hearken to the populist rallying cries denouncing the Court for resisting the will of the people, and of course the victors write the history books. What is too easily overlooked is that the most vocal critics of the *Lochner* Court repeatedly lost in the electoral arena that mattered most. The commitments of the "countermajoritarian Court" of the early twentieth century were eventually swept away only by the overwhelming force of the Great Depression. The New Dealers themselves perhaps saw with clearer eyes in contending that the old Court had lived beyond its prime. Although the Court might have been outgunned in its final battle against populist forces, it had been vibrant and active for more than three decades before the fall. Those years of strength also suggest why judicial review proved so resilient after the New Deal reversal.

Dahl's own approach to judicial review points to one possible political motive for supporting the institution. Dahl noted that though the appointment process could be expected to bring the courts into alignment with legislative majorities, there might be a lag during which a holdover Court might obstruct newly empowered lawmakers. Indeed, he attributed Roosevelt's difficulties with the Court to this effect.[40] In Dahl's story, these effects are largely accidental. In what is sometimes called the "entrenchment" or "insurance" thesis, however, they are intentional.[41]

Elected officials may lend their support to judicial review in hopes that the judges will outlive their coalitions and disrupt the legislative plans of their successors. Dahl may believe that in the long run the courts will converge toward the preferences of legislative majorities, but, as John Maynard Keynes might have responded, in the long run we are all dead. If lawmaking majorities are more heterogeneous than Dahl tended to assume in his analysis of judicial review, then the long run might become very long indeed as the appointment process becomes murkier than he portrayed. Likewise, the fractious nature of American politics frequently allows even defeated legislative coalitions to fight a rearguard action to preserve their judicially entrenched victories. Indeed, the entrenchment strategy was visibly employed quite early in American history as the Federalists "retired into the judiciary as a stronghold" after their electoral defeat in 1800, and Thomas Jefferson feared that "from that battery all the works of republicanism are to be beaten down and erased."[42] Similarly, a persistent fear of what one early American Bar Association president called the "tumultuous ocean of democracy" could and did lead even political incumbents to throw their weight behind the judicial "breakwater."[43] Judicial review might be a double-edged sword from the perspective of any given legislator, but it can win support from those who think that it will cut most deeply against their political enemies.

The Court has also proven adept at dividing majority coalitions and finding its own allies to support its independent use of the power of judicial review. Occasionally, the Court can effectively "go public" and appeal over the heads of elected officials to tap directly into the preferences of general public.[44] Political professionals protested loudly over the Warren Court's ruling against gross legislative gerrymanders in favor of "one person one vote," but they gained no traction with the general public, which found little cause for concern in such a decision.[45] More often, the Court can exploit the seams in the dominant legislative coalition, recognizing that American politics is less majoritarian than pluralistic. Thus, despite Jefferson's frustration with a Marshall Court whose Federalism "seems to assimilate" every new justice the Republicans appointed, the Court made its greatest gains when appealing to factions within the Jeffersonian majority itself.[46] More aggressively, the Fuller Court could safely strike down a congressional ban on "yellow-dog" contracts that had been a legislative sop to unions but had little real support within the Republican majority.[47] Likewise, the Rehnquist Court could count on conservative support for its federalism decisions invalidating superficially popular congressional statutes.[48] As Dahl could appreciate, judicial review may "accord with the preferences of one minority and run counter to the preferences of another minority," creating the semblance but not the substance of a countermajoritarian difficulty.[49]

The "ticklish question of federalism" that Dahl passed over in his analysis of judicial review is also of central concern for identifying sources of political support for the practice. In a narrow sense, judicial review of state legislation avoids some of the normative and political complications of judicial review of federal legislation. The Philadelphia drafters of the Constitution were centrally concerned with establishing checks on the states, and union and constitutional supremacy might reasonably be thought to require federal review of state laws. Even while urging general restraint in judicial review, Justice Oliver Wendell Holmes, Boston Brahmin and Civil War veteran, noted, "I do not think the United States would come to an end if we lost our power to declare an Act of Congress void. I do think the Union would be imperiled if we could not make that declaration as to the laws of the several States."[50] State legislation does not enjoy the presumptive support of national political majorities that federal legislation does, and the Court's claim to speak for "we the people" might be stronger when placed against merely local majorities. Nonetheless, it is the judicial review of state legislation that often sparks the greatest political controversy and involves the Court in national disputes. The Court's authority to interpret the Constitution in the context of reviewing state laws cannot be easily separated from its authority to "say what the law is" more generally, and the Court did not hesitate to follow up its declaration to state government officials that it was "supreme in the exposition of the law of the Constitution" with similar assertions directed at Congress and the president.[51]

Incorporating federalism into our field of vision makes particularly evident the reasons that national elected officials might place positive value on active judicial review. Judicial review is the primary mechanism by which national officials monitor the states for compliance with the national constitutional vision. American federalism allows dissenting political voices to find strongholds in state and local governmental institutions from which to launch contrary policy initiatives. Although some advocates of judicial supremacy, such as Daniel Webster, have recoiled from the imagined chaos of a multitude of "popular bodies, each at liberty to decide for itself, and none bound to respect the decisions of others; and each at liberty, then to give a new [constitutional] construction on every new election of its own members," it is significant that in practice the Court has tended to direct its constitutional fire primarily on state legislatures that are politically out of synch with the dominant national coalition.[52] The national political debate over the power of judicial review has been structured in part around that fact, and this federalism consideration has provided a persistent rationale for national officials to lend their support to the Court.

Defending an Activist Court in the Twentieth Century

Although more attention has been given to the late-nineteenth and early-twentieth-century critics of the Court and its constitutional decisions, the Court had supporters, as well, and they were willing, even eager, to come to the defense of an independent Court and an aggressive power of judicial review. Although Williams Jennings Bryan carefully insisted, in his 1896 speech accepting the Democratic presidential nomination, that he made "no suggestion of an attempt to dispute the authority of the Supreme Court," the Republicans seized the opportunity to paint their opponents as extremists.[53] The Republicans made respect for the Court a central theme of the campaign. In his letter accepting the Republican presidential nomination, William McKinley swore to defeat "the sudden, dangerous, and revolutionary assault upon law and order."[54] Former president Benjamin Harrison told his fellow Republicans, "I cannot exaggerate the gravity and importance of this assault upon our constitutional system of government" and the Democratic threat to "the high-minded, independent judiciary that will hold the line on questions of wealth and labor, between rich and poor."[55] After the Bryan nomination, a breakaway convention of conservative Democrats adopted a platform condemning "all efforts to degrade that tribunal or impair the confidence and respect which it has deservedly held."[56]

Of course, the Republicans won a crushing victory in 1896, ending twenty years of close electoral competition between the two parties. For the first time since U. S. Grant's reelection in 1872, a presidential candidate was able to win a solid popular majority. The image of the Democrats as the party of "radicalism" was entrenched, and the Republican victory was widely interpreted in part as a "determination on the part of the people everywhere to maintain the dignity and supremacy of the courts."[57] Entering the 1896 elections, the Court had thrown its weight behind "the constitutional position of the most conservative wing of the Republican party," and the GOP rallied around the Court and emerged victorious.[58]

Similarly, the reaction to Theodore Roosevelt's attacks on judicial review in the 1912 campaign was swift. The *New York Times* called one of Roosevelt's early articles criticizing the Court "the craziest article ever published by a man of high standing and responsibility."[59] President William Howard Taft, Roosevelt's successor, was a firm supporter of the courts, and his formerly close relationship with Roosevelt grew increasingly bitter during Taft's term of office as the new president cast his lot with the conservative wing of the party. Taft had, in fact, served as a federal appellate court judge through much of the 1890s, and his highest ambition was to serve on the Supreme Court. The impatient Roosevelt sneered at what he called the "lawyers' Administration."[60] In 1911, Taft vetoed statehood for Arizona and New Mexico in part because they had adopted recall provisions that the president regarded as "destructive of the independence of the judiciary," "injurious to the cause of free government," and encouraging of "tyranny of a popular majority."[61] Roosevelt's speeches hit Taft "like a bolt out of a clear sky"; Taft denounced his proposals as "absolutely impossible" and thought that Roosevelt himself was becoming "not unlike Napoleon" in his impatience with the law.[62]

Roosevelt's crusade against the courts turned even centrist Republicans against him, while motivating Taft to seek renomination and reelection himself. In letters, Taft avowed, "I represent a safer and saner view of our government and its Constitution than does Theodore Roosevelt, and whether beaten or not I mean to labor in the vineyard for those principles." Taft was convinced that he "represent[ed] a cause that would make it cowardly for me to withdraw now . . . the only hope against radicalism and demagogy."[63] More important than winning the election, Taft and his supporters were convinced, was "retain[ing] the regular Republican party as a nucleus for future conservative action."[64] In campaign speeches, Taft denounced Roosevelt for planting the seeds of "tyranny" and expressed confidence that the American people would "never give up on the Constitution."[65] The Democratic nominee, Woodrow Wilson, remained largely silent on the judiciary, though occasionally expressing opposition to judicial reform, and Roosevelt de-emphasized it as the presidential campaign of 1912 progressed. Taft, by contrast, continued to insist that the Constitution was "the supreme issue" of the election and that the "Republican Party stands for the Constitution as it is."[66] After leaving the White House, Taft accepted a position teaching constitutional law at Yale in order to continue the fight. Once the Republicans reclaimed the White House, Taft was rewarded for his service with an appointment to the Supreme Court as Chief Justice.

The 1912 election was not the clear-cut victory for the Court that the 1896 election was, but the effect was similar. The question of judicial review receded from electoral politics for another decade. The 1924 Progressive candidate Robert M. La Follette was a prominent critic of the Court, but he did not make judicial review a central theme of his campaign that year. Just two years before, however, La Follette had proposed a congressional override of the Supreme Court's constitutional decisions in order to overcome a "judicial oligarchy" that had "wrested sovereignty from the people."[67] Conservatives feared that 1924 might be a repeat of 1912, with La Follette pulling insurgent Republicans away from the party and allowing a Democratic victory. Both the Democrats and Republicans threw themselves behind the Court, however. Calvin Coolidge argued that "Majorities are notoriously irresponsible" and that judicial review was essential to prevent political majorities from voting away even the "most precious rights."[68] Stumping for Coolidge, Charles Evans Hughes warned that La Follette's proposals would leave "everything you have, the security of your person and life, . . . at the mercy of Congress."[69] As the reporter for the New York World concluded, the Republicans "did not want to permit La Follette to escape from the Supreme Court issue if it could be forced on him."[70] The Democratic presidential nominee was John W. Davis, a Wall Street attorney, past president of the American Bar Association, and no friend of court-curbing. His nomination found favor with Chief Justice Taft, who was confident that, if elected, Davis would hold to the "preservation of constitutional principles and the dignity and influence of the Court."[71] Coolidge won in a landslide, despite La Follette's relatively strong showing in the popular vote. Many observers attributed the Republican success in part to La Follette's perceived opposition to the Supreme Court.[72] Taft celebrated the "famous victory" and its lesson that the United States "is really the most conservative country in the world."[73]

Franklin Roosevelt avoided direct criticism of the Court in his presidential campaigns, noting merely that the judiciary in 1932 was also in the hands of the Republicans along with the other two branches of the federal government.[74] As president, of course, Roosevelt was in a better position to advance court-curbing proposals than were earlier progressives such as La Follette or Theodore Roosevelt. Although Roosevelt's 1937 Court-packing plan was dramatic, and dramatically rejected, it is worth noting how moderate it was relative to the standard progressive and populist proposals of the prior several decades such as the abolition of judicial review, a "judicial recall," or a congressional override of judicial constitutional decisions. By contrast, Roosevelt's proposal contained no provision requiring judicial restraint at all.

Rather than getting rid of judicial review, Roosevelt wanted to harness it. The Constitution had created a "three horse team" but "two of the horses are pulling in unison today; the third is not." The administration and the people simply wanted "the third horse to pull in unison with the other two."[75] The judiciary was being "asked by the people to do its part in making democracy successful."[76] What was needed was a "reinvigorated, liberal-minded Judiciary" that understood the "present-day sense of the Constitution."[77] As Robert Jackson later explained, "What we demanded for our generation was the right consciously to influence the evolutionary process of constitutional law, as other generations have done," to loosen the "firm grip" of a "past that was dead and repudiated."[78]

But even a popular president, fresh from a landslide electoral victory, backed by overwhelming partisan majorities in Congress, and faced with stern judicial resistance to his policy program in the midst of economic crisis, could not win passage of even a relatively tempered proposal to meddle with the Court. Many were distrustful of a plan that seemed to consolidate further power in the presidency, and congressional New Dealers rhetorically asked how they would have been expected to respond to such a proposal if a Republican president had made it.[79] Even supporters of the New Deal could foresee positive benefits from the power of judicial review. Referring to the Court-packing plan, the editor of the *Nation,* for example, wrote, "If I were a Negro I would be raging and tearing my hair over this proposal."[80] Others pointed to the value of the Court in protecting free speech and religion.[81] As soon as Roosevelt's appointments joined the Supreme Court, one of the architects of Roosevelt's Court-packing plan, the Princeton constitutional scholar Edward Corwin, began laying out a positive agenda for it. Corwin argued that judicial "self-abnegation" would be "less laudable in the long run" in such areas as the extension against the states of "certain rights which the Bill of Rights protects in more specific terms against Congress." The "enlargement of judicial review" had "its best justification" when the "Court empowered itself to give voice to the conscience of the country in behalf of poor people against local prejudice and unfairness." He singled out "freedom of speech and press and the right to a fair trial."[82] The justices generally agreed and quickly began laying the foundations for the Warren Court's constitutional resurgence.

Since the late nineteenth century, the Court has been routinely denounced as antidemocratic. Even scholarly friends of the Court, who generally favor the power of judicial review, have focused on the countermajoritarian difficulty as a critical normative concern. The countermajoritarian approach to understanding judicial review has sometimes suggested to empirical political scientists that the Supreme Court would, in fact, be fairly passive, unable to muster the political will and support for sustaining such an antidemocratic practice. And yet, the Court has been active and has been able to withstand persistent criticism of its most fundamental function. Contrary to some expectations, elected officials have seen value in an activist Court. Both voters and politicians have ultimately feared the unchecked power of the elective branches more than the power of judicial review. In particular, conservatives early in the twentieth century were eager to defend and encourage the Supreme Court and seemed to reap electoral dividends from doing so, and progressives gradually abandoned efforts to kill judicial review and instead looked to the ways in which the Court could be used to advance their own political interests. Like incumbent officials before them, liberals in power discovered the potential usefulness of judicial review. In practice, the Court has operated in concert with powerful elected officials, and those officials have in turn sought to preserve the "dignity and influence of the Court."

NOTES

1. Alexander M. Bickel, *The Least Dangerous Branch* (Indianapolis, IN: Bobbs-Merrill, 1962), pp. 16–17.

2. Abraham Lincoln, *Abraham Lincoln*, ed. Roy P. Basler (New York: Da Capo Press, 1990), p. 585.

3. See also Barry Friedman, "The History of the Countermajoritarian Difficulty, Part One: The Road to Judicial Supremacy," *New York University Law Review* 73 (1998): 333.

4. *Chicago, Milwaukee and St. Paul Railway Company v. Minnesota*, 134 U.S. 418,

457 (1890). The Court went on to indicate that the "reasonableness" requirement had a constitutional, as well as statutory, base. Eight years later, the Court struck down a rate schedule as "so unreasonably low as to deprive the carrier of its property without such compensation as the constitution secures, and therefore without due process of law." *Smyth v. Ames,* 169 U.S. 466, 526 (1898).

5. *Chicago, Milwaukee and St. Paul Railway Company v. Minnesota,* 462–463.

6. *In re Debs,* 158 U.S. 564 (1895).

7. *United States v. E.C. Knight Co.,* 156 U.S. 1 (1895).

8. *Pollock v. Farmer's Loan and Trust Co.,* 157 U.S. 429, 532, 583 (1895).

9. James B. Weaver, *A Call to Action* (Des Moines: Iowa Printing Company, 1892), p. 122.

10. Ibid., pp. 80, 81.

11. Quoted in Donald Grier Stephenson Jr., *Campaigns and the Court* (New York: Columbia University Press, 1999), p. 127.

12. Quoted in Barry Friedman, "The History of the Countermajoritarian Difficulty, Part Three: The Lesson of *Lochner,*" *New York University Law Review* 76 (2001): 1439–1440.

13. Walter Clark, "The Revision of the Constitution of the United States," *American Law Review* 32 (1898): 7.

14. James M. Ashley, "Should the Supreme Court be Reorganized?" *The Arena* 14 (1895): 221.

15. *Lochner v. New York,* 198 U.S. 45, 56 (1905).

16. Ibid., 76, 75.

17. J. Allen Smith, *The Spirit of American Government* (New York: Macmillan, 1907), p. 103; Louis B. Boudin, "Government by Judiciary," *Political Science Quarterly* 26 (1911): 242.

18. Matthew Franck has identified a few scattered earlier uses of the term in the constitutional context, but Edward Corwin seems to have popularized it. Edward S. Corwin, "The Supreme Court and the Fourteenth Amendment," *Michigan Law Review* 4 (1909): 643. Competing terms to describe the phenomenon were being suggested at the same time, including "judicial supremacy," "judicial veto," and "judicial nullification." Charles Grove Haines, *The American Doctrine of Judicial Supremacy* (New York: Macmillan, 1914), p. 16n2. Corwin himself had previously tried out "judicial paramountcy." Edward S. Corwin, "The Supreme Court and Unconstitutional Acts of Congress," *Michigan Law Review* 4 (1906): 620.

19. This was the original context for the term "judicial review," as legislatures provided for judicial examination of administrative actions to ensure their conformity with the law. See, e.g., *John Den et al. v. The Hoboken Land and Improvement Company,* 59 U.S. 272, 283 (1855); Frank Goodnow, "The Administrative Law of the United States," *Political Science Quarterly* 19 (1904): 112; Thomas Reed Powell, "Judicial Review of Administrative Action in Immigration Proceedings," *Harvard Law Review* 22 (1908): 360.

20. Haines, *American Doctrine*, pp. 5, 11.

21. Theodore Roosevelt, *The Letters of Theodore Roosevelt*, ed. Elting E. Morison and John M. Blum, vol. 6 (Cambridge, MA: Harvard University Press, 1952), p. 904.

22. Ibid., 6:904, 6:1393.

23. Theodore Roosevelt, *Progressive Principles* (New York: Progressive National Service, 1913), pp. 73, 47, 75.

24. Ibid., p. 120.

25. Arthur M. Schlesinger Jr. and Fred L. Israel, eds., *History of American Presidential Elections*, vol. 3 (New York: Chelsea House, 1971), p. 2188.

26. Ibid., p. 2202.

27. Quoted in Friedman, "Lesson of *Lochner*," p. 1446.

28. Barry Friedman, "The History of the Countermajoritarian Difficulty, Part Four: Law's Politics," *University of Pennsylvania Law Review* 148 (2000): 971.

29. Franklin D. Roosevelt, *Public Papers and Addresses of Franklin D. Roosevelt*, ed. Samuel I. Rosenman, vol. 4 (New York: Random House, 1938), p. 209.

30. Ibid., 6:126, 6:127.

31. Ibid., 6:331.

32. Quoted in Friedman, "Law's Politics," p. 1000.

33. Arthur S. Miller, "Policy-Making in a Democracy: The Role of the United States Supreme Court—A Symposium," *Journal of Public Law* 6 (1957): 277; Robert A. Dahl, "Decision-Making in a Democracy: The Supreme Court as a National Policy-Maker," *Journal of Public Law* 6 (1957): 279.

34. Dahl, "Decision-Making in a Democracy," p. 283.

35. Ibid., p. 291.

36. Ibid., p. 285.

37. Ibid., p. 282.

38. For research reexamining Dahl's specific argument, see, e.g., Richard Funston, "The Supreme Court and Critical Elections," *American Political Science Review* 69 (1975): 795; Jonathan D. Casper, "The Supreme Court and National Policy Making," *American Political Science Review* 70 (1976): 50. For more recent research following the Dahlian perspective, see, e.g., Gerald N. Rosenberg, "Judicial Independence and the Reality of Political Power," *Review of Politics* 54 (1992): 369; Barry Friedman, "Dialogue and Judicial Review," *Michigan Law Review* 91 (1993): 577; Mark A. Graber, "The Nonmajoritarian Difficulty: Legislative Deference to the Judiciary," *Studies in American Political Development* 7 (1993): 35; William Mishler and Reginald S. Sheehan, "The Supreme Court as a Countermajoritarian Institution? The Impact of Public Opinion on Supreme Court Decisions," *American Political Science Review* 88 (1993): 87; James A. Stimson, Michael B. MacKuen, and Robert S. Erikson, "Dynamic Representation," *American Political Science Review* 89 (1995): 543; Michael J. Klarman, "Rethinking the Civil Rights and Civil Liberties Revolution," *Virginia Law Review* 82 (1996): 1; Keith E. Whittington,

"Taking What They Give Us: Explaining the Court's Federalism Offensive," *Duke Law Journal* 51 (2001): 477.

39. Rosenberg, "Judicial Independence and the Reality of Political Power," pp. 398, 395.

40. Dahl, "Decision-Making in a Democracy," pp. 285–286.

41. J. Mark Ramseyer, "The Puzzling (In)dependence of Courts: A Comparative Approach," *Journal of Legal Studies* 23 (1994): 721; Ran Hirschl, *Towards Juristocracy* (Cambridge, MA: Harvard University Press, 2004); Andrew Moravcsik, "The Origins of Human Rights Regimes: Democratic Delegation in Postwar Europe," *International Organization* 54 (2000): 217; Tom Ginsburg, *Judicial Review in New Democracies* (New York: Cambridge University Press, 2003); Jack M. Balkin and Sanford Levinson, "Understanding the Constitutional Revolution," *Virginia Law Review* 87 (2001): 1045; Howard Gillman, "How Political Parties Can Use the Courts to Advance Their Agendas: Federal Courts in the United States, 1875–1891," *American Political Science Review* 96 (2002): 511.

42. Thomas Jefferson, *The Writings of Thomas Jefferson*, ed. H.A. Washington, vol. 4 (New York: John C. Riker, 1854), p. 424–425; Thomas Jefferson, *The Writings of Thomas Jefferson*, ed. Paul Leicester Ford, vol. 10 (New York: G.P. Putnam's Sons, 1899), p. 169.

43. John F. Dillon, "Address of the President," in *Report of the Fifteenth Annual Meeting of the American Bar Association* (Chicago: American Bar Association, 1892), p. 211.

44. Samuel Kernell, *Going Public* (Washington, D.C.: CQ Press, 1997).

45. *Baker v. Carr,* 369 U.S. 186 (1962).

46. Jefferson, *Writings,* ed. Ford, 10:140. See also, Mark A. Graber, "Federalist or Friend of Adams: The Marshall Court and Party Politics," *Studies in American Political Development* 12 (1998): 229.

47. George I. Lovell, "'As Harmless as an Infant': Deference, Denial, and Adair v. United States," *Studies in American Political Development* 14 (2000): 212.

48. Whittington, "Taking What They Give Us."

49. Dahl, "Decision-Making in a Democracy," p. 282.

50. Oliver Wendell Holmes, *Collected Legal Papers,* ed. Harold Laski (New York: Peter Smith, 1952), pp. 295–296.

51. *Cooper v. Aaron,* 358 U.S. 1, 18 (1958); see also *Powell v. McCormack,* 395 U.S. 486, 521 (1969); *U.S. v. Nixon,* 418 U.S. 683, 704 (1974).

52. *Debates in Congress,* 21st Cong., 1st sess., 1830, vol. 6, 78. See John B. Gates, *The Supreme Court and Partisan Realignment* (Boulder, CO: Westview Press, 1992).

53. Schlesinger and Israel, *History of American Presidential Elections,* 2:1853.

54. Quoted in William G. Ross, *A Muted Fury* (Princeton: Princeton University Press, 1994), p. 36.

55. Quoted in Stephenson, *Campaigns and the Court,* p. 127.

56. Quoted in Ross, *A Muted Fury,* p. 36.

57. James L. Sundquist, *Dynamics of the Party System*, rev. ed. (Washington, D.C.: Brookings Institution, 1983), p. 165; Indianapolis *News*, quoted in Alan Furman Westin, "The Supreme Court, the Populist Movement, and the Campaign of 1896," *Journal of Politics* 15 (1959): 38.

58. Gates, *The Supreme Court and Partisan Realignment*, p. 68.

59. Special to the *New York Times*, "The Short Way with the Courts," *New York Times*, 6 January 1912, 12.

60. Roosevelt, *Letters*, 7:113.

61. William Howard Taft, *The Collected Works of William Howard Taft*, ed. David H. Burton, vol. 4 (Athens: Ohio University Press, 2002), p. 150.

62. Quoted in Henry F. Pringle, *The Life and Times of William Howard Taft*, vol. 2 (New York: Farrar and Rinehart, 1939), p. 573; Archibald Butt, *Taft and Roosevelt*, vol. 1 (Garden City, NY: Doubleday, Doran, 1930), p. 346.

63. Quoted in Pringle, *Life and Times*, 2:764, 2:772.

64. Quoted in ibid., 2:808.

65. Quoted in Ross, *A Muted Fury*, p. 138.

66. William Howard Taft, "The Supreme Issue," *Saturday Evening Post*, 19 October 1912, 3; Special to the *New York Times*, "Taft and Root Assail Radicals," *New York Times*, 2 August 1912, 6.

67. Quoted in Ross, *A Muted Fury*, p. 195.

68. Calvin Coolidge, *Foundations of the Republic* (New York: Charles Scribner's Sons, 1926), p. 95.

69. Quoted in Alpheus Thomas Mason, *William Howard Taft* (New York: Simon and Schuster, 1965), p. 282.

70. Quoted in Ross, *A Muted Fury*, p. 268.

71. Quoted in ibid., p. 259.

72. Ibid., pp. 282–283.

73. Quoted in Russell Fowler, "Calvin Coolidge and the Supreme Court," *Journal of Supreme Court History* 25 (2000): 284.

74. Roosevelt, *Public Papers*, 1:837.

75. Ibid., 6:123, 6:124.

76. Ibid., 5:641.

77. Ibid., 6:133, 6:127.

78. Robert H. Jackson, *The Struggle for Judicial Supremacy* (New York: Vintage, 1941), p. xiv.

79. William E. Leuchtenburg, *Franklin D. Roosevelt and the New Deal, 1932–1940* (New York: Harper and Row, 1963), pp. 234–235.

80. Quoted in ibid., p. 235.

81. William E. Leuchtenburg, *The Supreme Court Reborn* (New York: Oxford University Press, 1995), p. 139.

82. Edward S. Corwin, *Constitutional Revolution, Ltd.* (Claremont, CA: Claremont College, 1941), pp. 110, 111–112.

13

The Significance of Cognitive and Moral Learning for Democratic Institutions

Ulrich K. Preuss

The idea that power is legitimate only when it is granted by the will of the ruled demonstrates the normative superiority of democracy above all other forms of governing. The basic idea that freedom and authority are reconciled with each other is constitutive only for democratic models of power and indicates their uniqueness. Other concepts of political rule may make manifold promises of salvation in order to justify the individual's subordination under the requirements of their respective pledges; only democracy is a model of self-rule of the people.

This unique quality makes democracy also, in a specific manner, vulnerable to the weaknesses of human nature. There are other forms of government, such as theocracies, monarchies, aristocracies, dictatorships, and rule through specially qualified individuals (holy persons, the Lord's anointed, warriors, the initiated and the like). In a democracy, it is the ordinary citizen who rules. That is, the functioning of democracy is founded upon the intellectual and moral ordinariness of people. It is then either by chance or because of a skillful institutional arrangement that democratic power is exercised by outstanding political leaders. The omnipresent complaints about the deficits or even failure of democracy can essentially be reduced to the basic argument according to which democracy has until now not found reliable mechanisms for the selection of the persons most able to exercise democratic rule. That is a serious problem, on which I, however, will not elaborate here, because there exists a graver problem, namely how democracy can perform its mission of both effective and legitimate rule despite the uncertainties about the appropriate qualities not only of the democratic leaders but of the people themselves, whose will in the last instance determines the course of democratic politics. In other words, does democracy dispose of equipment that protects it against the weaknesses and failures of the demos? This is, of course, a question about the relationship between persons and institutions in the democratic system.

In what follows, I start with a brief reminder of one classical answer to this problem in democratic theory, Rousseau's claim that the identity of the rulers and the ruled ensures the good quality of democratic decisions, and its fallacy (I). In a second step of the argument, I show that modern complex societies are increasingly confronted with cognitive and moral problems, which require methods of solution for which the democratic means of problem solving appear insufficient (II). I then turn to the issue of learning as a problem-solving method used not only by persons, organizations, and institutions but also by political systems (III). Thereafter, I deal with the relationship between learning and power. If, according to the famous statement of K. W. Deutsch, "power is the ability to afford not to learn,"[1] the question arises whether democracy—the form of government in which the people possess the supreme power—includes the right of the people not to learn. I make the claim that the legitimacy of democratic institutions in modern societies requires openness for generating, preserving, and enhancing both cognitive and moral knowledge (IV).

I. A Democratic Answer to a Democratic Problem, and Why It Fails

When we reflect on the possibilities of increasing the quality of democratic governance, we always have to take into account two discrepant elements: the moral and cognitive qualities of the people who rule themselves and the impersonal functioning of institutions—rules of action that impose themselves upon the subjectivity of the individuals and that protect the people against their inclinations toward myopia and irresponsible behavior.[2] It is the well-known tension between *ratio* and *voluntas* that is particularly relevant in democracies. The core element of democracy—the people's will as the source of supreme authority— embodies a deep tension: The people's will in its purest and most authentic quality requires its immediate presence, and, if this is not possible, its utmost mirror-image representation.[3] However, the popular will in its quality as the source of supreme authority requires the willingness of the people to mediate their more or less spontaneous intuitions, to launder, as it were, their preferences, to reflect on the effects of their will power on others who are not present but who are affected by their decisions; that is, to assume responsibility for their actions. In other words, while the former element—outwardly more authentically democratic—is prone to foster irrational and irresponsible behavior,[4] the latter—at first glance less democratic—is likely to be more beneficial to the people.

As we know, Rousseau and all democratic theorists who follow his line of reasoning deny this kind of tension. For them, the centuries-old question of what the ideal of a good and just government demands and by which criteria of justice the rule of one person over another should be evaluated has an amazing, simple, and suggestive solution. Since the end of the eighteenth century, democracy has been recognized as the form of just rule because it is tantamount to the self-rule of the people, that is, a political order in which those who are subject to the rule are at the same time its authors. Rousseau was the first who gave this answer of seducing simplicity: When all decide over all collectively, that is, when all give the laws to themselves, then no injustice can be done to anybody. In such a case the general will is always correct, because "there is no one who does not take that word 'each' to pertain to himself and in voting for all think of himself."[5] What comes into being is a complete mutuality among the members of the community, which prevents any kind of preference or discrimination whatsoever. In a strictly secular understanding of justice, this means nothing other than full identity of the people with itself, which signifies perfect self-determination as the means for perfect justice; one cannot be unjust to oneself. In this situation, the people "[are] in the position of a private person making a contract with himself."[6]

Unfortunately, this conclusion suffers from a serious flaw. It does not take into account that the formation of the general will does not mean only self-binding but also binding others and being bound by others. Those who bind themselves through agreement within a collective resolution cannot unbind themselves without the agreement of all others. Collective self-determination is much more heteronomy than autonomy. If this is so, then the idea of responsibility comes into the fore; while in a framework of self-determination responsibility is irrelevant, ruling over others requires a minimum of concern for their welfare. This in turn requires that the rulers' decisions be appropriate in terms of their problem-solving capacity, that is, they must be based on both the knowledge of the relevant information and the alternatives that are available and the consciousness of principles that serve as criteria for the choices among those alternatives. In other words, responsibility demands cognitive and moral qualities of the rulers. Rousseau offered only a theory that explained why the general will was inherently just; for this theory, the cognitive and moral truth of the general will was of no systematic importance, because even a cognitively and morally deficient decision would not impair the legitimacy of the rule of the general will. It was the authorship of the people and not the quality of the decisions of the general will that created the legitimacy of democratic rule. Moreover, and this was of utmost importance for Rousseau, it was this perfectly mutual character of the general will that safeguarded individuals' freedom even under the condition of social dependence. For Rousseau and his contemporaries, living under the despotism of a feudal-absolutist regime, the protection of individuals' freedom was certainly the essential criterion for the evaluation of the quality of the collective will of the people. Today, however, we value democracy not only because it embodies the best available conditions of individual freedom but also because it is a political system that embodies the most favorable conditions for the inducement of collective reason, wisdom, and morality.

Rousseau himself suspected that these different requirements for the quality of democratic resolutions do not always stand in harmony with one another. A just collective decision that does not violate anybody's individual autonomy may still be wrong and damaging for the community.

> How can a blind multitude, which often does not know what it wants, because it seldom knows what is good for it, undertake by itself an enterprise as vast and difficult as a system of legislation? By themselves the people always will what is good, but by themselves they do not always discern it. The general will is always rightful, but the judgment which guides it is not always enlightened. It must be brought to see things as they are, and sometimes as they should be seen; it must be shown the good path, which it is seeking, and secured against seduction, by the desires of individuals; it must be given a sense of situation and season, so as to weigh immediate and tangible advantages against distant and hidden evils. Individuals see the good and reject it; the public desires the good but does not see it. Both equally need guidance. Individuals must be obliged to subordinate their will to their reason; the public must be taught to recognize what it desires.[7]

Rousseau speaks here about wrong collective resolutions in a twofold sense: with respect to both their cognitive weaknesses and their moral faults. A decision is wrong in a cognitive sense if the people make a decision in the absence of a more enlightened account of what would be good and just ("the public desires the good but does not see it"). On the other hand, resolutions are morally insufficient when they have been made in a situation where the people have succumbed to the temptations of passions, where, in other words, the citizens recognize what is normatively correct but reject it. In the former case, the cognitive capacity is wanting; in the latter the control of reason over pure will is lacking. As we know, Rousseau pulls from this error-prone collective will the conclusion that a people actually require a superior intelligence that could safeguard the inherent cognitive and moral quality of the law, who "could understand the passions of men without feeling any of them, whose happiness was independent of ours, but who would nevertheless make our happiness his concern."[8]

Had Rousseau been less preoccupied with the idea that the people had to be physically present rather than being represented (e.g., in a parliament) in order to form a collective will, he might have been able to find a solution to this problem in the concept of institution. Institutions allow the conservation and the transfer of a person's knowledge and will to future generations. Just as much as, for instance, patents can be understood as private stores of knowledge[9] that continue to exist after the death of the person who created this knowledge, the constitution is a store of public knowledge in that it objectifies the will of the constituent powers for the use of subsequent generations.[10] Given that modern law (including modern constitutions) can be amended any time according to the very rules of the constitutions thanks to its positivity, constitutions can be regarded as the stores of the knowledge and experience of the chain of generations that lived under the same, if more or less, frequently amended constitution.[11] Depending upon the anti- or pro-institutionalist character of a political system, a people is doomed to gather experience for each generation anew or it can build upon the past experiences of its predecessors. Obviously, the former method is much more resource-consuming than the latter, which may account for the relative economic lag of some societies if compared with others that are more institution-friendly in their system of government.

It is plausible to assume that this correlation between knowledge and institutions, in particular between knowledge and the constitution, escaped Rousseau's attention because, for him, the question of how political power could be justified stood clearly in the foreground of his political philosophy. Since the rise of the modern European state in the seventeenth century, coercive power of the sovereign state had become the pivotal means of societal integration,[12] and political philosophers from Hobbes through Locke to Rousseau had developed systems of reasoning that aimed at limiting and legitimizing the state's sovereign power through the natural rights of its subjects. Hobbes was primarily interested in the unconditional supremacy of state power over a chaotic plurality and a conflict-ridden society; Locke aimed at restricting state power firmly to its purpose to protect the natural rights of the individuals; and Rousseau, most ambitiously, claimed to have reconciled sovereign power and individual freedom in the idea of the general will emanating from the collectivity of the ruled who had turned rulers.

Yet, beyond these stark differences among them, these three philosophers converged in one particular point: Power was the essential social and political energy whose quality determined the nature of the polity. When they argued for their respective conception of a good polity, they argued for or against a particular kind of power, which in their framework was, positively or negatively, the strategic resource for the shaping of the polity. In a political community whose social integration is mainly organized through the medium of power, the limitation and legitimating of this very power is the central concern. Hobbes was concerned about its supremacy, which he deemed necessary for the sake of imposing social discipline upon the society. Rousseau aimed at its preeminence because it secured the integrity of the general will. Locke, conversely, sought to limit it for the sake of the individual's freedom.

II. Problems That Cannot Be Solved by Power

Yet, power, understood in the Weberian sense of the "probability that one actor within a social relationship will be in a position to carry out his own will despite resistance,"[13] is not a resource that is able to solve all problems of a modern society. In particular, an increase of power does not mean an upsurge of problem-solving capacity, just as a reduction of power is tantamount to the weakening ability of the polity to cope with its problems. Unlimited power undermines sovereigns' authority because they cannot make credible promises, making them unable to allocate trust and, consequently, to engage in long-term social relations,[14] while self-limited power, as the case of Ulysses and the Sirens shows, can increase the range of options of the self-bound person.[15]

Moreover, coercive power has ceased to be the major force that ensures the social discipline of the individuals and the coherence of society. The basic conflicts of advanced contemporary societies cannot be understood in the conceptual framework of "individual freedom versus sovereign power."[16] The functional differentiation of modern societies; the acceleration of technological innovations and socioeconomic transformation; and processes of globalization, with its shifting patterns of production, trade, financing, migration, environmental use, cultural orientation, and political domination,[17] have changed the character of conflicts and problems with which these societies have to cope. Although the traditional conflicts around socioeconomic status and cleavages, distribution and social justice, persist (though in different modes),[18] a new class of problems has turned up that follow a different logic. These conflicts include the relationship of humans to nature and to humankind's own technology; the globalization of risks caused by people; the relationship between living generations as well between living and future generations; and the relationship between the two sexes, between various ethnic groups, and the like.

It is difficult to recognize a common positive attribute in these conflicts, but there is a negative one: None of these relationship problems can be solved with the characteristic and successful means of the modern constitutional state, namely power, law, and money.[19] Rather, we cannot fail to see that complex societies and their constituent parts exhibit a distinct functional need for responsible and ethical mass orientations, which can neither be compensated for by an ethic of responsibility on the part of elites and experts nor satisfied by falling back on the rountinized, everyday moral orientations of the "ordinary citizen."[20] More and more, the individuals' sociability is induced less by the coercive authority of the state and built instead upon their self-regulatory capacity, that is, their own reasonable view and judgment. Political communities, in which those capacities of citizens are valued or at least seen as important, can be denominated as primarily guided by morality and knowledge.

Of course, this does not mean that previous societies, regulated mainly through power and obedience, did not require cognitive and moral capacities of their members. No social and political system could survive without a minimum standard of intellectual and moral qualities of its members. This is why, after the establishment of the absolutist state in the seventeenth and eighteenth centuries in Europe, the princes set up compulsory education in order to safeguard elementary cognitive abilities among their subjects, whereas the moral qualities were created by the churches.[21] The objective was mainly the learning of obedience as commanded by the state and its officials. Yet after the transformation of the absolutist into the constitutional state, of the subaltern subjects of a statist power machine into the citizens of a democratic republic, and after the change of the agrarian into the industrial, urban, individualized, and interdependent modern mass society, the requirements on the moral autonomy and the intellectual judgment of the individuals had considerably increased.

In the postindustrial society, whose productivity is dependent on individuals' knowledge and their ability for methodic acquisition of knowledge and information, these demands have undergone a further transformation. The modern and knowledge-based society values the disciplined acquisition and application of knowledge about industrial machinery and processes, as well as the ability for cognitive and moral orientation in extremely expanded, specialized, and complex patterns of action. The chains of action in which the individual is involved are so long and complicated that it has become ever more difficult to evaluate the social effects of one's actions according to the logic of a linear causality. To live a responsible personal life increasingly requires an almost scientific attitude and reflection of everyday life observations and experiences and the capacity and readiness to refer complex, uncertain, and often litigious connections to one's own moral constitution and, finally, to draw practical consequences from it.[22]

I will briefly specify four life spheres in which this reflexive attitude plays a pivotal role and where regulative power is of inferior significance:

(1)   There are spheres of life that are significant for the society at large and whose order belongs to the field of the community's responsibilities but that are insensitive to the (legally established) power of the community. The education of the children in the family and the school belongs to this field just as much as the behavior of the sexes and the generations toward each other or their ability to cope with strangeness. Family and school have ceased to be special and paralegal spheres of internment in which parents and state rule over the bodies of children. Parents no longer possess the power to impose their will upon children with superior physi-

cal force in order to mold them into good members of the society. In order to achieve this goal today, responsible institutions must develop the ability for communication and interaction with the individual personalities of the children and young people and, most important, evoke in them the sense of the importance of this development process, which in earlier epochs would have been implanted within them more or less by authority through force.

(2) There are groups in society that have become insensitive to both the rewards and the negative sanctions of its institutions. They are not attracted by the promises of a vocational career or the temptations of a high consumer level as rewards for their adjustment to the norms of the society. Nor can they be pulled back into the center of the society through social punishments, by the neglect and discrimination of their fellow citizens, or through the inconveniencies of their material poverty. Such alienation and partly self-inflicted marginalization, should not leave society indifferent, because their existence demonstrates a loss of control within the community and thus a challenge to and a restriction on the validity of its social, moral, and even legal norms. In extreme cases, this kind of exclusion from the society may even challenge the universality of those norms and hence endanger the identity of the community. The civilized society cannot leave drug addicts, those who have lost out because of rapid modernization (marginalized and self-marginalized persons such as delinquents, the long-term unemployed, alcoholics, and homeless persons), and increasingly "ghettoized" immigrants to their fates without betraying its basic principles and, in the long run, undermining its social cohesion. Police control is no answer to this question. Should society choose a strategy of coercive integration, or should one simply tolerate the status of the marginalized at the edge of the society, or should one perhaps even recognize their status in a positive sense? Questions of this kind require reactions, for which the constitutional state with its guarantee of individual rights, separation of powers and welfare institutions is hardly prepared, because it does not dispose of the necessary instruments that could influence the moral infrastructure of both the society and the individual.

(3) But there are also configurations in which not only the marginalized but also those who live in the center of society are confronted with new challenges. The constantly accelerating scientific-technological revolution exercises a strong pressure on the individual to replace outdated knowledge with new. This develops, to a certain extent, a durable "stand-

by knowledge alert" so that one is always up-to-date with the conditions of the functioning of both workplace and consumer devices and with permanently changing vocational requirements. This situation asks for an epistemological attitude of experimentation, tolerance, or even indifference in relation to fixed knowledge and epistemological certainty that has up to now been seen only among scientists. Socially relevant knowledge is being accumulated less and less through experience and from perceptible, real objects (machines, books, hard currency) and more through power over immaterial information; this again requires a certain measure of theoretical knowledge about complex connections, which are transparent for a declining number of people. This is indicative of a new stage in the abstraction of social relations and knowledge about society.

The knowledge-sensitive basic attitude, which is necessary or at least useful in the spheres of occupation and consumption, has, however, an ambivalent character. As it applies to the role of the individuals as citizens it can have damaging and destructive consequences for the institutions of the community. The fulfillment of civic obligations and the observation of certain social responsibilities are based in the long run on the acceptance of ideas of legal commitment and moral certainty, and this again does presuppose an epistemology, in which knowledge, based on every day life experience, represents a stable and reliable basis of individual acting. This civic spirit cannot be created by authoritatively imposed rules and prohibitions. Hence, there is reason to suspect that traditional means of state regulation have become increasingly ineffective.

(4)   Finally, the extension and intertwining of the chains of action, mentioned earlier, require a new kind of social and moral sensitivity, which no longer can be achieved through the traditional pattern of congruence of control and accountability. Traditional social morality evaluated the moral and legal character of the individual's actions and its consequences on the basis of a concept of causality, in which each part of the chain was identifiable and attributable to the acting individual. Today we speak of "complex causality" when assessing the quality of our social, aesthetic and natural environment. Through this term we want to express that more and more conditions of our world are the effects of a combination of many different causal factors, so that only in the rarest cases is it possible to assign clear responsibilities. Attributions may be so general and vague that no one is able to derive active guidance from his or her individual conduct. If, for example, a considerable part of the ongoing climatic change is a consequence of the Western lifestyle, then the realization of

this complex chain of causality is more likely to discharge individuals of their responsibility for this result than to lead to a call for changes in human behavior, since no individual can reasonably be burdened with the task of changing the way of life of a whole civilization.

And yet, a well-organized society in the present requires a social and moral attitude that is willing to accept responsibilities for uncertain and remote consequences of individuals' behavior. What was until recently almost exclusively required of scientists working at the boundaries of knowledge will increasingly be expected of the layman: Since the life sciences have made the manufactured creation of human beings possible, the actual realization of this step depends now upon the moral maturity of the society, in the end upon the individuals. The considerations called upon in this area require a much higher level of moral reflection than those demanded from the individuals in agrarian and industrial societies.

III. Institutional Learning

So far I have spoken about the requirements that modern societies impose on their members and about the powerlessness of power in creating these qualities and appropriate social conduct. Power has only a limited importance for societal integration. What is required is individuals' capacity and willingness to act responsibly. Since the relevant cognitive and moral qualities of individuals are not innate, they have to be learned. Cognitive learning is a "process of acquiring information and knowledge";[23] moral learning is a social practice in which the normative orientations of individuals that affect their social conduct are formed.[24] Learning is a constitutive element of human beings' development and of their capacity to cope with the challenges of human life.

But not only human beings learn. Social institutions such as markets, organizations, firms, hospitals, governments, and networks learn,[25] at least in the cognitive sense of this term. Strictly speaking, only humans can acquire knowledge and moral orientations, but institutions "learn" when their system of incentives encourage their members to create, acquire, and disseminate knowledge and values to the benefit of the institution. Institutions store not only information but also moral convictions. Institutions create models of thinking, reasoning, and social behavior that impose themselves upon their members and develop a social environment and an institutional culture that may further or impede cognitive innovation and moral reorientation. There is plenty of research material with respect to firms and other organizations.[26]

In the field of political science, Karl W. Deutsch was the first to stress the role of communication, information, and value development in the understanding of political institutions, political behavior, and political ideas. Thus, power is seen not simply as the ability of persons or organizations to impose their will upon the environment but as "the most important currency in the interchanges between political systems and other major subsystems of the society."[27] Like monetary currency, its function depends upon the trust of the society, and its coercive dimension is only a kind of safety net for the sake of damage control in case social expectations for the normal functioning of this currency are thwarted.

In this perspective, it is not coercive capabilities that define the essence of politics but "the dependable coordination of human efforts and expectations for the attainment of the goals of the society."[28] This explains why, for democracy as a political system that is built upon the coordination of voluntary social interaction, learning—the response to the challenge of the given state of affairs—is of pivotal significance.[29] The institution that embodies the relevant communicative—both cognitive and moral— capacities of individuals living in a democratic system is citizenship. Despite the important role of collective representative actors such as parties, interest groups, and parliaments, "the quality of policy decisions and outcomes . . . will ultimately depend upon the quality of the citizens' thought and action."[30] The cognitive and moral resources of (active) citizens, as distinct from (subaltern) subjects, certainly depend upon their civic education both in formal institutions and in the social practice of civil society;[31] yet, arguably the basic prerequisite of citizenship is a constitutional structure in which the coercive element of power is minimized.

However, the traditional liberal constitutional paradigm of "limited government"[32] is hardly sufficient for the fulfillment of the requirements of citizenship outlined so far, although it remains, of course, important. "Limited government" focuses too much on the negative or positive role of state power for the organization of the society. This approach to the understanding of the constitutional state regards all other resources, and, above all, the cognitive and moral abilities of the citizens, as unproblematic givens. As mentioned earlier, they had to be created by the absolutist state, and modern societies must care about them no less, perhaps even more.

Citizens in modern societies are not embedded in a set of homogeneous and stable values and cognitive and moral perspectives; they are confronted with processes of accelerated transformations of their natural, social, and economic environment, with technological innovations, and cultural diversity. In order to face the resulting uncertainties, they have to understand and cope with a multiplicity of epistemological and normative perspectives; they have to acquire an attitude of cognitive and moral reflection over their own acting. Hence, the process of generating the cognitive and moral resources of the citizens requires modes of learning that take the heterogeneity and multiplicity of epistemological and normative orientations into account. The learning of learning—of generating, acquiring, and applying knowledge—becomes more important than the learning of knowledge.[33] The school—the basic institution in which the future citizens of the community are formed intellectually and morally—will then no longer be a place for the conveyance of traditional knowledge but a place for acquiring the ability to understand, to bear, and to cope with the variety and openness of knowledge and of values.

Citizenship is only one, albeit the most important institution of democracy that needs particular conditions for learning and that represents the polity's self-image of what is necessary and desirable to know and to store for future generations. There are other institutions that, albeit in different ways, reflect the necessity of the political system to learn. For instance, in all modern societies, the concept of law has undergone a considerable change. Rather than representing durability and generality (as an expression of universal truth), it has become more and more an instrument of regulating and reregulating specific situations and constellations depending upon changing circumstances. As a consequence, in Germany the procedures of legislation have been made reflexive in that the effects of the laws upon the regulated object are under permanent scrutiny by scientific institutes, work groups, and NGOs. The procedural rules of the Bundestag establish a mechanism of expert advice and of "Inquiry Commissions" in order to provide the lawmakers with appropriate knowledge, as distinct from their everyday experience and their common sense, needed for their regulative tasks. Also, the initiators of legislative bills have to designate the existing alternatives to their particular proposals. A major institutional innovation, to mention a last example, has been the longstanding jurisprudence of the German Federal Constitutional Court, which imposes upon the legislature the obligation to correct laws if the empirical assumptions underlying their normative regulations about future developments do not materialize on review; this is a particular case of institutional coping with the problem of uncertainty. Today, experimentation laws, revision clauses in laws, and time-limited laws serve as well-known instruments of the political system for dealing with cognitive uncertainty and for producing a constant readiness to correct decisions in light of better knowledge.

IV. The Evolutionary Risk of Voluntary Ignorance and the Democratic Duty to Learn

Not only individuals but also organization and polities can fail to learn. The demise of great empires has time and again been explained by the failure of the imperial elites to meet the challenges imposed upon them by new developments in their environment. Gibbon's *History of the Decline and Fall of the Roman Empire,* published between 1776 and 1788, has remained the outstanding and reputable work in this field. The history of the decline and fall of the Soviet Empire remains still to be written; it will certainly add another chapter to the grand book about the decline of great empires caused by their inherent incapacity to learn. But that does not mean that democracies have good reason for self-complacency and self-righteousness. They, too, are susceptible to self-destructive tendencies. Leaving aside here the conventional Tocquevillean concerns about the destruction of democratic freedom through the egalitarianism of mass democracy and the "tyranny of the majority," today we have to care about the danger of the elimination of democracy through democratic means[34] and about what today seems to be the more serious threat, part of the "evolutionary risks of democracy,"[35] a widespread sense of dissatisfaction and frustration with democracy among the popular masses in many democratic countries. I am afraid that we have to add to this listing the danger of unnecessary, that is, self-inflicted ignorance.

Both the political and the economic system within a society can occasionally be so resistant to learning that the society's knowledge of its own malfunctioning either disappears or remains without consequence; it fails to turn into an instrument of societal self-observation, self-regulation, and, finally, self-improvement.[36] When the political or economic power elites are able to let the knowledge about the society run dry by neglecting it, then it is not sufficient to shield the institutions of knowledge production from the effects of the noncommunicative quality of power. In such a case, mechanisms have to be found that pressure the centers of power to learn. I do not mean to suggest a political system governed according to merely technical, scientific, and objective criteria. What is at stake in a democratic polity is, rather, the principle that the public and controversial debate among the various social forces about different policy options should occur on the level of the best attainable standard of knowledge. In other words, in a democratic system, collective decisions can be considered as legitimate only if they are taken on the basis of an updated standard of the ability of the people's up-to-date awareness of both their collective problems and possible solutions to those problems.

This principle may appear simplistic, but if we put it into the framework of democratic theory, many difficulties arise. When does a social group use its power in a legitimate way in order to ignore a certain knowledge about the society or to interpret it in a sense that would benefit its interests, and when does this group go beyond the border of permissible dethematization or even suppression of knowledge? Behind this question we can discover a deeper problem, namely why it is that in a democratic society, the suppression of knowledge about the insufficiencies of the society is illegitimate if the political elites have been empowered by popular vote. Should not democracy include the right of the people to suppress or, for that matter, the right to tolerate the suppression of unpopular knowledge? Is not, to repeat Rousseau's statement referred to earlier, "the general will . . . always rightful," although "the judgment which guides it is not always enlightened"?

Obviously, two different legitimization principles compete here. Those who are unwilling to know derive their legitimacy from the democratic principle of the power acquired rightfully according to democratic rules—the government is elected, and interest groups are constitutionally recognized by the constitution as factors in an open political process. But which principle are invoked by those who insist upon the "duty to know"? The freedom of sciences protects, individually and institutionally, the process of independent, power-averse "knowledge-production," but not the transfer of knowledge from the system of scientific research to the political system, and quite rightly so, because the absence of such a guarantee is an indispensable element of the constitutional protection of the autonomy of science. But which other source of legitimization can be invoked to support the postulate that the modern democratic community must develop the ability and the willingness to learn?

If we understand democracy as the most advanced form of collective self-determination of a civil society, then we can derive from this starting point the postulate that individuals must be able to articulate and discuss their political will among themselves on the highest level of knowledge to which they have access. The power formed in and through democratic processes of will formation is democratically legitimized only to the degree to which the members of the society can decide freely whether they agree with the political groups that canvass for their votes; and "freely" today means with the awareness that society is constantly changing and undergoing a permanent knowledge revolution, that is, in the full knowledge of the possible continuities and discontinuities of the society's self-transformation. In other words, a legitimate process of will formation is not possible on the basis of self-inflicted ignorance; power based upon "willful" ignorance lacks democratic legitimacy. Therefore, the constitutional guarantee of the ability and willingness to learn is an inherent requirement of the democratic principle itself. In terms of constitutional law, this constitutional guarantee is an indispensable element of the legitimacy of the democratic public authority. If we add to the traditional rules about democratic competition for power the principle that cognitive and moral learning should be the rationale of democratic institutions, this enriches considerably the value and the functioning of the democratic principle. We could prevent political power from becoming knowledge-blind, that is, from becoming the privilege of having not to learn. This privilege, like all privileges, protects only those who hold power, to the detriment of the political community as a whole.

Yet, we have to consider the possibility that ignorance can be legitimate under certain circumstances. This proposition leads back to the problem of moral learning. Cognitive learning does not stand for the appropriation of as much new information as possible; rather, it suggests a methodical attitude of individuals, giving rise to individuals' judgment and evaluation of their own role in the process of acquiring and applying knowledge. It is a reflexive attitude, which indeed can include the moral decision to remain ignorant. For instance, I may decide not to know whether I am the bearer of a potential disease against which remedies will not be available during my normal life expectancy. This kind of ignorance has a reflexive character, which the individual has chosen on the basis of the knowledge about the significance of knowledge and of ignorance. It is, in other words, a deliberately chosen ignorance. Whether intentional ignorance can also be a morally justified decision on the collective level is a difficult question, which I will only raise, without examining it here in depth. For instance, should a democratic society forbid the cloning of human beings? I restrict myself to the suggestion that a criterion for a justifiable decision should be whether ignorance is based on the effectiveness of power or on the reflection of knowledge—admittedly an abstract criterion, but one that is susceptible to being concretized and operationalized.

V. Concluding Remarks

To conclude briefly: The power concentrated in the modern state which at its starting point was the secular problem solver in that it expelled all religious and moral questions from the public agenda, turned itself into a problem, whose solution since the end of the eighteenth century has been the modern constitutional state. Yet, today, the modern constitutional state is ill prepared to solve the serious problem of mass democracy—that democratic power can be unwise, corrupt, self-damaging, myopic, and irresponsible toward future generations. It is not well prepared for the inducement of cognitively and morally enlightened decisions and policies. To be sure, Lord Acton's famous statement is still true: "Power corrupts; absolute power corrupts absolutely." But even more suitable would be this updating: "Power stupefies; absolute power stupefies absolutely." And self-inflicted stupidity is immoral.

NOTES

1. Karl W. Deutsch (1963), *The Nerves of Government. Models of Political Communication and Control* (New York and London: Free Press/Collier-Macmillan), p. 111.

2. Cf. Jon Elster (2000), *Ulysses Unbound. Studies in Rationality, Precommitment, and Constraints* (Cambridge: Cambridge University Press); Stephen Holmes (1988), "Precommitment and the Paradox of Democracy," in J. Elster and R. Slagstad (eds.), *Constitutionalism and Democracy* (Cambridge: Cambridge University Press), pp. 195–240.

3. For the difference between a politics of presence as distinct from a politics of representation, cf. Anne Phillips (1995), *The Politics of Presence* (New York: Clarendon Press).

4. Joseph A. Schumpeter (1975), *Capitalism, Socialism and Democracy* (New York: Harper Colophon Books), pp. 256 ff.

5. Jean-Jacques Rousseau (1968 [1762]), *The Social Contract* (London: Penguin Books), II/4.

6. Ibid., I/7.

7. Ibid., II/6.

8. Ibid., II/7.

9. H. Albach and J. Jin (1998), "Learning in the Market," in Meinolf Dierkes et al., *Organisationslernen—institutionelle und kulturelle Dimensionen*, ed. Harost Albach (Berlin: Edition Sigma [WZB-Jahrbuch]), p. 369.

10. Ulrich K. Preuss (1995), *Constitutional Revolution. The Link Between Constitutionalism and Progress* (Atlantic Highlands, N.J.: Humanities Press International), pp. 109 ff.

11. It is therefore not just a matter of political style that France has experienced some fifteen constitutions after the revolution of 1789, while the United States has lived under one constitution that has undergone seventeen amendments in almost the same timespan.

12. Michael Mann (1986), *The Sources of Social Power*. Vol. I. *A History of Power from the Beginning to A.D. 1760* (Cambridge: Cambridge University Press).

13. Max Weber (1978), *Economy and Society. An Outline of Interpretive Sociology*, ed. Guenther Roth and Claus Wittich (Berkeley: University of California Press), p. 53.

14. Elster, *Ulysses Unbound*, pp. 146 ff.

15. Jon Elster (1984), *Ulysses and the Sirens*, rev. ed. (Cambridge: Cambridge University Press), pp. 87 ff.; Preuss, *Constitutional Revolution*, p. 113.

16. Preuss, *Constitutional Revolution*, pp. 115 ff.

17. D. Held, A. McGrew, D. Goldblatt, and J. Perraton (2000), *Global Transformations. Politics, Economics and Culture* (Cambridge: Polity Press).

18. Anthony Giddens (1981), *The Class Structure of the Advanced Societies*, 2nd ed. (London: Hutchinson).

19. Cf. Anthony Giddens (1992), *The Consequences of Modernity* (Cambridge: Polity Press); Giddens (1992), *Modernity and Self-Identity: Self and Society in the Late Modern Age* (Cambridge: Polity Press); U. Beck, A. Giddens, and S. Lash (1994), *Reflexive Modernization: Politics, Tradition and Aesthetics in the Modern Social Order* (Cambridge: Polity Press).

20. Cf. Claus Offe (1997), "Micro-Aspects of Democratic Theory: What Makes for the Deliberative Competence of Citizens?" in A. Hadenius (ed.), *Democracy's Victory and Crisis* (Cambridge: Cambridge University Press).

21. Rudolf Vierhaus (1988), *Germany in the Age of Absolutism*, trans. J. B. Knudsen (Cambridge: Cambridge University Press) pp. 72 ff.

22. Beck et al., *Reflexive Modernization*, pp. 174 ff.

23. Albach and Jin, *Learning in the Market*, p. 357.

24. Lawrence Kohlberg (1981), *Psychology of Moral Development* (San Francisco: Harper & Row) pp. 294 ff.; Lawrence Kohlberg (1984), *Psychology of Moral Development* (San Francisco: Harper & Row) pp. 170ff.

25. Albach and Jin, *Learning in the Market;* F. Leeuw et al. (eds.) (1994), *Can Governments Learn? Comparative Perspectives on Evaluation & Organizational Learning* (New Brunswick/London: Transaction Publishers).

26. Albach and Jin, *Learning in the Market.*

27. Deutsch, *Nerves of Government,* p. 120.

28. Ibid., p. 124.

29. Ibid., pp. 163 ff.

30. Offe, *Democratic Theory,* 81.

31. Claus Offe and Ulrich K. Preuss (1991), "Democratic Institutions and Moral Resources," in D. Held (ed.), *Political Theory Today* (Cambridge: Polity Press), pp. 143–171; Craig A. Rimmerman (1997), *The New Citizenship* (Boulder: Westview Press); Ian Davies et al. (eds.) (1999), *Good Citizenship and Educational Provision* (London and New York: Routledge).

32. Cf. Carl Joachim Friedrich (1974), *Limited Government* (Englewood Cliffs, N.J.: Prentice Hall).

33. K.-H. Ladeur (1997), "Post-Modern Constitutional Theory: A Prospect for the Self-Organising Society," *Modern Law Review,* Vol. 60, pp. 617–629.

34. Karl Loewenstein (1937), "Militant Democracy and Fundamental Rights," *American Political Science Review,* Vol. 31, pp. 417–432, 638–658.

35. Danilo Zolo (1992), *Democracy and Complexity. A Realist Approach* (Cambridge and Oxford: Polity Press), pp. 99 ff.

36. Cf. Deutsch, *Nerves of Government,* pp. 219 ff.

About the Contributors

CLAUS OFFE is a professor of political science at Humboldt University, Berlin. His fields of research are democratic theory, transition studies, EU integration, and welfare state and labor market studies. He has published numerous articles and book chapters in these fields. Recent book publications in English include *Varieties of Transition; Modernity and the State: East and West; Institutional Design in Post-Communist Societies* (with J. Elster and U.K. Preuss); and *Reflections on America, Tocqueville, Weber & Adorno in the United States* (Polity Press, 2005).

TERRY M. MOE is a professor of political science at Stanford University and a senior fellow at the Hoover Institution. He writes on public bureaucracy, the presidency, and political institutions generally, as well as on the politics of education. His books include *The Organization of Interests; Politics, Markets, and America's Schools* (with John E. Chubb); and *Schools, Vouchers, and the American Public.* Among his articles are "The New Economics of Organization," "The Politicized Presidency," "The Politics of Bureaucratic Structure," "Political Institutions: The Neglected Side of the Story," "Presidents, Institutions, and Theory," "The Presidency and the Bureaucracy: The Presidential Advantage," "The Institutional Foundations of Democratic Government: A Comparison of Presidential and Parliamentary Systems" (with Michael Caldwell), and "The Presidential Power of Unilateral Action" (with William Howell).

JOHN FEREJOHN is a senior fellow at the Hoover Institution and Carolyn S. G. Munro Professor of Political Science at Stanford University. He is the author of numerous articles and books, including *Pork Barrel Politics: Rivers and Harbors Legislation, 1947–1968; The Personal Vote: Constituency Service and Electoral Independence* (with Bruce Cain and Morris Fiorina);

and *The New Federalism: Can the States Be Trusted?* (edited with Barry Weingast).

ROGERS M. SMITH is the Christopher H. Browne Distinguished Professor of Political Science at the University of Pennsylvania. He has published more than seventy articles and is author or coauthor of the following books: *Stories of Peoplehood: The Politics and Morals of Political Membership; The Unsteady March: The Rise and Decline of Racial Equality in America* (with Philip A. Klinkner); *Civic Ideals: Conflicting Visions of Citizenship in U.S. History; Citizenship without Consent: The Illegal Alien in the American Polity* (with Peter H. Schuck); and *Liberalism and American Constitutional Law.*

PAUL PIERSON is a professor of political science at the University of California, Berkeley, where he holds the Avice Saint Chair in Public Policy. His most recent books are *Politics in Time: History, Institutions, and Social Analysis* and (with Jacob Hacker) *Off Center: The Republican Revolution and the Erosion of American Democracy.*

KATHLEEN THELEN is a professor of political science at Northwestern University. Her most recent books include *How Institutions Evolve: The Political Economy of Skills in Germany, Britain, the United States, and Japan; Beyond Continuity: Institutional Change in Advanced Political Economies* (edited with Wolfgang Streeck, Oxford University Press 2005); *Structuring Politics: Historical Institutionalism in Comparative Analysis* (edited with Sven Steinmo and Frank Longstreth); and *Union of Parts: Labor Politics in Postwar Germany.*

MARGARET WEIR is a professor of sociology and political science at the University of California, Berkeley, and a nonresident Senior Fellow at the Brookings Institution. She is the author of several books and edited collections, including *Schooling for All: Race, Class and the Decline of the Democratic Ideal* (coauthored with Ira Katznelson); *Politics and Jobs: The Boundaries of Employment Policy in the United States; The Politics of Social Policy in the United States* (with Ann Shola Orloff and Theda Skocpol); and *The Social Divide,* which examines social policymaking during the Clinton administration. She is currently working on a study of metropolitan inequalities in the United States, with a particular focus on the politics of coalition-building in metropolitan America.

ELISABETH S. CLEMENS is an associate professor of sociology at the University of Chicago. Building on organizational theory and political sociology, her research has addressed the role of social movements and voluntary organizations in processes of institutional change. Her first book, *The People's Lobby*, received the 1998 Max Weber Award and the award for the best book in political sociology in 1997–98. She is also coeditor of *Private Action and the Public Good* and *Remaking Modernity: Politics, History and Sociology*. Her current research addresses the relations between formal state institutions and private organizations in American political development.

R. KENT WEAVER is a professor of public policy and government at Georgetown University and a senior fellow in the Governance Studies Program at the Brookings Institution. He is the author of *Extending Welfare as We Know It; Automatic Government: The Politics of Indexation;* and *The Politics of Industrial Change.* He is also coauthor and coeditor of numerous books, including *Do Institutions Matter?: Government Capabilities in the U.S. and Abroad* and *The Government Taketh Away: The Politics of Pain in the United States and Canada.*

MARK TUSHNET is Carmack Waterhouse Professor of Constitutional Law, Georgetown Law Center. He is the author of *A Court Divided: The Rehnquist Court and the Future of Constitutional Law; The New Constitutional Order;* and *Taking the Constitution Away from the Courts.*

JON ELSTER is the Robert K. Merton Professor of Social Sciences at Columbia University. His publications include *Ulysses and the Sirens; Sour Grapes; Making Sense of Marx; The Cement of Society; Solomonic Judgements; Nuts and Bolts for the Social Sciences; Local Justice;* and *Political Psychology.*

KEITH E. WHITTINGTON is a professor of politics at Princeton University. He is the author of *Constitutional Interpretation: Textual Meaning, Original Intent, and Judicial Review* and *Constitutional Construction: Divided Powers and Constitutional Meaning;* he is the editor (with Neal Devins) of *Congress and the Constitution* and (with R. Daniel Kelemen and Gregory A. Caldeira) of the *Oxford Handbook of Law and Politics.*

ULRICH K. PREUSS is a professor of law and politics at the Free University Berlin and a judge at the Constitutional Court of the *Land Bremen.* He has worked on the constitutional transition in the postcommunist states of East and Central Europe; on the development of a European constitution, in particular on the concept of European citizenship; and on the relations between liberal constitutionalism and the multicultural society. Among his recent works are *Constitutional Revolution: The Link Between Constitutionalism and Progress; Institutional Design in Post-Communist Societies: Rebuilding the Ship at Sea* (with Jon Elster and Claus Offe); and, as co-editor with Ferran Requejo, *European Citizenship, Multiculturalism and the State.* His most recent book, *Krieg Verbrechen Blasphemie. Uber den Wandel bewaffneter Gewalt,* deals with the legal and moral questions of the terrorist attacks of September 11 and the role of the United States in international politics.

About the Editors

IAN SHAPIRO is Sterling Professor of Political Science at Yale University, where he also serves as Henry R. Luce Director of the Yale Center for International and Area Studies. He has written widely and influentially on democracy, justice, and the methods of social inquiry. His most recent books are *The Flight from Reality in the Human Sciences* and, with Michael Graetz, *Death by a Thousand Cuts: The Fight over Taxing Inherited Wealth*.

STEPHEN SKOWRONEK is the Pelatiah Perit Professor of Political and Social Science at Yale University. His publications include *The Search for American Political Development* (with Karen Orren); *The Politics Presidents Make: Leadership from John Adams to Bill Clinton;* and *Building a New American State: The Expansion of National Administrative Capacities, 1877–1920*. He is a managing editor of the journal *Studies in American Political Development*.

DANIEL GALVIN is a Ph.D. candidate in political science at Yale University. His dissertation examines presidential party building in the United States. His primary research interests are in American politics, with an emphasis on the presidency, political parties, and American political development.

Index

CPSIA information can be obtained
at www.ICGtesting.com
Printed in the USA
BVHW032351180119
538252BV00001B/118/P